The Eightfold Path (Buddhism)

The Eightfold Path is also called the Middle Way or Middle Path. By following these ideas, people can reach enlightenment.

- **Right understanding:** Understanding that the Four Noble Truths are noble and true.
- **Right thought:** Determining and resolving to practice Buddhist faith.
- **Right speech:** Avoiding slander, gossip, lying, and all forms of untrue and abusive speech.
- **Right conduct:** Adhering to the idea of nonviolence (ahimsa), as well as refraining from any form of stealing or sexual impropriety.
- **Right livelihood:** Not slaughtering animals or working at jobs that force you to harm people.
- **Right effort:** Avoiding negative thoughts and emotions, such as anger and jealousy.
- **Right mindfulness:** Having a clear sense of one's mental state and bodily health and feelings.
- **Right concentration:** Using meditation to reach the highest level of enlightenment.

The Ten Commandments (Christianity and Judaism)

Although the Ten Commandments for Christianity and Judaism are the same, each religion numbers them slightly differently. Here's one version of the Christian counting:

1. You shall not have any God beside me.
2. You shall not take the name of the Lord your God in vain.
3. You shall keep the Sabbath holy.
4. You shall honor your mother and father.
5. You shall not murder.
6. You shall not commit adultery.
7. You shall not steal.
8. You shall not bear false witness against your neighbor.
9. You shall not covet your neighbor's wife.
10. You shall not covet your neighbor's possessions.

BESTSELLING
BOOK SERIES

Religion For Dummies®

Cheat Sheet

Important Religious People

Person	Role	Religion
Buddha	Founder of Buddhism	Buddhism
Confucius	Philosopher and teacher; founder of Confucianism	Confucianism
Guru Nanak	First guru (divine leader) of Sikhism	Sikhism
Jesus	Prophet and Son of God	Christianity
Lao-Tzu	Attributed writer of Tao Te Ching; founder of Taoism	Taoism
Mahavira	Spiritual leader and last of the 24 Tirthankara (Jain saints)	Jainism
Moses	Prophet who talked to God and was given the Ten Commandments	Judaism, Christianity, Islam
Muhammad	Prophet to whom God revealed the Qur'an	Islam
Zoroaster	Founder of Zoroastrianism	Zoroastrianism

The Five Pillars of Islam

In Islam, commandment or obligation is a central religious concept. The most important duties that Muslims must perform are the Five Pillars of Islam:

- **Recite the shahadah correctly and deliberately:** There is no god but God, and Muhammad is his prophet.
- **Pray five times a day:** Pray at rising, noon, midafternoon, sunset, and before retiring, according to the proscribed ritual.
- **Observe Ramadan:** This month-long fast brings the faithful closer to God and purifies earthly desires.
- **Give alms:** Each Muslim donates 2½ percent of their money to others.
- **Make a pilgrimage to Mecca:** All Muslims should try to make this pilgrimage, or Hajj, at least once in a lifetime.

Four Affirmations (Shinto)

The basic beliefs in Shinto are the Four Affirmations (affirmations are positive declarations):

- **Tradition and the family:** Understanding that family is the foundation for preserving traditions
- **Love of nature:** Holding nature sacred
- **Ritual purity:** Ritual bathing to spiritually and physically cleanse oneself before entering a shrine to worship the kami. (In addition, festivals are held twice a year to drive out pollutants or impurities.)
- **Matsuri:** Worshipping and honoring gods and ancestral spirits

For Dummies: Bestselling Book Series for Beginners

by Rabbi Marc Gellman & Monsignor Thomas Hartman

Wiley Publishing, Inc.

Religion For Dummies®

Published by
Wiley Publishing, Inc.
909 Third Avenue
New York, NY 10022
www.wiley.com

Copyright © 2002 by Wiley Publishing, Inc., Indianapolis, Indiana

Published simultaneously in Canada

No part of this publication may be reproduced, stored in a retrieval system, or transmitted in any form or by any means, electronic, mechanical, photocopying, recording, scanning, or otherwise, except as permitted under Sections 107 or 108 of the 1976 United States Copyright Act, without either the prior written permission of the Publisher, or authorization through payment of the appropriate per-copy fee to the Copyright Clearance Center, 222 Rosewood Drive, Danvers, MA 01923, 978-750-8400, fax 978-750-4744. Requests to the Publisher for permission should be addressed to the Legal Department, Wiley Publishing, Inc., 10475 Crosspoint Blvd., Indianapolis, IN 46256, 317-572-3447, fax 317-572-4447, or e-mail permcoordinator@wiley.com

Trademarks: Wiley, the Wiley Publishing logo, For Dummies, the Dummies Man logo, A Reference for the Rest of Us!, The Dummies Way, Dummies Daily, The Fun and Easy Way, Dummies.com and related trade dress are trademarks or registered trademarks of Wiley Publishing, Inc., in the United States and other countries, and may not be used without written permission. All other trademarks are the property of their respective owners. Wiley Publishing, Inc., is not associated with any product or vendor mentioned in this book.

LIMIT OF LIABILITY/DISCLAIMER OF WARRANTY: WHILE THE PUBLISHER AND AUTHOR HAVE USED THEIR BEST EFFORTS IN PREPARING THIS BOOK, THEY MAKE NO REPRESENTATIONS OR WARRANTIES WITH RESPECT TO THE ACCURACY OR COMPLETENESS OF THE CONTENTS OF THIS BOOK AND SPECIFICALLY DISCLAIM ANY IMPLIED WARRANTIES OF MERCHANTABILITY OR FITNESS FOR A PARTICULAR PURPOSE. NO WARRANTY MAY BE CREATED OR EXTENDED BY SALES REPRESENTATIVES OR WRITTEN SALES MATERIALS. THE ADVICE AND STRATEGIES CONTAINED HEREIN MAY NOT BE SUITABLE FOR YOUR SITUATION. YOU SHOULD CONSULT WITH A PROFESSIONAL WHERE APPROPRIATE. NEITHER THE PUBLISHER NOR AUTHOR SHALL BE LIABLE FOR ANY LOSS OF PROFIT OR ANY OTHER COMMERCIAL DAMAGES, INCLUDING BUT NOT LIMITED TO SPECIAL, INCIDENTAL, CONSEQUENTIAL, OR OTHER DAMAGES.

For general information on our other products and services or to obtain technical support, please contact our Customer Care Department within the U.S. at 800-762-2974, outside the U.S. at 317-572-3993, or fax 317-572-4002.

Wiley also publishes its books in a variety of electronic formats. Some content that appears in print may not be available in electronic books.

Library of Congress Control Number: 2001012345

ISBN: 07645-5264-3

Manufactured in the United States of America

10 9 8 7 6 5 4 3 2

1B/QR/QY/QS/IN

Ⓦ Wiley Publishing, Inc. is a trademark of Wiley Publishing, Inc.

About the Authors

Rabbi Marc Gellman and Monsignor Thomas Hartman write a nationally syndicated newspaper column on faith and values and host their own cable television program, *The God Squad*. They appear regularly as religion consultants for many television and radio programs, including the syndicated radio show, *Imus in the Morning*. Their children's book, *How Do You Spell God?* was made into an animated children's special for HBO and won the Peabody Award. They also have written *Where Does God Live?*, *Lost and Found: A Kid's Book for Living through Loss*, and *Bad Stuff in the News*. At the foundation of their literary and media efforts is the central fact that Rabbi Gellman is a working rabbi and Monsignor Hartman a working priest.

Rabbi Marc Gellman: Rabbi Gellman has written two volumes of modern Bible interpretations (midrashim) for children: *Does God Have a Big Toe?* and *God's Mailbox*. He also has written *Always Wear Clean Underwear: And other ways your parents say "I love you,"* and *And God Cried, Too: A Kid's Book of Healing and Hope*. Rabbi Gellman is the senior rabbi of Temple Beth Torah in Melville, New York. He is also a past president of the New York Board of Rabbis. Rabbi Gellman holds an earned doctorate in Philosophy from Northwestern University. He is married to Betty Schulson and has two children, Mara and Max.

Monsignor Thomas Hartman: Monsignor Hartman's books include *The Matter of Life and Death: Surviving Loss and Finding Hope* and *Just a Moment: Life Matters with Father Tom*. Monsignor Hartman directs the diocesan television station, Telecare, for the Diocese of Rockville Centre on Long Island, New York, and celebrates Mass at Holy Trinity High School and St. Vincent de Paul Church. Monsignor Hartman holds an earned Doctorate of Ministry degree from the Jesuit School of Theology at Berkeley, California.

Dedication

We thought about dedicating this book to Don Imus, who definitely believed from the beginning that we were dumb enough to write it.

We thought about dedicating this book to all our friends who have not seen much of us during the past year and have had to endure our quoting from obscure Taoist sources at dinner parties.

Finally, we decided to dedicate this book to the teachers of religion everywhere on earth. Each day, they awaken to teach that life is more than getting and fighting. Each day, they try to awaken in us the better angels of our nature. Each day, they try to make the world better than it was yesterday according to a vision of the truth that will never die.

Authors' Acknowledgments

No matter how much we knew — and we didn't know nearly enough — there was no way for us to truly understand the deep meaning of every faith on planet Earth. Therefore, we truly and deeply thank all those whose wise contributions helped turn our minds and hearts to new understandings of ancient and modern faiths and whose editorial advice kept this book under 1,000 pages. We thank Tracy Barr; and also thank Fay Shapiro, Tracy Boggier, Kathleen Nebenhaus, Michelle Hacker, Patricia Yuu Pan, Michael Kelly, Marla Selvidge, William Young, Jamsheed Choksy, Kristin Cocks, Christine Beck, Diane Steele, Joyce Pepple, and Kevin Thornton.

Publisher's Acknowledgments

We're proud of this book; please send us your comments through our Dummies online registration form located at www.dummies.com/register/.

Some of the people who helped bring this book to market include the following:

Publisher's Acknowledgment
Tracy Barr, Consultant

Acquisitions, Editorial, and Media Development

Acquisitions Editor: Tracy Boggier

Editor: Mike Kelly

Senior Copy Editor: Patricia Yuu Pan

Editorial Supervisor: Michelle Hacker

Technical Editors: Marla J. Selvidge, Ph.D., Central Missouri State University
William Young, Westminster College
Jamsheed K. Choksy, Indiana University

Cover Photos: © ADAM SMITH/Getty Images
© Corbis
© PictureQuest

Production

Project Coordinator: Nancee Reeves

Layout and Graphics: Scott M. Bristol, Joyce Haughey, Barry Offringa, Jacque Schneider, Betty Schulte, Mary J. Virgin

Proofreaders: Laura Albert, John Greenough, Andy Hollandbeck, TECHBOOKS Production Services

Indexer: TECHBOOKS Production Services

Special Help:
Christine Beck

Publishing and Editorial for Consumer Dummies

Diane Graves Steele, Vice President and Publisher, Consumer Dummies

Joyce Pepple, Acquisitions Director, Consumer Dummies

Kristin A. Cocks, Product Development Director, Consumer Dummies

Michael Spring, Vice President and Publisher, Travel

Brice Gosnell, Publishing Director, Travel

Suzanne Jannetta, Editorial Director, Travel

Publishing for Technology Dummies

Andy Cummings, Acquisitions Director

Composition Services

Gerry Fahey, Executive Director of Production Services

Debbie Stailey, Director of Composition Services

Contents at a Glance

Cartoons at a Glance

By Rich Tennant

The 5th Wave By Rich Tennant

"I don't mean to appear unenlightened Mr. Grove, but I don't think an exorcism should be our first line of treatment."

page 335

The 5th Wave By Rich Tennant

"You don't have to tell me the kitchen's a spiritual center of the house. God knows I pray for a good matzo kugel every Passover."

page 237

The 5th Wave By Rich Tennant

DEATH

"I think you're on to something here."

page 7

The 5th Wave By Rich Tennant

"My sense of faith is always tested when confronted with bacon on sale."

page 73

The 5th Wave By Rich Tennant

"When did we stop giving an 'amen' and start giving the 'wave'?"

page 113

The 5th Wave By Rich Tennant

Spiritually, I believe I can manifest many good things in my life. But right now, I'd settle for being able to manifest a cab.

page 179

Cartoon Information:
Fax: 978-546-7747
E-Mail: richtennant@the5thwave.com
World Wide Web: www.the5thwave.com

Table of Contents

Introduction

● ●

*M*ost people have had some contact with religion. Many of us have grown up as Christians, Jews, Muslims, Hindus, Buddhists, or something else entirely. Our parents or grandparents raised us up in some religion or another. The holidays of some religion were probably our holidays; the beliefs, our beliefs; the foods, our foods. All that raising up makes it easy for us to understand religion because we already know a lot about it from our own lives. Others of us haven't grown up in any religion at all but have run into it, in some form or another, most of our lives.

What makes religion familiar also makes it strange. Many of us grew up doing religious things without really understanding what we were doing. Many of us grew up understanding our own religion but were clueless about the religions of our neighbors. Some of us grew up without any religion and kind of feel left out and maybe even skeptical of the whole religion thing.

Whether you're a believer or not (or want to be or not), religion affects your life. Your religion, your neighbor's religion, the religions within your culture, the religions in other cultures that interact with your culture — they all play an important role in how people view the world and their place in it and how they interact collectively and individually with other people. *Religion For Dummies* can help you understand what you've been doing all your life and what folks in other religions have been doing all of theirs.

About This Book

This book covers a lot of stuff about religion, but you don't need religious training to read it. In fact, you don't need to know anything about religion at all. This book gives you easy-to-understand information about various religions of the world and makes that information easy to find. It's a no-holds-barred reference that you can jump into and out of at will — just choose a chapter and enjoy, or go to the table of contents or the index to find the information you need.

Each chapter is divided into sections, and each section contains information that helps you understand some part of religion, including topics such as,

✔ The basic beliefs of different religions.

✔ The ideas and values that many religions share.

✔ The ways that people express their faith.

You also get all sorts of interesting tidbits about the cultures that religions come from.

Conventions Used in This Book

This book is straightforward. No fancy stuff here. The one thing that may throw you for a loop, though, the first time you see it, is how we designate years. You're probably used to seeing dates designated by the abbreviation A.D., which means *Anno Domini* (Latin for "In the year of Our Lord") or B.C. (before Christ). This dating system is fine, but it makes sense only to people who use the Christian event of Christ's birth to mark time — a thing that religions other than Christianity don't do. Therefore, in this book, we use the corresponding — but non-denominational — abbreviations C.E. (Common Era) and B.C.E. (Before Common Era). These designations refer to the same dates: 1959 A.D. is the same as 1959 C.E., for example; and 913 B.C. is the same as 913 B.C.E.

Foolish Assumptions

In writing this book, we made some assumptions about you:

- ✔ You want to know more about religion, whether you're a member in a religion or not.

- ✔ You're curious about religion the way you're curious about how penguins live. You're mildly interested, but it's not a really big thing in your life. On the other hand, you may want to understand your own religion better.

- ✔ You know someone who grew up in a religion different from yours and you want to know more about that religion.

- ✔ You may want to find a religion to belong to, and you're not sure which one is right for you or how to get hooked up.

- ✔ You want to understand why religion, which is supposed to be good, seems to be at the heart of so much conflict.

How This Book Is Organized

We set up this book so that you can easily skip around. Just find something you were wondering about and go straight to it. To help you find the information that you want, this book is organized into six parts, each covering a particular topic. Each part contains several chapters relating to that part.

Part 1: In the Beginning: Religion Basics

This part gives you the basics on several religions, explaining the religions' fundamental beliefs, important rituals, and holy books. This is the place to start if you want an overview of what draws people to religion, what makes a religion a religion, and how religions answer life's big questions.

Because religions offer a worldview for believers, outlining their place in the universe and their obligations to the Divine, this part also examines how religions have been used to spark conflict and justify atrocities.

Part 11: Religious Beliefs

This part is devoted to some of the most important beliefs of the world's religions and how these messages are shared. In this part, we also look at the different kinds of spiritual beings that supposedly inhabit the earth and heaven so that, if you bump into one, at least you'll be prepared.

Part 111: Religious Rituals

This part presents some of the rich variety of religious rituals that give color and taste, holidays and songs, structure and traditions to the world's religions. Some of the rituals are private devotions; others are meant to be performed in a group of believers. These rituals, both public and private, are what many people think of when they think of religious traditions.

Part 1V: Religious Ethics

Religious ethics are the values (or morals) of a religion. Many people call them virtues. Whatever you call them, they're the behaviors that spring from religious beliefs. In this part, we examine some of the main ethical teachings of the world's religions. We also cover some of the hot topics of our time and look at how religions — most of which are ancient — are dealing with issues of the modern age.

Part V: All (Other) Things Holy

This part fills in the pieces — beyond beliefs, rituals, and ethics — that give every religion its form and substance. In this part, you can find information about the sacred texts, holy people and places, and houses of worship of the world's religions.

Part VI: The Part of Tens

Every *For Dummies* book has a Part of Tens, and this one is no exception. Want to find fun and easy info about religions? This part is the place to go. Here, we include descriptions of ten jobs or vocations associated with the world's religions and regale you with ten great religious stories.

Appendix

Whereas this book arranges information by topic — rituals, beliefs, houses of worship, and so on — the appendix arranges information by religion, giving you a brief description of what several major world religions are all about. It describes core beliefs, major customs, and how you can give them money . . . (just kidding!).

Icons Used in This Book

To help you find information you're interested in or to highlight information that's particularly helpful, we've used the following icons:

✔ You find this icon next to important information that you'll want to remember.

✔ This icon appears next to information that you may find interesting but can skip without impairing your understanding of the topic.

✔ This icon highlights issues and problems that all — or many — religions face and deal with.

✔ This icon highlights more detailed, but essential, information about a topic. If you skip this, you'll miss something important.

✔ This icon points out passages that came lock, stock, and barrel, from the world's holy books.

Where to Go from Here

Religion For Dummies is like a spiritual buffet. You can sample faiths from all over the world. Just jump in where you want, read as much (or as little) as you want, and jump back out. This book is designed so that you can use it as a reference, flipping here and there willy-nilly. Of course, if you prefer, you can start at the beginning and read through to the end. We can't promise you much of a plot, but we can promise you a lot of good information.

Just decide what you want to know and head to that place. If you're not sure where to begin — or want a general overview before you delve into specific topics — why not start at the beginning? It's as good a place as any.

Part I
In the Beginning: Religion Basics

The 5th Wave   By Rich Tennant

"I think you're on to something here."

In this part . . .

Part I eases you into thinking about what makes something a religion and includes a section on how religions answer the biggest questions of life. We take on many of the big questions about Ultimate Reality, including the problem of proving the existence of gods and goddesses, and defining the nature of the Divine. In addition, we expose the problems that arise when a great and good religion is perverted, distorted, and twisted into a teaching of hate.

Chapter 1

Holy Smoke! Defining Religion

*I*f you travel to some remote part of earth and find a group of people who had never met anyone outside their tribe, you'd discover that these people have some type of food, shelter, and language. The group would also have some kind of religion, which is one of the basic parts of human life.

This chapter helps you understand what defines a religion; what the main components of a religion are; and how religion differs from other approaches to life — such as spirituality and philosophy — that, on the face of it, sound an awful lot like religion. Understanding religion helps you understand what it means to be human.

Religion: A (Relatively) Quick Definition

You could say that religion is a belief, except not all beliefs are religions. (Your Aunt Martha may believe that her potato salad is the best in the world.) You could narrow that definition and say religion is a belief in God. Well, that definition covers *monotheistic religions* (those that believe in one god), but it doesn't cover the religions that believe in many gods (*polytheistic religions*) or religions that believe in a chief god and other, lesser, gods and goddesses (*henotheistic religions*). You could say that religion is a way of behaving — being decent to others and caring for your environment; but not all decent, responsible people are religious. You could say that religion is the belief in the *truth*. But what's the truth? Different religions have different understandings of what is "true."

Basically, the definition of religion includes all of these definitions (expect for the potato salad, maybe): A religion is a belief in divine (superhuman or spiritual) being(s) and the practices (rituals) and moral code (ethics) that result from that belief. Beliefs give religion its mind, rituals give religion its shape, and ethics give religion its heart.

Basic theology

Every religion has a belief system. Each religion teaches or expounds its own truths about the world and humanity and God (or gods) as those truths are seen by that particular faith. These beliefs also explain how a religion's followers achieve salvation or enlightenment and why these are important goals for their spiritual journeys. From these fundamental beliefs flow the beliefs that establish authority and explain how the leaders of organized religions rightfully exercise the power of that authority.

Through these belief systems, religions teach their truths about life and death, suffering and hope, and whatever comes after death. These beliefs give meaning to the lives of the religion's followers and sustain hope in the face of suffering and loss.

Beliefs are the ideas that make any religion what it is. Of the three elements that make something a religion (beliefs, rituals, and ethics), beliefs are the most important because they give rise to and shape the ethics and the rituals of a faith.

A religion's *theology* (its religious teachings, or *doctrine*) and its stories connect the beliefs. A religion's theology is its handbook of beliefs (although many theologies are not even written down). Theology is important because it puts a religion's beliefs in an order that people can understand. Some religions, such as Christianity and Islam, have a long tradition of theologies that are complex and sophisticated. Other religions (such as Judaism and Hinduism) use stories, not systematic theologies, to convey their beliefs. For this reason, pinning down the essential beliefs of Judaism or Hinduism is much more difficult. Yet, other religions, such as Zoroastrianism and Buddhism, combine both.

Whether or not religions use theology or storytelling as the main way to teach their beliefs depend on the following:

> ✔ **Their history:** Both Judaism and Hinduism are very ancient and developed before contact with the Greeks, who first organized beliefs into a system. In the ancient faiths, stories convey beliefs, and the impulse to yank the beliefs out of the stories and put them down in some systematic order would have been an insult to the sacred texts.

✔ **How they define membership:** *Tribal religions* define members of the faith not by belief but by blood. Many Native American religions are like Judaism in this respect. You have to be born into the tribe or culture in order to share the faith of the tribe. If you're born into a tribal religion, what you believe doesn't matter very much; you're a member whether you like it or not and whether you believe in the religion or not. (See the related sidebar titled, "Judaism: Both tribal and open" in this chapter.)

In contrast, *belief-oriented (open) religions,* like Islam and Christianity, seek converts. These religions need to have clear and easily identifiable theologies because people need to understand the religion's beliefs in order to join up. A good example is the *shahadah,* the Islamic profession of faith: "There is no god but God, and Muhammad is his prophet." This simple and powerful statement of belief is all you have to say to enter Islam and become a Muslim.

For more about tribal and belief-oriented religions, see the section on joining religions in Chapter 5.

The beliefs of Western religions: Islam, Judaism, and Christianity

Judaism, Christianity, and Islam are the religions that many call *Western religions.* People sometimes call the beliefs of these three religions the *Judeo-Christian tradition,* but we dislike that term because it leaves out Islam. Because all three religions trace themselves back through Abraham — considered the first patriarch (father) of the ancient Hebrew families and, from his descendents, of the followers of Islam and Christianity — we think that the terms *Abrahamic tradition* or *Abrahamic religions* fit better.

The beliefs they share

Islam, Judaism, and Christianity share many common beliefs:

✔ All three religions believe that one single, all-powerful, all-knowing God (called *Allah* by Muslims) created the world out of nothing. This God made everything in the world and gave living things a special blessing. Human life was not only blessed by God but also made in the image of God, which gave it special sanctity.

✔ Abrahamic faiths — such as many Christian sects, Judaism, and Islam — believe that God gave human beings free will to decide how they would live and a code of moral laws and commandments for life that would set a path for living a good and holy life.

✔ Abrahamic religions believe that God will eventually redeem the world from all its sins and imperfections and usher in an age of universal peace, although this messianic age may be preceded by terrible wars.

✔ The three religions believe that God has worked and continues to work through the events of history and has commanded people to do his will in the world.

God revealed all this to humanity through prophets and, according to Christianity, through a Messiah, or savior, named Jesus. The written records of this revelation form the sacred texts of the Abrahamic religions:

✔ Hebrew Bible (called the Old Testament by some, but not by Jews)

✔ New Testament (for Christians)

✔ Qur'an (for Muslims)

Where they differ

These religions differ in important areas, however, and some of the main differences focus on the Christian idea of the Trinity and Christians' belief in Jesus as Messiah and Son of God.

✔ **The Trinity:** Christians believe in one God, as do Jews and Muslims, but they describe God as being made up of three persons: God the Father, God the Son (Jesus), and God the Holy Spirit. To the Jewish community, this idea of the Trinity looked like a belief in three separate gods, and it enlarged the break between early Christianity and Judaism. Muslims have the same problem with the concept of the Trinity: They believe the Trinity compromises Christianity's belief in one God.

✔ **Jesus as Messiah:** To Christians, Jesus is the Messiah (savior). Judaism, however, required that the Messiah bring world peace and a gathering of all Jewish exiles. Because Jesus didn't do this, another break occurred between Judaism and Christianity as the result of debate regarding whether Jesus actually was the Messiah the Jews hoped for. Muslims regard Jesus as one of the great prophets (those, like Moses, Abraham, and Muhammad, to whom miracles are attributed), but they believe that he was unable to complete his mission; therefore, another, final teaching — the Qur'an — was necessary.

✔ **Jesus as the Son of God:** The Christian belief that Jesus is the Son of God (and therefore is both God and man) differs from the Jewish and Muslim belief that God could never become human. To Muslims, Jesus was a prophet but not the Son of God. In fact, that Allah would have a son is, in the Muslim view, improper. *"It is not worthy of the Beneficent (Allah) that He should take to himself a son"* (Qur'an 19:92).

The sacred texts

Holy books form a tangible core for religions. Whether it's the Christian Bible, the Hebrew Bible, or the Qur'an, these sacred texts are a source of inspiration and guidance for the faithful. Following is a very brief introduction to the Jewish, Christian, and Islamic holy books.

Judaism: Both tribal and open

Judaism is one of the few religions in the world that is both tribal and open. You can convert to Judaism, and that makes it open like Islam, Christianity, and Buddhism. But Judaism is also tribal: You're Jewish if your mother is Jewish. Today, some Jews say that you can be Jewish if only your father is Jewish, but not all parts of Judaism today accept this change.

The Hebrew Bible (Tanakh)

The Hebrew Bible includes no personal Messiah, and its prophets proclaim an ethical, as well as ritual, duty to serve God. This holy book also includes a covenant with Noah that covers all peoples (not just Jews) and a covenant with Abraham that applies only to Jews. The book concludes with miscellaneous writings, the largest part of which are the Psalms, or sacred songs.

In the Hebrew Bible is the line, "There is one God called YHVH, Elohim, and El Shaddai." You pronounce YHVH something like YAH-way (Yahweh), but Jews don't do so. When this name of God appears in text, Jews replace it in public readings with *Adonai,* meaning "my Lord." (See the related sidebar titled, "God's names," in Chapter 3.)

The Christian Bible

Many denominations and sects within Christianity accept the holiness and divine revelation of the Hebrew Bible. Adopted into the Christian Bible as the Old Testament, it composes the first (and lengthier) half of the Christians' holy book. The New Testament makes up the other, shorter, portion.

The New Testament consists of

- ✔ **The four Gospels,** which relate the life and teachings of Jesus.
- ✔ **The Acts of the Apostles,** which chronicle the first years of the Christian church.
- ✔ **The Epistles, or letters,** which give advice and instructions for living a life according to Christ.
- ✔ **Revelations,** which describe how God has intervened throughout history.

The Qur'an

Made up of 114 chapters (called *surahs*), the Qur'an outlines what Muslims' moral and religious duties are in light of God's wishes and in preparation for the Day of Judgment. In other words, the Qur'an gives instructions on how to build a society that's compatible with the moral life that Allah demands.

The Islamic holy book accepts the divine revelation of the Hebrew Bible and the absolute unity and uniqueness of God as taught in the Hebrew Bible. The Qur'an does not recognize Jesus as the son of Allah (God) but does accept Jesus as a prophet of Allah. The Qur'an considers Muhammad to be the most recent and final prophet of Allah. The Qur'an traces the origins of Islam back to Hagar, who, according to Christian tradition, was a concubine of Abraham, but who, according to Islamic tradition, was Abraham's second wife. Muslims look to her son, Ishmael, as the founder of their religion and heritage.

According to Islamic belief, the Qur'an is the perfect transcription of the infallible Word of God. The Qur'an continues and culminates the revelations that God began in the Old and New Testaments. As the perfect earthly representation of God's words, Muslims believe that the Qur'an cannot be adequately translated and so should be read (or preferably) heard in Arabic.

The beliefs of Eastern religions: Hinduism, Buddhism, and others

Several religions and sects make up what are considered the *Eastern religions.* Chief among these religions are Hinduism and Buddhism, but this category also includes Taoism and Confucianism (the primary religions of China), and Shinto (a primary religion of Japan).

Their beliefs

The Eastern religions have rich and ancient traditions, dating back, in some instances, thousands of years. (See the related sidebar titled, "From East to West," in this section.) Following is a cursory explanation of the main tenets of some of these religions:

- **Taoism:** Founded more than 2,000 years ago in China by Lao-Tzu, the person credited as author of the Tao Te Ching (the book of Taoist philosophy), this religion advocates simplicity and selflessness in conformity with the Tao, the central or organizing principle of the universe. According to the law of Tao (literally, the Way), everything reverts to its starting point, and the whole is contained in its parts. Through the Tao, everything moves from a state of nonbeing to being to nonbeing. By allowing the Tao to flow unchallenged, the world becomes a tranquil place.

- **Confucianism:** A renowned teacher with thousands of students and 72 close disciples, Confucius (551-479 B.C.E.) believed in the perfectibility of humanity through the cultivation of the mind. His teachings emphasized devotion to parents and rituals, learning, self-control, and just social activity. Although more a worldview for living a just and moral life and not an organized religion in itself, Confucius' ideas became the standard in Chinese politics and scholarship and were eventually recognized as the Imperial ideology. Confucianism has had a huge impact on other Eastern religions, such as Taoism and Buddhism.

✔ **Hinduism:** Hinduism is the main religious tradition of India. Hindus believe in the *Brahman,* an eternal, infinite principle that had no beginning and has no end and is the source and substance of all existence. Hindus believe in *transmigration* (the soul passing into another body at death) and *reincarnation* (a cycle of death and rebirth). Hindus also believe in *karma,* the idea that your actions in one life have a direct effect on the events in your next life. To Hindus, salvation comes when they are finally released from the cycle of death and rebirth.

✔ **Buddhism:** Buddhism, an offshoot of Hinduism, is the primary religion of central and eastern Asia. For Buddhists, the world is a prison of suffering and illusion that keeps people from reaching freedom and enlightenment. Buddhists believe that the purpose of life is to learn that nothing lasts and that suffering comes from being attached to the things of ordinary existence. Until people learn this, they are destined to repeat the cycle of death and rebirth. Only by freeing themselves from desire and giving up their sense of self can people be free of this cycle.

Karma is the moral and spiritual result of our actions. Our karma is the sum of our deeds, and if it is good, we advance toward happiness, perfection, and enlightenment; if our karma is bad, we return to a former state of existence, a former life. Certain special people make it to the stage of perfect knowledge, which is called *moksha* in Hinduism and *nirvana* in Buddhism. Some of these enlightened souls return to teach humanity about the path to freedom; they are called *bodhisattvas* (in Hinduism) or *lamas* (in Buddhism).

✔ **Shinto:** The indigenous religion of Japan, Shinto emphasizes the worship of nature, ancestors, and ancient heroes. The religion stresses the virtue of living with a "true heart" — that is, with sincerity and uprightness — a state that is possible only by being aware of the divine.

Eastern holy texts

Following is a very brief introduction to some of the texts considered holy or, if not holy, of special significance to Eastern religions:

✔ **Taoism:** Two books in particular, the Tao Te Ching and the Chuang Tzu, inform Taoism.

  • The Tao Te Ching is the book of Taoist philosophy. Traditionally considered to have been written by Lao-Tzu, the founder of Taoism, it was intended to be a handbook for the ruler.

  • The Chuang Tzu, written by Taoist philosopher Chuang Tzu, an important early interpreter of Taoism, serves as a handbook for the individual.

These books both propose that acting in accordance with the Tao (the universal oneness of existence) brings peace and harmony to the individual and to society.

- **Confucianism:** Not strictly holy texts, The Five Classics are 2,000 year-old books that detail Confucian ideas on Chinese law, society, government, education, literature, and religion. These works became the core curriculum in Chinese universities in the second century and are still studied today.

- **Hinduism:** According to Hindus, neither man nor god wrote the Vedas (Books of Knowledge). Instead, seers heard them and then transcribed them into Sanskrit.

The books consist of four Vedas:

- Rig-Veda (Wisdom of the Verses)
- Yajur Veda (Wisdom of the Sacrificial Formulas)
- Sama Veda (Wisdom of the Chants)
- Atharva Veda (Wisdom of the Atharvan Priests)

Another important text for Hindus is the Bhagavad-Gita (Song of God), which explains the paths to salvation.

Other Hindu holy texts include the Sutras, the satras, and the smritis, which were written by man (unlike the Vedas) and which outline rules of conduct and behavior.

- **Buddhism:** Although not used in the same form by all Buddhist sects, the Tripitaka (Sanskrit for "Triple Basket") is the canon of southern schools of Buddhism.

The Tripitaka comprises three sections:

- **Vinaya Pitaka** (Basket of Discipline), which regulates monastic life
- **Sutta Pitaka** (Basket of Discourse), which includes the sermons and admonitions attributed to the first Buddha (Siddhartha Gautama)
- **Abhidhamma Pitaka** (Basket of Special Doctrine), a section of supplemental text

TECHNICAL STUFF

From East to West

A characteristic of many Eastern religions is that they don't believe in a one, true God. Some sects within Buddhism, for instance, believe in no gods, and many Hindus believe in hundreds of gods.

Unlike Western religions that see human history as the record of a single god's work in the world, Eastern religions don't believe that the world is the place where one god works out a plan of salvation.

Some Western religions believe in reincarnation, but the idea that our souls are reborn into other living beings or people after we die is a huge idea in Hinduism and Buddhism. Both of those religions teach ways to find release from the cycle of birth and death and rebirth.

✔ **Shinto:** The Shinto religion doesn't have a sacred text, as such. The works that come closest to being Shinto scripture are the Kojiki (Records of Ancient Matters) and the Hihon shoki (Chronicles of Japan). These books record the oral traditions of ancient Shinto and detail the history of Japan.

Acting It Out: Religion and Rituals

Rituals are important to religions because they provide a tangible way for believers to experience their faith. Beliefs are the province of your mind, but rituals get the rest of your body into the act. Through rituals, religions take physical form. These practices give texture and taste, form and function to a religion. (Check out Part III for loads of detail on religious worship.)

Religious rituals

✔ Establish the sacred calendar and its holy days.

✔ Set the ways followers celebrate the passages in life.

✔ Focus the mind in a spiritually disciplined way.

Religious rituals are also often limited to the people who make up a particular religion. In fact, many religions specifically forbid those of other faiths from practicing their traditional rituals:

✔ When Judaism instructs Jews to light candles on Friday night, it's a ritual meant especially for Jews.

✔ When some Christian groups, such as Roman Catholics and Greek Orthodox, offer Holy Communion (also known as the Lord's Supper or the Eucharist), only their members can receive it.

✔ The Muslim pilgrimage to Mecca, the Hajj, is only for Muslims. Non-Muslims are not even allowed to visit Mecca. (See the related sidebar titled, "You say Mecca; I say Makkah," in this chapter.)

You say Mecca; I say Makkah

People who speak Arabic, and most Muslims, prefer the more accurate transliteration of Makkah for what we have learned to pronounce as Mecca. To make things easier for Western ears, we use the term Mecca in this book. Also, the Arabic term *masjid* as the name of the Muslim place of worship is preferable to the French term *mosque*. Another preference is *Muslim* rather than *Moslem*. In fact, in the early days, Muslims were known by the now rejected word *Mohammedan*.

Happy holidays to you

Holidays are basic religious rituals and one of the main ways that religions define themselves. Whether these days are called festivals, holidays, holy days, or something else, religions celebrate or note a particular event that's important to them and mark it in a specific way. (See the related sidebar titled, "Sacred calendars," later in this chapter.)

Following is a sampling of important religious observances:

✔ **Easter:** This holy day (which celebrates the resurrection of Jesus after his crucifixion) is the most important holiday for Christians; Christmas (the day celebrating Christ's birth) is another big one, but Christians have a whole slew of other holy days.

✔ **Ramadan:** In addition to other dates of note, Muslims fast during the holy month of Ramadan (see Chapter 7 for more on Ramadan) and celebrate the night that the prophet Muhammad ascended to heaven and descended into hell (a trip he made so that he could tell Muslims about the rewards and punishments that awaited moral and immoral people).

✔ **Passover:** An important holy day for Jewish people, Passover commemorates God's deliverance of the Israelites from Egypt. Another Jewish holiday is Hanukkah, which celebrates the rededication of the Temple of Jerusalem.

Sacred calendars

Having a separate sacred calendar with separate holidays is one of the main ways that religions define themselves. These calendars also enable religions to set themselves apart from other religions and apart from the secular culture in which they live. When Christianity split off from Judaism and when Buddhism split off from Hinduism, one of the ways they did so was to make up a new calendar, thereby reinforcing the new and moving away from the old.

Some religious calendars go by the solar calendar, the calendar commonly used in secular life. Christmas, for example, is always on December 25 of the solar year. Many religions use a lunar calendar to fix their holy days because the phases of the moon are clear and easy to mark.

Ramadan is a holiday that is charted according to a Muslim lunar calendar. Jewish holidays are also fixed on a lunar calendar.

The challenge that comes with using the lunar year is that it is 11 days shorter than the solar year, although this inconsistency is no problem for Muslims. The holy month of Ramadan comes 11 days earlier than in the preceding year. However, for the Jewish holidays, many of which have to fall in a certain season, such a floating calendar is not possible. In Judaism, therefore, special calculations add a leap month every so often to ensure that the fall harvest holidays always occur in the fall and not in the winter.

✔ In the Shinto religion, which doesn't include a weekly service, worshippers make pilgrimages to shrines or temples on certain days to gives thanks for protection and good fortune; festivals occur throughout the year.

Head over to Part III for more information about a whole bunch of religious holidays.

Rites of passage

The rituals that accompany the rites of passage are another way that religions define themselves. In every religion, rituals surround the milestones of life: birth, adulthood, marriage, childbirth, and death. These rituals recognize (and even enhance) the importance of these events. As such, they serve as rites of passage that help their followers make the transition between what came before and what comes after.

Rites of passage accomplish the following:

✔ **Connect the followers to their ancestors,** their traditions, their beliefs, and their duties, and reinforce the religion's beliefs about the way life begins, progresses, and ends.

✔ **Help reinforce the value of the family** as a primary religious value (one of the main tasks and purposes of religion).

So important are these rituals that, many times, people who don't live particularly devout lives (that is, in strict accordance with the tenets of their faith) return to their religions to help them consecrate these special dates.

Prayers from the faithful

All religions include prayer. People pray to express thankfulness for life's blessings, to repent for sins, and to grant forgiveness to other people. They pray to clear and focus their minds. They pray so that they can achieve calmness and wisdom. They pray to express awe and wonder at the mystery of life and at the beauty of the world around them. They pray to find release from suffering. They pray while kneeling, while standing, with eyes downcast or lifted heavenward. They pray alone and they pray as a community. They pray at proscribed times and in proscribed ways, or they pray whenever the mood hits them:

✔ The Catholic Mass is a prayer service that includes the most important Christian ritual, the Eucharist, and defines the community that prays together.

✔ Many Buddhist and Hindu sects pray for many hours at a time. They find solace and release from stress by looking inside themselves in order to experience the great void or emptiness. This emptiness quiets them and frees them from the constraints of their own lives.

✔ Five times a day, Muslims remember Allah and their relationship with him (see Figure 1-1). The content of their prayer includes praise, gratitude, and supplication. The prayer's purpose is to keep life — and their place in it (submissive to God) — in perspective.

✔ Regular Jewish prayer must be said three times a day (although afternoon and evening prayers are often combined), with special prayers added for the Sabbath and holidays. A formal Jewish prayer service requires a *minyan,* which is a group of ten Jewish male adults. For more liberal Jews, a minyan consists of ten Jewish adults of any gender.

Regardless of how they do it or when they do it or what they're praying for, people pray to communicate with what their religion considers sacred or holy.

Figure 1-1:
Five times a day, Muslims pray to Allah, sometimes alone, sometimes in large groups such as this one.

Ethically Speaking: Religion and Ethics

If beliefs give religions their distinctive wisdom and rituals give religions their distinctive form, then ethics give religions their distinctive virtue. The ethics of a religion are both personal and communal. Some ethical teachings direct followers how to live their own lives, while other ethical teachings of a religion explain how to order society. (For a closer look at the role religion plays in ethics — both personal and communal — see Part IV.)

Ethics compose the moral code of life — the way people should live with one another and with nature. By following an ethical or moral code (we think ethics and morals refer to the same thing), any person can live a good, decent, compassionate, just, and loving life. Ethics give religion its moral force and universal message. And it all comes down to deciding on the right thing to do.

I've heard that before: Universal ethics

The beliefs and rituals of the world's religions are very different (see the earlier sections for details), so you may be surprised to discover that the ethics of the world's religions are almost identical. This similarity even holds for religions that haven't had much (or any) contact with the rest of the world. For example, in Talmud, a post-biblical commentary on Jewish law and legend, you can find the saying "sticks in a bundle are unbreakable, but sticks alone can be broken by a child." This ethical teaching about the value of community is found in exactly the same language in the Masai tribe of sub-Saharan Africa. The golden rule, "Do unto others what you would have them do unto you," appears in almost the same words in many different and geographically separated faiths. For some reason, religions that don't share a single common belief or ritual may share the same vision of human virtue.

Some theologians explain the common ethical teachings of the world's religions by a concept called *natural law*. The idea is that human life produces common ethical laws for the same reason that physical laws (like the law of gravity) are the same in any part of the universe. Natural law imagines a kind of universal law of human goodness. Somehow, the nature of human existence leads all people to derive the same ethical norms. Perhaps natural law is real; maybe it's some kind of divine revelation to all people; or maybe it's something we don't understand yet. What's important is that many of these teachings don't vary much from religion to religion. That similarity is a mystery to us, but a very wonderful mystery.

The Dalai Lama, the spiritual leader of Tibetan Buddhists, once said in a letter to us, "There are different religions because there are different kinds of food. People just need to eat what grows best where they live." So there will always be different religions. But the great thing about the fact that many religions have similar ethics is that these deep and powerful ethics link all the religions of the world together. When religions come together to do good in the world, it's usually because of their shared ethics. When you think of Gandhi, Mother Teresa, or Reverend Martin Luther King, Jr., you get the idea that coming from different religions doesn't make it harder for people to do good; it makes it easier. (For more information about these three religious influentials, see Chapter 14.)

Hand in hand in hand: Ethics, beliefs, and rituals

Some folks say that because the ethics of the world's religions are similar, we should just throw out all the different beliefs and rituals and stick with the ethical teachings. A religion called Ethical Culture, founded in 1876, tries to do just that.

One reason this approach probably wouldn't work in the long run is that many religious ethics are part of religious rituals. The Passover meal in Judaism is both a ritual and an ethical commentary on the importance of freedom. The Hindu practice of meditation is part of the ethical teaching of tranquility and patience. The tea ceremony in Zen Buddhism is both ritual and a way to teach the value of hospitality. Rituals that may seem to be nothing more than tribal rites end up containing tribal ethical wisdom when you look more closely.

Another reason that separating religious ethics from religious ritual and belief wouldn't work is because ethics are taught through sacred texts and stories that are particular to a religion — even though the ethic itself is universal. Some of the Jataka legends of the Buddha, for example, teach compassion by linking this particular ethic to a related story in the Buddha's life. Although you can make the same point — be compassionate to others — without the story, you rob it of the power of narrative. The tone of a *parable* (the short religious stories found in the Old and New Testaments), for example, is deliberately intended to be mysterious and suggestive, the better to drive home the moral or spiritual truths.

Why People Flock to Religion

In a world of high-pressure sales and a prove-to-me-I-need-it mentality, it's normal that some people expect religion to sell itself to them with promises of money, problem-free lives, and miracle cures. But for people of faith, religion generally offers something deeper. Some of these things are tangible;

most aren't. For example, one of the main beliefs of religions is hope — the hope that tomorrow will be better than today; the hope that death is not the end of us; the hope that good will win. In essence, religion offers people a way to navigate a broken world full of cruelty and disappointment.

Dealing with problems, big and small

Most religions maintain that one primary hurdle stops people from realizing their potential. By being able to overcome this hurdle, people can achieve whatever the ultimate reward in their religion is.

The hurdle is different for different religions, as is the goal:

- ✔ **In Buddhism, the biggest problem is suffering,** and Buddhism solves that problem by offering a path to enlightenment, where suffering is no more.

- ✔ **For the Abrahamic faiths, sin is the problem;** and Judaism, Christianity, and Islam offer a path to salvation from sin. The three paths to salvation are different, but the goal is the same.

- ✔ **For Hinduism, the problem is being repeatedly reincarnated.** Hinduism offers a solution to the problem of rebirth by offering a way to release, moksha, from the cycle of birth, death, and rebirth.

- ✔ **For Zoroastrianism, purity is the problem.** You need to combat evil while you're alive to ensure your salvation upon death. (Zoroastrianism was the religion Persians upheld until converting to Islam.)

Suffering, sin, and rebirth are cosmic problems affecting all people, and the solutions that a religion offers are solutions that apply to all people.

Religion also provides answers to the big problems that confound people: What is the meaning of life? What happens after death? Why do the innocent suffer? How can we live a decent life in a crummy world? These and other questions have vexed humans from time immemorial. To the faithful, religion provides the answers to questions like these, too.

Religions don't generally promise solutions to daily personal problems. Instead, they help people deal with the problems and accept the suffering the problems cause. Many people use religious faith as a way to maintain (or tap into) courage and patience as they work their way from sorrow or hardship into a time of joy and happiness. For many, living a life of faith is a way to deal with problems, not a way to magically sweep them away. (See the related sidebar titled, "Spiritual con artists," in this section.)

Finding joy

Many people find joy in religion. Hindus call the ultimate happiness moksha, the term that refers to finally having attained perfection and being released from the constant cycle of birth-death-rebirth. Christians call this state *ecstasy,* the time when the believer, through faith, experiences an inner vision or union with God. Jews call it *simha,* the joy they feel when they experience the Torah. This joy comes from immersing oneself in the divine and, from that immersion, being able to appreciate the beauty and wonder of life in all its forms and rejoicing at being alive to share that wonder.

This type of happiness is far different from the happiness that advertisers try to convince people will come if they just buy some new thing. Religious happiness points believers to lasting joy — to the joy of family and friends, the joy of rituals, and the joys of life's passages — by challenging them to examine the happiness that comes from selfishness and replace it with selfless acts of kindness and generosity. Religious people believe that the greatest happiness comes from helping others, seeking wisdom, and doing God's works.

Being responsible

Many people find in religion a guide that leads them to do good works by challenging and goading them to do their part to fix the broken world. This guide reminds people of their duty to the poor, the widowed and orphaned, and the homeless. This source impels them to accept duty as a way of serving the Divine, even when that duty is burdensome or exhausting.

In Islam, the link between a devout life and one of service is particularly notable. Humans, the noblest of God's creatures according to the Qur'an, have a tendency to fall into arrogance. Humans see themselves as self-sufficient, and, in their pride (the gravest sin in Islam), consider themselves God's partners. To help them remember the purpose of their existence (complete submission to God), Muslims must struggle against their pride. One way to do that is to go beyond themselves and serve people who are less fortunate. So important is this obligation to help others that the third of the Five Pillars (or duties) of Islam is to give to charity. (For more on the Five Pillars of Islam, see Chapter 5.)

A great nineteenth-century preacher once said, "Happiness is the natural fruit of duty," which suggests that religions can make you happy, but only if doing the right thing makes you happy. For example, if walking out on the people who love you and need you makes you happy, chances are you are going to be miserable in your religion.

REMEMBER

Spiritual con artists

Unfortunately, you don't have to look too hard to find charlatans of faith, spiritual hustlers, and con artists who prey upon suffering and gullible victims. We remember a preacher who sold prayer cloths to people who listened to him on the radio. If you sent in money, he would send you the prayer cloth, and you could rub it and get a brand new car, just like that! I guess if you didn't get the car, he could always say that you had not prayed enough or paid enough! Such hucksterism gives religion and the clergy a bad name, but really, when you think about it, if somebody believes that rubbing a prayer cloth is going to get them a new car, that isn't practicing religion at all, and religions shouldn't have to take the rap for gullibility and greed.

Accepting suffering

Suffering is a part of life. The illness of someone we love, the death of a child, and a hundred other defeats we suffer every day are often not caused by our choices and are not within our power to solve. If you didn't cause the suffering and you can't do anything about it, what lesson can you possibly learn from it — except to duck and run?

Every religious tradition answers the question of suffering differently:

- **Christianity teaches that the deepest help God gives people** is in suffering with them. Knowing that God is with them during the most difficult times of their lives is an immense comfort, but the lesson goes beyond that. Christians believe that God is compassionate, and Christianity teaches its followers to be compassionate to others. In this way, personal suffering can produce positive outcomes. Although accepting God when things are bad is difficult to do, Christians believe that this acceptance is essential if they are to acquire a mature faith.

- **At the end of a Jewish funeral service,** the last words spoken at the grave are, *Adonai natan, adonai lakach, y'hi shem adonai m'vorach.* (God has given and God has taken away. Blessed be the name of the Lord.) This simple phrase contains a spiritual truth: It is far easier to bless God when God is giving to us than it is to bless God when God is taking from us, but it is spiritually important to understand that the giving and the taking are both from God — that everything we have is just a gift, just a loan, from God and that it must be surrendered some day.

- **Theravada Buddhism teaches that suffering is an illusion** that comes from our desires. We make ourselves unhappy because we won't accept the pain that comes from being attached to the things, people, and feelings in our lives. We crave things that make us miserable when we don't get them. We love people whose death causes us pain when they die. According to Theravada Buddhism, the only way we can find peace is to abandon our attachment to our desires, hopes, and dreams. In this release of attachment, we will find the happiness we are looking for in our lives.

The Buddha once helped solve the problem of grief for a woman who had just buried her child. She came to the Buddha and asked him to comfort her. He put a tiny mustard seed in her hand and told her to go and collect one mustard seed from every one of her neighbors who had never lost a loved one to death. She returned with just the same one mustard seed and with the comforting awareness that every person has been touched by death.

✔ **Many who practice within the Hindu faiths** view suffering as having a purpose. The goal of Hindus is to find release from the cycle of birth-death-rebirth that continues until a person can finally free him- or her-self from desires, which keeps the cycle going. The suffering people experience in this life is a result of their actions (karma) in a former life. By acting to relieve suffering (or by having the suffering taken away by someone else), a person cannot escape the birth-death cycle. In addition, many Hindus believe that by taking away the suffering, a person might be reborn in a lower life form. So, although things might be easier in this life, they could be that much worse in the next.

Being healthy

Many followers of religion believe that their religion not only makes them happy but it also makes them physically healthy. Eastern religions deeply understand the connection between religion and health. Hindu, Buddhist, and Tao religious rituals help people unify their mind and their bodies; and these rituals have found their way into Western practice. For example, yoga came from Hindu religious life, and Westerners now embrace this life practice.

The power of prayer

Recently, some very interesting studies by internist Dr. Larry Dossey and others seem to indicate that prayer has a healing effect. The correlation doesn't make sense to many scientists, but for some researchers it is clear that prayer has a real effect in healing sick people. People who are the focus of other people's prayers seem to recover more quickly than those who are not prayed over. We don't know if this is true, but research is ongoing. Eastern religions have known for thousands of years that religion is good not just for your soul, but good for your body, too. It seems reasonable that Western religions should also realize this.

These Westerners feel that yoga improves alertness, flexibility, and strength, and provides a general feeling of well being. (See the related sidebar titled, "The power of prayer," in this section.)

Comparing Religion with Philosophy and Spirituality

Questions we hear a lot have to do with the differences between philosophy and religion. Many philosophies, for example, wrestle with the question "What is good?" and try to solve what it means to live a "good" life. Other philosophies try to explain the nature and meaning of existence — topics that fall well within the sphere of religion.

Spirituality is another area that ties into (but in some cases is separate from) religion. Religion is about spirituality, so when people say they're spiritual but not religious, what does that mean? What distinction are they making? This section helps you find out.

Philosophy and religion

Many philosophies take up the questions of what is good and how people should act. In providing guidelines on living, philosophies have ethics just as religions do.

Religions differ from philosophies in several ways:

- **Only a religion has rituals.** Only a religion has holy days. Only a religion has ceremonies to consecrate birth, marriage, and death. Rituals are the clearest way of differentiating religions from philosophies.

  Some religions, such as Buddhism or Confucianism, however, have often been termed philosophies because Westerners looked in these religions for an image of a transcendent God and didn't find it. Some Buddhist sects, such as Zen, don't teach a belief in a god or supreme being; their goal is to find enlightenment or happiness within themselves. Other Buddhist sects, such as Pure Land, do believe in a transcendent God, similar to Christianity, which leads to a rebirth in paradise. But because of their rituals, Buddhism and Confucianism are both clearly religions.

- **Philosophies use reason to figure out what is true, and religions use both reason and revelation.** Reason depends solely upon the use of unaided human rational thinking to determine what is true. Reason doesn't appeal to the authority of God or tradition to establish the truth. By contrast, religion often depends on *revelation,* a gift of knowledge given in a holy text or directly by God to a prophet. To accept reason you just have to think, but to accept revelation you have to believe. (See the related sidebar titled, "Natural Law of Theology and other ideas," later in this section.)

✔ **Religions teach that miracles, which appear to supersede commonly held beliefs about Nature, are actually true.** To the religious mind, miracles actually happen. These events are not simply metaphorical or symbolic tales that represent some divine principle. In Nature, bushes do not burn without being consumed, and people don't rise from the dead. Miracles are examples of God's power and love for people of faith. They're also classic examples of how religions can seem irrational to philosophers, who seek to prove all truth by reason.

Religions and philosophies are like two circles that intersect. The part they both share is the search for what is true about life here on earth. The belief that stealing and murder is wrong is in the part where the two circles overlap. The beliefs in Moses' splitting the Red Sea or Jesus' rising from the dead or Buddha's turning rain into a shower of flowers are in the part of a religion circle that does not touch human reason or secular philosophy.

One interesting thing to remember is that, although most current philosophies don't include a belief in God, history hasn't always been that way. Aristotle and Plato, two great Greek philosophers, believed that the existence of God could be proven. In fact, the belief in God was part of philosophy until about the sixteenth century. Thus, using reason and believing in God are not incompatible: You can do both at the same time. The main point to remember is that being religious does not mean that you're committed to being irrational, and being a philosopher doesn't mean that you're committed to being an atheist.

Spirituality and religion

Our opinion is that religion is just organized and ancient spirituality. Nowadays, however, you often hear people say, "I'm spiritual, but I am not really religious." This kind of distinction between religion and spirituality is hard to understand, but it's clear that they are trying to say something even if it's not always clear what that is.

In this context, a spiritual life can be different from a religious life in the following ways:

✔ **Spirituality does not require membership** within an organized religion, nor does it have the authority structure that religions do.

✔ **Spirituality is the willingness to follow rituals,** ethics, and beliefs of different religions that are personally appealing, and not just the rituals, ethics, and beliefs of one single religion.

> ✔ **Spirituality is deeply personal and not systematic,** while religion has all its ideas clearly set out and organized.

Beyond this, the distinctions are primarily ones of perception rather than reality. Both sides weigh in with their ideas on how one is better than the other. For us, religion and spirituality aren't two opposing ideas at all; they're just two ways of speaking about humankind's deepest yearning for the profound gift of hope and healing in a wounded world.

Natural Law of Theology and other ideas

In the Middle Ages, some religious thinkers — such as St. Anselm (the archbishop of Canterbury from 1093-1109); St. Thomas Aquinas (1225-74), Italian theologian and philosopher; and Maimonides (1135-1204), Spanish rabbi and physician — tried to show that both reason and revelation came to the same conclusions. This school of thought is called Natural Law Theology. However, some philosophers such as the German philosopher Immanuel Kant (1724-1804) said that if you do something because God said so, it couldn't be right or moral even if it is the same as the truth of reason. Religious rationalists say that how you come to the same truth doesn't matter, just as long as you get there, and that God would never reveal something to human beings that was irrational.

Chapter 2

Four Big Mysteries and a Couple of Recent Conundrums

*W*hy are we here? How should we live? What happens after we die? Why does evil exist? These are life's great mysteries, and the ones that almost all people, at some time in their lives, ponder.

Of course, some people seem to live happy lives without giving much thought to such life-and-death questions. These people aren't tormented by the need to find out the meaning of life or to know what happens after they die. Is it bad to not care about the big questions? No, but we don't really believe that most people can actually get through life without occasionally thinking about these things. When somebody you love dies, it's natural to wonder if there is life after death. When somebody does something so reprehensible that it makes you sick, you wonder if goodness truly is rewarded and evil is really punished. Moreover, at some time, you're going to wonder why you were put here on Earth.

Helping people form spiritually constructive responses to these questions is one of the hallmarks of all religions. Religions confront and provide answers to the deepest questions people ask about life and death. To the faithful, religions provide answers that have not only the power of ancient wisdom, but also the weight of Truth.

This chapter examines the four biggest mysteries of life and the responses of some of the world's religions to them. This chapter is also a good place to look at the relationship between religion and science and some of the big issues confronting religions today.

Why Are We Here?

What is the meaning of human existence? What is our place in the universe? Are we alive for some purpose, or are we, in the words of Psalm 90 in the Old Testament, "like a blade of grass that in the morning grows up and in the evening withers"?

The one point all the religions of the world agree on is that we are here for some reason. Our lives have some real purpose, and religion invites us to embark on a spiritual journey that can help us realize that purpose. This journey is one of the greatest gifts that religions offer. Religions affirm our uniqueness and remind us of all the things we have in common. In this way, religions enable people to become spiritually realized human beings who can serve others and live a life of joy, thankfulness, and serenity.

Now you have an idea of what all religions do for their followers. Beyond that, each religion has its own wisdom about the spiritual journey we must all make.

Keeping your eyes on the prize

For all religions, the spiritual journey that gives meaning to our lives is a journey from a place of need and limitation to a place of freedom and fulfillment:

- ✔ For Christians, our journey and the reason we are here is to find salvation from sin and life everlasting in heaven.

- ✔ For Muslims, our journey is a way to prove our loving surrender to the will of Allah as taught by his prophet Muhammad, so that after being judged on the Last Day, we may cross the bridge that leads to the gardens of paradise.

  Both Christianity and Islam are thought to have picked up the idea of heaven or paradise (plus hell) from Zoroastrianism, an ancient Persian religion.

- ✔ For Hindus, we are here to make a spiritual quest so that we can find release from the cycle of being reborn over and over again and in that way escape the impermanence of human existence.

- ✔ For Buddhists, we journey away from suffering and toward a "state of being" in which we have realized true wisdom and enlightenment.

- ✔ For Jews, our journey is a way to show love of God by performing his commandments, which will change and save us, as well as change and save the world.

No matter how a religion defines the biggest obstacle people face — whether it is sin or death or ignorance (or all three) — it helps people transcend or cope with those limits and, in that way, gives life meaning.

Understanding human nature

As a whole, religions reject the idea that humans are just material beings living in a purely material world. We are more than just animals or clumps of DNA, and our lives have more purpose than just eating and sleeping and working and dying. Of course, most religions don't deny our material existence, but they do change the emphasis. Instead of thinking of ourselves as bodies that happen to have souls, religions teach us to see ourselves as souls that just happen to have bodies.

Each religion brings home this lesson through its belief system, and because people are physical as well as intellectual beings, the beliefs gain substance through the religion's rituals and its ethics. (See Parts III and IV for more on those topics.) By accepting a religion's beliefs and acting out those beliefs through its rituals and ethics, followers find deeper meaning and purpose in their lives.

Most religions teach the belief in something more by showing their members how to live: how to live in what we call *sacred time* (time measured not by the clock but by joy, loss, holidays, and fasting days); how to show compassion and generosity; and how to have hope that the best part of us can survive even death.

Therefore, the answer to the question "Why are we here?" links inextricably to the question, "How should we live?" — another mystery that religion addresses.

How Should We Live?

How we should live is one of the great mysteries of life, and religions address this issue by providing codes of ethics and morality. The first and most amazing characteristic about the ethical teachings of the world's religions is how similar they all are, despite the differences in their theologies (beliefs). Different religions have their own visions of the spiritual journey, different ideas about the divine, and different perceptions of the world. But when it comes to teaching compassion, condemning murder and theft, promoting charity for the poor and good works in general, and reproaching the harm of others, they're all pretty much on the same page.

We don't know why this similarity exists. Perhaps the moral laws of the universe are universal for the same reason the physical laws of the universe are universal (like the law of gravity). (This idea of the universality of moral law is called *natural law,* and it played a big role in some Christian and Jewish theologies, such as those of St. Thomas Aquinas and Maimonides.) Maybe the ethical teachings are similar because the experience of living as human beings is pretty much the same everywhere, and so ethics are the same everywhere. Maybe it's just a lack of options: You can believe lots of strange things, but when it comes to loving and serving others, there just aren't a lot of different ways to do it. Perhaps the answer is as simple as this: The ways we are different are less important than the ways we are the same. (For more information about Maimonides and St. Thomas Aquinas, see Chapter 14.)

Whatever the reason for the similarities among religions' ethics, the important thing is that they *are* alike. In this section, you explore just a few common religious virtues. We consider these and other virtues in more depth in Part IV.

Respect for others

You'd be amazed at how many disparate religions have some version of the golden rule: "Do unto others as you would have them do unto you." Some religions, such as Judaism, phrase it positively: "Do unto others as you would have them do unto you." Some put the same ethical insight negatively: "What is hateful to you, do not do to your neighbor." Some version of the golden rule appears in the New Testament (part of the Christian Bible), the Udanavarga (a Buddhist sacred text), the Mahabharata in Hinduism, the Sunan in Islam, the Confucian Analects, and many other sacred texts.

The basic idea of the golden rule is respect or compassion for others. Compassion comes from two Latin words meaning, "to suffer with." When we are able to feel the pain of others the way we feel our own pain, we cannot inflict that pain on them. The ability to feel another person's pain also enables us to feel another person's joy. When we learn to avoid inflicting pain, then and only then, can we learn to give and receive love.

The golden rule reminds us that only by getting beyond our own selfishness and self-absorbed isolation can we enter a compassionate and loving relationship with anybody.

Bottom line? What hurts us hurts others. What heals us heals others. Morality begins with this shared sacred truth.

Respect for all life

For the Western faiths (Judaism, Islam, and Christianity), the idea of the sanctity of life is rooted in one God who created all life and endowed all life with a measure of God's holiness. This holiness has levels in the Abrahamic faiths:

✔ The things of the world are due a measure of respect because God creates them.

- ✔ The living things of the world are both created and blessed by God to procreate and sustain themselves.
- ✔ Human beings are created, blessed, and made in the image of God.

In Western religions, life is sacred because God made it, and we have no right to end what God has made. Still, this ladder of sanctity puts humanity at the pinnacle.

Eastern religions apply the sanctity of life more universally. In Buddhism, Hinduism, and others, for example, life is sacred because they believe that the Divine is present in all living things. In fact, many Eastern faiths teach vegetarianism as a way to support the ethical value of *ahimsa,* that is, non-violence to all living creatures.

In Eastern religions, reverence for life comes from the idea of *karma.* Karma is the belief that you get what you give. So if you live a life of violence, you will suffer violence either in this life or in the lives you will have after you're reborn. Life is to be respected and protected because respecting life is part of living an enlightened, non-violent life.

Although life is sacred, some religions (both Eastern and Western) teach some exceptions to the sanctity of life. One exception is killing in self-defense. Some religions teach that if somebody is going to kill you, you have a right to kill that person if that is the only way you can defend yourself. Some religions teach that you can kill animals for food. All religions teach that it is better not to kill and better to eat things that don't feel pain . . . such as asparagus. (Some folks, however, believe plants do have feelings . . . but we won't go down that path!) See the related sidebar titled, "Respecting life reincarnate" in this chapter.

You may be wondering why — if religions, as a whole, teach the sanctity of life — there is (and has been) so much violence in the world. One answer is that humans are flawed. Religions provide the guidance and framework for living good lives, but people are the ones ultimately responsible for what they do. So what about the times when religious belief itself seems to be the instigator (or defender) of violence and schisms that divide people? For more information about that, head to Chapter 4.

Practice charity

All religions of the world teach that what we are given in life must be shared with those in need.

In Eastern religions, charity is a way to get good karma. The idea is that the good we do here and now helps us in our spiritual journey through death and rebirth. In addition, by being charitable, we show that we aren't so attached to our stuff that this attachment should hold us back in our spiritual journey. By giving things to the poor, we not only help them, which is a noble virtue in itself, but we also declare our independence from the material things in this world.

In the Western religions, the commandment to give charitably to poor people comes from the belief that God owns everything because God made the world; we really own nothing (even though we may think we do). Instead, everything is on loan to us from God. We work hard to get some things, like material possessions. Other things, like our health, intelligence, and talents, come to us as clear gifts from God. Whatever we have we must share, because charity is the way we show God that we are happy to share what God has shared with us. *Tzedaka* is the Jewish word for charity, and it is a huge part of Jewish practice. Alms-giving, called *zakat,* is one of the Five Pillars of Islam and is one of the most important aspects of the observance of the holy month of Ramadan.

Forgive others

Forgiving people who have hurt us may be the hardest and most important lessons that religions try to teach. The natural impulse of people who have been hurt is to hurt the other person back. Religions try to restrain these impulses and teach people to forgive those who harm them.

In the West, the command to forgive comes from this belief: Because God has forgiven us for our sins, we should forgive others for their sins against us. The reason is that asking God to do something for us that we are not prepared to do for others is foolish and hypocritical. In Christianity, Jesus sets the example for this forgiveness by forgiving those who murdered him. In Judaism, the holy day of Yom Kippur is devoted to offering forgiveness and seeking it from God and from others. In Islam, the sacred month of Ramadan is devoted to acts of charity and the seeking and granting of forgiveness.

Respecting life reincarnate

Reincarnation is the idea that we are reborn after death into a new form of life. This tenet is also part of the reason that Eastern religions respect life so highly. If that steak you are about to eat is really the back part of a cow that was your Uncle Harry in its last life, you may want to order just the salad. Some of the Eastern religions take nonviolence *(ahimsa)* to inspiring levels. Highly pious or orthodox Jains, for example, sweep the roadway before them as they walk so that they won't crush even a lowly bug under their feet. Jains even wear cloths across their mouths so as not to inhale a living creature, and, of course, they do not kill animals for food.

Create community

Many religions teach that people reach their highest potential as spiritual beings not alone but in sacred communion with others. The Talmud and the Masai tribe of Africa have a saying: "Sticks in a bundle are unbreakable. Sticks alone can be broken by a child." What this adage means is that alone, a person is a vulnerable being, but when bundled into a community, people are stronger and our lives are given a purpose that we could never discover alone. (For information about how prayer can help keep a family together, see the sidebar titled, "The family that prays together . . ." in this chapter.)

Communities teach children the traditions and beliefs of their ancestors; communities build houses of worship; and communities help feed the hungry and lift up those who have been bowed down. In Judaism, formal prayer requires the presence of a *minyan,* a gathering of ten adults, which reinforces the importance of community. In Theravada Buddhism, the community of monks is called the *sangha;* one of the main spiritual elements of the sangha is to come together for meditation and prayer. Religious orders of priests and nuns in Catholicism sustain community with each other and the Church through prayer and service.

Some religious communities separate themselves from the general society. Hasidic Jews, some Buddhist monks, Trappist and other Catholic monks, and Amish Christians, for example, choose to live very isolated and contained lives.

These religious groups separate themselves from the larger, secular society to

- ✔ Preserve their ways of life.
- ✔ Concentrate on their prayer life.
- ✔ Protect their spiritual communities from the seductions of the outside world.

The family that prays together . . .

The most basic form of community is the family, but religions all teach that the family is not enough. Families bundle us together so that we, as individuals, don't break; religious communities bundle families together so that they don't break. Staying bundled is difficult for modern families to do when all their members are so busy and so involved in their own work and interests. All this hustle and bustle is why the old saying, "The family that prays together, stays together," is so true. Statistics show that divorce rates are much lower for families that take part in some religious community. A recent study in Cleveland revealed that the divorce rate in the Jewish community was around 50 percent, but among Jews who went to synagogue regularly, the divorce rate was 22 percent.

Not all religious communities insist on the same degree of isolation, however. Communities that are more open allow their members to move in and out and participate in secular life. Both types of communities face challenges: The challenge of the isolated communities is to be open to what the outside world is learning. The challenge of open religious communities is to preserve and teach their religious identity. Both challenges are daunting. The two paths are very different, but they both try to bundle people spiritually against the cold of modern civilization.

What Happens after We Die?

Religion helps people overcome their deepest fears, and one of the situations people fear most is public speaking. Next up on the fear-factor lineup is death. Religion helps people deal with this fear by letting them know what to expect when they die.

Most religions have a different answer as to what in particular happens after death (the soul is absorbed into the cosmos, it's reborn, it waits for judgment, or it heads straight to heaven or hell, for example). What's interesting is that despite all the ways religions may disagree on the particulars, they are all of the same mind about this: Death is not the end. People consist of bodies and souls, and only the body dies.

Body and soul: 'Til death do us part

The soul (called *nefesh* or *neshama* in Judaism and *atman* in Hinduism) is the entity that lives after death. Eastern and Western religions have different ideas about what the soul is, however:

- ✔ In the Eastern religion of Hinduism and Buddhism, the individual souls are not really souls; rather, they are just a part of the great world soul.

- ✔ In the Abrahamic faiths (Judaism, Islam, and Christianity), souls are both real and separate from God, who made them as a potter makes a pot. In Judaism, the soul is often spoken of as spirit, breath, or wind. (Zoroastrianism shares the belief that each soul originated from and should return to God.)

Whether the soul is a piece of God or something else is a matter of dispute. (Many philosophies, for example, claim the soul is the same thing as the mind, although no philosophical systems teach that the mind lives on after death.) What the soul is exactly isn't as important as the fact that, by dividing what we are into physical and spiritual beings, life after death is possible.

After life, after death

Just as many religions' conceptions of the soul are different, so are their conceptions of the afterlife.

For some religions, the afterlife consists of places — heaven and hell for Christians and Jews, for example, and the Garden (paradise) and the Fire (hell) for Muslims. The Hindus and Buddhists, on the other hand, don't really have an "afterlife," per se. Hindus believe that the soul continues to be reincarnated until it reaches a state of perfection, at which time it is released from the cycle of birth-death and rejoined with the world soul, which represents the universe. Buddhists believe the soul continues to be reincarnated until it achieves enlightenment, at which point, it, too, is freed from the birth-death cycle. For both Hindus and Buddhists, the individual soul ceases to exist upon reaching perfection or enlightenment by becoming part of everything. After that reunion, nothing relating to our world matters or exists for the soul.

For more information on heaven and hell and other afterlife topics, head to Chapter 5, where we touch on each religion's take on paradise and perdition.

Why Does Evil Exist?

Before you can understand why evil exists, you need to understand what evil is. Most dictionaries give you synonyms such as wickedness, sin, and depravity. In this section, you find out how religions view evil and how they respond to it.

The nature of evil

Every day, news reports tell of horrific, sad, or deeply disturbing events worldwide, and we wonder why such things happen. Is it humanity's own doing? Is it evil at work?

Following are the primary explanations of evil:

(A) A mistake made by basically good and decent people

(B) A natural response of our deeply sinful basic natures

(C) The result of the devil's seductions of basically weak people

(D) An illusion

(E) A mistake in our past life

(F) Nonexistent

(G) Proof that there is no God

Different religions choose different answers about what evil is:

- ✔ **For Judaism, the answer is A.** Evil is basically a mistake made by people who have been given the freedom to choose between good and evil, life and death, blessing and curse, and who sometimes tragically choose poorly.

- ✔ **For Christianity, Islam, and Zoroastrianism, the main answers are A, B, or C.** People's sinful nature is the reason why Christ's death, which atones for humankind's sins, is so crucial to salvation for Christians. For Muslims, in addition to being good, people are also prideful and easily seduced by the devil or Satan (also called *Iblis* in Islam) into forgetting their rightful place.

- ✔ **For Hinduism and Buddhism, the answer is D, E, or F.** Evil is just one of many illusions we harbor because of our low level of spiritual understanding.

- ✔ **Atheists often choose G.** Indeed, for many people the presence of evil in the world is the main reason they don't believe in God or religion.

Responses to evil

The responses to the mystery of evil take many forms. Consider the following:

- ✔ Evil is a test of faith.

- ✔ Evil is punishment for our sinful nature.

- ✔ Evil is punishment for our bad choices.

- ✔ Evil is a way for each of us to emulate the suffering of Christ.

- ✔ Evil is a way to help us to see the illusion of evil and everything.

- ✔ Evil is proof that there is no moral order in the universe and a challenge to give up the childish illusions that goodness is rewarded and evil punished.

Religions with many gods and goddesses, including many devils and demons, have an advantage in explaining evil because they don't have to reconcile how evil can exist in a world created by a single, all-powerful God who is accepted as good. For polytheistic religions, like Hinduism, evil comes from the "bad" gods and goddesses; and goodness comes from the "good" gods and goddesses, who are at war with the bad gods but sometimes lose. Polytheistic religions have the problem of figuring out which of their many gods is the most powerful at that particular time and place. In those religions, humans play important roles in assisting the bad divinities to do evil things.

Monotheistic religions, such as Judaism and Christianity, however, have to explain evil in such a way that its existence doesn't negate their beliefs about an omnipotent (all-powerful) God who is infinitely good. Here's the dilemma:

If God can rid the world of evil but won't, he isn't infinitely good. Moreover, if he would rid the world of evil but can't, he isn't omnipotent. The response? Evil doesn't come not from God, but from the choices and actions of the beings he created.

Islam regards both good and evil as originating ultimately from God, who is both the wrathful and the merciful and who is the source of both infinite good and all evil. Thus, Muslims stress the singular and all-encompassing nature of God as the source of everything. Other religions, like Zoroastrianism, attempt to answer this dilemma by viewing God as all good but not all powerful. Humans then become necessary in waging battle against evil to help God.

Religion, Science, and a Basic Mystery: Who Creates Life?

The advances in science today are so amazing that the neat divisions between science and religion are breaking down again, and this time the fight is very serious. (For more detail about science versus religion, see the related sidebar titled, "Can religion and science coexist?" in this chapter.) Most of the contention lies in the area of biotechnology, which is the science of rearranging the stuff of life.

Genetic engineering, cloning, genetically altered food — all this seemingly science-fiction stuff is now real, and it runs right up against the religious question, "Are we the creations of God, or are we our own creators?" This question is profoundly new and profoundly important.

This question brings religion and science into conflict, but it is a good conflict, for a change. This conflict isn't like the one that led the Catholic Church to excommunicate Galileo for casting doubt on the biblical idea of the earth as the center of the universe. This conflict is about the moral and spiritual limits of science, and it raises new questions for scientists and theologians to debate:

- ✔ Just because we can make copies of human beings, does that mean we should?
- ✔ Who owns our clone? Does a clone have rights?
- ✔ Is a clone made in the image of God?
- ✔ With the advancement of bioscience, what does it mean to be a human being?

We discuss these important questions (and more hot topics) in Chapter 12. For now, the important point is realizing that, in the inevitable conflict between modern genetic science and religion, the debate requires new kinds of scientists and new kinds of theologians. We need scientists who are sensitive to moral and spiritual values, and we need theologians who are scientifically trained and who understand that medical therapy and scientific possibilities are coming in new and challenging forms.

Now, more than ever, the future of religion and the future of science depend on a mutual exchange of information. With that exchange, the problems and mysteries of our life here on planet Earth will serve both the cause of wisdom and of love.

Can religion and science coexist?

The attack on religion as being a crutch for the intellectually weak and fearful had its beginnings in the sixteenth century with

✔ The end of the medieval world and its close connection between church and state.

✔ The rise of science and the opposition of religious leaders to its early discoveries.

✔ The creation of secular democracies that put a new emphasis on individualism and individual rights.

By the eighteenth century — and with it, the coming of the Age of Reason — many of the great thinkers of the time believed that truths could be discovered only through reason. To be considered viable, all ideas and concepts, even

religious tenets, had to withstand the rigorous examination of rational thought. During this time, influential philosophers taught that because God couldn't be rationally proven and because religious ethics were not the result of human rational thought, they could not be considered true or even necessarily paths to truth.

The rise of science in the eighteenth and nineteenth centuries produced a schism between religion and the artistic and intellectual communities that, in many ways, continues today. By the end of the nineteenth century, many major thinkers and artists were atheists, and this anti-religious prejudice still exists in some ways.

Chapter 3

The God Questions: Does He Exist and What's He Like?

In This Chapter

▶ Looking at how people of faith prove the existence of God

▶ Divining the nature of God, gods, and goddesses

▶ Understanding why we refer to God as a he

Consider this verse from the prophet Isaiah in the Hebrew Bible:

> *You are my witnesses, says the Lord, and my servant whom I have chosen,*
> *that you may know and believe me and understand that I am He. Before me*
> *no god was formed, nor shall there be any after me (Isaiah 43:10).*

This simple statement of the monotheistic faith of Judaism reveals the point of spiritual humanity in the West: We are here to bear witness to one true God. Our faith begins with God, is animated by God, and is informed at every stage by God.

This verse, however, may have little meaning to a Hindu, a Buddhist, a Taoist, or to the faithful of many other Eastern religions. For these people, the spiritual journey isn't to find the God that the Christians, Jews, and Muslims revere, but to seek enlightenment and reunion with the divine essence that imbues everything in the universe.

No matter how you look at it, all religions — monotheistic and polytheistic — offer a way for their followers to connect with the Divine. The Divine, of course, is different for different religions. Moreover, because you have to believe in the existence of a god before you can believe in a particular god, this chapter begins by showing how people of faith prove the reality of God.

The Proof Is in the Pudding

The terrible suffering of innocent children. The Holocaust, slavery, and a million wars. Disease, famine, and homelessness. Earthquakes, floods, hurricanes, typhoons, lightning, forest fires, pestilence, and elevator music. All refute the divine . . . or so you would think.

The question is: Does God (or do gods and goddesses) exist? The answer for most people is a resounding yes. A whopping 90 percent of people in the United States believe in the divine, for example. The following sections explain the evidence that, to these believers, proves God's existence.

Cosmological proof: The existence of time proves God

Everything in the world, at this present moment, seems to have been caused to exist by something that came before it. The question arises: Was the series of causes that led up to the present moment infinite or finite? In other words, was there infinite time before this moment, or was there a moment when all time began?

If the sequence of causes leading up to the present moment is infinite, we have a huge problem, because an infinite series can never be completed! You cannot, for example, count from 1 to infinity. So, if there was an infinite series of moments and causes before this present moment, we could never get to the present moment. Nevertheless, we *are* at the present moment, which is proof that the series of moments that began at the creation and went from that moment to this is not an infinite series, but a finite series.

Consider the following:

- Time and the world of causation must have a beginning, a moment when some force/being/thing began the series of time and chain of events that eventually led to the present.

- The force/being/thing that caused everything to start must have had no cause itself. Nothing created it, and nothing came before it.

- The force/being/thing must be the *only* thing that had no cause, no creator, and nothing that came before it because if that force/being/thing had a cause, then we are still going backward in time, and the problem of getting to the present comes up again.

- Our certainty that we are here now (pinch yourself if you aren't sure) requires us to be equally certain that there was some force/being/thing that created everything from nothing.

In a nutshell, the cosmological proof is this: Something had to begin the chain of events that led to the present, or we could not have arrived at this moment. Obviously, we are in the present moment, so God must have started everything way back then. It doesn't matter how far back the first moment of time occurred. It just matters that God began it, and nothing began God.

Teleological proof: The existence of the world proves God

Teleology is the study of design or purpose in nature. The best way to explain a teleological proof is to imagine that you are walking along a beach when suddenly you see something shiny in the sand. You pick it up and discover that it's a watch.

Here's the question: Do you *know* that the watch is the product of a watchmaker, or do you just *suppose* that someone made the watch? Obviously, the answer is that you know, with absolute certainty, that *somebody* made that watch. Things like watches show purposefulness, design, and function, and they don't just *poof!* into existence. Even if you never meet the watchmaker or learn his name, you still know he exists because that watch could not exist without him. Your knowledge of the existence of a watchmaker is not an assumption, and it's not a belief. It's a fact.

So, turn from the watch to the world. The world is like the watch, in that it shows design and purpose. It is complex and intricate. Everything works according to plan. Flowers don't bloom in the winter, and birds don't fly north in the fall. In addition, the human body shows far more complexity, purpose, design brilliance, and structure than any paltry watch.

If we know that a watchmaker exists when we look at the design of a watch (because we are sure that such a thing could not exist without a watchmaker), then all we have to do is look at the designs and patterns of the universe and everything in it to know a world maker, a creator of all that we see, does exist.

The ontological proof: The idea of God proves God

Ontology concerns the nature of being or existing. In the ontological argument, the idea of God proves the existence of God.

Here's how the concept works: What we really mean by "God" is a being greater than anything else that can be conceived. That idea either exists in our mind alone or in the world. If the idea of God exists only in our mind, then it isn't as great as a God that also exists in the world. However, since we have an idea of God as the greatest being we could possibly imagine, God must also exist in the world.

The ontological argument is simple and complex, and, not surprisingly, it attracts the most interest by philosophers. The idea is that when we think about God, we are not thinking nonsense concepts such as a married bachelor or a square circle. When we think about God, we are thinking about the greatest and most perfect being imaginable; and such a being must exist because we can think about it, and we could not think about it if it didn't exist.

This concept may seem strange and perfectly ridiculous at first. After all, we can, and do, think about unicorns and Minotaurs and the Cubs winning the World Series and other notions. Thinking about such matters doesn't make them exist, but that misses the point of this abstract proof. According to the ontological proof, the idea of God is the only idea that requires existence of the thing we are thinking about. The idea of God is all about perfection, and perfection requires existence.

The moral proof: The existence of morality proves God

The moral argument begins from a fact about animals on earth: Only people can choose between good and evil. No animals other than human beings, as far as we can tell, have free will and make moral choices. Lions don't choose to kill antelopes; they're driven by instinct to kill antelopes. All other animals obey the laws of nature and the compulsions of nature: They mate with whom they want; they eliminate body waste wherever they want; they eat when and what they want; and they kill when they want. Only people can resist animal urges for the sake of some moral good.

One God or many?

Not all religions believe in a single God. A monotheistic God is a basic idea in Judaism, Christianity, and Islam, but not in some sects of Buddhism, Taoism, and Confucianism, none of which believe in any God. Other religions, such as Hinduism and Shinto, and many tribal religions around the world believe in many gods.

If you grow up thinking that the Abrahamic faiths (Islam, Christianity, and Judaism) are the only faiths, you may be surprised to realize that many religions get along just fine without the idea of a single creator God who is all powerful and all good.

The question of this proof is simple: Where does the human capacity for moral choice come from? It can't come from nature, because nothing else in nature shows this capacity. So it must come from some force beyond nature, from God who made nature but who isn't a part of nature.

Therefore, God must exist in order to explain the existence of morality in human beings. See the related sidebar titled "One God or many?" in this chapter.

The Nature of the Divine

In Islam, Judaism, and Christianity (the Abrahamic faiths), God is more than the world in the same way that the potter is more than the pot, the painter more than the painting, and the plumber more than the plumbing. God pre-existed the world (and by the *world,* we mean the universe, not just planet Earth) and created the world at some moment in time. God is totally different than the universe but present in it completely. This belief is called classical theism.

Other religions believe that God is the universe and nothing more. God is the spirit of the universe, its purpose, and its deepest meaning, but not its creator. This belief is called *pantheism.* Pantheistic religions can believe in many gods, as in Hinduism, or in just one god, as in Taoism. The advantage of pantheism is that when we see the universe, we see God. We don't have to struggle with the concept that an invisible creator God made the world but isn't the world.

These distinctions seem simple enough, but they lead to a lot of confusion and misunderstanding among faiths. For example, the belief about God in the Abrahamic faiths produces a distance between God and the world. God created the world but is not defined by it or dependent on it, and this belief is the reason why Christianity, Judaism, and Islam oppose idolatry. Idolatry is making a god out of something God created. Idolatry confuses the created with the creator.

In Hinduism, the gods are each a part of the world, and no god is beyond the world. Hinduism has no trouble worshiping parts of nature because they are all really gods. To the Abrahamic faiths, Hindu practice looks like idolatry, and to Hinduism, the Western religions look excessively abstract and removed from human existence. For Jews and Muslims, the Christian worship of Jesus looks like idolatry because it seems to be the worshiping of a human being. To Christians, Jesus is a part of the mystery of God, and worshiping Jesus is not idolatry. Some Protestants who have no trouble worshiping Jesus think that the worship of Mary in Catholicism is idolatry; but to Catholics, Mary is also a part of the mystery that is God, although Mary, the mother of Jesus, is not a part of the Trinity. See the related sidebar titled "M, as in Mary" later in this chapter.

To help eliminate some of this confusion, see Table 3-1, which outlines the current state of belief in God among some of the religions of the world.

Table 3-1	God Beliefs
Religion	*Divine Being(s)*
Judaism	One God (but you can be Jewish and not believe in God; see Chapter 1).
Christianity	One God represented in three parts (the Father, the Son, and the Holy Spirit).
Islam	One God (no ifs, ands, or buts).
Zoroastrianism	One chief god and many divine entities created by that god.
Hinduism	Hundreds of gods and goddesses, but one divine essence.
Buddhism	Find God in yourself, in community, in everything. Some forms of Buddhism, especially the Mahayana form, have spiritual beings who assist humans.
Jainism	Various gods, subordinate to 24 perfected souls that have attained liberation from corporeal bodies. Even insects and other animals contain some divine essence.
Taoism	The Absolute Tao, an unknowable, transcendent reality that produces all things.
Confucianism	Humans are essentially good and can be led by the ancient ancestors in making good decisions about life.
Shinto	There are doorways in Nature through which you can walk and find the divine Kami (deities), which are present in every aspect of existence.
Indigenous religions	The Divine is present in the sky, the water, and the trees. We are all part of this divine essence.

M, as in Mary

Within some Greek Orthodox and Catholic traditions, Mary is almost equal to Jesus and God the Father. She has been portrayed as cradling the two in her arms. Greek Orthodox churches regularly portray the Virgin Mary holding the baby Jesus. Because the story of Jesus in the Bible takes him to adulthood and to the cross, these depictions of Mary sustaining Jesus may be viewed as a very strong image of mother and intercessor on behalf of believers.

God in Western religions

The basic idea of God as developed in Judaism, Christianity, and Islam is that God (as in Allah, Yahweh, and so on) is an invisible being who has three very big and unusual traits. God is omnipotent, omniscient, and omnibenevolent. In plain English, this means that God is all powerful, all knowing, and all good. Alternatively, God is absolutely and completely perfect. God knows everything, God can do anything, and God is absolutely good.

God shows these big three traits by:

✔ Making a perfect world.

✔ Revealing a perfect way to live.

✔ Promising to take care of our souls when we die.

✔ Promising to send a Messiah (or *Mahdi* in Islam) someday to fix what's still wrong with the world.

That, in a very broad nutshell, is God for Jews, Christians, and Muslims. As you look more closely at Western religions, however, you also notice some differences in their idea of one God. These differences show that even among religions that believe in a monotheistic God, the devil, as the saying goes, is in the details.

God in Judaism

In Judaism, God is completely different from the world and from human beings. As such, God would not become a person; in fact, Jewish people believe that we cannot see God and live. (This is one of the reasons why Jews don't believe that Jesus was God. The other reason is that he didn't do what the Messiah was supposed to do, according to Jewish belief: bring world peace and defeat evil.) Jews also believe that we cannot speak his true name. For more detail, see the related sidebar titled, "God's names" later in this chapter.

Jews believe that God

✔ **Is the creator of the world,** and because of this, he owns everything. He will one day send a Messiah to redeem the world from evil and usher in an age of peace and tranquility. (Some Jews also believe that God may then resurrect the dead and bring them back to life.) Because he is the God of all people, he grants the blessings of heaven to the righteous of all peoples.

✔ **Is the source of everything,** including all goodness and all evil, but he has given people free will. God offers the choice of life and goodness over death and sin, but he does not compel us to choose.

- **Revealed a *Torah,*** a code of law, and a group of spiritually enlightening stories to order our lives and provide us with commandments (*mitzvot*) that we should follow to show our love and obedience to him.

  Judaism has a long tradition of arguing with God. In the Bible, Abraham argues with God to save the cities of Sodom and Gomorrah. The questioning of God's ways isn't a sin; such questioning is encouraged as a way of coming to understand the sacred texts and the ways of God in the world.

- **Is the source of law (*halacha*) and legend (*aggadah*).** He demands justice in this world. In our daily lives and businesses, he commands honesty and integrity. God's revelation of the Ten Commandments in the Hebrew Bible is the cornerstone of Western religious understanding of morality.

- **Chose the Jewish people as vessels of his covenant** and as witnesses of his love. Being chosen as part of his covenant doesn't make the Jewish people more holy or better than other people. Their relationship with God makes them only a carrier of God's words and will, an awesome spiritual responsibility.

The Jewish conceptions of God are the ground, the trunk, and the foundation for the ideas about God in Christianity and Islam, both of which revere the Hebrew Bible as the revealed word of God.

God in Christianity

Christianity took the Jewish idea of God and changed it in a daring and revolutionary way, teaching that God had become human in the person of Jesus. In this way, Christianity broke with Judaism. (See the related sidebar titled, "Jesus in the Old Testament," later in this chapter.)

One challenge facing Christianity was whether this change made Christianity a polytheistic religion (that is, one that believed in more than one God) that, in effect, established God, Jesus, and the Holy Spirit as separate gods.

God's names

In Judaism, God's name, made up of four Hebrew letters, YHWH, is unpronounceable. Some scholars translate the name as Yahweh, although no Jew would use that word. Speaking the name of God is forbidden. When the name of God appears in the Hebrew Bible, another word, *adonai,* which means my lord, is said instead. The Bible also has some other names for God that can be pronounced such as *Elohim* and *El Shaddai.* Jewish mystics call God *Hamakom,* the place, or the *Ein Sof,* the endless one. Some Jews will not even write the word God, replacing it with G-d instead to visually remember that God's power cannot be captured or contained by a few letters in any single word.

The concept of the Trinity is at the root of this challenge. Christians believe in a single God in three parts (called the Triune God):

✔ **God the Father:** The Father is God as the Creator. This is roughly equivalent to the God of Judaism. God the Father is the closest Christian belief to the beliefs about God in Judaism and Islam. God the Father is the notion of the invisible creator God who is all-powerful and supernatural and beyond our understanding. He is the creator of the world and the revealer of law spoken of in the Hebrew Bible. He is the all-knowing, all-powerful, benevolent God depicted in the Hebrew Bible.

✔ **God the Son:** The Son is God as Jesus Christ, who is both man and God at the same time. Jesus came to earth to die for our sins. Whether Jesus had the bones and blood and physical parts of a man, or whether Jesus was never really a man but came to earth appearing to be a man is the source of many doctrinal disputes in Christianity.

✔ **God the Holy Spirit** (which used to be called the Holy Ghost): The Holy Spirit is God as an indwelling presence. This part of the Trinity is roughly equivalent to the Jewish idea of *shechinah* (glory of God) or *ruah Elohim* (the spirit or wind of God), which describe the way God touches human affairs and our own lives. The Gospels speak about the Holy Spirit descending on Jesus at his baptism. For some Christians, the Holy Spirit is believed to also descend on ordinary people and cause them to speak in tongues, to heal, to expel demons, and to prophesy.

To non-Christians, these three parts of the Trinity may appear to be three different and separate gods. Most Christians, however, believe that the Trinity represents three parts of the one God and not three different gods. It is something like the three branches of a single clover, or like three ways of imagining the one God. Each part of the Trinity represents one aspect of God. Together, they represent the fullness of God's power and love.

The question of the Trinity has been one that Christian theologians have wrestled with, too. It wasn't until a Christian church council in Nicea (in Turkey) in 325 C.E. fixed the Christian belief that Jesus was of the same substance as the Father. Later, in 381C.E., another council (this one in Constantinople) included the Holy Sprit in the Trinity as also having the same substance as God.

God (Allah) in Islam

Islam shares the same idea of God as Judaism. In both religions, God is the single creator, revealer, and redeemer of the world.

Many people are under the mistaken impression that Muslims worship a different God than Jews and Christians do. They don't. Allah is an abbreviation for the Arabic term *al-ilah,* which means "the God."

Jesus in the Old Testament

Some Christians wanted to prove that Jesus had been present from the beginning of time and began to find Jesus on every page of the Old Testament. These Christians maintain, with the writer of the Gospel of John, that "In the beginning was the Word, and the Word was with God, the Word was God" (John 1:1).

Therefore, they began to teach that the Old Testament prophesied, foreshadowed, and was written with Jesus in mind. Of course, this particular type of interpretation is not historical, because it ignores the original writers, their historical situation, and the reasons for writing many of the books in the Old Testament.

Muslims take the notion of God's unity and uniqueness to a level of absolute purity and commitment:

- **God is not a person and does not commune with people.** He has no equals, no partners, and no gender. This immutable Oneness of God is revealed in the Qur'an: "He, Allah, is One. Allah is He on Whom all depend. He begets not, nor is He begotten; And none is like Him" (Surah 112). To deny the unity (*tawhid*) and uniqueness of Allah is the one great and unforgivable sin.

- **Despite the Oneness that makes Allah infinitely different and separate from humans, he is also a personal God,** watching over all, responding to people in need or despair, and showing them the "straight path." Allah loves the righteous, the compassionate, and the charitable.

- **As the immaterial (has no physical form), invisible creator of an inherently moral universe, Allah's awesomeness inspires fear,** and demands not submission to his will but surrender to his will. It is not a slavish submission that Allah wants, but a loving sacrifice of our evil ways and a full dedication to the will of Allah.

Even Muslims, who believe that Allah is absolutely one and indivisible, have 99 names for him. Each name represents an aspect of Allah and includes appellations such as the Merciful One, the Wise, the Seer, the Witness, the Protector, the Benefactor, the Creator, the Judge, the Rewarder, the Forgiver, and so on. These many names are a way of expressing the idea that Allah, or God, cannot be contained by one simple name, word, or thought.

Muslims affirm God by reciting the shahadah: "There is no god but God, and Muhammad is his prophet." Saying the shahadah is the first of the Five Pillars of Islam. At least one time during his or her life, every Muslim must say the shahadah aloud, correctly, and with purpose. Complete surrender to the will of Allah, which is unquestionable, is the goal of Islam and the single way to affirm Allah in the world. By reciting the phrase, a person acknowledges that he or she is Muslim.

Deities in Eastern religions

Most Eastern religions are polytheistic. That is, they believe in many gods rather than one God. For many of these religions, all parts of the world have their own god. If the world has a zillion parts, then there are a zillion gods. This concept explains the diversity of the world pretty well.

One characteristic that polytheistic religions share is that many paths and truths exist; there is no room for one person dominating another with the insistence that only one thing can be considered the Truth.

In Hinduism

In Hinduism, there is a god who is the creator (Brahman), a god who is the destroyer (Shiva), and a god who is the affirmer (Vishnu). Hindus also venerate a goddess, Kali, who is another destroyer god. The Hindu religion includes hundreds of other gods and goddesses that divide responsibility for all the other parts of life in the world.

The Hindu gods are not jealous, fighting gods, and they don't demand reverence only to them. Because of this openness, Hindus seek to include people of other faiths. For example, if a Christian or Jewish person moved to a city in India, the Hindu neighbor might invite the Christian to the temple. It would not matter that the Christian worshipped a God by another name. The Hindu neighbor would encourage the new neighbor to bring a picture or representation of the God to the temple to add it to the pantheon (group of gods). Most Hindus will explain that they do worship many gods and goddesses, but all of these images are part of one divine essence that permeates the universe. That essence is Brahman or Parusha.

Brahma

Brahma, the creator god, is also called *pitamaha,* which means grandfather. Hindus regard Brahma as the ancestor of all the other gods and demons. He was born in a golden egg and created the earth and every thing on it. Some later Hindu legends tell of Brahma being born from a lotus flower that grew from the navel of Vishnu. (We favor the golden egg theory, but we have many good friends who are lotus/navel followers.) Brahma is also the god who represents the priestly class of Hindus called Brahmans.

Brahma was the major god of Hinduism for about 1,000 years, from 500 B.C.E. to 500 C.E., but as Hinduism grew and changed, Brahma was not as central to Hindu worship as was Shiva, Vishnu, and the Great Goddess. Today, no part of Hinduism worships only Brahma, but all temples dedicated to Shiva or Vishnu have images of Brahma in them. Brahma is often depicted as having four faces and four arms and is often standing on a lotus flower throne.

Shiva

Shiva is the destroyer god of Hinduism, but he is also the restorer god. Shiva is represented by a lingam, an image of a penis. Shiva is a paradoxical god because he can symbolize both the virtues of abstinence and the sensual values of sexual union. He is a herdsman of souls and an avenger of wrongs.

Shiva has three eyes, two for vision, and the third for inward vision. This third eye also has the ability to burn people with its gaze. He has a blue neck from swallowing poison. His hair is a coil of matted locks, and he is the one who brought the sacred Hindu river, the Ganges, to earth by allowing it to flow through his hair.

Shiva has a woman partner god, whose name is Kali (also known as Uma, Sati, Parvati, Durga, and Sakti). Shiva and Kali have two sons, Skanda and Ganesa. Shiva and his divine family live at the top of Mount Kailasa, one of the highest mountains in the Himalayas.

Vishnu

Vishnu is the protector and preserver of the universe. He is the lawgiver who establishes the *dharma,* the moral code and ritual practice of Hinduism. Vishnu is known and worshiped mainly through his manifestations as Krishna and Rama. As Brahma faded from primacy, Vishnu rose. He appears when evil needs to be overcome, and he is by far the most popular Hindu god and the focus of most Hindu worship. Vishnu also has female gods as his companions. They are Laksmi (also called Sri) and Bhumidevi (symbolic of the earth). His home in the heavens is Vaikuntha.

In Buddhism

Theravada Buddhism came into existence in order to reform some aspects of Hindu traditions. This movement sought to give an equal voice to women, wipe out the inequalities of the caste system, and do away with the concept of reincarnation *(samsara).* Somewhere along the way, it didn't meet its goals, but it did develop into a religious tradition that venerated the words of Siddhartha Gautama, the first Buddha.

While Siddhartha was not the only Buddha, he is the most important. He taught followers to seek release from their stresses in life by looking inside themselves. One of the favorite sayings of a Buddhist is, "Be a lamp unto your own feet." That saying means you don't need an outside light or a transcendent deity to lead you down the path. You can do it on your own.

Mahayana Buddhism developed as it spread from India to Sri Lanka and eastward. Mahayana means "greater," and this division of Buddhism contains many, many beliefs that Westerners would consider *monotheistic* (relating to one god), *polytheistic* (relating to many gods), and *humanistic* (relating to the idea that humanity is capable of self-fulfillment without the help of the divine). Mahayana Buddhism tends to be more interested in elevating and solving the problems of the human community. For instance, the Buddhist sect of Soka Gakkai believes that it can change the world through doing peaceful things. These Buddhists spend their time on education, art, and bringing people together from all over the world.

Each country that was touched by Buddhist teachings changed it. The Buddhism in Tibet, for example, is remarkably different than the Buddhism of China or Japan. Theravada Buddhism encourages the adherent to find the divine within the self. Yet, Mahayana Buddhism has a wide spectrum of beliefs in deities, essences, and self.

In Confucianism and Taoism

If we attempt to find deities within Confucianism, we may come up short. Confucianism and Taoism teach that humans are essentially good and that all they need to do to create peace, prosperity, and happiness is to follow their inner longings. Confucius saw life in a structured way that kept society educated, organized, and running. Taoism taught various approaches, but some of the more popular ones taught that if you tap into the power of Nature you may just live forever.

While Westerners look hard for a transcendent deity in the teachings of these religions, they sometimes miss the concept of "heaven." Both of these religions offered sacrifices and rituals to the ancients during various periods of Chinese history. Ancestors were venerated in much the same way as we venerate deities. Both of these religious traditions also believed in the essential "divinity" or "genetic goodness" of humanity.

Other Questions about God

Based on their religious texts and the traditions of their faiths, people form pictures of God, describing him in human terms and defining the relationship their faith has with him. Whether God is the omniscient, omnipotent creator of the universe (as in the monotheistic religions) or a group of gods who hold sway over different domains (as in the polytheistic religions), most people see themselves in a personal relationship with the divine.

Does God have a gender?

In polytheistic religions, the question of whether their gods have gender is easy enough to answer: Yes. Some gods are male and some are female. Brahma, Vishnu, and Shiva in Hinduism are all characterized as male, for example, while Kali is female. The Zoroastrian chief god, Ahura Mazda, also is described as male, with male and female divine entities under him. In Western monotheistic religions, the answer to that question is a little more complex. In the Abrahamic faiths of Judaism, Christianity, and Islam, God isn't a guy or a gal. So here's another question: If God doesn't have gender, why refer to God as "him"? (Most kids in Western societies grow up with the image of God as an old man in the sky with a long, white beard.) See the related sidebar titled "Gender-neutral language in the Bible" later in this chapter.

Following are some reasons God is a generally considered a "he":

- **Our language requires us to make everything in the world a he, she, or it.** God, however, is unique and not like anything else in the world, so he-she-it language isn't quite accurate, but it's the only way our language works. You can circumvent the problems by not using pronouns at all to refer to God, but then you'd end up with something like, "And God rested from the work that God had done."

- **The primary authors and translators of the Bible were men** who used masculine language and masculine imagery in describing God. As a result, we get things like, "the Lord is a man of war" and the description of God as King and Father.

- **Christians believe Jesus to be divine, or the Son of God, or a part of God; and Jesus was a man.** This suggests to some that God wanted to come to earth in the form of a male. Dispensing with masculine God-talk is difficult to do if God chose a male as the form of his incarnation.

While tradition often portrays the Divine in Christianity and Judaism as a male, many verses in the Bible suggest that the Divine is androgynous (having both male and female characteristics). For instance, in the creation narratives found in Genesis 1, the Hebrew Bible says, "So God created humankind in his image, in the image of God he created them; male and female he created them" (Genesis 1:27). The Bible includes many examples in which the Divine is described in terms of suckling a child or carrying someone in a womb. God is like a mother bird or a hen that gathers chicks under her wings. The Hebrew word for God's compassion (*rahamin*) comes from the root meaning "womb" (*rechem*) suggesting that some basic divine attributes in the Bible are feminine.

Gender-neutral language in the Bible

With the rise of gender equality and the feeling that this masculine God-talk is discriminatory against women, a new movement has emerged demanding gender-neutral language in references to God. Some people are even starting to talk about God as "she" to try to balance the centuries of male references to God. Several new translations of the Bible include gender-neutral language. Some use "humankind" in place of "mankind," for example, or "Father-Mother" in place of "Father" that refers to God. In some, references to the Son (meaning Jesus) become references to the Child.

Does God play favorites?

The idea that some people or religions are more beloved of God than others is one that many people contemplate. In religious texts and traditions of the Abrahamic religions, God singles out certain people and groups for special attention. Prophets and Messiahs, for example, are individual human beings who have a closer relationship to God than other human beings:

- **Prophets receive the revealed word of God.** Among the prophets, some are considered closer to God than others, depending on the religion. The Bible teaches that Moses was the only prophet who was allowed to speak to God "face to face like a person speaks to his neighbor," for example. In Islam, although all prophets should be recognized as people especially chosen by God, some prophets are more important than others because of their roles in society as messengers for God. Examples of the great prophets include Abraham, Noah, Moses, and Jesus. Muhammad is believed to be the last and greatest prophet of God.

- **Messiahs are sent to redeem the world from sin and suffering.** In Christianity, Jesus is believed to be the Son of God.

In religious tradition, the people whom God chooses aren't necessarily more holy than other people, but they have been touched with certain spiritual powers that other people do not possess. The chosen ones are like spiritual geniuses, but their lives are not more valuable to God. They have special gifts, but they do not have special status with God.

When it comes to religions, the question of whether God plays favorites is more controversial and contentious. Many religions have some kind of belief that God has chosen them above all other nations and peoples and faiths. Judaism, Islam, Christianity, Shinto, and Sikhism all include beliefs that they are chosen by God.

Following are some beliefs of religions that consider themselves in a special relationship with God:

- **Judaism teaches that the Jewish people are the chosen people of God.** A covenant exists between God and the Jewish people. Jews willingly accept special obligations to obey their part of this divine relationship. Exodus 19:5-6 has the classic statement about Jews as the chosen people of God: "If you will obey my voice and keep my covenant, you shall be my own possession among all peoples. Although all the earth is mine, you shall be to me a kingdom of priests and a holy nation."

- **In the Qur'an (3.110), we read the Muslim version of this same idea: "You are the best community that has been raised up for mankind.** You enjoin right conduct and forbid indecency; and you believe in Allah/God."

- ✔ **In Shinto, this belief of being chosen is deeply connected to the land of Japan: "The land of Japan is the divine land.** Through the divine protection of the gods, the country is at peace. And through the reverence of the nation, the divine dignity is increased" (from the records of Princess Yamatohime).

- ✔ **Christianity teaches that Christians are the "new Israel" and that the special relationship between God and the Jewish people is fulfilled in the life and mission of Jesus.** Jesus founds the church on Peter, the first Pope: "You are Peter and on you I will build my church, and the powers of death shall not prevail against it. I will give you the keys of the kingdom of heaven, and whatever you bind on earth shall be bound in heaven, and whatever you loose on earth shall be loosed in heaven" (Matthew 16:15-19).

- ✔ **Followers of Latter-day Saints (commonly referred to as Mormons) also believe that they are the new Zion: "And the Lord called his people Zion,** because they were of one heart and one mind, and dwelt in righteousness; and there was no poor among them" (Pearl of Great Price, Moses 7:8, also Book of Mormon 3 Nephi 21).

These chosen people believe that they have been given a special gift and are responsible to take that gift and share it with the peoples of earth. This belief in the truth of one's religion, and the implication of being chosen doesn't always exclude the believers in others faiths. Many religions believe that good people who live kind, loving, and compassionate lives will receive the same blessings as those who follow the one true faith. Still, at various times in history, people have used this "chosen-ness" — the idea that they have a special relationship with God because they adhere to the "one truth faith" — to justify spreading their idea of faith through force or coercion. See Chapter 4 for more information on how religions can be perverted in this way.

The idea of "being chosen" seems to originate within monotheistic religions. For many people outside monotheistic traditions, the idea of being chosen is not a matter of "truth." Buddhism and Hinduism place the responsibility of being "religious" upon the shoulders of its adherents. Individuals choose the path on which they walk; they are not chosen or taken down a path. Certainly, individuals within Hindu traditions can have special relationships with individual gods or goddesses, but the gods/goddesses are not in control of individuals. Some *sannyasins,* or holy people, within Hinduism appear to be chosen; yet it is they who choose a life of poverty, restlessness, and meditation in order to find their own happiness and liberation. Even in Taoism and Shinto, people can find direction by listening to Nature, but Nature doesn't dominate them.

Can you be good without God?

All of us know good people who don't believe in the divine, as well as not-so-good people who do. You don't need to believe in a God to be good.

A centuries-old whole field of philosophy, called ethics, offers many theories about what is good and how we can do good. The two big nonreligious ethical theories are called *utilitarianism* and *deontology.* These big words describe two very simple ideas:

- ✔ **Utilitarianism** is the idea that we can know what is good by rationally deciding what action will produce the greatest good for the greatest number of people.

- ✔ **Deontology** is the idea that what you do is right if you are doing it for a good reason.

Utilitarians care about what happens, and deontologists care about why you are doing it. Both theories claim to be able to show people what is good without having to believe in God.

Still, some religious people say that even if reason can show you how to do the right thing, the same ethical rules are right there for us to learn in God's revealed word. "Do not steal" and "Thou shalt not steal" reflect the same moral law, one derived from reason and one from revelation. Good is good, no matter how it's determined.

Chapter 4

When Good Religions Go Bad

*T*he ethics of the world's great religions are strikingly similar: They all teach love, compassion, hope, tolerance, and healing. (For more detail about religious ethics, see Part IV.) The unifying force of religion comes not just from a common set of high moral principles, however, but from other aspects of religion, as well. Religions give people a foundation for their human dignity and human rights that goes beyond nationhood: The belief of the Abrahamic faiths (Islam, Christianity, and Judaism) that all people are made in the image of God is a way of reinforcing the inherent value of each human life, regardless of color, religion, or any other trait. In this way, religion is a powerful source of unity for human rights. In the Eastern religions, the unifying bond is the idea of karma, which makes all people equally responsible in exactly the same way for their choices and actions. The ideas of *ahimsa,* or nonviolence, and vegetarianism also create a powerful respect for all living things that unifies all people.

Still, religious differences seem to fuel, not quell, the fires of intolerance, hatred, war, and violence in the world. Too often, self-seeking politicians and religious leaders quote the sacred texts of the world's religions to justify harm not healing, contention not compassion, and hatred not hope. When holy words are used like whips, it's hard to see their holiness and harder to believe in the healing power of any religion, especially those that use their texts to spread suffering and oppression. This chapter takes an honest look at religion and examines why it so often seems to be at the root of contention between people and nations.

Every great religion demands modesty and humility in the way its followers profess their faith. Deeds of compassion and tolerance have always been far more effective tools of conversion than the point of a sword or the barrel of a gun. So when people hurt, subjugate, or kill others in the name of their God, they're perverting, rather than representing, the true teachings of their faith.

Can't We All Just Get Along?

Look at the conflicts in the world today, and the answer to the question, "Can't we all just get along?" seems to be, "Obviously not." Consider the danger of fanatical Islam and its war on the West. Or the conflict between Protestants and Catholics in Northern Ireland. Or the fight between Hindus and Muslims in Kashmir. Or the bloodletting between Jews and Arabs in the Middle East. Even when you think back in history — to the Crusades in the tenth through thirteenth centuries, or to the Inquisition of the fourteenth to sixteenth centuries, or to the Biblical justification that the American South used to support slavery in the nineteenth century — the picture doesn't get much brighter. With this history, it's hard to say that religions bring people together.

Yet, most religions possess a message of unity. So why does religious belief seem to be the root of division among people? The following sections look at some answers for this question.

Making unholy alliances

One historical reason that the authentic religious message of unity gets twisted is the merging of religion and political power.

Religion is, at its heart, not about seizing and using political power. Religion is about personal and communal liberation from idols, illusions, and seductions that draw people away from a religious truth, freedom, and salvation. Historically, though, the institutions of organized religion have meshed with the political institutions that govern countries.

When religious institutions make deals with monarchs and rulers to support their reigns in return for the ruler's support of the religion, they forge an alliance that can often pervert the true meaning of religion.

The medieval European divine right of kings, which held that the royal authority to rule comes from God, is one such example. In this scheme, the church supported the king's power (as the ruler selected by God), and the king supported the church, often by banning other religions or restricting their practice, building cathedrals or other religious buildings, and financially supporting the clergy. This idea is not limited to western countries; it was present among the ancient Babylonians and Persians (Zoroastrians), for example, and is still present in those Islamic countries in the Middle East, such as Saudi Arabia, that have monarchies.

This alliance drew religions into medieval wars. The wars between Catholic France and Protestant England, for example, distorted and perverted both branches of Christendom, because religious leaders became cheerleaders for often-corrupt secular rulers.

Putting hands in the cookie jar

Another way religions can divide people is when a religion takes and holds secular power for itself and becomes distorted in the process. The crusades, or the holy wars waged against Muslims by the Catholic Church during the eleventh through thirteenth centuries, are an example of the corrupting influence that political power can have on a religion.

From its humble beginnings as a relatively small sect that attracted people from the lower classes, the Catholic Church grew in influence both spiritually and politically. When the Western Empire fell in the fifth century, the Church and its pope were the only effective force for order in the West. From there, the Church grew to an empire in its own right, holding dominion over all secular, political, and spiritual realms in Western Europe. The Church even had its own army, which it used to maintain its holdings. When the Muslims conquered the Holy Land, the Roman Catholic Church considered this not as much a religious insult as it was a theft of the Church's wealth. Pope Urban II authorized the first crusade to reclaim the land "for God." In reality, it was a war to keep the Church rich.

Politicizing religion

Sometimes, the real differences among religions aren't so much religious as they are political or economic, but religion is used to justify or explain the conflicts that result.

Catholics and Protestants, for example, live peacefully together in Ireland, but because of the politicizing of their faiths in Northern Ireland, conflicts arise. Jews and Muslims live peacefully together all over the world, but the political/religious conflict in Israel and Palestine make that common life impossible in the Middle East. The same is true in Bosnia. Muslims, Orthodox Christian Serbs, and Roman Catholic Croats are fighting for a slice of a very small economic pie, and so they use religion in their battle to secure economic equality or security.

Intertwining culture and faith

Sometimes, a religion becomes so deeply woven into the culture of a country that separating the culture from the faith is impossible. This type of meshing is true in the relationship of Hinduism to India. *Hindu*, in fact, means India, and it is simply true that the culture of India is a Hindu culture, just as the culture of Italy and Ireland are Catholic and the culture of Saudi Arabia is Muslim.

For Muslims, this link between culture and religion is not only a matter of tradition, but also a matter of faith. Here's why: The Qur'an outlines God's will, which is eternal and unchangeable. In addition to the Qur'an, Muslims also look to *hadith,* the sayings and deeds attributed to the prophet Muhammad. In these two things, Muslims find explicit instructions and guidelines regarding how to live in a way that is pleasing to God. Every Muslim is also directly responsible to God for acting in accordance with these rules and creating a "good" society as defined by Allah and the Qur'an. In this way, the Muslim identity is inextricably linked to the social and, therefore, political order. Islam is not only a guide for each believer; it's also a guide for the societies they build.

In some ways, the United States is different. This country is Christian in the sense that most Americans are Christian, but it has separated church and state and committed itself to respecting religious diversity. Still, even in America, non-Christians often express feelings of isolation and exclusion. If you are a Jew or a Muslim or a Hindu during Christmastime in the United States, feeling included is difficult to do.

In all of these instances, the culture and the dominant religion are not just superficially connected; they are woven together at the deepest levels. As a result, people who are not of the majority faith have a hard time feeling comfortable or accepted. Part of the conflict between Muslims and Hindus that led to the 1947 partition of India into Hindu India and Muslim Pakistan (and Bangladesh) was a cultural and religious conflict that made it impossible for India to continue to be as pluralistic as it had been.

The intermixing of religion and the culture isn't necessarily bad, nor is separating a culture from the religious forces that had a significant part in establishing its identity necessarily good. (Besides, taking Catholic influences out of Irish culture or Hindu influences out of Indian culture would be practically impossible.) Still, the future of our world depends upon people of differing cultures being able to walk the fine line between religious discrimination and loving observance of old and honored traditions.

Confusing conversion with indoctrination

Another reason that religion seems to be root of contention between people and nations concerns *triumphalist beliefs,* beliefs that one religion is superior to all others. Christianity in the past and the radical Islam of today are examples of religions that have had to struggle against triumphalism.

All religions consider their teachings to be true for all people, but some believers go quite far in declaring that their religion is the only true faith and that all people need to convert to that faith if they want to be saved from sin and allowed into heaven.

Following are some examples of Christian triumphalism, also called *supercessionism:*

✔ From John 14:6-9 in the New Testament we have, "I (Jesus) am the way and the truth and the life," and, "The only way to the Father is through Me."

✔ From Catholic teachings we have, "Outside of the Church there is no salvation."

Since 1964, when the papal encyclical (letter to bishops) *Nostra Aetate* (Latin for *In Our Time*) specifically absolved Jews of any responsibility for the death of Jesus and thus reduced the impulse in the Church to demean other faith traditions, the Catholic Church has made great strides to a kind of spiritual generosity that fosters unity among the Abrahamic faiths.

✔ Some fundamentalist (or evangelical) Christian groups do not worship or associate with people of other faiths because they believe that their way of thinking, acting, and worshipping is the only true way to salvation.

Unity, from Isaiah

The following passage from the prophet Isaiah (Isaiah 40:17-31) reveals the unifying power of religion:

17. All the nations are as nothing before him, they are accounted by him as less than nothing and emptiness.

21. Have you not known? Have you not heard? Has it not been told you from the beginning? Have you not understood from the foundations of the earth?

22. It is he who sits above the circle of the earth, and its inhabitants are like grasshoppers; who stretches out the heavens like a curtain, and spreads them like a tent to dwell in;

23. who brings princes to naught, and makes the rulers of the earth as nothing.

24. Scarcely are they planted, scarcely sown, scarcely has their stem taken root in

the earth, when he blows upon them, and they wither, and the tempest carries them off like stubble.

28. Have you not known? Have you not heard? The Lord is the everlasting God, the Creator of the ends of the earth. He does not faint or grow weary, his understanding is unsearchable.

29. He gives power to the faint, and to him who has no might he increases strength.

30. Even youths shall faint and be weary, and young men shall fall exhausted;

31. but they who wait for the Lord shall renew their strength, they shall mount up with wings like eagles, they shall run and not be weary, they shall walk and not faint.

Christianity and Islam (and, to a minor extent, Buddhism) — unlike Judaism, Zoroastrianism, and Hinduism — are faiths that actively encourage converts, but sometimes this encouragement becomes violent and leads to forced conversions or religious war:

✔ Although Islam, in general, tolerates other religious beliefs (believing that each person should choose his or her path and that conversions should be voluntary and not forced), the Muslim teachings about *kafirs*, or unbelievers, has led fundamentalist Muslims to the idea that the only religion for the world must be Islam and that Muslims must endeavor to make this happen.

✔ Christian conversion efforts sometimes make the intended convert feel attacked and demeaned. These conversion efforts can also make Christian missionaries insensitive to the wisdom of other religious traditions.

Religions that claim one true faith find it difficult to find room for other faiths. Although we honor this belief and the right of people to hold it, the new movement in spirituality is a movement to reclaim the unifying elements of religion and set aside those who imagine that there is just one way up the mountain. (See the related sidebar titled, "Unity, from Isaiah," in this chapter.)

Understanding "Bad" Religion

No sacred books or any of the world's great religions teach that innocent people should be murdered or that poor people should starve. But the sad fact is that some religious leaders and followers warp this legacy of spiritual unity. In its warped form, good religion becomes bad religion.

Bad religion is the result of three conditions that have gone wrong inside a religious tradition:

✔ **Bad beliefs within the religion:** In this case, a religion actually believes and teaches morally corrupt ideas. These ideas may have seeped into the religion from outside influences or they may have been part of the beliefs of the founder of the faith. Either way, they are like a bad virus that makes the religion morally and spiritually sick. These bad beliefs need to be rejected in order for the religion to be well again

✔ **Twisted interpretations of religious doctrine:** This situation arises when fanatics hijack a healthy and good religion. These fanatics invent ideas the religion never taught and teach these ideas as if they were ancient and authentic. This type of religion is a perversion of a good faith, not the natural and ancient teachings of a bad faith.

✔ **Cults parading as religion:** Cults are not religions at all. They are not ancient, and they are just scams pretending to be a religion. Cults are brainwashing and moneymaking centers run by groups of power-seeking, money-hungry leaders who are merely working to increase their own power and wealth. Cults use the laws in the United States that protect religions as a cover for their corrupt and unspiritual activities.

Bad religion

Every religion has some morally embarrassing text or belief in it. After all, Hinduism is over 5,000 years old; Judaism over 4,000 years old; Christianity 2,000 years old; and Islam over 1,400 years old. Such religions bear both ancient wisdom and ancient prejudices. In this section, you explore some examples of religion-sanctioned beliefs and practices that caused a great deal of suffering.

Somebody saying that a religious belief is bad doesn't necessarily make that belief bad. For example, nowadays, a lively and important debate is going on between those who believe that the world religions have wrongly condemned homosexuality and lesbianism and have preserved prejudices leading to discrimination against women and those who say that these ancient beliefs may not fit the modern temperament but they are still morally correct. Although the subject matter differs (sometimes it's about racism, sometimes it's about sexism, sometimes it's about something else), the argument itself has a long history, and the fact that the debates are still going on speaks to the vitality and influence of religions today.

The caste system in India

Hinduism includes the caste system. The castes (*varnas*) divide people into these categories: the priests and scholars (Brahmin); the warriors and rulers (Kshatriya); the shopkeepers and farmers (Vaisya); and the laborers, artisans, and servants (Sudra). Those at the bottom, the Unscheduled Classes (formerly called Untouchables), are forced to live a life of extreme poverty and misery. A person's caste is determined by birth.

Both the Buddha and Mahavira (the last of the Jain saints), who were born into the Kshatriya caste, opposed the caste system but couldn't change it. Guru Nanak, the founder of Sikhism, also fought against the caste system. Mahatma Gandhi, (1869-1948; Hindu nationalist leader and social reformer who taught nonviolent resistance) also tried to eliminate the varnas but failed. Although today the rigidities of the caste system have eased in urban areas, thanks to the work of Gandhi and later Indian governments, castes still hold a great deal of influence in the countryside where most of India's people live. The ancient caste system has been adapted so that modern occupations and social groups can fit into that religiously determined hierarchy, despite attempts by religious reformers to eliminate it.

The blame for Christ's death

The authentic but bad Christian belief that Jews were responsible for the death of Jesus has caused Christianity to be the carrier of anti-Jewish teachings and to be the supporter of violence against Jews in the past.

In John 8:44-45, we read one of the most painful statements of Christian anti-Jewishness. Referring to the Jews, Jesus is said to have remarked,

> *"Ye are of your father the devil, and the lusts of your father ye will do. He was a murderer from the beginning, and abode not in the truth, because there is no truth in him. When he speaketh a lie, he speaketh of his own: for he is a liar, and the father of it. And because I tell you the truth, ye believe me not."*

This — and other similar Christian teachings that the Jews should be punished because they killed Jesus and are devils and the anti-Christ — spurred Christians to persecute the Jews:

- The reading of some of these anti-Jewish texts, especially on Good Friday (the day of Christ's crucifixion) was the cause for many pogroms in Europe. A *pogrom* is an attack on a minority group, especially the Jewish community.

- The First Crusade killed 50,000 Jews in the Rhine valley towns of Worms and Spier, and the various crusades from the eleventh through the thirteenth centuries caused great suffering. Although economic and political motivations were clearly part of the crusades, the anti-Jewish beliefs helped justify this carnage.

This Christian belief in the guilt of the Jews was not only cruel, it was also untrue: The Romans killed Jesus. Pope John XXIII began the work of cleansing Catholicism of its anti-Jewish teachings in 1964 at the Second Vatican Council. This healing work continues through the work of Pope John Paul II.

Other bad beliefs

For many years, Mormonism taught that dark skin was the mark of Cain (who killed his brother Abel and was cursed by God), and that Africans were Cain's cursed descendents. This belief kept African-Americans out of the church and out of church leadership positions.

Defending some of the teachings of native religions as morally acceptable can be hard. Some tribes in New Guinea and other isolated areas of the earth, for example, still have tribal faiths that justify cannibalism, human sacrifice, scalping, and head shrinking as sacred and respected religious rituals.

Perverted religion

People with terrible hatreds who are able to pervert a good religion through that hate hijack some religions. Such people are not appealing to ancient bad teachings of a religion (see the preceding section); they are introducing bad beliefs of their own that they have based on ignorant and misguided interpretations of sacred texts.

Although these people are often clerics, their teachings don't reflect or express the mainstream teachings of a religion. Unfortunately, because of their positions or titles, people naturally assume that what they preach is indeed taught by the religion.

In bad teachings, the religion has been honestly presented by teaching its real but bad beliefs. In perverted religion, good teachings have been betrayed. The difference between bad and perverted teaching may seem very small, but it's really quite large. The results of both, however, can be equally painful and deadly.

Support for racism

One clear example of a perversion of authentic Christian teaching occurred in white Protestant churches in the southern United States. In the 1800s, these churches used the Bible to justify slavery as authentic Christian teaching. (They claimed that African-Americans were the descendents of Ham, Noah's second son, who was cursed because of the disrespect he showed to Noah when he saw Noah drunk and naked.) Unlike the church's unfortunate anti-Jewish teachings, Christianity never defended slavery. The fight against slavery by abolitionist churches reflected the basic Jewish and Christian teaching of the humanity of all peoples, as found in the Bible, where we read in the prophet Amos that God says to the Israelites, "You are like the black Ethiopians to me."

The rise of extremism

Of course, the most painful example of perverted religion in our time is the hijacking of Islam by fanatical Muslim extremists and the rise of terrorism as the means by which they try to achieve their goals. Islam isn't the first religion to be beset by extremist movements, and it undoubtedly won't be the last. Extremism in any religion generally seeks to eliminate perceived corruption within the religion, return the faith to its roots, and return believers to a purer form of worship. In doing so, the extremists at times view other faiths and their practitioners as different and unacceptable.

Islamic fundamentalism has several branches, all of which believe that the only true expressions of Islamic experience are in the principles of the Qur'an and the *Sunnah* (actions and sayings attributed to Muhammad). Although

Islamic fundamentalism is a valid religious movement, some groups have radicalized their messages and their ways of bringing this purity of religion to pass, using tactics like *jihad* (holy war) and the use of force (or threats of force) to attain their goal: a pure Islamic state.

The West tends to interpret jihad as holy war or struggle against unbelievers, similar to the religious underpinnings of the Crusades waged by medieval Christian leaders. Although this interpretation is indeed one sense of the word, jihad also has a more personal significance to Muslims: The term refers to the struggle to turn away from sin and sinful temptations. Therefore, jihad as a concept initially meant a struggle for personal religious piety.

Nevertheless, the radical groups use the Qur'an to justify their actions, even those actions that conflict with ancient Islamic teaching. For example, the Qur'an outlines what a just war is: One that is fought to right a wrong or one that is fought in defense. Islamic tradition also forbids the killing of women, children, and the old, even during a holy war. The Qur'an states that conversion should not be forced ("Let there be no compulsion in religion" [2.256]) and that the different religions are the result of Allah's will: "For every one of you We appointed a law and a way. And if Allah had pleased, he would have made you a single people. . . . So vie with one another in virtuous deed" [5.28].

By employing Islamic beliefs for their own political and social goals, Muslim radicals and those mullahs, ayatollahs, and imams who support them pose a threat to the majority of Muslims who reject their teachings and violence. Islam does not teach that killing non-Muslims is the will of Allah, nor does it teach that terrorists will be received in heaven as holy martyrs. True Muslim leaders have made these points, but their words are often drowned out by words of hate wrongly spoken in the name of one of the great religions of the world. As a result, an ideological and doctrinal struggle is going on between the vast number of moderates and the fewer radicals within Muslim societies.

Cults: False religions

Cults are not religions, although they may look like religions and they may act like religions. Cults may have holidays and clerics, sacred texts, and places of worship, but cults are *not* religions. Why? Because they take away the freedom of will that every religion gives its followers. Cults use very carefully developed psychological tools to brainwash people into joining the cult and then to keep them in the cult after they're captured. Religions have followers; cults have victims.

You know that you have encountered a cult and not a religion when the group

- ✔ Cuts off its members from contact with their families.
- ✔ Engages in all-night sessions and sleep deprivation in order to teach its lessons.
- ✔ Threatens those who disagree with it.
- ✔ Demands that you transfer all (or nearly all) your money or assets to them.
- ✔ Uses its members to go out begging or raising money all the time.
- ✔ Hides its true identity in parts of its work.
- ✔ Doesn't tolerate internal dissent.
- ✔ Funnels most of the money to leaders of the group, despite claiming to do charitable work,
- ✔ Keeps all finances secret.
- ✔ Engages in "love bombing." Cults take in lonely or confused people and surround them with members who don't know them but say they love them. This friendly group seduces these lonely people into joining them.
- ✔ Is constantly being investigated by the media or government organizations.

Cults are dangerous because they take away a person's ability to critically evaluate what is happening. The cult becomes the total and exclusive environment of its members, cutting them off from every element of their life that could help them pull out and regain control.

If your child or friend is caught up in something that makes them into a zombie, cuts them off from reality, deprives them of sleep and freedom, and keeps them brainwashed, they're in a cult. Do everything way in your power to get them out.

A Final Thought

If you view history honestly, you can see that economic motivations and imperialistic national ambitions are the source of far more wars than religion ever was. In fact, religious reasons were often brought out just to cover what were, at base, just reasons of greed and power.

Still, part of what it means to have a faith and be a member of a religion is to own all the history of that religion, both the good and the bad. Just because you may have had an ancestor who was a horse thief doesn't mean you have to abandon your family. Religions are like a family. Only by accepting and trying to change bad and perverted teachings can we help religion purify itself and fulfill its true mission of healing and comfort, compassion and justice, hope and love.

Some religious texts are misunderstood. Some are the result of historical prejudices seeping into pure revelation. Whatever the source of the bad stuff — misinterpretations or ancient prejudices — we own them if we are a part of that religion. We must all take responsibility for saying, "I do not hear God through that text" or "I don't understand this text" or "I am sorry for the harm such a text has done."

Part II
Religious Beliefs

The 5th Wave · By Rich Tennant

"My sense of faith is always tested when confronted with bacon on sale."

In this part . . .

Obviously, religious beliefs differ from religion to religion, but they're not as different as you may imagine. This part shows you that differences in belief produce some consistent ideas about the way life works and the way you achieve salvation, freedom, and/or enlightenment.

Chapter 5

The Foundations of Faith

All faiths are built on a foundation of beliefs. Although the beliefs differ from one religion to the next (and often from one sect to another within a religion), all religions have at their core an overarching principle or concept that unites believers. In addition, every religion influences the culture of the societies in which it is practiced.

If you get past these differences, you discover that all religions address many of the same topics: Life's mysteries, the obligations of the faithful, the nature of the Divine will, the presence of the Divine, our relationship to the Divine, our roles and responsibilities within society and within the family, and our relationships with other humans. In essence, these topics reveal each religion's concept of what the world is really like and what our place in it should be. These beliefs form the foundations of faith.

Joining Up

The first point to understand about religious beliefs is that, for some religions, getting everybody to have the same beliefs is very important. Identity in these *belief-oriented religions* comes from the shared belief. If you don't believe something central to such a religion, you can't be a part of it. In other religions, called *tribal religions*, membership comes from birth, not belief. You're born into these religions the way you are born into citizenship of a country. Your identity comes through your parents.

Belief-oriented religions: Sign me up, Scotty

Christianity is a pure belief-oriented religion, as are Islam and Buddhism. The fundamental belief in Christianity is that Jesus was the Messiah who came to earth to die for humanity's sins. If you don't believe this, you simply can't be a Christian, even if you like Santa and his reindeer and love chocolate Easter bunnies.

Christianity over the years has had many creeds that express the belief in Jesus as the Messiah:

- **Apostle's Creed:** Statement of faith of the Roman Catholic Church, Anglican Church, and major Protestant churches

- **Nicene Creed:** Statement of faith of all other Christian churches, plus the Eastern Orthodox Church

- **Athanasian Creed:** Profession of faith in the Roman Catholic and some Protestant churches

Although you don't have to believe in these or later Christian creeds, one thing is definitely true: If you don't believe that Jesus was the Messiah who came to earth to die for your sins, you're not a Christian.

Islam is another belief-oriented religion. You join Islam by stating that you believe that Allah is God and Muhammad is God's prophet. This affirmation of Muslim faith is called the *shahadah*. If you say the shahadah and believe the shahadah, you're a Muslim. If you don't, you aren't.

You affirm Buddhism by expressing your belief in the Four Noble Truths, which explain the origin of suffering and the path to enlightenment and the end of suffering. (For details on the Four Noble Truths, head to Chapter 14.)

Tribal religions: Who's your daddy? Who's your mamma?

Religions, such as Judaism and Hinduism, and almost all the native religions of the world do, of course, have beliefs, but they don't use their beliefs to determine membership. These tribal religions use birth and not belief to count their members. You can be part of a tribal religion and not believe a single thing. In Judaism, for example, if your mother was Jewish, then you are Jewish, no matter what you believe. (Some liberal Jews are now teaching that if your father was Jewish, you could also be Jewish, but this change is hotly debated within Judaism, and more orthodox Jews don't accept it.) Anyway, Jews who are Jewish only by birth and believe nothing that Judaism subscribes to are often called *secular Jews*. They're Jews, but they're not religious Jews. (See the related sidebar titled, "You are Jewish forever!" later in this chapter.)

Judaism is unique in that it is both an open, belief-oriented religion and a closed tribal religion at the same time! It's a tribal religion in that you're Jewish by birth and not belief, but it's also an open, belief-oriented religion in that you can convert to Judaism. Judaism doesn't aggressively seek converts, but it does accept them. This combination of being open and closed has made Judaism hard to understand for many people and is a source of conflict within Judaism. (If you want an in-depth look at Judaism, get a copy of *Judaism For Dummies,* by Rabbi Ted Falcon, Ph.D., and David Blatner, published by Wiley.)

Hinduism is the biggest closed religion in the world. When you are born into this religion, you are also born into one of the four castes (varnas), or classes. (For more information about this social structure, see the section titled, "The caste system in India," in Chapter 4.)

Many indigenous cultures also have closed religions. To have the religion of the Hopi or the Inuit of North America, for example, you need to be born a Hopi or an Inuit. For indigenous people, the religion is the spiritual part of their cultures.

It's a Mystery to Me: Religion and the Search for Answers

The world has mysteries that we confront and problems that we try to solve. However, mysteries are different from problems. The questions, "Does life have meaning?" "Is evil punished and goodness rewarded?" and "What is the cause of suffering?" are mysteries. No matter how many times philosophers and prophets provide answers to these and other of life's big questions, the questions remain real and pressing in every generation and in every life.

You are Jewish forever!

A little-known Jewish law says if any woman on your mother's side ever was Jewish, then you are fully and completely Jewish. In this case, if you ever decided to become Jewish, you wouldn't have to convert. The bestowing of Jewishness by the mother lasts forever, even if you don't know it and even if you come from a long line of people raised in other faiths, such as Christianity, Hinduism, or Islam.

Mysteries versus problems

The beliefs of a religion are not beliefs about the problems of life; they are beliefs about the mysteries of life. The French philosopher, Gabriel Marcel, understood the differences between problems and mysteries. A problem, he believed, was a question we ask about something that is outside ourselves. A mystery is a question we ask about something that is within us. When we answer a question, it disappears. When we respond to a mystery, it remains, deepening and defining our life.

Consider, for example, the question of what causes combustion. People used to think that a substance called phlogiston caused combustion, but then, French chemist Antoine Lavoisier proved that oxygen causes combustion, and nobody asked what caused combustion again.

Religions are about mysteries. Science is about problems. That's why science and religion can coexist and why all cultures have both. The need to understand how the world works drives science. The need to understand what the world means drives religion.

The questions "What causes lightning?" and "How will I spend my evening if the cable goes out?" are problems. Of course, not all problems are this easily answered or (to be honest) this irrelevant. "How will we feed the children if I lose my job?" and "Where should we go if the war comes to our front door?" are some of the bigger problems that people face.

For many folks, including us, trying to find answers to life's mysteries is the place where the religious impulse begins. When we understand mystery, we come to understand God more as an ongoing action than as a thing and the religious life more as a quest than a destination. Comprehending such mysteries helps us figure out how to survive life's problems and enjoy life's blessings. (See the related sidebar titled, "Mysteries versus problems," in this chapter.)

Searching for meaning

Every culture has some kind of religion, and all faiths answer the question "What is the meaning of life?" Humanity's search for an answer to this question is one of the main reasons that people are drawn to religion. The answers, although different from religion to religion, give people's lives purpose, meaning, and hope. (See the related sidebar titled, "What a downer! Nihilism," in this section.)

The different religions have their own views on the meaning of life:

TECHNICAL STUFF

What a downer! Nihilism

All the religions of the world may be wrong. Maybe nothing more than dirt and worms and a cold universe await us after death. Maybe goodness, life, and hope have no edge over evil, death, and despair. Maybe what we can physically see is all there is. The belief that life has no meaning, that no God exists in the universe, that there is no revelation, no prophecy, no redemption, no salvation, and no purpose or inherent value in human existence — no nuthin' — is called *nihilism,* or nothing-ism.

Nihilism is a belief that completely contradicts all religions and all religious beliefs. In concluding that life has no meaning or purpose and that all beliefs and values are unfounded, nihilists (people who believe in nihilism) point to the abundance of evil in the world, the injustice of human existence, and the idea that no proof for any higher power exists.

The question to ask yourself is not whether nihilism is true, but whether you could live your life if you believed that it was true. What's the sense of living, of hoping, or of fighting for justice and freedom if life has no meaning or purpose or value? Religion may be ultimately wrong, but it is humanly necessary.

Some forms of Buddhism have an idea that looks like nihilism but isn't. It is called *shunyata,* nothingness. The idea here is that nothing has independent existence; everything depends on everything else. The main point of shunyata is that much of what we see in the world isn't the ultimate truth. Only by seeing through the illusions and attachments of life can we reach enlightenment. Shunyata is a very hopeful idea and, unlike nihilism, takes us to serenity not despair, to wisdom not cynicism.

- ✔ **Hinduism:** Gain release from the cycle of rebirth and merge with the eternal Divine, thus escaping an inhospitable world.

- ✔ **Buddhism:** Gain enlightenment and, in that way, free yourself from the sufferings that come from illusions and attachments to life.

- ✔ **Judaism:** Do God's commandments.

- ✔ **Christianity:** Try to love the way Jesus loved.

- ✔ **Islam:** Submit oneself to the will of Allah.

- ✔ **Taoism:** Achieve inner harmony.

Accounting for sin and suffering

"Why is there suffering in the world?" That's another big mystery that religion addresses. For most religions, suffering is the result of human failing or the lack of human understanding. In monotheistic religions, suffering is wrapped up in the concept of sin and human failing. In the Eastern religions, suffering is the result of humankind's lack of understanding, or enlightenment. Whatever the source of suffering and death is — human failure or human "blindness" — religions give their members hope by offering ways to overcome suffering and death. In Western religions, the goal is salvation; in Eastern religions, it's enlightenment.

Sin: The devil made me do it

One of the most powerful reasons people come to religion is to find salvation from sin. Monotheistic religions use the term *sin* to describe the brokenness of human existence. The belief is that humans, in and of themselves, are not whole. Only by living through God's commandments or in accordance with God's will can humans be complete. Sin is a human failing, the result of human rebelliousness and arrogance and the source of evil in the world.

What makes a sin depends on the religion:

- ✔ **An action:** All monotheistic religions agree that sins are actions that violate God's law. By behaving in ways that contradict divine will, a person sins. In Judaism and Islam, sin is *always* an act, a wrong act, and an immoral or impure act.

- ✔ **A thought:** In Judaism, a thought cannot be a sin, but a thought can lead to a sin. In Christianity, a thought can be a sin.

- ✔ **A state of being:** In some Christian traditions, sin is not only a thought or an act; it is also a state of being, represented in the concept of *original sin.* Original sin is a condition that humans are born to because of Adam's disobedience (he ate the forbidden fruit) in the Garden of Eden. (See the related sidebar titled, "Paul, Augustine, and original sin," in this section.)

Whether sin is an act, a thought, or a condition, it is, at its heart, distance from God.

Atonement and salvation: Getting right with the Lord

For monotheistic religions, sin and suffering are the results of choosing badly, of allowing selfishness and grasping to overcome what we know to be the will of God. By willfully and deliberately violating the divine will, we distance ourselves from God.

By atoning for bad deeds, people can cleanse themselves from the effects of sins and reconcile with God. Also called *reconciliation,* atonement requires repentance (being sorry for what you've done) and a change of behavior to conform to a religiously prescribed one. Through the process of atonement, people can reconstruct their relationships with God and those they have sinned against. By teaching people how to forgive others, religion helps people ask forgiveness themselves. In this way, these faiths address the basic human need to admit moral failings and move forward to a better way of living.

TECHNICAL STUFF

Paul, Augustine, and original sin

Saint Paul, who interprets the creation story in Genesis (in the book of Romans in the New Testament), makes the first connection between Adam's fall and original sin. Hundreds of years later, Augustine, a theologian within the Roman Catholic Church, popularized the idea of original sin. According to Augustine, no person can cleanse the original sin that damns us all and blocks our salvation. Only Jesus' atoning death and resurrection saves people from original sin and opens the way to salvation — but only for those who believe in Jesus and his sacrifice.

For most religions, salvation is a lifelong process, aided by both the discipline of ritual and the moral teachings of the faith.

Being negative

Buddhism doesn't concern itself much with sin as a separate issue. For Buddhists, the goal isn't to find salvation from sin but to achieve enlightenment and release from all human issues, including sin. Negativity or attachment to material life, Buddhists believe, is the obstacle that holds people back.

Within some Buddhist sects, negativity is expressed in the teaching of *tahna* (craving) and *dukkha* (suffering or imperfection). Our human desires, illusions, and attachments cause our suffering.

The reason people are so unhappy is that they want or crave things: love, adventure, and material possessions, chocolate, whatever. When people don't get what they want, they become sad. The idea is that we are our own source of unhappiness, and we can change how we feel by changing our attitude and desires.

Some Buddhist sects teach that life is a constant process of overcoming this suffering by learning why we suffer and giving up our attachments and our illusions. Dukkha, which describes the source of all human suffering, is the first of the Four Noble Truths of Buddhism.

Being born again . . . and again . . . and again . . .

In Hinduism, the nature of human limitation is that we are all trapped in the world of *samsara,* which forces us to die and be reborn endless numbers of times. Hinduism also offers hope that we can stop the process of rebirth and death. With proper practice, a person can attain release (*moksha*) from the suffering of samsara and find freedom and oneness with the infinite, the ultimate goal in most Hindu sects.

Practicing holiness

The word *holy,* which means sacred or hallowed, comes from Judaism and appears in the other monotheistic faiths. The sense of holiness, however, cuts across all religions and even goes beyond them. Many people who reject organized religion describe themselves as spiritual, indicating that they want to find some way to express and connect to holiness in the world.

The term *holiness* means a state of moral and spiritual perfection, but even that doesn't adequately convey the deep sense of mystery that imbues the word. The root meaning of the Hebrew word for holy, *kadosh,* is "something set apart from ordinary things." The objects of the Temple in Jerusalem, the ark that held the tablets of the law, the food of the priests — all these things were set apart and untouchable by non-priests. These objects somehow communicated the power of absolute holiness that is God.

Holiness means many different things and is understood differently in different religions.

(Not quite six) degrees of holiness

Holiness is also usually seen as having degrees. Among holy things, some are more holy than others. For example, in the creation account in Genesis, the order of holiness is as follows (from least to most holy):

- ✔ All things in the world are minimally holy because God makes them. This includes rocks, plants, the land, and so on.
- ✔ Animals are more holy than the inanimate items because they are alive.
- ✔ People are more holy than animals because they are both alive and, according to the belief of the three monotheistic faiths, are "made in the image of God."
- ✔ God, of course, is absolutely holy.

For inanimate objects and animals, holiness is a natural expression; they can't be anything other than they are. For people, holiness is a struggle because of our dual natures: part strivers toward God and part sinners against God.

Holiness and the avoidance of impurities

The Eastern faiths don't use the word *holiness,* but the idea of something set apart and closer to absolute purity and perfection is a basic part of the faiths. A Buddha is one example, and a *bodhisattva* is another. (A bodhisattva is an average person who reaches nirvana but chooses to fulfill a vow not to enter Buddhahood and instead turns back to help others.) The Buddha and bodhisattva have gone beyond the struggles of human existence and have attained the higher realm of the truth.

Holy things

All sorts of things can be holy:

- **Time:** Holy days and holidays are a part of every religion. These days connect followers of the faith to holy events and the turn of the seasons and the cycle of the moon.

- **People (in certain religions):** In Hinduism, for example, probably the most holy or sacred person is the *Sannyasin,* or renouncer. Sannyasins give up everything to search for the Divine and become conveyers of spiritual wisdom to all who would be taught by them. Whole communities adopt sannyasins and take care of their needs. In monotheistic religions, on the other hand, people can't attain absolute holiness; see the sidebar titled, "Close but no cigar," for details.

  Within some religious communities, ancestors are venerated. In Taiwan, Mexico, and Central American communities, special holidays are set aside to remember the dead. Even in the United States, we do not step or deface a grave. We consider the space to be sacred ground.

- **Objects:** Consider the sprinkling of holy water at a Roman Catholic or Greek Orthodox service. The Orthodox believe that the hands of the priest become the hands of God during the service.

- **Places:** In India, the city of Banares (or Varanasi) is holy because it is where holy rivers find their homes. For many in India, the river Ganges is a holy goddess.

- **Nature:** Native Americans consider all of life and the earth to be holy. Taoism and Shinto also share this immense respect and awe of Nature.

Close, but no cigar

Monotheistic faiths don't believe that people are holy. This concept surprises many people who think that if things like trees and the seas can be holy, then surely people can be holy. Nowhere does the Bible state that people are holy. People are made in the image of God, but because people have free will and can decide to disobey God and sometimes choose evil over good, people aren't holy. In Jewish law, a dead person is holy, perhaps because, after you're dead, you can't choose evil.

The Christian belief that Jesus was the Son of God is a departure from Jewish and later Islamic ideas of human holiness. Jesus represents a singular and remote human achievement — Jesus as a purely holy human being. Judaism and Islam have ideas of saints and righteous people and prophets, but none go beyond the normal human impulses of good and evil. Jesus is different, and the Christian beliefs about Jesus represent a new idea of human holiness. Still, Christianity never taught that any human being could become holy like Jesus. Jesus was human and holy, but Jesus was also unique. (Being the Son of God can do that to you.)

Hanging On to Faith

When people think of religion as a set of beliefs, they often use the word faith to describe what they mean: When someone makes the simple statement "I am of the (fill-in-the-blank) faith," they reveal what religious belief system they consider true. In this definition, faith is the group of ideas that a religion holds to be true. People learn this type of faith because their parents taught them the faith of their ancestors, or because they convert to a religion that they come to believe is true.

Faith is also trust. In Hebrew, the word for faith is *emunah,* which has as its root meaning, trust. The word *amen,* spoken by Jews and Christians after prayer, comes from emunah. This idea of trust is found in the New Testament, for example, "Now faith is the assurance of things hoped for, the conviction of things not seen" (Hebrews 11:1). This type of faith means trust in a God or gods, trust in the truth of a religion's teachings, trust in a teacher, and trust in the traditions of one's ancestors. Although many of the beliefs of the world's religions can be proved true by using reason, the essence of faith is trust.

Faith versus works

Martin Luther, the founder of Lutheranism, stressed the idea of justification by faith. What justification by faith means is that doing good deeds and living a good life (that is, following God's commandments) isn't enough for salvation. When you stand before God, you stand there as a sinner. The only redemption comes from God's grace (and, according to Luther, not from a particular church or bishop). To get that, you have to have faith; for Christians this specifically means believing that Jesus died for humankind's sins. To put it more simply, as a Christian, the trust you put in God and Jesus for salvation produces your salvation.

Many Christian theologies contrast salvation by faith with salvation by works. The question is, "Is faith in God and Jesus' atoning death enough to get into heaven, or does the Christian also have to do good deeds?" Christian sects are divided on this issue, and biblical support can be found for both arguments:

- James (one of Jesus' Twelve Apostles) taught, "Even so faith, if it hath not works, is dead, being alone" (James 2:17). Faith alone may or may not be enough for salvation, but faith is most often accompanied by works that flow from the goodness that faith instills within us.

- The Christian doctrine that faith and not works is essential for salvation finds expression in Paul's letter to the Ephesians: "For by grace you have been saved through faith; and this is not your own doing, it is the gift of God — not because of works, lest any man should boast. For we are his workmanship, created in Christ Jesus for good works, which God prepared beforehand, that we should walk in them" (Ephesians 2:8-10).

The relationship between faith and works in Christian theology is subtle and complex. Those who say faith matters only for salvation don't understand that good works are the fruit of real faith, and those who say only works matter don't understand how the belief in Jesus' atoning death itself leads to salvation.

The central belief in Islam is stated in the shahadah: "There is no god but God, and Muhammad is his prophet." Everything in the faith reaffirms this belief in a single, omnipotent God who has revealed his will in the Qur'an; Muslims don't have the dilemma of choosing between works and belief as the paths to salvation. The two — faith and works — are inseparable. They know what leads to paradise: Surrender to Allah and his will. One way to show this surrender is to share the blessings that Allah has bestowed. So important is this concept in Islam that almsgiving is one of the faith's Five Pillars.

In Buddhism, faith is connected to the idea of trust. You must find the courage to travel down the path toward enlightenment by looking inside your own heart or mind and trusting that you can find enlightenment.

Going on "blind faith"

Many people of faith have what some call "blind faith." That is, they trust that the teachings of their religion are true, without the need for rational proof. Scientific proof is unnecessary, they say, because of the following reasons:

- **The record of sacred history:** The events recorded in sacred texts (and for Muslims the existence of the sacred text, the Qur'an, itself) are proof enough.

  - The Hebrew Bible, for example, often introduces a commandment with the phrase, "You have seen what the Lord your God has done for you by bringing you out of the house of bondage. . . ."

  - In the case of Christianity, the resurrection of Jesus and the appearance of Jesus to the women and disciples after his death aren't only stories; Christians believed they are proof of the credibility of the Christian claims.

  - For Muslims, the Qur'an isn't a record of God's law and presence in history; it is *literally* the transcribed word of God as spoken through the angel Gabriel to Muhammad. The fact that it even exists is ample proof of God's existence and will. Many people of faith trust that the historical record of God's actions is proof that the God who would perform miracles and redemptions would not reveal falsehoods.

- **Faith's effect on the faithful.** People of strong faith, such as the Dalai Lama or Mother Teresa, seem to possess a wisdom and serenity based on their faith. The compassion and love that radiate from them and uplift all who behold it is both inspiring and convincing.

✔ **Faith's antiquity.** Scientific truths can be absolutely true even though they were discovered just this morning, but when it comes to wisdom and ethics, the older a tradition is, the more likely it is to be true because it's proven its reliability over time. Hinduism is over 5,000 years old, Judaism traces its roots back some 4,000 years, Christianity is more than 2,000 years old, and Islam 1,400 years old. Wisdom that has withstood the passage of time and the challenges of the ages does not require scientific proof to be real. "New and improved" may be high praise for soap, but not for wisdom.

Knowing through Revelation

The way we know things in philosophy is through logic or experience. The way we know things in religion is through revelation. *Revelation* is the way God or gods make known what humans are supposed to know and do; it's his (or their) way of communicating to us. Revelation is the idea that the way we understand the Divine is the way the Divine wants to be understood. The word revelation comes from the Latin word *revelatio,* which means, "to uncover or lay bare." In essence, revelation is the uncovering of the divine.

Types of revelation

The way in which the Divine reveals itself is different in different religions. For some religions, the universe itself is the medium through which the Divine reveals itself to humans. Also called *natural revelation,* this type of revelation is evident in the interconnected patterns and systems of the cosmos. The beauty of a sunset, the majesty of the stars and planets, the miracle of birth — all are revelations in that you can see the essence or nature of the divine within them. (See the related sidebar titled "Psalm 19" later in this chapter.) Natural revelation is a big part of Hinduism, Native American religions, Shinto, and Taoism. In Hinduism and many other *pantheistic religions* (religions that believe that God is the combined forces and laws displayed in the universe), the divine or the infinite permeates all living things and unites them in one cosmic mind.

The other main type of revelation is historical revelation. In religions that see a significant distance separating the sacred from the secular, revelation is a matter of historical events in which God or the gods reveal the divine will through human interpreters, otherwise known as prophets. For this reason, this type of revelation is also called prophetic revelation. (For information on the role of prophets in religion, see Chapter 6.) Another type of revelation is the personal revelation, where at some time in your life, you experienced a moment of purity, clarity, or joy.

FROM THE HOLY BOOKS

Psalm 19

The classic example of natural revelation is Psalm 19 from the Old Testament:

1. The heavens are telling the glory of God; and the firmament proclaims his handiwork.

2. Day to day pours forth speech, and night to night declares knowledge.

3. There is no speech, nor are there words; their voice is not heard;

4. yet their voice goes out through all the earth, and their words to the end of the world.

The three great monotheistic religions, Islam, Christianity, and Judaism, believe that, at some point in human history, God spoke to human beings and revealed his will. Whether that event involved Moses on Mount Sinai, Jesus at Calvary, or Muhammad at Mecca, at some point God said or did something that was never said or done before. The creation story is another example of historical revelation: It was a particular event that happened at a particular time. Similar examples are the Hebrew exodus from Egypt and the lives of Jesus and Muhammad.

When one revelation supplants the last

BIG ISSUE

Many Christians believe that the revelations in the Hebrew Bible were fulfilled in the life, death, and resurrection of Jesus, who was the Christ, or the Messiah. This idea that Judaism is "fulfilled" in the revelations of Christianity has caused much friction between the two communities. Similarly, the Islamic belief that the Qur'an is the culmination (and correction) of revelations of both the Jewish and Christian traditions created quite a stir in its own right.

Religions that believe divine revelation began at some point also have to figure out some way to prove that it stopped. Otherwise, another new religion can come along and say, "You were good for a while, but now God has sent us to replace you." (See the related sidebar titled "Revelatory updates" later in this chapter.) You can't run a religion that way, and you can't always be fighting about who is and isn't a bona fide prophet. In the Hebrew Bible, the stopping idea was Moses' uniqueness. In Christianity, it was the idea that there was only one Son of God, and in Islam, it was the idea that Muhammad was the last prophet. Whether these stopping ideas work depends upon whether you are in or out of the religion.

Revelatory updates

Many religious traditions claim to have special insight or revelation from the Divine. Early Quakers in England believed that they had an "inner light" from the presence of the Holy Spirit in their lives. This inner light gave them courage to challenge the sexism and authoritarianism of the Puritans. Mother Ann Lee, the founder of the Shakers, believed that she had received a divine revelation from a Mother-Father God and so created a celibate Christian community that, at one point, reached as far west as Kentucky. Mary Baker Eddy, the founder of Christian Science, and Myrtle Fillmore, co-founder of Unity, claimed that the Divine had healed them and so began to practice what is termed today as "New Thought" religion. They taught mind over matter. The ideas for the power of positive thinking came directly from these traditions.

Throughout the history of the world, when current or historic religions are not meeting the needs of people, new religions come into existence. Often, these newer religions build upon the foundations of beliefs from the past to create a newer system that fits into the lives of those seeking something different. For example, astrology, spiritualism, and charismatic Christianity claim to have a special link with the divine spirit or world in some way.

Revelation versus reason

Much of medieval theology in all three monotheistic faiths focused on the difficult task of reconciling reason and revelation. The central problem that the medieval scholastics had to deal with was that if human beings could rationally understand God's intentions, why would we need sacred scriptures and organized religion? On the other hand, if we need God to figure out everything we're supposed to do, why did God give us the power to think in the first place? What is the role of human reason in determining the truth? What is God's role? These are not just medieval problems; they continue to vex us today.

One solution is to believe that God commanded only rational truths, and all the other stuff (rituals, miracles, snake worship, and so on) is just human invention to jazz up God's truths. The problem with this solution is that the Bible has rational and irrational things together in the same book, and all of it is supposed to be the word of God.

Another way of fitting reason and revelation together is to think of them as two different ways of getting to different parts of the truth. Reason gets us to the religious truths that are universal, the truths that are true for everyone whether they are a part of the religion or not. Revelation is a way of getting to universal truths, as well as truths that are deeply felt by the followers of a religion. The Mass is true for Catholics, the Hajj is true for Muslims, and Passover is true for Jews in ways that reason cannot describe. For those who think that the only truth is that which applies to all people all the time, a good dose of yoga or Eucharist or matzo (bread) may help them see the truth in a new way through the eyes of revelation.

Consider these examples:

- ✔ Texts written by Taoist priests hundreds of years ago explore the foundations of the universe in search of immortality. In their quest, these priests devised ways to vaccinate people for smallpox and monitor people with diabetes.

- ✔ Ancient Muslim researchers charted the nervous and circulatory systems long before Europe understood human physiology. The researchers studied the minute details of the universe because they believed that Allah spoke to them through his creation.

Heeding the Divine Commandment

Some people come to religion because they want to believe in God; other people come to religion because they want to do for God. Faith and works, creed and deed, beliefs and commandments are not necessarily opposed to each other (although this issue has long divided Jewish and Christian theologians). Even though some commandments are good deeds, the essence of the idea of commandment is not goodness but obligation. When you do something because you believe God wants you to do it, that is a commandment. What you do for God may be ethical or it may be ritual, but its main meaning is that you are acting out of obligation to God.

Every religion has some tradition of sacred obligation, of the path to salvation or release or enlightenment that we must walk, not just imagine or think about: Theravada Buddhism's Eightfold Path, the Tao Te Ching of Taoism, and the Law Code of Manu in Hinduism all define the path to freedom. The Confucian Analects reminds average people that it is better for society if they accept their position in life. Harmony or peacefulness can be attained only if all people accept their social status and respect their neighbors and the emperor. Both the Law Code of Manu and the Confucian Analects were written in order to bring some type of order to society. In a sense, they outline the obligations believers have in the practice of their faith.

The idea of commandment is important in Judaism and Islam, and less so in Christianity.

Obligations in Judaism

If you ask Orthodox Jews what they do to be Jewish, they will answer, "We do mitzvot," which means that they seek out God's commandments and try to do as many of them as possible in their lives. That is the Jewish religious quest.

Judaism traditionally lists 613 total mitzvot, or commandments, as enumerated in the Hebrew Bible and Talmud that every Jewish male should follow. Of these commandments, 248 are positive, meaning that they tell a Jewish person that God wants them to do something; 365 commandments are negative, meaning that God wants them *not* to do something. Some of the positive commandments have to be performed at a set time during the day or the year (morning prayers, reading from the Torah scroll, and so on). In Orthodox Judaism, these time-bound positive commandments are not obligatory for women so as not to cause a conflict with maternal duties and ritual obligations.

Obligations in Islam

In Islam, commandment or obligation is a central religious concept. Muslims have two fundamental obligations:

- Show gratitude for life, which is a gift from Allah.
- Surrender (or submit) to God.

The following texts outline how Muslims perform these obligations:

- The Qur'an, Islam's holy book
- The hadith, the record of sayings and actions attributed to Muhammad
- The sharia, the holy law of Islam (itself based on the Qur'an and hadith)

The most important duties that Muslims must perform are the Five Pillars of Islam:

- Reciting the shahadah, the Islamic profession of faith
- Performing the five ritual prayers in a particular way and at a particular time
- Giving to charity for the benefit of the poor and needy
- Fasting during the month of Ramadan
- Making a pilgrimage to Mecca

Ranking commandments

The big question about commandments is whether all of them have the same importance. The prophets in the Hebrew Bible strongly represent the view that ethical commandments are more important than ritual commandments.

Judaism teaches that whenever a ritual commandment conflicts with an ethical commandment, the ritual commandment is set aside in order to fulfill the ethical commandment. For example, if the ritual commandment to fast on Yom Kippur conflicts with your doctor's order to eat in order to preserve your life or health, then you're actually commanded to eat on Yom Kippur.

Islam makes a similar distinction. Although Muslims are expected to perform their ritual obligations and observe the rules of the faith, if doing so is impossible, the failure is not seen as a transgression.

Following are examples of how these obligations make allowances for special circumstances:

- ✔ Muslims observe certain dietary restrictions (derived from Jewish ones); they can eat only the food that is allowed (halal). They can eat meat that has been ritually slaughtered, for example, but they must never eat meat from animals that have died of themselves or that have been clubbed to death or gored by other animals. Nor can they eat pork. If no other food is available, however, Muslims can eat even the forbidden foods, as long as they don't enjoy it or get used to it.

  Then whoever is driven by necessity, not desiring, nor exceeding the limit, no sin is upon him. Surely, Allah is Forgiving, Merciful (2.173).

- ✔ Fasting during the month of Ramadan is the Fourth Pillar of Islam. People who need nourishment and would suffer from fasting, however, are exempt. These people include young children, pregnant or nursing women, the sick, and soldiers in battle. The mentally handicapped, if they don't understand the religious reasons behind the find, are also exempt.

For Muslims, these exceptions (and others like them) don't diminish Allah's power; they illustrate his mercy and compassion. (See the related sidebar titled "Micah.")

Micah

According to this classic passage from Micah, ethical commandments are more important than ritual commandments:

6. "With what shall I come before the Lord, and bow myself before God on high? Shall I come before him with burnt offerings, with calves a year old?

7. Will the Lord be pleased with thousands of rams, with ten thousands of rivers of oil?

Shall I give my first-born for my transgression, the fruit of my body for the sin of my soul?"

8. He has showed you, O man, what is good; and what does the Lord require of you but to do justice, and to love kindness, and to walk humbly with your God?

Providence and Karma: The Consequences of Our Actions

One of the few ideas that is found in all religions is the idea that what happens to us is the result of what we do. In the Western religions, this idea is called *providence,* and it means that God judges us and rewards our goodness while punishing us for our sins. In Hinduism and in some Buddhist sects, this same idea is called *karma,* and it's the idea that how we act in this life determines how we will live in our next life. In both East and West, this is a distinctive religious belief, and many people come to faith because they hope (or fear) that providence and karma are true.

Consider providence and karma as the religious version of the law of cause and effect: What goes around, comes around.

Providence

In Judaism, Christianity, and Islam, the idea of providence takes both individual and collective forms. In Judaism, this idea first emerged as a way to describe how God punished or rewarded the whole nation of Israel. For example, the destruction of the Temple in Jerusalem by the Babylonians in 586 B.C.E., and then again by the Romans in 70 C.E., were both seen as punishment from God to the people of Israel for their collective sins: "Because of our sins, we were exiled from our land."

Later in the Hebrew Bible, the idea of providence became more individualized, but was still a worldly idea. Ezekiel and Jeremiah revealed the new idea that "Each man shall die because of his own sins." The sins of others would no longer affect an individual's spiritual possibilities. Finally, in the rabbinic period at the beginning of the Common Era, providence was pushed into "the world to come," as well as this world. By creating the idea of heaven and hell, the problem of righteous people such as Job who suffered in this world could be solved. After death, the souls of the righteous would be totally rewarded and the souls of the wicked totally punished.

Christianity developed the ideas of heaven and hell to a much greater degree than Judaism, and Islam followed Christian teachings in this regard by creating the idea of paradise. Most practicing Jews do not believe in heaven and hell; therefore, it's not a topic of much rabbinic speculation, as opposed to Christianity, where it is a major focus of the faith.

The walled garden: Heaven

The teachings of the monotheistic faiths about heaven are similar. Heaven is, first of all, God's neighborhood. Heaven is the abode of the most high; it is

God's home and the home of the souls of the righteous. Heaven is described with every possible glorious adjective. It is a place of peace, joy, and tranquility, and above all else, it is a place of closeness to God. So wonderful is heaven, the Talmud teaches, that "one hour of bliss in the world to come is equal to all the bliss we experience in this world." The Islamic idea of heaven (or paradise) reiterates this idea: Paradise is a walled garden, open to those who do good, avoid evil, truly repent for their transgressions, and believe in the Qur'an.

Into the fire: Hell

Hell is the final state of torment and punishment for the souls of the wicked. Christian thinkers and writers such as Dante (1265-1321, the Italian poet who wrote *The Divine Comedy*) were much more lavish in their descriptions of hell than were Jewish thinkers. In Judaism, hell is called *sheol* or *gehinom,* and it is just generally a kind of wastebasket for misused souls, where the souls are destroyed. (See the related sidebar titled *"Dante's Inferno"* in this chapter.)

For Muslims, hell (al-Nar; literally, the fire) has seven divisions. Some Muslims believe each division holds a particular type of sinner:

Level	Occupants
Jahannam	Unrepentant, wicked Muslims
Laza	Christians, misers, and those who turn their backs on the truth
Al-Hutamah	Jews
Sa'ir	Pagans
Saqar	Zoroastrians
Al-Jahim	Idolaters
Al-Hawiya	Hypocrites

Karma

Hinduism, Buddhism, and Jainism believe that we are all bound up in a cycle of birth-death-rebirth. This is called *samsara*, and freedom from it is called *moksha*, or release. Buddhists and Jains have subtle differences from Hinduism on the precise workings of karma, but all endorse it as the most honest and accurate description of moral reality. The ethical fruits growing from the plant of our past deeds determine our present life. If we live a good life — which means that we live true to the laws set forth about our caste — then we are reborn into a higher caste or station in life. If we ignore the rules of the caste system, then we may be reborn at a lower station in life.

Dante's Inferno

The *Inferno,* the part of *The Divine Comedy* that deals with hell, remains one of the most imaginative descriptions of perdition that ever graced the pages of literature. According to Dante, hell has nine levels — concentric circles that become smaller as they descend. The torments these sinners suffer are poetically just: Those who remained on the fence their whole lives and never took a stand (which is a sin, according to Dante), for example, spend eternity chasing flags that represent causes.

Each circle of hell holds particular sinners, and the sins become graver as you move though hell to the last circle. The inhabitants of the final circle (which, by the way, is ice and not fire) are Satan himself and the three most vile betrayers of all time: Judas Iscariot (who betrayed Christ) and Brutus and Cassius (who betrayed Caesar).

The laws regarding caste, however, are not the only factor determining the extent of good or bad karma. Hinduism offers many paths that you can take to break the bonds of samsara. You can choose to follow your caste, you can devote your life to a god or goddess, or you may take the path of a sannyasin and abandon life in search of the Divine. All of these, and more, influence karma and the possibilities of the next life.

The Jains have an especially vivid and unique idea of karma. They see karma as a force in the universe that holds down the life force of our souls. Any bad act is karma, and it blocks the soul from rising to the top of the universe like a spiritual balloon and resting there in eternal peace. According to the Jains, karma actually colors our souls black, blue, gray, yellow, red, or white. Black, blue, and gray are the colors of the souls of bad people, while yellow, red, and white are the colors of the souls of good people.

To gain release for your soul, you must practice restraint from any act of violence or confrontation that could produce karma. Jains take the practice of nonviolence to the extreme. Some sects wear facemasks to prevent bugs from entering a person's nose or mouth and thus committing suicide. Many will not cook in the evening for the same reasons. Some shed clothing as a symbol of their asceticism, and many spend long hours meditating in a trance-like state in order to find a better birth.

Love, Love, and More Love: Grace

The Greek word for sexual love is *eros.* Love of friends is *philos.* Divine love is *agape,* as in "grace" or "self-sacrificing love." The religious meaning of grace is that God loves us not because we deserve to be loved but because God's nature is to love. Humans simply benefit from that superabundant unmerited grace. Grace is simply the word we use to describe the love God has for humankind collectively and individually. Perhaps more than any other thing, the possibility of divine love attracts people to the monotheistic faiths.

One of the basic tenets of Judaism, Christianity, and Islam is that an all-powerful, all-knowing, all-present entity loves each person like a parent loves a child.

Seeing God's love on earth

Each religion points to certain events or conditions that reveal God's love for humankind.

✔ Jewish people see God's love in the gift of the covenant *(brit)* that God establishes with them. To Jews, God's gift of the covenant, as well as the exodus from Egypt and other miracles, produce a human commandment that they love God in return. Human love for each other and for God is called *ahavah*: "You shall love *(v'ahavta)* the Lord your God with all your heart and with all your soul and with all your might" (Deuteronomy 6:5). This love supports all Jewish ethical teachings and, particularly, the golden rule, "Love your neighbor as you love yourself." (Head to Part IV, where we look at religious ethics, to find out more).

✔ Christians see God's love in the incarnation and resurrection of Jesus. In Christianity, grace is called agape, which means the freely given and unmerited love of God as was connoted in the divine grace, but it also includes a sacrificial element that is seen in God's decision to send his only begotten Son to die for the sins of humanity (John 15:13; also Mark 12:29-31). The only proper response to such a gift is to love God in return. (See the related sidebar titled, "Ideas of love: Thoughts from Christian theologians.")

✔ Muslims see God's love in the revealed word of the Qur'an, which itself was a gift from Allah to Muhammad through the angel Gabriel. The only thing Allah wants in return for the gifts he has bestowed is the absolute faith of humans.

For Islam, Christianity, and Judaism, the spiritual response to God's unmerited love is praise, humility, and thanksgiving.

If God loves us so much, . . . ?

Misunderstandings abound about what God's love and grace really mean. Following are some of the responses formed by the monotheistic religions:

If God's love us, why does he judge us? A central Jewish prayer for the penitential season is *Avinu Malkeinu*, "Our Father, Our King." This duality is always present in God's love. God is both parent and sovereign, both protector and judge.

God's love is present in both roles. Just as a parent must occasionally judge and punish his or her children so that they grow morally as well as physically, God judges us for our sins and demands that we acknowledge them and seek repentance, after which, we receive his forgiveness.

If God loves us, why do we have pain or burdens? Sufferings and burdens are not a denial of love; sometimes they are a challenge to deepen our ability to love both God and other people. In Jewish theology, there are sufferings of love *(isurin shell ahavah)*, which are challenges that God places in our lives so that we may love more deeply. The sufferings of Jesus on the cross are not a violation of God's grace; they are its most exquisite fulfillment. They show how people can live through their sufferings because of their belief that God loves them and will not place burdens in their life that are too heavy for them to bear.

If God loves us, why do we die? Death is not a violation of God's love; it is a part of God's love. Death is not a mistake or a defeat or a betrayal. Death is part of life and part of God's plan. Why death comes too soon to some is one of the mysteries of that divine plan, but death is a part of the giving and the taking that are the twin movements of God's presence in the world and in our lives. The belief that God's love extends beyond the grave is, however, one of the main elements of God's love as understood by the Abrahamic faiths. The belief that our souls will live on in heaven (as it's called in Christianity), paradise (as its called in Islam), or the world to come (as it's called in Judaism) is a conclusion that the monotheistic faiths have come to because of their belief in God's love.

Love in Eastern religions

Love takes on a different flavor in religions of the East. Confucianism emphasizes family and the giving up of personal and individual desires in order to show love of your family and to maintain harmony. While people in the West prize individualism, many in the East know the values of community.

Following are some of the ways that Eastern religions view and show love:

- In Mahayana Buddhism, an example of self-sacrificing love is the Bodhisattva, a person who has attained enlightenment, has tasted the sweet fruits of freedom, but comes back to the physical plane of existence to help others find the same experience.

- In Hinduism, Krishna, who is an avatar (human incarnation) of Vishnu, calls the animals to his side as a way of showing love. He can also satisfy as many as 10,000 cowgirls who worship him. Finding the Mind of the Divine can be a form of love also.

- Preeminently, the concept of *ahimsa,* or nonviolence to any living thing, demonstrates love on a grand scale. Both Hinduism and Buddhism reject violence and believe that animals, birds, and all sorts of beings become your friend when you cease to kill and eat them.

> ✔ For many Buddhist sects, love is just one of many attachments that are to be transcended if you want to achieve spiritual freedom. "Let therefore no man love anything; loss of the beloved is evil. Those who love nothing, and hate nothing, have no fetters" (Dhammapada 16).

The grace of God, the unmerited love of the creator of the universe for each one of us, is not just a religious belief; it is a religious challenge. We must find some way to repay this extraordinary gift.

People of all faiths strive to replicate the concept of divine love. They do it in different ways, based on their faith traditions and the cultures in which they live: by loving other people, by loving God directly through prayers of adoration and thanks, and by performing acts of charity and compassion, which are considered in more detail in Part IV.

Ideas of love: Thoughts from Christian theologians

Roman Catholic bishop and theologian, Saint Augustine (354-430 C.E.) used the Latin word *caritas,* or sometimes *dilectio,* to describe love. Augustine was in agreement with Paul about the foundation of Christian faith: "Love and do what you will" (On the Epistle of John 7). Augustine made a distinction between self-love, which he labeled *cupiditas,* and love of others, which is caritas. (The English word charity comes from the Latin caritas.)

Caritas for Augustine is love of God directly or the love of other people because they are made in the image of God. Caritas is always love for the sake of God. Cupiditas is the love of one's self or others for some reason other than God. All real, spiritually authentic love goes to God as a response to the belief that all love came from God.

Martin Luther (1483-1546 C.E.), the biblical scholar who is credited with starting the Reformation, also believed that only God's love is pure, unmerited, and freely given. For Luther, human love is always tainted with some self-interest and is always directed at some object other than God. When humans love, we want to be loved in return. God, on the other hand, loves without needing us to love God in return.

The Italian theologian and philosopher Thomas Aquinas (1225-1274 C.E.), more than Augustine, saw the ethical implications of love. Love, for him, was the source of all morals. We explore the ethical implications of love in Part IV. Here, it is important to understand just how deeply love is at the understanding of faith for the monotheistic faiths and particularly for Christianity, beginning with Paul, who set forth in his long poem in I Corinthians 13 the belief that love was the greatest and most important virtue of the three great Christian virtues of faith, hope, and love.

Chapter 6

The Amazing Variety of Spiritual Beings

• •

In This Chapter

▶ Introducing angels and other divine messengers

▶ Understanding Satan and his demon horde

▶ Taking a look at people especially touched by the Divine

• •

In all religions, the supreme divinity — whether it is a single omnipotent God, quarreling gods of different powers, or a transcendent awareness that encompasses everything — is separate from human beings. To help people bridge the gap, most religions have some form of intermediary. Sometimes, these intermediaries are divine themselves; sometimes they're people who have achieved a spiritual awareness or perfection that eludes most others. This chapter takes a look at these beings.

Nevertheless, before you read this chapter, be forewarned. Some of these religious beliefs are spooky or weird. Some are spooky *and* weird. Some folks think that these beliefs are just foolish superstitions, more befitting fairy tales. Truth be told, we thought about leaving out this chapter, but a visiting angel with really big wings told us to keep writing.

Angels: Direct Line from God

Angels are part of nearly every religion's belief system. Winged angelic figures appear in the earliest human writings from Sumer around 3,500 B.C.E. Egyptian tombs and Assyrian carvings show angels doing their thing. Angels appear in more than half the books of the Christian Bible. For example, it was an angel who rolled the stone away from Christ's tomb. The existence of angels is a fundamental belief in Islam: "The righteous is the one who believes in Allah, the Last Day, the angels, the Book, and the prophets" (Qur'an 2.177).

Many people mistakenly think that good people become angels when they die. In Islam, Judaism, and Christianity, however, angels are actually separate beings; they're not just good dead people with wings and a halo. Angels, as beings with souls but no physical body and no desires, bridge the gap between God, who is absolutely holy, and humans, who are a mixture of divine essence and animal urges because of our physical bodies.

Angels at work

The main job of the angel is to act as a transition figure between the divine and the human. The Hebrew word for angel is *malach,* which means messenger. Angels bring messages to people from God, and they serve God in other ways. For example, Muslims believe that angels listen and record the prayers of the faithful and testify for or against people on the Day of Judgment.

Angels are also

- ✔ **Administrators for God's universe.** Each angel has its own responsibilities in the governance of the cosmos and human affairs.

- ✔ **Representatives of the Divine in a form that humans can comprehend.** Angels scale down the awesome power of God into smaller, less terrifying, more intimate forms.

- ✔ **Physical representations of God's love.** It is hard to imagine the maker of galaxies and black holes really being concerned about the death of our pet hamster, but angels, guardian angels particularly, are figures that make a transcendent God more personal, intimate, and caring.

Types of angels

Different theologians in the Abrahamic faiths of Judaism, Christianity, and Islam have imagined the angel architecture of heaven differently. In Judaism and Christianity, angels fall into three types: the ministering angels, the guardian angels, and the human angels. (See the related sidebar titled "Choirs of angels" later in this chapter.

Islam, on the other hand, doesn't have an elaborate hierarchy that divides classes of angels, but it does consider four angels to be archangels (chief angels):

- ✔ **Jibra'il (Gabriel):** Considered the greatest of all angels because he is the one through whom Allah revealed the Qur'an to Muhammad. According to Islamic tradition, Gabriel showed Noah how to build the ark, he lured the pharaoh's troops into the sea, and he interceded on Abraham's behalf to save Abraham from a fire.

Gabriel is the archangel of revelation and communication between God and humans, par excellence, in Judaism, Christianity, and Islam. His counterpart in Zoroastrianism is Vohu Manah.

- ✔ **Izra'il (Azreal):** He is the principal Islamic angel of death. Although he doesn't bring death, he is the one responsible for separating the soul from the body after a person's death is signaled by a leaf falling from a tree beneath Allah's throne.

- ✔ **Mika'il (Michael):** He, with Gabriel, instructs Muhammad. He also watches over places of worship.

- ✔ **Israfil (Israfil):** The angel who sounds the horn that ends time.

Ministering angels

In Hebrew, the ministering angels are the *Malachai ha-sharet*. There are actually two types of ministering angels, the cherubim and the seraphim. These angels never leave heaven, and their main job is to help God administer the universe. In some schemes, they are also called archangels. The archangel Michael, for example, is believed by Jewish legends to be the angel who watches over God's people in Israel. Raphael is one of the seven angels who, according to the Book of Daniel, are always ready to enter the closest realm of the presence of God (Daniel 3:49).

Guardian angels

Guardian angels are your garden-variety angels with wings and halos (both retract so as not to attract too much attention here on earth). These angels are assigned to protect people, and billions and billions of them are around all the time.

Some of these earthly angels have special jobs to do.

- ✔ An angel with a flaming sword guards the entrance to the Garden of Eden.

- ✔ Three angels came to tell Abraham that Sarah was going to give birth at the age of 90. (It probably took three to convince him!)

- ✔ A man who was also probably an angel wrestled with Jacob and changed his name to Israel.

Human angels

Although not strictly angels, sometimes people can act as angels when they carry a message from God for some particular person on earth. Therefore, any person can be a messenger from God. The message can be of any kind, and these human messengers don't even know that they're working for God. They're just doing what they normally do, but God is using them to give a message.

Choirs of angels

In the sixth century, a mystical theologian named Pseudo-Dionysus of Areopagite wrote a complex and imaginative description of the Christian angel hierarchy, called *The Celestial Hierarchy*. Pseudo-Dionysus divided the angels of heaven into three hierarchies, with each one having its own rank (called *choirs*).

The first hierarchy is closest to God:

- **Seraphim:** Angels with three pairs of wings who guard God's throne.

- **Cherubim:** Angels with human or animal characteristics who guard sacred places and continually praise God.

- **Thrones:** Angels who bring justice.

The second hierarchy seeks to balance opposing forces (good and evil, for example):

- **Dominions (or Dominations):** Angels who regulate life in heaven.

- **Virtues:** Angels who work miracles.

- **Powers:** Angels who protect humankind from demonic attack.

The third hierarchy looks over us humans:

- **Principalities:** Angels concerned with the welfare of nations.

- **Archangels:** The heralds of great, important news. Some are also rulers or princes of angels. Well-known archangels include Gabriel, Michael, and Raphael.

- **Angels (including guardian angels):** Angels who serve as guides and messengers (on a lesser scale than archangels) to individual human beings.

That's a great number of angels, but then, the religious universe is a lot of territory to cover!

The message could be "Would you like to meet a nice person?" who then turns out to be your spouse, or "You would make a great doctor," which then turns out to be your job.

When Jacob sent Joseph to find his brothers (a story in Genesis), his brothers had already moved on. Joseph met "a stranger in the fields." This stranger pointed Joseph in the right direction to find his brothers, which resulted in Joseph's being sold into slavery in Egypt and later saving his family.

Devils, Demons, and other Bad Guys

All religions provide an explanation of why evil and death exist in the world, and for many religions, the answer involves, in one form or another, the idea of an adversary of the Divine. In Judaism, Christianity, and Islam, this adversary takes the form of Satan and lesser demons, a belief that seems to have originated in Zoroastrianism. In polytheistic religions, the adversaries take the form of various evil gods who work against the good gods.

TECHNICAL STUFF

Satan in Paradise Lost

John Milton wrote his famous epic poem *Paradise Lost* in 1667. In *Paradise Lost,* Milton gave the devil a fully modern character as being unwilling to submit to the will of God because of his pride and his desire for personal freedom. In the poem, Lucifer/Satan leads a rebellion against God and is kicked out of heaven, which, it seems, suits him just fine. "Better," he says, "to reign in hell than serve in heaven." Of course, his power is only illusion; he can't do anything that God doesn't allow him to do, and even in his primary triumph — corrupting Adam and Eve — he turns out to be the loser.

In a way, Milton's description of the devil can be seen as a symbol of modern man, aware of his divine nature, but rebellious, individualistic, and stubborn. Milton's Satan is not just a figure of myth and faith; he's a projection of our deepest fears. Because Christians can't imagine evil coming from the one God, they imagine it coming from the devil, who is slightly removed from God. Because they can't accept that death is a part of life and therefore a part of God's plan, they imagine death as being the mission of the devil on behalf of God.

In monotheistic religions

BIG ISSUE

The issues of death and evil remain a huge problem for the monotheistic faiths. If just one God created everything, then everything comes from God, and that means evil too. The really big question for the Abrahamic faiths is this: Is the devil a creation of God? If so, then, evil is under divine control, but if the devil is an independent opponent of the Divine, with more or less equal powers, then there are two forces in the universe: a force for good and a force for evil, and with that idea, monotheism goes right down the drain.

To explain this dilemma, Christianity, Judaism, and Islam have Satan beginning as an angel, who, because of his own nature and free will, falls from grace. In Christian and Jewish tradition, his name was Lucifer (which means Bearer of Light), before he was booted out of heaven. In Islam, he was an angel who refused to bow before Adam. In all three religions, Satan is a tempter and spiritual enemy of humankind whose goal is to lead people away from God. Although he is the ruler of hell and all demons, he is subordinate to God. (See the related sidebar titled "Satan in *Paradise Lost*" later in this chapter.)

Whatever you call the devil — Satan, la Diable, Beelzebub, Lucifer, Shaytan, Iblis, or Angra Mainyu — he is considered the supreme adversary of God in Judaism, Christianity, Islam, and Zoroastrianism. (See the related sidebar titled "A devil by any other name . . ." later in this chapter.)

A devil by any other name . . .

The word *satanas,* translated as "devil," finds its way into Judeo-Christian traditions through the Book of Job (in the Hebrew Bible/Old Testament), when Satan asks God to test Job. Additional references include I Chronicles 1:21 ("And Satan stood up against Israel and moved David to number Israel"). Zechariah includes another brief reference to Satan as an opponent to Joshua — and that's it!

Many speculate as to the origins of the name and dualistic view of the universe that divides all of life into good and evil. Some suggest that adherents of Zoroastrianism, who lived in the same area around the fifth and sixth centuries B.C.E., influenced ancient Jews. A prophet by the name of Zoroaster, living near what is now Iran around the seventh century B.C.E., began to proclaim a monotheistic faith in Ahura Mazda. He claims that he was tempted to leave this new faith by an evil spirit, Angra Mainyu. In the Gathas, he explores places like the "House of Lie," or hell, and the conflict between good and evil, with predictions that the world would come to a blazing end.

In Christianity

In the New Testament, the devil isn't just present; he's one of the main characters. The Gospel according to Matthew includes the story of Satan's tempting Jesus in the wilderness. In this tale, Satan competes directly with God as the supreme object of worship. (For a closer look at this story, see the sidebar titled "A Tale of Temptation" later in this chapter.)

By the time of the New Testament, not just Satan but Satan's assistants had become much more a part of the spiritual landscape. In addition to the temptation of Jesus by the devil himself, for example, Jesus is described as casting out devils.

In some places in the New Testament, Satan is described as "the lord of this world" or "the god of this world" (John 12:31; 14:30; 2 Corinthians 4:4; Luke 4:6). This idea of Satan pushes the limit of Satan as a creation of God and as a second, evil God.

The idea of a lower, evil god at war with a higher, good god came from a popular religion of the time, which has since vanished, called Gnosticism. The belief in Gnosticism was that an evil god, called the Demiurgos, ran the world, which was a prison, and that a good god, who was out of touch with this world, ran a higher world.

The basic power of Satan, as developed in the New Testament, is the power of death. This is the power that Jesus came to conquer.

FROM THE HOLY BOOKS

A tale of temptation

In Matthew 4:1-11, Jesus rebuffs Satan:

Then was Jesus led up of the Spirit into the wilderness to be tempted of the devil. And when he had fasted forty days and forty nights, he afterward hungered. And the tempter came and said unto him, If thou art the Son of God, command that these stones become bread. But he answered and said, It is written, Man shall not live by bread alone, but by every word that proceedeth out of the mouth of God. Then the devil taketh him into the holy city; and he set him on the pinnacle of the temple, and saith unto him, If thou art the Son of God, cast thyself down: for it is written, He shall give his angels charge concerning thee: and, On their hands they shall bear thee up, lest haply thou dash thy foot against a stone. Jesus said unto him, Again it is written, Thou shalt not make trial of the Lord thy God. Again, the devil taketh him unto an exceeding high mountain, and showeth him all the kingdoms of the world, and the glory of them; and he said unto him, All these things will I give thee, if thou wilt fall down and worship me. Then saith Jesus unto him, Get thee hence, Satan: for it is written, Thou shalt worship the Lord thy God, and him only shalt thou serve.

Then the devil leaveth him; and behold, angels came and ministered unto him.

The devil is the symbol of our fear of death, and Jesus the symbol of hope that death will not be the end of us as death was not the end of Jesus. Of course, for Christians, Jesus is much more than a symbol of hope. Jesus is the reality of that hope.

In Islam

As in Christianity and Judaism, Satan (also called Shaytan from the Hebrew Satan, or Iblis, meaning the devil) in Islam is a tempter who tries to lead people away from the straight path. He's the one who tempted Adam and Eve in the Garden of Eden, which led to their fall. He's also the one who tried less successfully to tempt Abraham, Hagar, and Ishmael, to disobey God. He is also an accusing angel, one who speaks up against people by reminding God of their sins. *Sufis* (Muslim mystics) regard Satan not as a fallen angel but as the angel who tests humans to see if they can be tempted away from God!

According to Islamic tradition, Satan has the characteristics of the angels, who are made of light, and the jinn, supernatural spirits that are made of flame. (People are made of clay.) As in the biblical account, Muslims believe that Allah cast Satan out of paradise for being the one angel who refused to acknowledge Allah's creation, Adam.

Beyond Satan, Islamic tradition holds that devils of all kinds appear in human form to tempt people away from the will of Allah and help to punish people in the fiery bowels of hell. Satan will be destroyed by the Messiah to come (*Mahdi*) in a great war that will signal the arrival of the Day of Judgment.

The debate over Jesus

The final Messiah was to be part of the line from King David, was to end evil, gather all the exiled Jewish people into the land of Israel, and usher in a time of world peace. Because Jesus didn't do these things, the Jewish community rejected the claims of his followers that he was the Messiah sent by God. The Christian community, particularly Paul, was moved and utterly convinced by the miracle of Jesus' resurrection and felt that the second coming (parousia) of Jesus was imminent. With the second coming, Jesus would then fulfill the Jewish criteria for "Messiahship." This debate has lasted 2,000 years and shows no signs of letting up.

In polytheistic religions

Each religious tradition has its own challenges when it comes to the devil or devils. Whereas the big question for monotheistic religions is how a God that is absolutely good and absolutely powerful created (or allows) evil, in polytheistic faiths, the big question is whether the devils or destroyer gods are more or less powerful than the good gods. If they are stronger, confidence in the ultimate triumph of good over evil goes down the drain.

In Buddhism, for example, the god Mara personifies the devil. Mara is lord of the realm of desire, who came to the Buddha as he sat under the Bodhi tree, where he (the Buddha) would finally achieve enlightenment.

Mara, in various disguises, tried to tempt Buddha to give up his quest for enlightenment. When he failed, Mara sent his daughters to seduce Buddha, but they also failed. After Buddha achieved enlightenment, Mara tried to talk him out of preaching, echoing Buddha's own doubts that others wouldn't be able to understand the truth. The good gods interceded, though, and begged Buddha to preach the dharma. Persuaded by the good gods, Buddha agreed, and the rest is history.

Although Mara and his horde of demons are described as actual entities that act against people, they are also described as the internal vices and desires that plague people seeking enlightenment.

Prophets: Direct Lines to God

Prophets are people who receive the messages from the Divine and share them with others. Many religions, ancient and modern, have people who would be considered prophets. The power of prophecy is often associated with the spiritual leaders or mystics in a community, including shamans and seers. Prophets receive divine messages in a variety of ways: visions, dreams, physical manifestations of the Divine, and so on. Although prophets are just human beings, not special spiritual beings like angels, their role is so unique that they push the spiritual envelope between humans and the Divine.

Famous prophets in Western religions

Judaism, Christianity, and Islam each consider certain people to be great prophets. Take a look at the top tier:

- **Abraham:** The first Hebrew patriarch, Abraham is believed to have been the first to acknowledge the one true God. In Judaism, it is through Abraham that the Israelites got the power to communicate with God. Christians revere Abraham as the father of all believers. Muslims see Abraham as the prophet through whom God revealed his oneness, proving monotheism, and as the person who (with his son Ishmael) built the Ka'bah, considered by Muslims to be the most sacred spot on Earth, in Mecca.

- **Moses:** Of all the prophets recognized by Judaism, Christianity, and Islam, Moses is unique because he is the only one who spoke to God directly. Through him, God revealed the Ten Commandments.

- **Jesus:** In Islam, Jesus is considered one of the great prophets. Through him, God revealed the golden rule (Do unto others as you would have them do unto you), which states the fundamental principle of how people should treat others.

To Christians, of course, Jesus is more than a prophet; he is God incarnate. Many Christians believe that the revelations in the Hebrew Bible were fulfilled in the life, death, and resurrection of Jesus, who was the Christ, or the Messiah. Although many in Islam believe that Jesus was born of a virgin, performed many miracles, and went to heaven after his death, they don't believe that Jesus was the Son of God or that he was crucified.

- **Muhammad:** In Islam, Muhammad is referred to as the "Seal of the Prophets," because he is the final prophet. Most Muslims believe that no other prophet will follow him. (Some Muslim sects, however, such as splinter groups from the Shi'ites, are looking for another prophet to come in the future.) The revelation Muhammad brought from Allah — the Qur'an — completed and corrected the revelations that had come before.

Islam has several prophets, and although all should be revered as messengers of God, a few prophets are considered great. God used miracles to validate the authenticity of the revelations these prophets made: Abraham was saved from fire. Moses was saved from the pharaoh. Jesus was born to a virgin (Mary) and, according to Islamic tradition, was saved from crucifixion. The miracle God worked through Muhammad was the Qur'an.

Another, non-Abrahamic religion, Zoroastrianism also holds that revelation was granted to a prophet—Zarathushtra—whose image parallels that of Moses, Jesus, and Muhammad in many ways, such as wandering in the wilderness, hearing from angels, being scorned by his own people, and eventually establishing a community of believers.

Will the real prophets please stand up?

The problem with prophecy is that distinguishing between the real prophets of God and the people who had just a little too much wine with dinner is hard to do. The Hebrew Bible solved this problem by making the revelation of God to Moses different from all other revelations. Only Moses spoke to God directly, "the way a man speaks to his neighbor," and heard clearly God's revelation. (Moses didn't see God's face, though, because God was a burning bush at the time of the conversation.)

According to Jewish belief, of the prophets, only Moses can be trusted completely, because all the others received their messages from God through dreams or visions, which may have been distorted. Moses, however, received God's revelation directly from God. In addition, Moses is the one who went up Mount Sinai to receive the Torah and all the laws in it. For this reason, any prophets who contradicted the revelation of Moses had to be false prophets, even if they came with miracles, signs, and wonders that supported the new revelation.

The problem with this Jewish idea of the supremacy of Moses' prophecy is that as Judaism grew and changed — as the Temple in Jerusalem was destroyed and new beliefs and rituals were needed — the biblical text was limited. The solution in Judaism was a teaching of the rabbis that, while on Mount Sinai, Moses received both the written Torah and an oral Torah. The oral Torah was all the new ideas not in the Bible that Judaism needed to survive. What the idea of the oral Torah did was to invest all the leading rabbis with the authority of Moses' revelation. The Talmud came into existence both in Babylon and Palestine as a way of preserving interpretations of the rabbis. This solution kept the law of Judaism vital and flexible while still guarding against new ideas that would undermine Judaism.

Messiahs: Anointed by God

The term *Messiah* comes from the Hebrew word *moshiach,* which means to anoint. A Messiah, therefore, is God's anointed one.

Anointing is the process of pouring sacred oil over the head of a person to indicate that person's initiation into some special religious status. In the Hebrew Bible, both King Saul and King David were called anointed ones, because they were specially chosen to serve as king. Priests in the Temple were also referred to as anointed ones.

Someday our prince will come:
Messiahs in Judaism

The Hebrew Bible doesn't really include the idea of a personal Messiah who will end evil and usher in a time of peace. Instead, there is the idea of a "Day of God" — a kind of messianic age that would bring peace to the earth. Later, in the chaos that followed the Roman destruction of the Temple of Jerusalem (around 70 C.E.), when rabbinic Judaism gradually arose to replace the priestly sacrificial offerings, the idea of a personal Messiah developed. This idea became a part of both rabbinic Judaism and, obviously, Christianity. (Rabbinic Judaism is based on the Talmud, which was written between the fourth and seventh centuries C.E.)

The rabbinic idea was that there would be two Messiahs:

✔ A Messiah, the son of Joseph, who would die in the great battle of the end of days fighting the forces of evil.

✔ A Messiah, the son of David, who would come and defeat evil, gather the scattered exiles of the Jewish people into the land of Israel, bring world peace, resurrect the dead to eternal life, and usher in the end of suffering death and strife.

In general, Judaism taught that trying to bring the Messiah or to even calculate the time when God would send him was a sin. Of course, people speculated about the signs of the Messiah's coming, which were called "the birth pangs of the Messiah." Often these signs took the form of horrible catastrophes for the Jewish people or the world. (See the related sidebar titled "The debate over Jesus" earlier in this chapter.)

God, savior, man: The Messiah
in Christianity

Christianity elevated the idea of the Messiah well beyond a political leader of Jewish independence. Messiah, in the Christian understanding, was not just a person, but also a spiritual messenger from God who shared directly in God's divinity. In Christianity, the Messiah (specifically in the person of Jesus) is one who

✔ Is a bearer of God's grace and a sacrificial lamb whose death erased original sin and saved all humanity.

✔ Is a kind of spiritual being who bridges the gap between God and humankind.

✔ Is a visitor from the divine realm who brings the good news that humankind is loved and saved.

Christ is the Greek word for the anointed one, and Jesus, along with God the Father and the Holy Spirit, constitutes the Trinity.

Al-Mahdi: Messiahs in Islam

Although not mentioned in the Qur'an, a Messiah, called al-Mahdi (the divinely guided one), figures into Islamic tradition. The Mahdi is one who will come to earth, bringing peace and justice, restoring the true religion, and ushering in a golden age that will last between seven and nine years before the end of the world.

Both major sects of Islam — Sunni and Shi'ism — believe in the idea of al-Mahdi, but the concept is more developed in the Shi'ite sect. A major branch of Shi'ism is the Twelvers (Imamis). The Twelvers believe in the succession of twelve Imams, religious leaders who are divinely guided and therefore infallible in their interpretation of Allah's laws. The first Imam, according to the Shi'ites, was Ali, Muhammad's son-in-law and husband of Muhammad's daughter Fatima. Other Imams followed, and the last Imam disappeared in 873. According to tradition, this last Imam is still alive and in hiding. His reappearance will herald the coming of the golden age and the Last Day.

Buddhas, Bodhisattvas, Lamas, and Saints

When the Buddha, Siddhartha Gautama, was asked if he was a god or a king, he said, "No, I am merely awake." Despite his modesty, the Buddha and all other enlightened ones are, like Jesus in Christianity, human beings who blur the boundary between people and spiritual beings.

The Buddha and other enlightened ones

Buddhists believe that Siddhartha Gautama, the first Buddha, was born in the sixth century B.C.E., lived many previous lives, and that he was just one of many Buddhas in the universe.

The wisdom that a Buddha achieves is so vast and deep, that it's not reasonable or accurate to say that a Buddha is just a person anymore. In a way, a Buddha has transcended all boundaries and lives completely in the truth.

Bodhisattvas

In some cases, someone who has achieved enlightenment, achieved Buddhahood, will voluntarily decide not to disappear into the realm of nirvana but remain in the world of the senses to help others learn the way to enlightenment. These returned Buddhas are called *Bodhisattvas.* The gift of a Bodhisattva is an example of unmerited love bestowed upon unworthy people because of the great spiritual generosity of a great spiritual being. In that way, it is akin to the idea of grace in Christian, Jewish, and Islamic theologies.

One of the most democratic ideas within Buddhism is the idea that every human being has a "Buddha nature" (Tathagata). Every human being has a kind of embryonic Buddha inside him or her and thus every human being has the possibility of achieving full Buddha status and enlightenment. No one can become Moses, Muhammad, or Jesus, but any person can become a Buddha; it just takes a great deal of spiritual working out.

Lamas, dalai and otherwise

A lama (the Tibetan word that means superior one) is a spiritual being and teacher in Tibetan Buddhism. Originally, the term meant the same thing as guru (venerable one), but people use it in two ways now:

- ✔ **Developed lama:** The head of a monastery or any venerated Buddhist monk can be called a lama because of his own great wisdom. The term is, of course, also used to refer to the Dalai Lama, who is the fourteenth incarnation of a previous lama — in his case, he is believed to be the reincarnation of the Bodhisattva of light and compassion, Avalokitesvara.

- ✔ **Reincarnate lama** (sprul-sku lama): A lama who is a reincarnation of a previous lama. Another famous reincarnate lama is the Panchen Lama, who is the head of the Tashilhunpo Monastery and is believed to be the reincarnation of the Amitabha Buddha.

Lamas are both teachers and possessors of spiritual powers, who transmit these powers to their disciples. After the death of a lama, several young children who are born at a special time and may be reincarnate lamas are brought together for a test. The child who picks up an object that was owned by a previous lama is selected as the new lama. The child is then given special training and education until his maturity as a reincarnate lama.

Saints preserve us!

A very broad definition of a saint is simply a holy or godly person, but in the major religions of the world, people identified as saints are those who have a special connection to the Divine:

✔ The Hindu and Buddhist idea of an *arhant* (a person who, through several lifetimes, achieves nirvana) is close to the idea of a saint in the western religions.

✔ Confucianism, Taoism, and Shinto all recognize saints as sages who have achieved high moral perfection as well as obedience to the Way.

✔ In Islam, the term for saint is *wali. Awliya* (the plural of wali) are holy men who perform miracles and teach the truth of the Qur'an. While Sufism (Islamic mysticism) recognizes an entire hierarchy of saints that Muslims venerate, more mainstream branches of Islam view this practice with suspicion, believing that the practice borders on idol worship.

✔ In Judaism, the closest term to saint is *tzaddik,* which means an especially righteous person. In the teachings of Hasidism, a tzadik is a person who is incapable of sinning because he or she is righteous. A rebbe is a Hasidic rabbi who can do miracles and has special spiritual powers to heal and curse.

In all these traditions, sainthood is a combination of intellectual and moral perfection. The ability to perform miracles is also a common characteristic of saints in the East and West. Christianity, and particularly Catholicism and Eastern Orthodoxy, take the theology of saints a few steps further, outlining requirements for being a saint.

To qualify for sainthood in the Catholic Church (and to be canonized — that is, officially recognized as a saint), a person must

✔ **Be dead:** No living people can be saints.

✔ **Have performed two miracles:** One miracle gets the candidate to the stage of beatification (where the Church, after declaring the person has attained the blessedness of heaven, gives him or her the title "Blessed"). The second miracle (or more if they're discovered) gets the candidate to canonization as a saint. (*Note:* The miracles have to be witnessed by others.)

Once canonized, saints can have churches named after them. They're also given a holy day of commemoration in the Church's liturgical calendar. The Christian tradition has thousands of canonized saints.

Many people wrongly believe that it's proper to pray to a saint and not to God. Saints are merely doorways to the Divine; they're not semi-gods. Saints are models of ideal lives; they lived at the outer limits of human moral, intellectual, and spiritual perfection.

Part III
Religious Rituals

The 5th Wave   By Rich Tennant

"When did we stop giving an 'amen' and start giving the 'wave'?"

In this part . . .

Rituals are what separate religions from philosophies. To many people, rituals are the most clearly identifiable parts of a religion. Doing good is not always seen as a religious command (although it clearly is), but lighting candles, taking communion, offering sacrifices, and saying particular prayers are. Rituals also mark life passages from birth to adulthood to marriage and, finally, to death.

Some religious rituals are communal. Such rituals require a community or a setting in a house of worship. Other rituals are personal, and they require only a single, searching heart. In this part, we discuss communal and personal rituals, and we look at the rites of passage that give our lives its sacred shape.

Chapter 7

Rituals of Communal Worship

. . . .

In This Chapter

▶ Looking at the power (and forms) of prayer

▶ Examining the art of self-sacrifice

▶ Reaching the divine through movement and music

▶ Exploring spiritual healing

▶ Focusing on fasting

▶ Understanding the role and purpose of the Eucharist

. . . .

Rituals form religious communities, giving members a kind of spiritual choreography for their lives. Performing these ritual acts binds worshipers together in two spiritually significant ways: by creating a bond with all believers of that religion who are doing the same thing at the same time, and by reinforcing the bond between the believers and their ancestors, who performed the same rituals at the same moment in their lives. These two ways of being bound together form religious traditions.

Rituals give people spiritual longitude and latitude and, in doing so, position them in the history of their people and their faith. Rituals also create a kind of third place for believers; they give people a place where they can be more than workers and more than family, where they can actually be a part of the work of redemption in the world.

Understanding Prayer

Prayer is by far the most important and common form of communal ritual in the religions of the world. For some, prayer is a way of repeating the stories of tradition; for others, it's a way of thanking God for blessings and for asking for divine help in life. Others use it as a way of showing submission to the will of God. Others use it as a way of sharing in communion the mystery of God's gifts to humankind.

The communal form of prayer is necessary in some religions and optional in others. Although the structure and guidelines for prayer vary, the desired result is still the same: When someone prays, she or he is seeking to make contact with the holy and the sacred. In essence, prayer is a relationship for the person of faith who tries to touch on the transcendent in life while binding himself or herself to a community.

The goals of prayer

From the earliest times, people have been preoccupied with understanding the forces behind nature. People found the presence of something supernatural in the wind, rain, sky, and earth. These natural instincts gave way to fear and awe. In time, religionists developed prayers and rituals to respond to their gods or God in many and elementary ways. Prayer became linked to sacrifice. People sacrificed animals, possessions, and time to make their gods happy. They tried to gain the attention and the good will of the deity of supernatural powers. Some chose magic as a way of manipulating the divine favor. They created formulas and rituals that had to be adhered to in a strict sense.

Some religions, on the other hand, offered not magic, but rituals that connected the prayer to the force of the supernatural. Literatures explained the stories of creation, destruction, redemption, and faith. Armed with these new stories, people began to build altars, churches, synagogues, mosques, temples, and shrines. People went to these places to give homage to the supernatural. In prayer, people sought not only to connect with the divine but also to transform the human.

Congregations gather together to pray to God for four reasons:

- ✔ **Adoration:** They offer praise to the Divine, surrender to the Divine, while offering a life of love and devotion in return.

- ✔ **Penance:** They ask for forgiveness of their sins and the means to overcome their faults, eliminate the evil side of their lives, and make amends to the Divine and to people for their failures.

- ✔ **Petition:** They come to ask a divine favor and for healing in times of illness, pain, tragedy, and human need. They ask for food, for a good life, for health, and for courage.

- ✔ **Thanksgiving:** They acknowledge that the Divine is the source of blessings. They come to thank the Divine for those blessings and ask the Divine to watch over them as a special favor.

Prayers in these four contexts are sometimes vocal and sometimes nonverbal.

A sampling of prayers

Thinking about the diversity of the countless prayers being offered each day throughout the world in mosques, synagogues, temples, churches, personal shrines, and any of the sacred spaces is awe-inspiring.

You can find many wonderful prayers in the different religions:

Bhagavad-Gita (12:13-14, Sir Krishna): That one I love whom is incapable of ill will, who is friendly and compassionate. Living beyond the reach of I and mine and of pleasure and pain, patient, contented, self-contented, self-controlled, firm in faith, with all his heart and all his mind given to me — with such a one I am in love.

Shema (Deuteronomy, 6:4-9): Hear, Israel, the Lord is our God, the Lord is One.

The Lord's Prayer (Matthew 6:9-13): Our Father which art in heaven, hallowed be thy name. Thy kingdom come. Thy will be done in earth as it is in heaven. Give us today our daily bread, and forgive us our trespasses, as we forgive those who trespass against us. And lead us not into temptation but deliver us from evil. For thine is the kingdom, and the power, and the glory, forever and ever. Amen.

Al Fatihah, (The Opening) (Surah 1 from the Qur'an): Praise be to Allah, the Lord of the worlds, the Beneficent, the Merciful, Master of the day of Requital. Thee do we serve and thee do we beseech for help. Guide us on the right path, the path of those upon whom thou hast bestowed favors, not those upon whom wrath is brought, nor those who go astray.

A Zoroastrian Prayer (Asham Vohu): Righteousness is good, it is best. As desired it is, as desired it will be. Righteousness is for one who represents the best righteousness.

We gather together: Communal prayer

In the Qur'an, the most holy book in Islam, you can find a proverb that says to pray and to be a Muslim are synonymous. In Christianity, prayer is at the center of the spiritual life. In Judaism prayer, study, and acts of compassion are the three pillars of the world. Among all faiths, communal prayer — the active communication between an individual through a spiritual community to some higher power — is a basic and transforming spiritual experience.

How the prayer proceeds depends on the religion and on the needs of the person praying. Sometimes people begin with prearranged prayers that they learned from their family or place of worship. These prayers often come from sacred books, sacred ceremonies, or formal liturgies printed in prayer books. In time, the prayerful person may begin talking to God in his or her own words, using the events and circumstances of life. In another important form of prayer, people read from a book of spiritual significance and meditate or reflect on the words written; they pray more by their presence than by their words. Finally, some people discover a form of prayer called contemplation or meditation, in which they sit in the presence of God, not asking anything and not speaking. (See the related sidebar titled, "A sampling of prayers," later in this chapter.)

Christian prayers

Among many Christian religions, the act of communal prayer is the deepest way that the religious communities define themselves. Christians pray communally on Sunday morning. In all Christian prayer services, men and women pray together.

Protestant services

Protestant services feature hymn singing, communal prayers, readings from the Bible, and, occasionally, the celebration of the Eucharist in which Protestants take communion.

Hymn singing is a major feature of Protestant worship services, and the hymnal provides the words and music for the worshippers. Hymns for the service are usually posted on the wall of the church. In many African-American Protestant churches, fervent and inspiring gospel singing adds an ecstatic and joyful exuberance to the prayer service.

The preaching of an inspirational sermon is a centerpiece for Protestant worship. (The influence of the sermon as an important part of service has spread from Protestantism to Judaism and Catholicism, which didn't traditionally feature the sermon.)

In Pentecostal churches, baptisms may be performed during the service, and in some, almost trance-like speaking in tongues occurs. Some Protestant churches have mid-week services in addition to the Sunday services.

The Catholic Mass

Catholics celebrate communal worship in the Mass, which is the reenactment of the Last Supper. Catholic churches celebrate Mass every day and several times during the day on Sunday. The Mass involves eating bread that has been changed (transubstantiated) into the body of Christ and drinking wine that's been changed into the blood of Christ.

Worshippers sing hymns, listen to readings from the Bible, and participate in a penitential rite in which they repent for their sins. The priest gives a sermon, which is called the homily.

Other services

Icons adorn Greek Orthodox churches. During the service, incense is lit. The scriptures are read from a gold-covered Bible. The prayer book is called The Divine Liturgy of St. John Chrysostom.

The Mormon prayer service is called a sacrament meeting, which includes songs and prayers. Bread and water are used for communion. Laypeople often offer the sermon.

The Society of Friends (commonly called Quakers) has two types of meetings: programmed and unprogrammed:

- **Unprogrammed Quaker prayer:** The Friends sit in silence in a Quaker meetinghouse that has no icons, no crucifix — no religious symbols whatsoever. When the spirit moves a worshipper, he or she will speak or sing.

- **Programmed Quaker meetings:** The Friends sing hymns and read the reading. A pastor gives a sermon.

Jewish prayers

In Judaism, prayer must be offered three times a day: morning, afternoon, and evening. Usually, however, observant Jews pray twice: once during the morning (*shaharit*) and then once again, using a combination of the afternoon prayers (*minha*) and the evening prayers (*ma'ariv*). On Friday night through Saturday night, Sabbath prayers expand the prayers of the three prayer times and add additional prayers (*musaf*). Holidays add other prayers to the order of Jewish prayer.

All three parts of the Hebrew Bible are included in the Sabbath and holiday liturgy:

- Selections from the Torah, the first five books of the Hebrew Bible (Genesis, Exodus, Leviticus, Numbers, and Deuteronomy), are read in the daily prayer service on Monday, Thursday, and Saturday.

- On Saturday, additional readings called the Haftorah (from the prophets, the second part of the Hebrew Bible) are also included.

- Rabbis begin their sermons on the Sabbath and holidays with readings from the Psalms, from the third part of the Hebrew Bible, called Ketuvim.

The central prayer in all Jewish communal prayer is called the *amida*. This prayer is consists of 18 separate prayers of petition, thankfulness, and atonement. On the Sabbath, all the prayers that request something more of God are taken out of the Jewish liturgy.

The Jewish prayer book for daily prayers and Sabbath prayers is called the *Siddur*. The prayer book for communal prayers for the high holidays of Rosh Hashanah and Yom Kippur (New Year's Day and the Day of Atonement, respectively) is called the *Mahzor*.

Jews don't have to say their prayers in a synagogue; however, they do have to have at least ten adult Jewish males (for traditional Judaism) or ten Jewish adults male or female (for liberal Judaism) present. In traditional Jewish prayer, a divider called a *mehitzah* separates men and women. In liberal Jewish prayer, men and women pray together.

Jews face Jerusalem when they pray, unless the ark with the Torah in it in the synagogue faces in a different direction. In that case, the community faces the ark and not Jerusalem.

Islamic prayers

Muslims reinforce the passion of their commitment to Allah during the course of their daily prayer schedule. According to the Qur'an, a practicing Muslim must offer prayer to Allah five times each day — at dawn, noon, mid-afternoon, sunset, and evening. In Muslim countries, the faithful are called to prayer by the *muezzin,* or crier, who calls from a minaret, the high tower of a mosque.

The prayer ritual is highly formalized. At the appointed time, Muslims prepare themselves for prayer by closing their minds to worldly concerns. They do this by purifying themselves with water (the practice is called *wudu'*) and finding a suitable place to pray. They also remove their shoes. Muslims don't have to attend a mosque to pray; a clean place will do, but they do have to face Mecca in prayer.

The prayer consists of cycles involving recitation of parts of the Qur'an (which are memorized) and body movement to show respect and supplication before God. The prayer begins with Muslims standing with hands raised to the ears while proclaiming God's greatness. They then stand while reciting the opening chapter of the Qur'an. As worshippers recite certain other verses from the Qur'an — some prescribed by tradition and some selected on their own — they change their position from standing (to show alertness) to bowing (to show respect, as well as love, for God) to prostrating themselves (to show surrender), to sitting (to show tranquility and acceptance), and finally to a second prostration.

Although Muslims can pray in a mosque, they don't have to. Nor do they need a certain number of people together before they can pray (unlike Judaism). However, the community usually gathers for *jumma* prayers on Friday at noon. These prayers are offered in the mosque and last about an hour. They may include a sermon by the imam (the leader of the mosque). Men and women usually pray in separate areas.

Unlike Judaism, Christianity, Buddhism, Islam doesn't generally have full-time clergy. The imam is usually a learned Muslim who takes on this responsibility in addition to his ordinary work. Among Shi'ite Muslims, however, the mullahs come close to being priests in the traditional sense. If Muslims aren't praying in a mosque, then the most learned man or oldest man in the group leads the prayer. Women can lead the prayer only when no men are present, for other women and for children.

> ✔ **Prayer rug:** Muslims often use prayer rugs, which are characterized by the prayer niche, or *mihrab* — an arch-shaped design at the end of the carpet. This design, accompanied by other religious symbols (but never

depictions of living things), serves the worshipper as memory aids to support the recitation of the prayers specified in the Qur'an.

✔ **Rosary *(subhah):*** In their personal devotions, Muslims sometimes use a subhah, a string of 99 beads. Each bead represents one of the revealed 99 names for Allah. The beads are divided into three sections, and as they pass their fingers over the beads in each section, they say "Glory be to Allah," "Thanks be to Allah," and "God is most great."

Zoroastrian prayers

Zoroastrians gather for prayer in fire temples, so called because a ceremonial fire burning in an altar serves as the focus of their devotions (much like a cross and altar in a church). Prayer occurs while standing or seated, is led by at least one priest who is male, and involves both men and women praying together. In the absence of a priest, a learned layperson leads the prayer service to God, just as in Judaism and Islam. Food offerings are consecrated during prayer service and then shared in a communal meal by the congregation.

Prayers in Eastern religions

Buddhist communal prayers can take many forms: They can be silent meditations or communal prayers and sermons by a Buddhist monk. Chanting together is very common, and offerings of food and gifts are often placed at the foot of a statue of the Buddha. Incense is lit to fill the air with fragrance. The service can last up to two hours.

Hindu communal worship centers on temples, each of which is dedicated to a particular Hindu deity. The service is called *puja,* and during the service, flowers are placed around the statue of the god, which is usually in the center of the Temple. The statue is also anointed with oil. Incense is lit. Prayers are recited and holy food, *prasad,* is served to the worshippers. In Hinduism, the entire community doesn't go through the worship service together; instead, worshippers proceed in their sacrificial offerings at their own pace.

In Shinto, people go to shrines to get the attention of the *kami* (the gods) to ask for favors, as well as for health or educational success. Worshippers clap their hands and bow, offer prayers, make a donation, leave food at the altar, and hope that the gods hear them. In many ways, the Shinto form of prayer is associated with purification and offerings.

Adherents of Eastern religions recognize the divine and all things holy by praying to various deities and visiting holy temples such as the Mahabodhi Temple (Buddhism) and the Golden Temple at Amritsar (Sikhism).

In addition to temples, many followers of the Eastern religions build altars within their homes or at sacred locations; mountains and other beautiful natural settings are deemed suitable for placement of altars to spiritual figures such as the Buddha. The Buddha statuary found in community shrines and personal altars represents the role of ceremonial objects in religious rituals such as prayer.

Among indigenous or primal religions, carved statues of ancestors or family are often placed in sacred spaces and used as focal points for prayer. The indigenous religions also find a spiritual kinship with nature. For example, references to sacred mountains can be found in the mythology of Native Americans, among the African religions, and in the mythology of the Australian Aborigines.

Making Sacrifices

Although many people hear the word *sacrifice* and think in terms of punishment, in the religious context, the word means to give up something of value in exchange for something of greater value. As a result, sacrifice isn't a punishment, but a reward. A parent giving up a kidney for a sick child is an example of such a sacrifice: The reward — a healthy, living child — far outweighs the loss of a kidney.

The origins of the act of sacrifice are rooted in religion as a way to recognize the Divine. While many may view sacrificial acts as barbaric — such as the sacrificial rituals of killing animals and human beings as offerings to the gods — you need look beyond the obvious. People of faith used the ritual of sacrifice because they believed they were returning life to its divine source, thus enabling the regeneration of the power of the source of that life. In fact, the Latin definition of sacrifice is "to make sacred."

Sacrifice as celebration of life

Sacrificial acts result in extraordinary good, ranging from Jesus' giving his life for humanity (as written in the Christian scripture) to the Vedic sacrificial stories about the creation of the universe.

In some of these Vedic stories from Hinduism, the universe is viewed as a cow. In primordial time, the cow was sacrificed and cut into pieces that became all the elements of the universe. This same idea is present in the division of Parusha into different body parts, which are symbols of the castes. For thousands of years, the Hindu philosophy of faith has been based on the religious idea that sacrifice strengthens the cosmic order.

This notion, however, is not unique to the Hindu. Looking back to the days of the Mayan sacrifices (both human and nonhuman), the ritual sharing of an assortment of plant, animal, and human edibles (typically blood) was done to sustain the cosmos in a state of ordered existence. Based upon religious beliefs, people performed ritual sacrifice to maintain the balance between the underworld and the king, who represented a positive, divine influence.

Sacrifice as a celebration of the divine

People throughout the world have embraced the notion of sacrifice as a means of getting closer to divinity. Human beings perceive that a distance exists between the sacred and the profane. They believe that in order to touch the soul of humanity, they need to be in touch with divinity. This sense moved the ancient Greeks to sacrifice animals such as sheep, goats, horses, and cattle as a way of communing with the gods they worshiped. In Judaism, the ritual of animal sacrifice — for atonement and for thanksgiving — was part of the religious culture until the destruction of the Temple in Jerusalem in 70 C.E.

The Chinese offered human and animal sacrifices to their ancestors. Since the days of the Han Period (circa 206 B.C.E. to 220 C.E.), the ruling classes of China have offered ritual sacrifices in acts called *feng-shan,* defined as wind and mountain, at sacred places such as Mount Tai and in temples. When our ancestors did these things, it was more than blood, violence, and the taking of life that motivated them. It was a desire to worship the divine in the best way they could think of. They offered gifts that were special to them, to their gods, in hopes that their gods would give back health, wealth, and peace of mind.

Sacrifice as a celebration of faith

In Judaism and Islam, the figure of Abraham stands out as a forefather of faith. He's called to sacrifice his time, his comfort, and his family's convenience. In Jewish tradition, God asks Abraham (in Chapter 22 of the Book of Genesis) to sacrifice his son Isaac as an act of supreme sacrifice to God. In Islamic tradition, Abraham dreams that God wants him to sacrifice his son Ishmael. In both versions, Abraham is willing to comply and stops only when God stays his hand. God's stopping Abraham from sacrificing his son teaches the lesson that God wants the *willingness* for sacrifice but never the sacrifice of a human being.

Christians, for example, believe that God sent his only son Jesus to earth to suffer and die on the cross for the forgiveness and sins of humankind. God initiated this heroic act of self-sacrifice. When Jesus rose from the dead and returned to God the Father in heaven, he left behind the Eucharist (also known as *communion* or the Lord's Supper). Roman Catholics view communion as taking the very flesh and blood of Jesus into your body (believing that the bread and wine are literally changed into the body and blood of Christ during the priest's blessing). Many other Christian faiths see the act as symbolically taking the Christ's flesh and blood, and they interpret the ritual of communion as a way of remembering the past. Christians believe that, when they receive communion, they're drawing the life of God into their souls. In Christian theology, God sacrifices himself for humanity, and humanity becomes better for it.

Gettin' Down with God: It's All about Noise and Movement

You don't necessarily have to pray and worship quietly. Many people communicate with God through noise and movement. Singing and chanting — otherwise known as letting your voices be heard — are part of the histories of most world religions. This "beautiful noise" often combines with movement such as dancing — ranging from the Native American Sun Dance to the Sufi whirling dervish — to create an experience that enables the participants to transcend beyond themselves. It's about letting go, giving yourself up to the divine ecstasy that is found in God's love. These actions are often part of the rites of passage found among most religions. Singing, chanting, dancing, and whirling can bring people together, part of the communal experience that unites people of faith. (See the related sidebar titled, "The Welsh Revival of 1904," later in this chapter.)

Singing and chanting

At some point in your life, you've probably participated in — or witnessed — some religious celebration that involves the singing of religious songs. Songs and prayers have a close connection in scripture because some songs are prayers and some prayers are songs. Nearly all religions have some tradition, song, or chant, used as a part of prayer and worship.

Om . . . : Chanting and sound in Eastern religions

Chanting crosses international boundaries. Among the Hindu religions, chanting dates back to ancient times. For Hindus, the chanting of the Rig-Veda and the Yajur Veda (created to be chanted by priests during sacrifices) is a methodical rearrangement of many of the verses of the Rig-Veda with the addition of prose. The chanting is based on various tones and syllables with a type of heightened speech and one syllable to a tone. Brahmin priests chant the Vedas during rites of passage such as weddings and funerals.

Although Vedic chanting (as well as devotional songs called *bhajans*) has been a prominent part of the Hindu religious culture for countless generations (almost 3,000 years), in the twenty-first century, the majority of Vedic chanting is found in India. Today, the Hare Krishna movement is bringing many of the teachings of the ancient Hindu scriptures — primarily derived from the Bhagavad-Gita ("Song of the Lord") — into Western society.

In Japan, the Shinto faithful perform chants, known as *norito,* during rituals. These chants are part of the music Shinto worshippers offer the gods as praise and entertainment. Chanting Buddhist hymns is known as *shomyo.* In both Shinto and Buddhism, chanting enables adherents to participate in their own divine communication.

Sing, sing a song: Music in Western religions

You can find chanting among the Western religions, too. In Judaism, you can find a wonderful example of the interweaving of singing and chanting into the religious experience. The *hazzan,* or cantor, directs all liturgical prayer and chanting when Jews come together in the synagogue. If no cantor is present, a skilled layperson, called the *ba'al tefilah,* chants the prayers, which the congregation then repeats. If you have the opportunity to visit a synagogue during prayer services, you can see for yourself the power of this rhythmic back and forth chanting of praise and devotion to God.

Chanting became part of the Roman Catholic Church during the days of Pope Gregory I (circa 590-604 B.C.E.). The Gregorian chant is the monophonic liturgical music of the Catholic Church; it was first used to accompany the text of the mass. The Gregorian chant has evolved over the centuries, becoming one of the many lyrical ways that Christian faithful offer praise or prayer to God.

The Muslim *Qari* (professional class of reciters of the Qur'an) become so focused and impassioned in their recitation of the Qur'an that they appear to be "chanting" as they communicate with Allah. While singing is not permitted among the Muslim faithful, the chanting to Allah is viewed as a powerful form of prayer. The Qari seem to lose themselves in this form of prayer. This intoning or chanting of the Qur'an is known as *tajwid.*

Today, responsorial singing (style of singing in which a leader alternates with a chorus) is part of many Christian worship services. However, you can find this type of singing in traditions beyond Christianity, commonly among the folk music of many cultures, including the indigenous religions of the world.

Today, the music of the church includes both chants and songs, such as religious psalms. *Psalm tone* is the melodic recitation that is used in the singing of psalms and canticles (or text) of the Bible. Think of the psalm tone as a two-part formula that enables the faithful to use the proper intonation to express the feelings in their heart.

Song and sound in indigenous religions

The combination of chanting and singing is present among the tribes of the North American nations, the thousands of African tribes, and the first peoples of Australia.

Many of the sacred songs, such as the ones sung by the Native Americans — such as the Hopi or the Zuni (from the Pueblo Nation) — are affiliated with rituals and rites of passage. Through these songs, worshipers ask the gods to listen to their pleas for rain, crops, and other elements needed for survival.

Many indigenous religions combine singing and chanting with dancing in order to create a highly energetic offering to the spirits. One of the most famous rituals was the Ghost Dance of Native American tribes in the western United States. Using music and dance, and performing the ritual over a period of four or five consecutive nights, Native Americans sought to rejuvenate their traditional cultures, oust the white man from the land, and return to their traditional way of life. The combination of song — actually, sounding like repeated chanting — and prayers ask for intervention from the divine. White Americans, blaming the Ghost Dance on Native American uprisings, outlawed its performance.

Dancing and whirling

Movement is inextricably tied with the music and songs of prayer. Although some restrictions may be placed upon specific types of dancing — for example, in orthodox Judaism, men and women are not allowed to dance together, and during the Middle Ages, the Christian church didn't allow dancing (some groups, such as Southern Baptists, still prohibit dancing) — dancing remains popular throughout many religions today.

Dance is a form of celebration. If you've ever attended a Jewish wedding, you've probably witnessed the horah, a communal dance in which family and friends raise the bride and groom onto chairs to honor the unity of their love and their roles in perpetuating Judaism (with marriage comes the promise of children). Still, dance as part of religious rituals and rites of passage is most common in indigenous religions and in the religions and cultures of the Middle East:

✔ In Africa, dance is as varied in style and function as the music of Africa. Dancing plays a critical role in rituals such as naming of infants, weddings, and funerals. African dancing includes both individual and group dancing.

✔ Among Native Americans, the rain dance is one of the most well-known rituals. A group performs this dance to ask for divine intervention in bringing rain. This dance is nature-oriented, and dancers usually perform it outdoors so to be closer to the power above. In Native American culture, both men and women perform the ritualistic circle and line dances.

Circle dancing was popular among the once great hunting peoples, such as the Navajo nation. Line dancing was found among the people who were the great agriculturists — such as the Iroquois and the Pueblo nations. Line dancing is also found among the first peoples of Australia.

✔ In the East, one of the most well-known forms of religious dance is the *dervish* (defined as doorway), founded in the thirteenth century. The whirling dervish is a Sufi dancer (an Islamic mystic) who performs the intoxicating religious ritual. In the dance, the dancer goes into a prayer trance to Allah. The dance of the dervish is accompanied by music and chanting as his movements build in intensity. At the height of the ceremony, the dervish is considered to be spinning in ecstasy.

People in Middle Eastern countries believe that the dervish goes so deeply into prayer that his body becomes open to receive the energy of God. Dervishes derive not only energy from Allah but also words and messages, which they transcribe and rehearse for others. According to Sufis, the dervish is considered an instrument of God, who retains God's power only during the solemn ceremony.

As the communities of the faithful continue to grow, the celebration of prayer through actions such as singing, chanting, dancing, and whirling will forever be part of the rituals and rites of passage of the world's religions.

Healing Is Believing

In the context of religion, healing describes a journey of both the physical and spiritual self. Healing can be a private moment of faith sought, for example, by an someone who needs the strength to accept and overcome a devastating illness (such as cancer or AIDS) or who needs divine intervention and guidance in overcoming a spiritual crisis (such as the sudden, unexpected death of a loved one).

Spiritual healing is about overcoming pain, fear of the unknown, anger, loss, depression, shock, denial, and the other emotions that are obstacles to internal peace. In addition, many see healing as an expression of the purist form of love — the love God has for them.

People seek this healing in many ways, among them:

✔ **Pilgrimages:** Common to many religions, a pilgrimage is a journey to a sacred place in search of divine intervention.

✔ **Meditation:** Common to many eastern religions, meditation allows practitioners to achieve a heightened awareness and a transcendent peace.

✔ **Faith healing through prayer:** Common to Christian Science and other Christian sects, faith healing is based on miraculous cures attributed to Jesus and his apostles in the New Testament.

✔ **Sweat lodge ceremonies:** Common to Native Americans, these ceremonies serve as a way to purify the body and the mind.

The common theme among all religions — both Eastern and Western — is that the journey toward healing is possible because of a powerful belief in the Divine. Without this passion of spirit and faith in a supreme being, pilgrims would not journey to sacred places looking for more direct access to God, and people would not participate in the various indigenous rituals and prayers in search of the healing of their bodies and spirits.

On the road again: Pilgrimages

Healing and faith have been intertwined for thousands of years. Ancient Greeks and Egyptians, for example, erected temples to the gods of medicine and good fortune. In times past and even more recently, people in search of healing often make pilgrimages to places considered sources of divine power.

Today, the world is filled with pilgrimage sites, many of them renowned as places of spiritual healing:

✔ One of the most famous Christian pilgrimage sites is Lourdes, France, where, according to Catholic literature, the Virgin Mary appeared 18 times to a young girl. Shortly after this (around 1858), miraculous healings began to be reported in the area. Today, millions of pilgrims make the journey to Lourdes each year in search of healing.

✔ Buddhism has several pilgrimage sites: Some are ancient sites associated with the life and death of Buddha Gautama; others are sites of natural beauty or splendor. One of the most famous pilgrimage sites is the Temple of the Tooth in Sri Lanka, which is supposed to possess one of Buddha Gautama's teeth.

✔ In Islam, the most important pilgrimage — the Hajj — is one of the Five Pillars of faith. Although the purpose of the Hajj is to celebrate particular events in Muslim history, pilgrims can also experience, through the several-days-long act of submission to Allah, spiritual healing. On the second day of the pilgrimage itself, for example, pilgrims reach the Mount of Mercy, where they stand before God, think about him, and pray for his mercy, resulting in a feeling of being wrapped in love and cleansed.

✔ Hinduism celebrates the sacredness of the Ganges River, shown in Figure 7-1. Each day, thousands of spiritual pilgrims wash in its waters for purification. The sick and the dying are brought to its waters so that they may taste liberation after death in this world. These waters not only purify in this world, but Hindus also believe the waters enable them to avoid rebirth in the next.

Figure 7-1:
The Ganges
River is
a holy
tributary
for Hindus.

Mind over matter: Meditation and prayer

Among the Eastern religions — such as Buddhism, Taoism, Shinto, Hinduism, Sikhism, and Jainism — the process of healing involves an extensive use of meditation. Through meditation, people are able to look within themselves to their "higher" selves. From this, they can begin the spiritual examination needed for healing. Numerous forms of meditation exist — ranging from the privacy of silent Zen (Buddhist) to Vedic chanting (Hindu).

Among the Western religions — such as Christianity, Judaism, Islam, and the indigenous religions — healing is also a primary goal of prayer. The peacefulness of prayer enables believers to seek God's intervention in physical and/or spiritual healing. In Judaism the healing prayer is called *refuah shlema,* in which the community prays for a "healing of body and a healing of spirit" for those who are ill. In Catholicism, the healing prayer is called "the sacrament of the sick." In this rite, the priest anoints the sick person, hears her confession, offers her communion, and says prayers for healing and for a return to the community.

Other paths to healing

Among the Eastern religions, you can find extensive literature about the energy that radiates from every person. The study of this energy source includes the study of the *chakras* (the energy points of the human body) and their relationship to the way we exist. By moving the divine essence through the chakras, people can achieve spiritual wholeness — in other words, self-illumination.

In Shinto, the official Japanese religion, the healing process includes religious amulets, or talismans, that people who are searching for purity of spirit use. In addition to the amulets, food and drink play a strong part in the ritualistic healing process. For example, tea — especially green tea — has achieved worldwide recognition for its medicinal or healing value.

Adherents to Jainism, on the other hand, believe that healing of a body and/or spirit is achieved through excessive denial to allow a cleansing of the individual. In terms of healing, the Jains consider fasting particularly important.

A Dieter's Delight: The Joy of Fasting

Fasting is one of the more rigorous religious experiences. By fasting, a person achieves an enhanced sense of self through the deprivation of food, drink, or other worldly comforts. Within the framework of the various world religions — including Christianity, Judaism, Islam, and others — fasting enables followers to achieve a heightened sense of spiritual awareness.

TECHNICAL STUFF

Fasting: A historical overview

Historically, priests and priestesses undertook fasting when they wanted to contact the deities. In the Hellenistic mystery religions, for example, gods would reveal themselves in dreams and visions only after a devotee would engage in a complete fast. Mystery religions are so called because they involved secret words or secret rituals. The reason for this secrecy is that during the first century C.E., several Roman emperors outlawed every religion except emperor worship. Remnants of these religions survive within Christianity itself, and in secret societies such as the Masons (or Freemasons) and the Greek societies on college campuses.

In indigenous religions, people often fasted during initiation rites. By fasting, they joined those from their nations who went before them, entering into a demanding ritual through which they could prove that they really wanted to be a part of the community.

Similarly, many Native American tribes engaged in the ancient rite of the vision quest, a rite of passage that is often achieved through isolation and self-deprivation (such as fasting). The person on a vision quest seeks to make a connection with the spirits beyond this world.

Fasting for political ends

Many people have used fasting as a way to achieve social and political ideals. Many of the civil rights activists fasted during the marches of the 1960s when they were fighting for the rights of the African-American community in the United States. In India, Mohandas Gandhi conducted a fast in prison to atone for the sins of those who would not live in a nonviolent way. Many religious leaders within North America and throughout the world protested the Vietnam War with prolonged fasts.

Now if we could just get politicians to starve themselves.

The benefits of fasting

Fasting teaches believers the discipline of giving up "stuff" for the sake of religious faith. Whether the fasting period lasts for a day (for example, Yom Kippur, the Day of Atonement in Judaism) or longer (for example, Ramadan, the month-long fast celebrated in Islam), many gifts can result:

- ✔ **Appreciation for what you have:** Fasting leads people to realize how they take food, possessions, words, and thoughts for granted. By giving things up for a period, they're able to look at life's gifts with new awareness and thankfulness.

- ✔ **Spirit of generosity toward others:** By feeling deprivation themselves, people (it is hoped) will recognize it in others and act to relieve it. When they see someone who's hungry, for example, they won't pass him by; when they hear that someone's in the hospital, they'll understand the fear and loneliness and, as a result, will choose to visit the person.

The point of fasting isn't suffering; it's attaining a heightened sense of purification. The cleansing creates focus. The focus enables awareness. The awareness means that a soul has opened the door to his/her spiritual self.

Fasting reminds us that this world is passing. It encourages us to wonder what we are doing with our lives and why we are making the choices that we have. When we give up something through fasting, we begin to live without it for a while and frequently realize that we don't necessarily need it — as least as much as we thought we did. This insight has led many to give sweaters to the poor, to move out of stressful jobs, to spend more time with their families, and to become less hedonistic. The changes in a person's life are initially subtle, but over time, those familiar with the person experience a deepening of the soul, transcendence in thinking, and peacefulness about the transition from this world to the next.

Whether to touch divinity or to find one's soul, fasting is a clear way of getting closer to the inner self. (See the related sidebar titled "Fasting: A historical overview" earlier in this chapter.)

Fasting traditions

The Jains use fasting as a way of moving from meditation into trances, which enable them to disengage themselves from this world and arrive at a more transcended state. Buddhists monks of the Theravadan school fast on certain days of the month and after noon on every day. In India, the Hindu sannyasins are known for their fasts, and in China, people used to fast and abstain during the night of the winter solstice to invoke the positive energy of yang as a new cycle of life was beginning. In the West, the Zoroastrians prohibited fasting because they believed that it wouldn't help a person in the struggle with evil. Contrast this with Judaism, Christianity, and Islam, where fasting is a way of life. (See the related sidebar titled, "Fasting for political ends," earlier in this chapter.)

Fasting in Judaism

Judaism has a tradition of fasting to commemorate certain events:

- ✔ Yom Kippur (the Day of Atonement): This is the most important fast day in Judaism. During Yom Kippur, Jews forgo eating in order to spend the whole day in spiritual introspection and prayers seeking atonement for sins.
- ✔ The fast of Tishah B'Av: Fasting in the Hebrew Bible is sometimes done in a time of sorrow, such as the fast of Tishah B'Av, which commemorates the destruction of the temple in Jerusalem in 586 B.C.E. and 70 C.E.

Generally, fasting in the Hebrew Bible means going without food or drink for one day — from sunrise to sunset. The prophets sometimes challenged those who fasted to not only externally observe God and sacrifice for God but also to change the way they faced life. Isaiah (Hebrew Bible, Chapter 58) makes this important spiritual point and Jews read this passage on Yom Kippur to remind them that physical fasting is only the beginning of letting go of sins.

Fasting in Christianity

The New Testament has a more casual attitude toward fasting. Jesus' disciples fasted, but he encouraged them to not let the fasting get in the way of doing good works. For Jesus, fasting became a private and personal experience: He admonished followers not to walk around with long faces and obvious discomfort so that others might be aware that they were fasting. Additionally, a person might fast when seeking divine assistance for an important decision.

Roman Catholicism has two important fast times:

  ✔ Lent: A 40-day period of fasting in preparation for Easter.

  ✔ Advent: A penitential period, preparing for Christmas.

Ash Wednesday, which marks the beginning of Lent, and Good Friday, which marks the day in which Jesus died, are other important penitential days in Christianity.

Since the Vatican Council (1962-1965), Catholics have modified their requirements for fasting and have allowed greater individual choice. People are encouraged to complement fasting with a commitment to good works.

Many Protestant groups do not include fasting as one of their rituals.

Fasting in Islam

In Islam, one of the Five Pillars of Faith is fasting during the month of Ramadan, the ninth month of the Islamic year. Here are some things to know about Ramadan:

  ✔ During the month of Ramadan, Muslims fast from sunrise to sunset each day. If in good health and not aged or pregnant, they are expected to give up all food, drink, smoking, and sex during these hours.

  ✔ Fasting during daylight hours may not seem like such a hardship until you consider that the Muslim calendar is a lunar calendar, which means that Ramadan falls eleven days earlier each year. In some years, Muslims fast during the shorter days of winter; in other years, they fast during the extremely long days of summer. And they do it for a whole month.

  ✔ The physical aspects of the fast are accompanied by giving up vices. Many Muslims also renew their commitment to charity and their willingness to embrace a way of life that sacrifices not only for Allah, but also for people.

Ramadan is an important month for Muslims because it is when Allah selected Muhammad to be his prophet and revealed the first chapters of the Qur'an.

Receiving the Eucharist: It's a Christian Thing

To Christians, Jesus Christ is the Savior, who, knowing that he would be betrayed and crucified, shared a final meal with his disciples. At this meal, Jesus broke bread and poured wine (pretty common fare at the time), blessed it, gave it to his disciples to eat and drink, telling them that it was his body and blood. This event is the foundation for the Eucharist, a celebration passed on by Christians through the centuries as the most direct way of encountering the risen Lord, Jesus Christ.

Eucharist, Communion, Lord's Supper — Different names for the same sacrament

The Eucharist is at the center of the Christian faith. Christians celebrate the Eucharist on Sunday because it was on Sunday that Jesus rose from the dead. When Christians receive the Eucharist, they're giving thanks to God for the gift of Jesus and professing their faith in Jesus. The reception of the Eucharist is a sacrament.

- ✔ For Roman Catholics, the Mass or Eucharist is a re-enactment of the Last Supper. During the blessing by the priest, the bread or wafer and the wine are believed to become the body and blood of Christ, which the parishioners, like the disciples, ingest.

- ✔ For Protestants, the Eucharist is often called the Lord's Supper. Many Protestants use bread and wine. The partaking of the Lord's Supper symbolizes their Christian commitment and serves as a reminder of Jesus' death and sacrifice.

- ✔ Lutherans believe that they receive grace with the bread and wine. (For more about grace, check out Chapter 5.)

During a Catholic mass, parishioners walk up to the altar and receive a wafer, which is the body of Christ, and sometimes drink from the chalice, which contains the blood of Christ (see Figure 7-2). Then they return to their seats to recognize that like Mary — the mother of Jesus, who was invited to carry Jesus in her womb — the person who receives the Eucharist has been invited by God to carry God in their souls. They become Christ bearers. They are meant not only to be a light of God in the world, they are meant to be transformed to do the work of God in this world.

When Christians receive the Eucharist, they draw on the Jewish experience at the seder meal where the participants give thanks to God for creating the world, calling Moses to lead his people from slavery to freedom, and ultimately, for bringing the Jewish people to the Promised Land. The Eucharist is the part of the historical foundation of the Christian church. By partaking, Christians indicate their willingness to become part of the worshipping community and to do the work of God that dates back to the time of Jesus — when it all began.

The meaning of the Eucharist

Today, as Christians of all denominations receive the Eucharist, a spiritual challenge exists. Through the Eucharist, Christians not only receive Jesus, but they are asked to examine how open they are to humanity. They should ask themselves, "Is there anyone that I am excluding from my life? Is there anyone I haven't forgiven? Is there anyone I should be helping?" The answers to these questions help them realize that more work is to be done and that they're the ones to do it.

On another level, receiving Communion carries with it the implied promise to be present to others the way Jesus would. Believers should review each day their relationships with others and ask the simple question, "Did I make the people of my life happier, healthier, and holier?" Such an examination is extremely challenging, and most people discover that they're not measuring up. So, they return to the Eucharist repeatedly to ask for more help from God to do what they know they're supposed to do.

Chapter 8

Rituals of Individual Devotion

· ·

In This Chapter

▶ Going beyond the physical with yoga

▶ Understanding the Stations of the Cross

▶ Using prayer beads, such as the subhah and the rosary

▶ Knowing how a pilgrimage ties into individual devotion

▶ Examining private prayer and study

· ·

*J*ust as communal worship is a large part of religious expression, so is personal devotion. Many religions have rituals that enable individuals to seek God or gods on their own and in private. Some of these rituals focus on prayer, some on meditation, others on movement. Regardless of the method, all involve contemplation and introspection as people try to experience an intimate connection with the Divine. This chapter takes a look at some of the main rituals people use for individual devotion.

There may come a time in your life after you've read the books, gone to the classes, and listened to your parents enough that you're ready to go off on your own, take what you've been taught about your religion, and put it to the test. If so, you may find the information in this chapter helpful as you further your personal spiritual evolution.

Getting Bent into Shape: Yoga

For Hindus, the goal of life is *moksha,* release. When you arrive on earth, you enter the natural world and begin to wrestle with ego, desire, and selfishness. These things are the products of the natural world, as opposed to the eternal world. As you remain tied to things in the natural world, you are destined to continue in the cycle of death and rebirth. Only by releasing attachments can you be freed from this cycle and return to the eternal.

In Hindu theology, to achieve moksha, you must direct the soul to make a full commitment to the Divine — to put aside the distractions of the mind and allow the soul to become more transparent so that it can rejoin the ultimate reality. One way to do this is through yoga.

Yoga is a form of physical and spiritual self-expression that offers the practitioner focus, strength (literal and metaphysical), and the awareness of soul needed to overcome the distractions of daily life. Through yoga, people can achieve the ultimate form of self-development — self-mastery.

Yoga by numbers: (1, 2, 3, . . .)

People who practice yoga claim that yoga gives them a sense of peacefulness and serenity. Without distractions, they can look for meaning. Traditional Hinduism believes that the proper practice of yoga helps you in the search for meaning by making a direct connection with the Divine.

Making this connection requires growth, in one set of guidelines through eight stages:

1-2. **Restraint *(yama)* and discipline *(niyama):*** These first two stages refer to preparation of the mind. In the first stage (yama), the person rejects vices such as lying, stealing, greed, and lust. The second stage (niyama) requires not only cleanliness of the body but also a devotion to God.

3-4. **Proper posture *(asana)* and control of breathing *(pranayama):*** These two stages refer to preparation of the body. In asana, the person practices body movement and postures that make the body flexible and healthy. Pranayama helps the person control breathing so that he or she can enter a state of relaxation.

5. **Detachment *(pratuahara):*** This stage involves controlling the senses so that attention can be drawn inward to the mind.

6. **Concentration *(dharana):*** This stage involves confining awareness to a single object for an extended period.

7. **Meditation *(dhyana):*** This stage involves increasing the concentration on the object to the point that awareness of the self disappears.

8. **Trance *(samadhi):*** This is the final stage, in which a person comprehends the true nature of awareness and ceases to recognize a distinction between himself (or herself) and the object.

Of course, reaching the upper stages of growth requires years of study and practice. People who seriously commit to yoga are willing to make this journey, devoting themselves to study, purity, and self-discipline.

Types of yoga

Yoga, in its many forms, has become popular today for many people looking for a spiritual base.

- ✔ **Karma yoga,** called "the way of action" helps individuals develop the right attitude toward actions; become detached from the results of actions, as determined by dharma; and devote actions to the Divine. Karma yoga invites us to mediate on the good that we do, our station in life, what needs improvement, and how some of the evil that we've done has brought unhappiness to our lives.

- ✔ **Raja yoga,** called "the way of meditation," is for those who are facing severe illnesses or the end of their lives. You learn how to concentrate in an almost trancelike way by eliminating sensory experience and being totally present to the future, the great unknown. This deep form of contemplation unifies the person who is preparing to pass from this life with the god who is waiting in faith to receive that life.

- ✔ **Bhakti yoga** is for those for whom religion is an important way of expressing devotion. With bhakti yoga, the person surrenders his or her will to do a spiritual exercise for the Divine or for the community. The person seeks to become selfless, giving the Divine the glory. Ritualistic practices such as singing the Vedas (Hindu chants), fasting, bodily torture, enacting plays, or making pilgrimages are all directed to the supernatural.

- ✔ **Jnana yoga,** called "the way of knowledge," is for the person who wants to develop the mind. In this form of yoga, people study the scriptures, philosophical systems, and rational arguments, and try to comprehend ultimate reality, or rather, go beyond comprehension to the experience of ultimate reality.

- ✔ **Hatha yoga and Kundalini yoga.** Hatha is popular among a great number of spiritual seekers. This form of yoga offers ways of physically controlling the body. Many who begin this process move on to kundalini yoga. Kundalini yoga is a process that moves beyond the physical discipline of hatha yoga to awaken the latent spiritual power that resides in the base of the spine.

Yoga presents a challenge to the modern person — particularly those (common in the West) who see it primarily as an exercise form. Beyond the physical benefits, the spiritual power of yoga

- ✔ Reminds those who practice it that getting caught up in a whirlwind of activity is easy.

- ✔ Teaches that peace comes from within.

✔ Helps you discover a discipline of a physical, emotional, and spiritual nature that takes time and effort to perfect.

✔ Offers an opportunity for study and commands good actions.

✔ Serves as a reminder that the issue of spirituality isn't just an afterthought.

Walking the Stations of the Cross

If you walk into a Catholic church, you'll find 14 pictures or frescoes on the wall, depicting the stories of the last days of Jesus' life and death. Called the Stations of the Cross, or the Way of the Cross, these images recall holy events when Jesus was put to death on a cross on Good Friday (the Friday before Easter Sunday). For Catholics, Good Friday is both a sad and a joyful day. It's sad because Jesus died; it's joyful because he died for people's sins and redeemed them. Recognizing the painful and holy dimensions of the story, Catholics reconstructed picture snapshots of these events, and they walk from station to station, contemplating the meaning of the life and death of Jesus.

The 14 stations are the following:

1. Jesus is condemned to death by Pontius Pilate.

2. Jesus is asked to take up a cross.

3. Jesus falls down on the journey.

4. Jesus meets his mother.

5. Jesus is too weak to carry the cross, so a man named Simon is engaged to help him.

6. A woman named Veronica, watching the blood drip down Jesus' face, brings a shroud and wipes his face clean, only to see the image of his face imprinted on the shroud.

7. The rigor becomes too much, and Jesus falls a second time.

8. Jesus gets up and meets some women from Jerusalem. He encourages them to do God's work.

9. As Jesus nears the crucifixion site, he falls for the third time.

10. At the site, Jesus is stripped of his garments.

11. Jesus is nailed to the cross — between the crosses of two thieves.

12. Jesus dies on the cross.

13. Jesus is taken down from the cross.

14. Jesus is placed in a tomb.

This devotion frequently consists of a simple prayer by someone in the quiet of the church when no one else is around. Walking the Stations of the Cross can be a supplication for comfort or help (by a parent whose child has gone off to prison, for example, or by a person just diagnosed with a terminal illness). It can also be a prayer of thanksgiving, given by someone who wants to thank God for the blessing in his or her life. The exception to this solitary journey of walking the Stations of the Cross is usually around the time of Lent. Worshippers usually attend Mass more often; and they sacrifice and fast, with many doing so as a group.

Whether celebrated by many or one, this form of prayer is akin to walking to the Wailing Wall in Jerusalem: This particular devotion is an invitation to open one's heart and soul to the God who already knows pain, suffering, and death.

Praying with Beads

Over the centuries, people have found various ways to count the prayers that they utter to God. When Marco Polo visited the King of Malabar, he noticed that the King had a rosary of 104-108 stones. St. Francis Xavier was surprised to realize that the Buddhists of Japan had rosaries. The monks of the Greek Church usually carried a chord with 100 knots used to count the prayers that they were saying. Those following the Hindu way and some Buddhists use beads to keep track of their prayers. These examples reflected, over the years, a very practical way of beginning and ending prayer.

The subhah (tasbih)

Muslims have a string of beads, called *subhah,* or *tasbih,* that they use in devotional prayer. The subhah holds 99 beads (some hold fewer), made from bone, wood, semiprecious stone, glass, precious gems, or now even plastic. Each bead represents *al-Asma al-Husna,* "the most beautiful names" of Allah, which come from the Qur'an and are used as the basis for meditation.

Three larger beads divide the 99 smaller beads into three sections. As Muslims touch each bead one by one, they say a short prayer, the most common being "Subhanallah" (glory be to God). The other prayers are "hamduallah" (praise be to God), and "Allah Akbar" (God is great).

Because prayers can be recited in the one's heart, however, saying the prayers aloud isn't necessary. The action of running your fingers over the beads is also considered a form of prayer.

The evolution of a prayer

The Hail Mary is a beautiful prayer, citing the greeting made to Mary by the Angel Gabriel, "Hail Mary, full of grace, the Lord is with you" (Luke 1:28). Over time, the greeting given to Mary by her cousin Elizabeth was added: "Blessed are you among women and blessed is the fruit of your womb, Jesus" (Luke 1:42). In the fifteenth century, the prayer was expanded to include, "Holy Mary, Mother of God, pray for us sinners now and at the hour of our death."

The rosary

Early Christians wanted to recite the 150 Psalms from the Hebrew Bible on a daily or weekly basis. Finding this task impossible, they came up with this solution: They created the rosary — a string of 150 beads — to help them remember, and they substituted the "Our Father" (a prayer that Jesus gave to his disciples) for the Psalms. Using the 150 beads as counters, the early Christians recited one Our Father for each bead. When they were done, they would have recited the prayer 150 times.

The term *rosary* comes from *rose,* and Mary (the Blessed Mother) is considered the Mystical Rose because she was the first to be redeemed by Christ.

In the Middle Ages, Christians added the "Hail Mary" (a prayer commemorating Jesus' mother) to the Our Father. The rosary was divided into 15 *decades* in which the worshipper would recite one Our Father (denoted by a large bead), followed by ten Hail Mary prayers (denoted by ten smaller beads). See the related sidebar titled "The evolution of a prayer" later in this chapter.

Later, other prayers were added to the rosary. One is called the "Apostles' Creed," a summary of ancient Christian belief. Another prayer, the "Glory Be to the Father," praises the Trinity of Father, Son, and Holy Spirit. Finally, the prayer, "Hail, Holy Queen" is recited at the end of rosary.

The rosary in many ways is like a mantra in which a person prays the Hail Mary and Our Father repeatedly. To keep the person focused, the church offers joyful, sorrowful, and glorious mysteries for the person to think about.

The full rosary is 15 decades long. A decade is composed of one Our Father, ten Hail Marys, and one Glory Be to the Father. (Most rosaries today contain a shorter version that is five decades long.) Practicing Catholics who say the rosary reflect on different biblical mysteries each day:

✔ On Mondays and Thursdays, they contemplate the joyful mysteries.

✔ On Tuesdays and Fridays, the sorrowful mysteries.

✔ On Wednesdays and Saturdays, the glorious mysteries

✔ On Sundays, they follow the Church calendar: From Advent through Lent, they choose the joyful mysteries:

- The announcement that Mary would be the mother of God

- The visit of Mary to her cousin Elizabeth

- The birth of Jesus

- The bringing of Jesus to the temple

- The finding of Jesus at the Temple

✔ For Lent, they choose the sorrowful mysteries:

- When Jesus prays in the Garden of Olives before his death on the cross

- The scourging of Jesus

- The crowning of Jesus with thorns

- The carrying of the cross by Jesus

- The crucifixion

✔ For the Sundays of the rest of the year, they choose the glorious mysteries:

- The resurrection of Jesus

- The ascension of Jesus

- The sending of the Holy Spirit

- The assumption of Mary into heaven

- The crowning of Mary as queen of heaven

Whether reflecting on the names of Allah or thinking about the life of Jesus, using the rosary or the subhah is a personal and spiritual way of spending time with God in the depths of one's soul.

Goin' on a Road Trip: Pilgrimages

Many people express private devotion by undertaking a pilgrimage. A pilgrimage is a religious journey, in which the believer travels to places that his or her religion considers holy. These pilgrimage sites can be special structure, such as shrines and monasteries; places of importance to that religion; or places that, because of nature beauty, seem to be closer to the Divine. A Hindu will travel to one of that faith's holy rivers or places, such as the Ganges River. A Jew will go to Jerusalem. A Muslim will go to Mecca. A Christian will make a pilgrimage to the Holy Land. A Buddhist may go to Bodhgaya. Regardless of where they go, pilgrims believe they're going to places where earth and heaven link.

Pilgrims often "begin" their journey months before they actually leave. They read about and study the place they're going to. They start to pray and maybe even fast.

Although their expectations are generally vague, people undertake pilgrimages for many reasons:

- ✔ A cure of an illness
- ✔ The burial of sacred remains
- ✔ The fulfillment of a vow
- ✔ Honoring an expectation of their faith
- ✔ Commemorating the anniversary of a special day

Whatever the reason that compels them, many people on pilgrimage claim that they feel they rediscover their souls.

The Hajj

In Islam, the pilgrimage to Mecca is called the *Hajj*. Although people may go as many times as they can afford and are able, every Muslim is expected to make the trip at least once if he or she can.

In the Qur'an (3.97) it is written: "And a pilgrimage to the House is a duty unto Allah for mankind, for him who can find a way thither."

Each year, about one-and-a-half million Muslims journey to Mecca during the last month of the Islamic calendar. (A pilgrimage taken at another time during the year — encouraged for Muslims who make the pilgrimage more than once — is considered *al-umrah,* or the Lesser Pilgrimage).

During the Hajj, pilgrims perform certain acts:

1. **Purify themselves.**

   Pilgrims cleanse and purify themselves by

- Bathing for ritual purity, indicating his or her intent to perform the pilgrimage.

- Donning *ihram* clothing. For men, this clothing consists of two unstitched, seamless, white cloths, one around the waist and falling to the ankles, the other draped over the left shoulder. Women wear a modified version of the two cloths or modest dresses that cover everything except for their face, hands, and feet).

- Adhering to certain rules of behavior, such as abstaining from sexual intercourse, that reflect human beings' status as servants to Allah who are focusing exclusively on God during the pilgrimage.

2. **Circle the Ka'bah (shown in Figure 8-1).**

Figure 8-1:
The Ka'bah, in Mecca, is the holiest site for Muslims.

Muslims consider the Ka'bah, believed to have been built by Abraham and Ishmael, the most sacred place on Earth. Upon reaching the Ka'bah (regardless of the time), pilgrims must circle it seven times, running for three circuits if they can, and touch, kiss, or salute the *al-hajar al-aswad* (the Black Stone) that the shrine holds.

According to tradition, God gave this stone to Adam. Originally white, it turned black after absorbing the sins of all the pilgrims who touched it. The pilgrim is expected to make a personal prayer either while facing or better still while touching the Ka'bah. Other prayers at the Station of Abraham, and drinking from the well of Zamzam are prescribed, as well.

3. **Perform the Sa'i.**

   In this ritual, pilgrims run or walk quickly seven times between two small hills, Safa and Marwah. This ritual represents Hagar's (Ishmael's mother) desperate search for water after Abraham abandoned her and Ishmael at Sarah's (Abraham's first wife) urging. According to tradition, when Ishmael, near death, scratched the ground, water came bubbling forth, a gift from Allah, proving that, even when things seem their bleakest, he is still present.

4. **Make a stand at Arafat.**

   Standing on the plain of Arafat is the most important part of the pilgrimage. On the second day of the pilgrimage, all pilgrims must stand before God for several hours outside on the plain of Arafat near the Mount of Mercy, from noon to dusk. Throughout this, they pray for mercy, just as they would do in God's presence at the final gathering of Muslims at the end of time.

5. **Throw stones at the pillars that symbolize Satan.**

   This ritual represents Abraham's, Hagar's, and Ishmael's rejection of Satan. According to tradition, Satan is in disguise as he tries to sway Abraham, Hagar, and Ishmael from obedience to God. Satan claims (to Abraham) that God wouldn't require such a sacrifice; (to Hagar) that Abraham must not love her or Ishmael if he was willing to sacrifice his son; and (to Ishmael) that his father must be mad to consider such a sacrifice that Ishmael could escape. All three drove Satan away by throwing stones at him.

6. **Fast or sacrifice an animal.**

   Sacrificing a sheep, goat, or young camel recalls Abraham's willingness to sacrifice his son Ishmael and God's mercy by substituting a ram for the boy at the last minute. This sacrifice (made only by the pilgrims who can afford it) is accompanied by a worldwide feast that lasts for three days. A fast can replace the animal sacrifice.

7. **Circle the Ka'bah again.**

All in all, the pilgrimage takes six to ten days and includes almost constant prayer.

Other pilgrimages

In Judaism, each of the three biblical holidays of Passover, Sukkot (Feast of Booths), and Shavuot (Pentecost) were called *hag,* the Hebrew term meaning both holiday and pilgrimage. In biblical times, Jews were required to make a pilgrimage to the temple in Jerusalem to offer grain and animal sacrifices to atone for sins, give thanks for births, and honor the holiday. After the Romans destroyed the Temple (in 70 C.E.), such pilgrimages were no longer possible. The rabbis, who replaced the priests as leaders and teachers of Judaism, transformed these holiday sacrifices into holiday prayers.

When Hindu pilgrims travel to a shrine, a temple, a lake, or a mountainside, they're often seeking relief from pain and looking for the removal of karma and detachment from worldly concerns. They also make pilgrimages to honor deceased ancestors. During the pilgrimage, pilgrims worship, bathe in sacred waters, and bring mementos of the deceased. In many ways, the Hindu pilgrimage is a foreshadowing of the next world, in which they hope to move to a better level of karma, or they hope to move beyond rebirth.

For Christians, in the early centuries, the Holy Land and Rome were the two most popular pilgrimage sites. The visitors would visit places where Jesus celebrated Mass, called his disciples, performed miracles, and died on the cross. Rome, over time, became a special place to visit because of the history of the papacy. In modern times, many Christians travel to Guadalupe in Mexico, Lourdes in France, and Fatima in Portugal to visit sites where the Blessed Mother (Mary) is thought to have appeared. Pilgrims to these sites frequently bring their sick with them and pray for healing.

In Japan, pilgrims generally wear special coats and hats and go to various temples acknowledging the kami and ancestors. (Kami are spirits or divinities that serve the ancient goddess Amaterasu.) You can find 88 temples on the island of Shikoku. On a book or on their coat, pilgrims stamp a seal of the temple that they are going to visit. When they arrive at the temple, they put slips of paper with their names and hometowns on the temple pillars and walls. They sing a special hymn at each temple and frequently leave behind some charity.

Private Prayer

The most intimate connection with the Divine is found in prayer. In prayer, believers open up their hearts, their minds, and their souls to the Divine. Prayer is sometimes formal and public, but prayer can also be an intensely personal experience whether the person praying is alone or in a group. (See the related sidebar titled "Contemplating contemplation.")

Contemplating contemplation

In meditation, a person takes a spiritual book, reads it, and pauses and asks, "What is God saying?" and "What is God saying to me?" This form of prayer encourages people to be totally open to God, to allow God to take over their lives, and to shape them in God's way. It is not a sudden transformation, but it brings about peace. Over time, the person learns how to contemplate. In contemplation, a person sits in the presence of God, not asking anything, not thinking anything, and not seeking anything. This is a very difficult form of prayer because most people are used to being active. Most people say it takes years to learn how to quiet our minds and become one with God. Those who have done so tell us the journey is worth it.

Having a private prayer life is a common characteristic of many spiritual seekers. Public prayer creates spiritual communities of faith, but private prayer creates individuals with a living faith inside them. Even within the public liturgy of all organized religions, the individual worshipper is encouraged to offer up prayers that are not formal and not written in any book.

Private prayer takes many forms. Following is a sampling of the ways you can pray when you're alone:

- ✔ **Speaking to the Divine:** This type of prayer may include uttering prayers that you may have been taught as children or uttering requests that come from your everyday living.

- ✔ **Listening to the Divine:** In this type of prayer, you contemplate religious texts. For example, you'd read a passage of the Bible or the Qur'an and ask the questions: "What is God saying?" and "What is God saying to me?" Then you listen over time for an answer.

- ✔ **Giving attention to the Divine presence:** Rather than speaking or listening, this type of prayer is considered contemplation. In contemplation, you sit before the Divine and, like a piece of clay in the hands of an expert potter, ask only to be shaped by the Divine. This form of prayer unites you with the Divine in a wordless and unstructured way.

Chapter 9

Holy Days in Our Lives: Rites of Passage

• •

In This Chapter

▶ Finding out how religions celebrate birth

▶ Knowing when you are considered an adult

▶ Looking at love and marriage

▶ Crossing over into the next life: Death and mourning

▶ Appreciating the differences and similarities of the human experience

• •

Religions offer many ways to understand life and celebrate its meaning. One way is to bring people together to celebrate life's most important moments. For most religions, those moments are the milestones of life: birth, the beginning of adulthood, marriage, and death. Many religions also consider a person's initiation into its faith to be a rite of passage.

Hindus outline the traditional four stages of a Brahmin's (upper caste) life. In the first phase, you learn about life. In the second phase, you develop a business, run a home, and have a family. In the third phase, you start to give back to the community. In the fourth phase, you retreat from your job and family to become a *sannyasin,* one who seeks the infinite. That pretty succinctly expresses the life stages that all people experience.

In this chapter, you discover the different ways in which the major religions help people celebrate or mourn the passing of the phases of their lives.

Christian Life Cycle Rituals

The various churches that fall under the heading of Christianity today have built faith-based communities that are grounded in their own distinct rituals and rites of passage.

Baptism: Water, water everywhere

A timeless ritual among the Christian churches is the rite of baptism, which is the way a person becomes a Christian. A minister of the church, acting in the name of Jesus, performs the baptism, which usually involves water (to signify cleansing of both the body and the soul) and an invocation of the Trinity. ("I baptize you in the name of the Father, and of the Son, and of the Holy Spirit.") In this action, the person's sins are washed away, or exorcised, and he or she is dedicated to God for life.

Methods of baptism vary:

- **Sprinkling:** A minister of the church sprinkles a few drops of water on the person's forehead.

- **Dunking:** The minister submerges the person's head.

- **Complete immersion:** The person's whole body is submerged in the water. Some Protestant groups, such as Southern Baptists, urge their members to be baptized in flowing water.

In addition, different Christian religions baptize at different times. Some baptize babies; others hold off baptism until the person being baptized is old enough to understand the meaning and significance of the rite.

- **Baby baptism:** In some Christian traditions (Lutheran, Catholic, and Episcopalian), parents are encouraged to bring their child to the church to be baptized. During the baptism, parents promise to teach their child about Christianity, and two godparents promise to assist the parents in their spiritual responsibility. The family receives a candle to remind them that the light of God is in their child's life. The child sometimes receives a bib signifying the new life that she or he embraces in Christ.

According to Catholic teaching, children are born affected by original sin. Original sin is attributed to all humankind for the disobedience of Adam and Eve to God. This sin is washed away in baptism, and the child emerges from the ceremony to begin a life of doing the work of God. This life frequently calls the child to reject evil, to embrace good, and to live in faith. Interestingly, when individuals are baptized, they not only become a member of the Christian community, they also enter into the priesthood of Christ in the sense that they are meant to be living the way Jesus did and helping others to get to know the Christ message.

- **Adult baptism:** During the Protestant Reformation, many church groups rejected infant baptism as unscriptural. These groups contended that only those old enough to know and profess their faith should be baptized. One of the groups was the Anabaptists, who were the forerunners of the Amish, Mennonite, and Bruderhof communities. Today, the two largest Christian sects that practice adult baptism are Baptists and the Disciples of Christ.

Some Protestants groups believe that people must have a salvation experience (be "saved") or speak in tongues before they are baptized.

Regardless of these differences, you can find some type of baptism among all Christian churches. Today, the ritual of baptism continues to expand the Christian community. Every participant in the church is baptized. (See the related sidebar titled "The origins of baptism" later in this chapter.

Confirmation: 1 do believe (1 think)

During adolescence, the church invites pre-teens and early teens (who, up until this time, have probably been going to church because their parents brought them) to make decisions for themselves, to confirm their faith. This rite is called *confirmation*. Lutheran, Catholic, and Episcopalian churches usually confirm young people at about age 13.

The word confirmation suggests a meaning that includes strengthening. In this regard, people come to the church and ask to be strengthened in their faith. They study the Bible, attend classes about the Christian life, and are asked to do a special work of charity in preparation for receiving the gift of God's spirit at confirmation.

Traditionally, in Roman Catholicism, people being confirmed were given the title "soldiers of Christ." Today, due to the obvious problems with that image, many are seen as becoming mature disciples of Christ. They go to the church to meet the bishop, who is the leader of faith in the community. The bishop talks to them about living out their faith in the contemporary world. He then invites them to be anointed with the special oil that is reserved for people who want to do the work of God in the world. He shakes their hands and wishes them God's peace. They are sent out from the church to practice their faith.

The origins of baptism

Christians borrowed the custom of the initiation ceremony from both Judaism and the mystery religions (so called because of their secret rites). Religions have used water rituals for millennia as a symbol of cleansing or making clean.

For many people, the baptismal ceremony is a pivotal point in their life of faith; for others, however, it's just a ritual that they embrace because they are Christian in name only.

A baptism is meant to imitate the moment in which Jesus went to the River Jordan. Jesus entered the water to meet his cousin, John the Baptist, who was calling for the people of his time to repent. At that moment, Jesus received a spiritual message from God, telling him that he (Jesus) was God's beloved son. Jesus came out of the water and began his public ministry.

Who's marrying whom?

Who marries the couple? The minister does. At least that was the traditional answer. Nowadays, however, couples are encouraged to realize that they actually marry each other. The priest and minister only *witness* the marriage.

Although many young people think of confirmation as the end of study of faith (yippee!), this is actually the opposite of what confirmation is about. Confirmation invites and challenges people to embrace their faith in a serious way and to embrace prayer, holiness, and helping the community as part of the core of their beings. Confirmation is the beginning of a deeper faith, not the end of it.

Marriage: You've got to be yoking

In the Gospels, Jesus invites his followers to love God and love people. This, along with the story of Adam and Eve in Genesis, is a spiritual foundation for the ritual of marriage

"But from the beginning of creation, 'God made them male and female.' For this reason a man shall leave his father and mother and be joined to his wife, and the two shall become one flesh. So they are no longer two, but one flesh. Therefore what God has joined together, let no one separate" (Mark 10:6-19).

Many people come to know and love God through prayers, rituals, meditation, sacrificing — in other words, through faith. Another aspect of love is equally important in the Christian community. People frequently discover how to love people by falling in love. Two people, attracted to one another, find themselves doing things for each other that previously they wouldn't have done for anyone else. When they sense that they want to do this for the rest of their lives, they come to the church to be married.

In Christianity, marriage is an important moment; it's a moment to be blessed by God. Churches offer programs for marital preparation. While they vary in length and scope, many programs introduce the couple to married couples, who talk about communication, sexuality, and spirituality. The minister, priest, or deacon will talk about the theology of marriage and the marriage ceremony itself. ("See the related sidebar titled, " Who's marrying whom?" later in this chapter.)

During the ceremony, family and friends witness the couple's vows, and the officiating minister reminds the couple that

✔ Their commitment is forever ("for better, for worse . . . for richer, for poorer . . . in sickness and in health . . . .")

✔ The marriage isn't simply a union of two people, but also the union of the two of them with God.

✔ They will form a home, begin a family, and help each other to walk back to God together.

The minister also encourages them to have children, to raise those children in faith, and to return to the church to get the strength they need to achieve what is probably the best — and hardest — thing they've ever done.

Death: Grieving through a happy time

Many people view death as a time of mourning, a time of sadness, and a time to pray as a community through the pain and tears. This view is challenged by the Christian belief that death is a passing from this world to a better world — a belief reflected in Christian funerals in New Orleans, where a music band leads the way to the grave. The point? Death should be a time of rejoicing that the deceased is with God.

The funeral practices themselves can be simple or elaborate, depending on the branch of Christianity and the desires (and wallets) of the surviving family. The funeral usually include the following:

✔ **The calling:** The calling (or wake) takes place one and sometimes two days before the funeral service. During the calling, mourners come to pay their respects to the family of the deceased. The body of the person who has died is generally present and the casket can be either open or closed.

✔ **The service and burial:** The service can take place in a church or at the funeral home and it generally involves a minister giving a service and people eulogizing the dead. Following the service, the body is taken to the cemetery for burial or taken away for cremation.

✔ **A reception:** Following the funeral, mourners gather to remember, honor, and celebrate the life of the person who has died.

Christianity also has traditions that remember the dead. For example, All Souls Day (November 1) is a Roman Catholic holiday that remembers the souls of people who have died and who can benefit from the prayers of the faithful. In many Latin American countries, this day is the Day of the Dead, during which people picnic at the graves of dead family members and hold other festivities commemorating those who have passed on. Latter-day Saints (Mormons) baptize the names of people who have died in order to place them in paradise.

Jewish Life Cycle Rituals

Beginning with Abraham and continuing through Moses, the Israelite people became a close-knit community. God established a covenant with Israel in which God said, "I will be your God and you will be my people." Blood and faith connected the 12 tribes of Israel to each other. This faith was — and continues to be — expressed through the Jewish life rituals. (For full coverage on Judaism, get a copy of *Judaism For Dummies*, by Rabbi Ted Falcon, Ph.D., and David Blatner, published by Wiley.)

Birth: Welcome to the community

Great rejoicing goes on when a Jewish child is born. Within eight days of the birth of a baby boy, a Jewish family arranges for a circumcision rite, called a *brit*, which means covenant (it's short for *brit milah*, which means covenant of circumcision). This religious ceremony signals the transition of a child from being a child of Abraham to a member of the Jewish community. The brit is a rite of initiation that unites a family because the child symbolizes the next generation of the faithful.

This ritual welcomes the child into Judaism and reinforces the covenant of Abraham with the male child. The family gathers during the brit and does the following:

1. **The family passes the child around.**

2. **The *mohel* (a specially trained male — sometimes a rabbi or physician) places the child on a chair and delicately performs the circumcision (in which the foreskin of the boy's penis is removed).**

   The chair symbolizes the chair of Elijah, which represents the hope of redemption.

3. **After the circumcision, the mohel hands the child to his father and recites blessings that praise God and ask for the welfare of the child.**

4. **The boy is given his Jewish name.**

   This name is the name that will be used when the child is called to read the Torah during his bar mitzvah. This name will also appear on his tombstone at death.

From antiquity, some Jews have had two names signifying their commitment to function in both the secular and religious communities. Ashkenazi Jews name the boy after his deceased relative. Sephardic Jews do not adhere to this custom and name after living relatives, but Jewish boys are never named after a living father. (Ashkenazi Jews usually have roots in Eastern or Central Europe, while Sephardic Jews claim ancestry from Western Europe, North Africa, and the Near or Middle East.)

5. **The entire community prays out loud: "Just as he has entered the covenant, so may he enter the study of the Torah, the wedding canopy, and do good deeds."**

The naming of a girl occurs in traditional practice during a Sabbath service within a month of her birth when her father is called up to read from the Torah.

In more liberal Jewish traditions, the girl is named in a ceremony similar to the traditional naming ceremony used for boys. This ceremony, called a *simhat bat,* offers ritual equality to girls and involves mothers and fathers. Of course, during the simhat bat, the girl isn't circumcised. Instead, wine is touched to her lips, often using the silver pointer that points to the holy words of the Torah. She is given a Hebrew name, and then everybody sings and eats! (See the related sidebar titled, "Dietary laws in Judaism.")

Adolescence: Bar mitzvahs and bat mitzvahs

Girls are considered adults at age 12 and boys at 13. Whether or not they have a ceremony marking this passage, they're full adults.

As adults they are

- Counted in a minyan of ten Jewish adults for prayer. (Girls are not counted in a minyan for prayer in Orthodox Judaism.)
- Obligated to follow all the commandments of Jewish law that apply to adults. (In Orthodox Judaism, girls are exempt from all time-bound positive commandments that might conflict with child rearing.)

The bar mitzvah (or bat mitzvah in liberal Judaism) is just a public acknowledgment of the physical fact of the child's new status as an adult. (Bar mitzvah literally means "son of the commandments" and bat mitzvah means "daughter of the commandments.") In order to emphasize the importance of this transition, however, the child studies for years in order to be able to perform difficult adult tasks like reading from the Torah scroll (the first five books of the Bible) and leading a prayer service.

From a Jewish perspective, the handing on of the Torah and all its wisdom is one of the deepest gifts any young man or woman can ever receive. From that perspective, as in Christianity's rite of confirmation, bar mitzvah and bat mitzvah mark the beginning of a deeper commitment to Jewish life than ever before. After the ceremony in the synagogue, friends, relatives, and members of the community gather for a feast.

Dietary laws in Judaism

The Torah provides a lengthy list of which foods are kosher and which are not. (See Leviticus 11-15 and Deuteronomy 14.)

What You Can Eat	What You Can't
Animals with cloven hooves and animals that chew their cud	Pork
Fish with fins and scales	Eels, shrimp, or shellfish
Flying birds that eat grain and vegetables	Birds of prey
Separated milk and meat product	Cheeseburgers
Properly killed animals	Road kill

Marriage: Contracts and vows

If you've ever been to a Jewish wedding, you most likely have seen a *huppah,* or wedding canopy. This beautiful structure symbolizes the new home of the bride and groom.

In Judaism, as in other religions, a wedding is a moment of celebration. Two people brought together by love make a commitment to their faith. The ceremony comprises two distinct rituals:

- ✔ The *kiddushin,* or betrothal
- ✔ The *nissuin,* or the wedding blessings and the feast that follows it

Jewish weddings can't occur on the Sabbath or on holidays. In traditional practice, weddings can't occur during the seven weeks from Passover to Shavuot (except for one special day called Lag b'Omer).

When weddings do occur, here's what happens:

1. **The couple arranges for a rabbi or cantor to lead the ceremony.**

2. **The couple signs a *ketubbah.***

   The ketubbah is the Jewish wedding document that describes the rights of the husband and wife.

3. **The rabbi utters the seven blessings, which extol the beauty of creation and the joy of companionship.**

4. **The couple exchange vows and rings.**

   In a traditional Jewish wedding, only one ring (for the bride) is used and in a liberal ceremony, two rings (for both bride and groom) are used.

5. **At the end of the ceremony, the groom breaks a glass, and friends and relatives then usually shout out "Mazel tov!" which means "Good luck!"**

   The breaking of the glass symbolizes the destruction of the Temple in Jerusalem.

In Jewish law, the rabbi doesn't actually marry the couple. The legal binding force of a Jewish wedding comes from two witnesses called, in Hebrew, *eidim*. These witnesses represent the Jewish people who, in an act of great spiritual democracy, actually sanctify the marriage. (See the related sidebar titled "The debate over intermarriages" in this chapter.)

Death: The way to Eden

When death approaches, observant Jews recite the final confession. Called the *vidui* in Hebrew, the confession's main sentiment is to ask God that the dying person's death be atonement for his or her sins.

Before the funeral, the deceased undergoes a purification ritual and is dressed in simple white shrouds. According to Jewish tradition, the casket must be made of only wood; such caskets don't prevent the body from returning to the earth. (Even metal nails are prohibited in a kosher Jewish casket, because nails are made of a substance that's used in warfare.)

In Judaism, speedy burial is a law and a firm tradition. Burial within a day is preferred, but the burial can be delayed if a mourner has to come from another city. (In Jewish law, a mourner is someone who has lost a father, a mother, a sister, a brother, a son, a daughter, or a spouse.) Ribbons or clothing that have been cut identify mourners. If a parent has died, the cut is made on a person's left side. The cut is on the right side if the death was of any other relative.

During the funeral service, Psalms are read (usually Psalm 122 and Psalm 23) and the rabbi and often (nowadays) family members and friends offer eulogies. At the cemetery, mourners and friends place earth on the coffin in the grave as a way to fulfill with their own hands the commandment of burying the dead. (Jews must be buried in a Jewish cemetery. Cremation is against Jewish law.)

Upon leaving the grave, the mourners pass through two lines of family and friends. The proper greeting to a Jewish mourner is, "May the Almighty comfort you, together with all the mourners of Zion and Jerusalem."

The debate over intermarriages

Jewish law doesn't permit rabbis to marry Jews to unconverted non-Jews. Such a marriage is called an *intermarriage.* (If the non-Jew converts, having a Jewish wedding ceremony isn't a problem at all.) Nowadays, however, some liberal rabbis perform intermarriages, which is perhaps the most divisive and contentious issue in modern Jewish life.

Rabbis who perform intermarriage say that they're just reaching out and compassionately accepting people where they are. Refusing to officiate at an intermarriage, they argue, only alienates the couple and their families from Judaism.

Rabbis who oppose intermarriages and don't officiate at them point to statistics that show that less than 20 percent of the children of intermarriages and only about 5 percent of the grandchildren of intermarriages are raised as Jews. In addition, over half of the American Jews who got married in recent years have married unconverted non-Jews. These rabbis contend that intermarriage is diminishing the number of Jewish people and that rabbis shouldn't participate in anything that reduces the Jewish population.

You may hear one of two Jewish prayers for the dead:

- The *el moleh rahamim,* which means "God full of mercy." This prayer asks God to take the soul of the departed into the Garden of Eden, one of the synonyms for heaven in Judaism. Heaven is also called *olam habah,* "the world to come." The decedent's Hebrew name is included in that prayer.

  A traditional Hebrew name has three parts, your first name in Hebrew, followed by *ben* if you're a man or *bat* if you're a woman, followed by your father's first name: David ben Moshe or Rivka bat Moshe, for example. Your mother's Hebrew names are used for prayers of healing in Judaism but never at funerals.

- The *kaddish yatom.* Mourners recite this prayer every day for 11 months and one day in a minyan (group of ten adults). The kaddish yatom, which doesn't include even a single reference to death, is just a pious reciting of many merciful attributes of God.

After the funeral, the community cares for the mourner, visiting the home during the first week after the burial, a time called *shivah* in Hebrew. During that time, mourners don't work or venture out. During the first month, men don't shave, and, during the first year, public celebrations are minimal.

Yizkor (memorial) services are held four times a year, on Yom Kippur, Shavuot, Passover, and Sukkot.

The biblical Jacob set a tombstone for his wife Rachel, beginning the custom in Judaism to set a headstone. Mourners can set a headstone up to a year after the death. Jewish families often visit the graves of their loved ones before holidays and on the anniversaries of their deaths, called *yahrzeit* (Yiddish for "a year's time"). At home, family members light a yahrzeit candle (which burns for 24 hours) for the deceased.

Islamic Life Cycle Rituals

For the Islamic community, Allah, the Qur'an, and faith are the reasons for living. The source for all Muslim ritual is found within the pages of the Qur'an (the most holy book in Islam). The Muslim faithful are passionate in their quest to serve Allah and to live their lives in submission to God. From the earliest moments of a child's life, the Muslim family begins to introduce that child to the Five Pillars of Islam.

Birth: Surprises maybe, but no accidents

In Islam, children are gifts from God. For this reason, Muslims don't consider any child's birth to be an accident or the child to be unwanted. A child's birth signifies the beginning of the next generation of the faithful to Allah.

Before Muslim couples make love, they utter *"Basmala,"* that is, "in the Name of God, the Merciful, the Compassionate." This prayer of devotion to God articulates that everything important comes from God and should be returned to God.

When a child is born, the first thing the child hears is the name of God: The parents recite the *adhan,* the call to prayer *(Allahu Akbar!)* including the *sha-hadah* — the same incantation that Muslims hear five time a day, summoning them to pray — into the baby's ear. They may also recite the command to rise and worship. They also touch the baby's lips with honey to make him or her sweet and kind.

Seven days after the baby's birth, the parents shave the baby's head and give alms, equal in value to the weight of the hair, to the needy. To show thanks, they sacrifice an animal (two for a boy) and give the meat to the poor. The family also names the baby (Muhammad and Ali being the most popular boys' names; names of women in Muhammad's family — such as Fatima and Aisha — being the most popular girls' names).

Although the customs differ slightly in different areas of the world, boys are circumcised. Some are circumcised as infants, others before they turn 10. In Turkey, for example Muslim males are dressed in their finest clothes and taken to their favorite places before they are circumcised.

Interestingly, the Qur'an says nothing about circumcision *(khitan)*. Instead, the act is probably a holdover from ancient traditions within the cultures within which Islam grew. Some areas of the Islamic world, especially places influenced by African cultures, also circumcise females (that is, they remove the clitoris). This practice has nothing to do with Islam.

Adolescence and religious education

Muslims teach their children about Islam and the Qur'an as early as they can. Between the ages of 3 and 5 years, some families hold a ceremony, called a *Bismallah,* in which a devout relative or an imam (an Islamic holy man) has the child write the Arabic alphabet and recite the al Fatihah (The Opening), the first chapter of the Qur'an (quite a mouthful for a young child):

In the name of God, the merciful, the compassionate

Praise to God, Lord of the worlds,

The merciful, the compassionate,

King of the day of judgment.

We worship you, we beseech you,

Guide us on the right path,

The path of those upon whom you have bestowed favor,

Not of those upon whom your wrath is, nor those who go astray.

After the Bismallah, Muslim children learn how to perform the *wudu'* (the ritual washing for purification before prayer) and begin their official study of Islam. By the time they reach age 10, Muslim children should be able to recite the five daily prayers on their own, take part in the fasting rituals, know what foods are acceptable and what foods aren't, and know how to behave according to their faith.

Muslims train their children to read and recite the Qur'an. Through this recitation, the child exhibits knowledge of God's teaching and becomes a full member of the *umma,* the family of the Muslim faith. This spiritual moment enables the young person to feel at home in his faith and requires that he or she take the responsibility of defending and propagating the faith seriously.

Marriage: A match made at home

In Islam, marriage is considered the natural way of life, but not one that should be entered into lightly or under the cloudy judgment of romantic love. For this reason, parents frequently act as matchmakers, a role that they have held for centuries. Although couples today are more likely to find their own mates, families still negotiate marriages.

Muslim men can marry women from other monotheistic faiths, but women can't. The reason for this is that children are usually raised in the father's faith. Therefore, the children of a union between a Muslim woman and a non-Muslim man would less likely be Muslim. Muslim men can marry women from other faiths, such as Buddhism and Hinduism, as long as their wives convert to Islam.

In addition, Muslim men can marry up to four women, but only if they can provide for all equally. This means if you give one wife a home, a child, or a trip around the world, you have to do it for all of your wives. Many interpret this rule to apply to emotions as well as possessions and actions. For this reason, many Muslim men have only one wife, and some Muslim countries, such as Tunisia, have outlawed multiple marriages. Muslim women may marry only one man.

The wedding ceremony itself is more a civil affair than a religious one, involving the creation of a contract between the couple. The bride doesn't even have to be present; she can send representatives, instead. Although no specific ceremony is required, the wedding usually includes readings from the Qur'an, as well as an inspiring talk. Witnesses for both the bride and groom attend the ceremony. A government official supervises the transaction. In order for the marriage contract to be valid, it must include a bride price, or dowry *(mahr)*. The bridegroom gives this dowry to the bride. It is hers to keep fully if the couple divorces after the marriage has been consummated. She can keep half if the marriage is dissolved before consummation.

Within three days after the wedding, some Muslims throw a party to celebrate the wedding and announce to the community that the couple has been legally joined and can live together.

Death: Solemn and simple

As Muslims near death, they turn their faces toward Mecca and say, "There is no God but Allah." During this final rite of passage — traveling from this world to the next — Muslims believe that the angels of death, Munkar and Nakir, will question the deceased in the tomb, giving him or her a preview of how they will fare in the next world.

The deceased person receives a ritual burial performed according to rules specified in the Qur'an, but with local variations:

1. **The body is cleansed with water and wrapped in a shroud.**

   In general, male family members perform the ritual preparations for their male relatives, and women for the bodies of their female relatives. Professional corpse-washers of the same sex as the deceased may also be used. The exception is that a husband can prepare his wife's body, and a wife can prepare her husband's. Embalming is not permitted.

   Many Shi'ites believe that martyrs don't need to receive the final ablution because they will be taken right to heaven. Pilgrims who die while making the hajj are also considered martyrs.

2. **A funeral service is held at the mosque, with or without the corpse. Then, family and friends follow the funeral procession to the grave-yard where they remain standing during the burial ceremony.**

   If possible, burial must occur on the same day; however, it can't take place after sundown. Burial at sea is permitted only if it's unavoidable.

3. **When the body first arrives at the gravesite, a male family member or an imam recites the first sura or shahadah of the Qur'an.**

4. **The person presiding over the funeral may whisper the shahadah into the ear of the deceased.**

   This action serves as a reminder to the deceased of the proper answers to be given to the questioning angels in the tomb.

5. **The body is placed in the grave, lying on its right side, facing Mecca.**

   The traditional grave is 4 to 6 feet deep, with a shelf hollowed out on one side. The corpse is placed on the side with the shelf, with his head turned toward Mecca. It's not necessary to place the body in a coffin.

6. **A reception is held in honor of the deceased.**

According to Muslim tradition, the prophet Muhammad did not encourage mourning. In common practice, however, reflecting human needs and emotions, men and women are expected to mourn their spouses for four months and ten days. For other deaths, the mourning time is three days and nights. Family members and friends are encouraged to visit the cemetery to remain mindful of God and their common destiny and to recite the shahadah on those occasions

Buddhist Life Cycle Rituals

Buddhism presents a challenge to the Western way of thinking. The West generally favors Aristotelian philosophy. Put simply, something either is or isn't.

Buddhist theology allows something to be and not be at the same time. While this concept is difficult for many Westerners to understand, Buddhists say that much of life is an illusion, and the desire to possess material things as though they were permanent leads only to suffering.

In many ways, Buddhism links birth to death to suffering. In order to understand birth, you have to understand the Buddhist concept that all people are destined for many rebirths. To understand death, you have to understand that people go through many deaths before getting to nirvana. To understand suffering, you need to put aside your desire for permanence.

Buddhism seeks a balanced way of life, one that offers awareness, moderation, and a comprehension of the mystery of life. Understanding that mystery enables you to find happiness by balancing life's problems.

When you find the Infinite, you display the following attributes:

✔ *Metta:* Caring, loving kindness displayed to all you meet

✔ *Karuna:* Compassion or mercy, the special kindness shown to those who suffer

✔ *Mudita:* Sympathetic joy or being happy for others, without a trace of envy

✔ *Uppekha* (or *Upeksa*): Equanimity or levelness; the ability to accept others as they are

Birth and adolescent rituals galore

Buddhists celebrate 11 traditional rituals beginning at birth and finally finishing up by the time the child is 12 or 13 years old:

✔ A pregnancy ceremony

✔ A birth ceremony performed during labor

✔ A head-washing ceremony several days after the birth of the child

✔ A hair-shaving ceremony

✔ A cradle ceremony — when the child is placed in a new cradle

✔ A naming ceremony

✔ A cloth-wearing or first-dressing ceremony

✔ A rice-feeding ceremony

✔ An ear-piercing ceremony for girls

✔ A hair-tying ceremony for boys

✔ An initiation as a novice monk for boys

In these ceremonies, monks sometimes chant or visit the home, preach a sermon, or help feed the child cooked rice. The monks are a reminder of the Buddha, his teaching, and the monastic order. The monk doesn't usually officiate but sometimes participates in the ceremony.

Joining a monastery

The goal for some Theravadan Buddhists is to join a *sangha* (Buddhist community). Those who want to be liberated from the cycle of rebirth and to take their faith life seriously are likely to join a Buddhist monastery for a short period of time to live the Buddhist teaching more deeply.

Boys generally decide to join a monastery when they reach puberty. They may join for several reasons:

- ✔ To show how serious they are to be part of the Buddhist community
- ✔ To learn the Buddhist values of discipline and quality
- ✔ To better learn the teachings of the Buddha

In the monastery, the initiate learns

- ✔ Respect for authority.
- ✔ How to read and write.
- ✔ More about the Buddha.
- ✔ Proper ritual knowledge.

Although time in the monastery can lead to ordination in the community, many young Buddhists see it as a stage on their way to marriage and family life. Those who do decide to be ordained into the community of Theravada monks shave their heads, don the monastic robes, receive a begging bowl, and renounce the life of a householder.

Marriage, the community, and the Three Jewels

Marriage is the principal rite of young adulthood and is extremely important to Buddhists because it provides an opportunity to recommit to Buddha and to the community to which the couple belongs.

While a religious leader does not conduct the marriage ritual itself, a Buddhist monk is often invited to the ceremony to do a reading or recite a chant. A strong infusion of ritual and spiritual practice reinforce the commitment to Buddha.

During the marriage ceremony, the bride and groom, as well as the assembled guests, recommit themselves to the Three Jewels: Buddha, the teachings of Buddha (*dharma*), and the community of Buddhism (*sangha*). They renew their moral commitment to the sanctity of life and to avoiding stealing, sexual misconduct, false speech, and intoxicants. After the monks chant, the marrying official "calls the spirits of the bride and groom." The center of the ritual, this call focuses on the virtues of married life, and the spirits are symbolically tied to the bodies of the bride and groom. A sacred cord connects the Buddha with a bowl of food offerings, and the ceremony concludes hours later with the bride and groom presenting food offerings to the assembled monks who have concluded the ceremony with a last blessing.

Funerals: It ain't over 'til it's over

The awareness that we pass from this world to someplace else plays an important role in Buddhism. Buddhists believe that people are reborn over and over until they are ready for nirvana.

Funeral rites tend to be elaborate, including various recited *sutras* (verses or poems) that focus on the impermanence of life. Every Buddhist hopes that, in death, they'll have completed the life cycle and will never be reborn again. Therefore, in many ways, death points to a higher existence. It also leaves the surviving family and friends wondering whether another rebirth is in the offing.

As a result of this uncertainty, the purpose of many of the rituals surrounding death is to help the deceased get to nirvana, or obtain release from the cycle of death and rebirth: In Tibetan Buddhism, for example, the lama (a spiritual leader) whispers into the ear of the dead to help him or her on the journey to the afterlife.

The Tibetan Book of the Dead (Bardo Thodol) outlines procedures to help the dying person confront past selves while passing from one state to another. (*Bardo* means, "intermediate state," and *Thodol* is "the great liberation by hearing.")

A lama or yogin usually comes to the dying person's home and reads from the Bardo Thodol. For up to four days after the person's death, the lama returns and continues to read from the book, in the presence of the dead body. After four days, the body is taken away, but the lama may return for up to 49 days.

During this period, Tibetan Buddhists believe that the dead person tries to resolve karma problems by struggling with the demons in his or her person's life. These demons are projections of the many faces or experiences of the self that the person had lived previously. If the person is successful, he or she will become one with the Western Paradise of Amitabha.

Hindu Life Cycle Rituals

The basic concept of the Hindu view about life is that an individual's existence or lifetime is part of a wider experience. A child is born not just into this world but also into the stream of life that will carry him or her through many subsequent rebirths. While each culture and each religion pays ritual attention to life cycle events, Hindus recognize that the journey is not a singular one and that the goal of life is liberation from continual rebirths. During the journey, each Hindu seeks to live within his or her caste, to maintain certain rituals, to learn, to have a family, to create a business, to do good things for the community, and to prepare to pass from this world to the next. While each person faces samsara individually, he or she is also part of a wider community of relatives and friends, males and females, who are journeying into eternity.

Conception and pregnancy

On the fourth night after a marriage, a couple is supposed to make love to create a child. The husband prays with the wife:

May Vishnu prepare the womb, may Tvashtar mold the embryo's form, may Prajapati emit seed, may Dhatar place the embryo. Place the embryo, Sinivili, place the embryo, Sarasvati! May the Ashvins garlanded with lotuses provide the embryo, the Ashvins with their golden fire-churning sticks, the embryo that I know place for you to bear in ten months (Jaimaniya Grihya Sutra 1:22).

In the Hindu notion of marriage, the woman is viewed as a crop field, and the man is considered the provider of seed. The new being is brought forth from the father's bones, teeth, bodily channels, and semen, as well as the mother's blood, flesh, and internal organs. If the father's characteristics are dominant, the child will be a boy. If the mother's are dominant, it will be a girl.

A number of customs and celebrations occur during the pregnancy. In the third month, for example, the parents perform a ritual to determine the sex of the child. In the fourth month, the father parts the hair of the mother, and people sing hymns as they further prepare to welcome the child.

Birth: A blast from the past

When the child is actually born and the umbilical cord is severed, the father touches the baby's lips with a golden spoon or a ring dipped in honey, curds, and clarified butter. The father prays for a long life for the child and invokes the goddess of sacred speech, Vach, by whispering into his child's ear three times.

After the umbilical cord is cut, the child receives a sacred name from his parents, which only they will know in life. Ten or twelve days after birth, the child receives his everyday name, often based on astrological information. The name serves as a cover for the real (secret) name. Hindus believe that children should be protected, not only by name but also by action, against the forces of evil that are in the world.

Rites of passage through various stages of growth occur. These rites vary according to the established practices of local communities and families. By the fourth month after birth, the parents can take the child outside to see the sun. At this age, the child is ceremonially fed solid foods such as rice either at home or at a temple. Between the fifth month and the first birthday, a boy's right ear and a girl's left ear are ceremonially pierced. A male child's head is tonsured (shaved) as a form of dedication to the community, and the family prays for the sacred life of the child, usually between the ages of 1 and 3 years. (When a boy turns 16, he returns to the temple to be tonsured again as he prepares to embrace manhood.) The beginning of schooling, again a ceremonial occasion occurs, around the age of 4.

Religious education: The thread

Between birth and death, Hindus celebrate a coming-of-age rite called *Upanayana,* or the sacred thread ceremony. In this ceremony, a boy is brought to a guru for religious instructions. This education in classical Hinduism is indispensable for members of the Brahmin, Kshatriya, and Vaisya classes. Usually, boys in the Brahmin class receive their thread as early as age 8, the Kshatriya receive it at 11 years old, and the Vaisya receive it when they turn 12 years old. Essentially, initiation marks religious adulthood; full membership in the community should occur before puberty. The thread is placed over the left shoulder, and the young man is taught not only the sacred text but also how to make a sacred fire. He is not only part of a community, but he is also beginning to assume responsibility of understanding the world and its order. (Zoroastrians also have a similar initiation — of both boys and girls — prior to puberty, by wearing a white undershirt and a white cord around the waist.)

The child is taught to live in a different way: He is to take on the values of the Brahman, he is to commit the Vedas to memory, and he is to view himself as an adult in his faith. When the young man returns home, he is prepared to get married.

In traditional Hindu families, girls don't participate in such an elaborate educational process, though education is spreading rapidly even among the most orthodox. Their coming-of-age ceremony occurs the same day that they are married. On that day, the bride receives the thread as part of the wedding ceremony.

Marriage: Months to prepare; days to enjoy

Marriage in the Hindu tradition is a great celebration and usually takes months to prepare.

Before the ceremony, both the bride and groom have their bodies anointed with oil, a sign of fertility.

The ceremony occurs at night in the house of the bride's father, often under a ritual booth of banana and mango leaves. The bride wears a thread around her wrist. She places her foot three times on the family grinding stone as a sign of fidelity. The couple creates a ritual fire to signify the hearth that will be in their new home. They observe stars together, which signify loyalty and steadfastness. Finally, the bride's hair is parted, to signal that her marital status has changed and that she is preparing to become a mother.

The ceremony also includes a wide range of prayers and rituals and can last for days.

Death: A way station to a better you

Hindus may cremate or bury their dead, although cremation is the preferred method. Many spread the ashes or remains of the dead in the Ganges River. The Ganges, or Ganga, has life-giving eternal properties, and Hindus worship it as a goddess.

Because Hindus believe that the deceased will live other lives, they have a sense that the self will endure. A funeral is sacred, therefore, because it represents the completion of a stage in the life. In other words, death for Hindus marks the beginning of a new journey, influenced by how they lived in this world.

Through the funeral ceremony, the surviving family helps to usher the dead into the his or her next life:

1. **The family prepares the body at home.**

2. **A procession carries the body to the burning ground or the cemetery.**

   The procession usually passes by a river considered sacred by Hindus.

3. **The pyre is lit (in the case of cremation), or the body is placed in the grave (in the case of burial).**

   Higher castes are more likely to cremate their dead; lower castes are more likely to bury their dead. (See the related sidebar titled, " I love you to death . . ." later in this chapter.)

4. **The chief mourner (usually the eldest son) walks around the body.**

   This action symbolizes offering the dead to the next world.

5. **A large ceramic pot of water is broken over the fire or grave.**

6. **Mourners ritually bathe.**

7. **The family gives a cow as a sacred offering.**

8. **After the person is cremated, the family gathers the bones and disperses them into a sacred river.**

Life Cycle Rituals of Confucianism, Taoism, and Shinto

The veneration of ancestors is a common thread found among the sacred texts and writings of the religions that have their roots within the East Asian cultures. Consider China and the profound ancestral cult that has been built over thousands of years. Or Japan, where ancestral veneration is the primary religious activity of the family. Historically, the motives for performing rituals have been to receive aid and support from ancestors.

Today, ancestor worship continues to drive the rituals found among the East Asian religions because it illuminates the importance of the life process, from the early stages of life to its culmination with death.

Birth and childhood

East Asian cultures have always placed a great deal of emphasis on the family and the group. The birth of a child is cause for rejoicing, but very few rituals are associated with it. In China, for instance, a person's birth isn't really celebrated until he or she turns 60 years old. All people in China, for example, celebrate their birthdays on New Year's Day, when life is renewed and everyone is counted a year older.

In Japan, parents announce births to their ancestors by performing certain rituals and saying particular prayers before a home altar. Because the Japanese believe that the child's first month is filled with taboos and health dangers, an infant stays home until the first month is over. Then parents take the baby to the temple shrine, where they present it to the kami. (The Japanese believe that, when a child is born, its spirit or soul comes from a kami, divine entities that are the source of life.) After this, the child belongs spiritually to that kami and will grow up to revere the kami and participate in annual festivals related to the kami.

I love you to death . . .

For hundreds of years in India, people practiced a ritual known as *sati* (faithful wife). When a father died, leaving his children and wife, the wife was supposed to throw herself on the burning ashes of her husband, thus eliminating the need for someone to take care of her. Her suicide was to have demonstrated her devotion to her husband and her virtue. While sati was outlawed in British India in 1829, it continued with relative frequency for 30 more years. People in rural villages in India still occasionally practice this ritual.

In Japan, an interesting tradition is that the family preserves the umbilical cord of the child. That sacred cord is sometimes used to heal the child if an illness occurs in later life. In some sections of Japan, the umbilical cord is buried with the mother.

When the child turns a year old, the family celebrates with a doll festival for girls and a festival for boys, as well. In addition, special children's festivals are held on November 15, called *Shichigosan*, which is translated "seven-five-three," or the ages at which the children attend the festival. Children dress in their finest clothes and go to the shrine of their kami. They pray that the kami will oversee them and recommit themselves to their kami.

Adolescence: Moving from child to adult

People in China don't have many ritual ceremonies in temples to signify life cycle events. Centuries ago, the Chinese developed an initiation rite for young men and women. The young adult would receive a new adult name; a boy would receive a special cap, and a girl would get new clothes and a special hairdo. That custom, however, has been absorbed into the marriage ceremony, when a young person is thought to come of age. For the Chinese, the celebrations of individual rites of passage aren't as important as how these passages fit into the overall well-being of the community.

In Japan, a rite of passage exists for adolescents as they move from being children to being young adults willing to shoulder adult responsibilities. When a young man begins to help at the festival by carrying around portable altars and generally taking responsibility for people other than himself, he is granted a loincloth as a sign of his newfound adulthood.

As the adolescent moves toward adulthood, children and their parents customarily go to the shrines to pray for successful examinations in lower secondary schools or to obtain admission into college, the finding of a job, and good health.

GOING DEEPER

The kami

In Japan, a close connection exists between kami and the believer. Kami is the name given to anything that has extraordinary or awe-inspiring qualities. Isanagi and Isanami were kami that frolicked in the ocean and created Japan, for example. The spirit of the kami infuses the earth, the sky, the mountains, and the very being of Japanese people. Before World War II, the Emperor of Japan was the divine face of the kami. The kami represent an eternal link to the past.

Although young men and women have their own birth dates, these dates don't officially signal their coming of age. Instead, the important coming of age date in Japan is January 15. This date marks the official coming of age of anyone who is 20 years old. At this point, young men and women can then marry without parental consent. Also around this time, young men and women start looking for their own jobs.

Marriage (in which the guest list includes dead relatives)

Marriage is essentially a contract between two families in which the parents frequently act as matchmakers. The families choose those to be married. In China, the bride and groom frequently don't see each other until the day of the wedding. Before the marriage, the families frequently consult with an astrologer to determine if the couple is compatible.

On the day of the wedding, the families exchange gifts and agreements, followed by a festival at the groom's house. The bride is brought in on a sedan chair together with furniture for the new home. When the bride first enters the groom's home, the couple bows briefly before the wooden tablets that hold the names and the dates of births and deaths of relatives. The Chinese believe that these tablets contain the spirits or essences of these ancestors. Although the bride and groom don't exchange vows and priests don't bless the wedding, the ceremony includes a sense that in the introduction of one family to the other, the marriage has occurred.

In Japan, although marriages can occur in halls, they traditionally occur in the home because the Japanese consider marriage to essentially be an agreement between families. Sometimes, the wedding takes place in a shrine where the ceremony can be performed before the kami. The families consult the almanac to determine the day of the wedding.

The pivotal moment in the ceremony is when the bride and groom exchange sake (rice wine). The bride generally wears a white kimono, which may symbolize the cutting of ties with her own family; the groom can wear anything he chooses.

In addition to uniting a couple, marriage in Japan unites two families. In many ways, for the Japanese, marriage is as much the preservation of the family as it is the uniting of two individuals.

Funerals

In many East Asian religions, funeral rituals are complex and often take days to complete. Chinese and Japanese families try to help the dead transition to a peaceful afterlife and ensure that the person who died is at peace with the other deceased ancestors.

An open casket is displayed in the main room of the house. People offer food to the spirit of the deceased, praying to the gods of the underworld for a safe transition. The family then goes to the grave, with mourners joining them. At the gravesite, a ritual places the spirit in its ancestral tablet, which is followed by a community feast. After the coffin is buried, the family returns home with the tablet, which is placed on the family altar and blessed with a second feast. (See the related sidebar titled "Tea and rice, anyone?" later in this chapter.)

Tea and rice, anyone?

Many Eastern religions include rice and tea ceremonies to honor ancestors and to celebrate sacred events and people. The importance of rice goes back more than 10,000 years. According to ancient mythology, rice (because of its popularity and accessibility) is the grain that links heaven and earth, gods and mortals. Rice, a staple of the Asian diet, dominates the customs, beliefs, rituals, and celebrations found among the practitioners of Buddhism, Taoism, Confucianism, Shinto, and most of the other religions traditions in the area.

The tea ceremony, or *sado* ("way of tea"), is yet another example of the importance of food in ritualistic and/or cultural traditions. Ritual tea drinking originated in China, and Zen monks introduced it in Japan during the Kamakura period (circa 1192-1333 C.E.). The tea ceremony is a time-honored institution in Japan and is rooted in the principal of Zen Buddhism. Actually a way of meditating, this ritual helps people find *satori,* or enlightenment. The ceremony takes hours and because each part is fixed, or predetermined, participants can become lost in the process and, in doing so, gain enlightenment.

In Chinese culture, death is seen as a time in which to strengthen respect for ancestors. It is also a time to pray that the ancestors will intercede and that new children will be sent to the family that experienced the death.

When a person dies, the general notion is that the soul leaves the body and prepares for the next world. To help, family members do the following:

- Place a bowl of rice by the body to help sustain the person in the next life
- Place a sharp instrument next to the body to ward off evil spirits

Friends bring the body to the funeral and help to wash it, clothe it in white, and place it in a coffin. Because the corpse is considered impure, the friends clean the body through ritual. Buddhist priests celebrate the funeral rites by reciting Buddhist scriptures and accompanying the family to the burial ground or crematorium. (The family consults the Chinese almanac for a favorable day for a funeral.)

At the time of the burial, the Buddhist monk gives the dead person a name, which is written on a temporary memorial tablet. After the funeral, the family sets this tablet in front of the house. The family mourns for 49 days, the amount of time Buddhists believe it takes a person to travel through purgatory, after which the dead person enters into his or her ancestral spirit. At this time, the family removes the temporary tablet and replaces it with a permanent tablet. People then remember the deceased on the annual anniversary of the death, until the person has been dead for 33 years.

Japanese religions believe that an individual who dies loses individual identity but joins with the ancestral kami of the family. This ancestral kami is responsible for the birth of new children, and the deceased is sometimes reborn in another body, which is part of the ongoing cycle of life. In Japan, the goal is to live a full and spiritual life with a connection to one's kami, and in death, to become an ancestor and maybe even eventually a kami. Families, in the meantime, are encouraged to pray the Buddhist scriptures for the deceased and to learn from the death of their loved one that they too will someday undergo the passage from this life to the next.

Sikh Life Cycle Rituals

For the Sikh faithful, the various rites of passage are considered part of the process that supports the perpetuation of the faith. At the core of this religion is the heartfelt belief that the rituals that have carried from generation to generation enable this male-oriented society to remain true to the religious foundation that was established in the *Adi Granth* (the most holy book in

Sikhism). Today, the *ardas* (Sikh prayers) continue, and the word of the Adi Granth remains as the beacon for the Sikh community, one that is enriched by the religious rituals that are very much a part of everyday life.

Many ritual ceremonies signify the sacredness of each phase of life and the importance of uniting the individual with the community, with a great deal of respect for ancestors as well as elderly members of the community. These ceremonies bring a wisdom and understanding of the law and a religious spirit to the main events of family life.

Birth: Girls are good; boys are better

The birth of a child in the Sikh faith is considered a gift from God. Because the society is patriarchal and all inheritance is through the male line, it is a special blessing to have a son. Daughters are received well, but quietly. When a child is born, the birth usually occurs in the wife's parents' home. Families decorate the house with leaves from the *sirin,* or mango tree. Sweets are distributed, and family members sing songs celebrating the birth of a boy.

In five weeks, a big feast begins, called *chhati,* in which the entire family on both sides is invited to demonstrate the importance of family receiving and protecting the child. Boys and girls are prepared for distinct roles. Girls tend to cook and sew, but in recent times have been allowed to pursue advanced education. Grandparents give children their names. Customarily, Sikh families go to a spiritual leader and ask for an initial letter of the Gurmukhi alphabet from the Adi Granth in order to choose the name. The spiritual leader opens the Adi Granth at random and reads the hymn on the page. The first letter of the first word of that hymn is now the first letter of the child's new name. That name will be announced on the following Sunday at services. Children who are born into Sikh families are called *Singh* (literally, lion) if a boy, and *Kaur* (literally, princess) if a girl.

Initiation: For men only

As a sign of dedication to their faith, many Sikh men identify with the *Khalsa,* or military tradition within Sikhism, and do not cut their hair or beards. They must manage the hair in some way, so they wrap it in a cloth that Westerners have called a turban. When a boy is about 11 or 12 years old, his family organizes a tying-the-turban ceremony. The family gathers in prayer in the presence of the Adi Granth. They recite ardas and ask the *granthi* (a spiritual leader) to tie the turban on the boy's head. The congregation chants, *"Boley so nihal-sat sri akal"* (One who says God is immortal is a happy person). In the Sikh religion, the turban is such a sign of sacredness that if one insults a person wearing a turban, it is regarded as an insult to the Sikh faith.

Marriage: Ordained by God

Marriage is considered a cornerstone of Sikh society. In marriage, not only are two people joined, but two families of social and caste status are also united. The marriage is considered a sacred bond. The two become one, and the relationship is considered to be pre-ordained by God.

Most Sikh marriages are arranged. Parents ask relatives or employ a matchmaker to find a suitable marriage partner. When the young person is chosen, the families meet so that the boy and girl can see each other. If all goes well, an engagement ceremony is arranged. This ceremony is a feast with fresh fruit and Indian sweets. The celebration includes singing and reading of selections from the Adi Granth. Before the marriage, a ceremony of *milni* takes place, which signifies the bringing together of two families. The families exchange gifts and say prayers. The ritual is restricted to those who are related through blood and marriage.

After the milni ceremony, the marriage ceremony occurs with the reading of the Adi Granth. The father of the bride joins the couple by using a scarf worn by the groom. The father of the bride gives his daughter away, and the couple listens to hymns from the Adi Granth that stress the permanence of marriage. At a ceremony called *muklawa,* the couple finally consummates the marriage. Women are expected to produce children, particularly sons, who will inherit the father's property and the social status of the family.

Death and mourning

Sikhs believe in the transmigration of the soul, which is a gradual transition from the human state to another state, depending upon one's conduct in this world. The soul is considered immortal, and the body is usually cremated. In India, funerals occur shortly after the death. The family gives the deceased a last bath to purify the body before cremation.

The sons and brothers of the deceased carry the pyre, and the oldest son leads. Women are forbidden to take part in the ceremony. It is the ritual duty of the son to light the fire. In the absence of the son, a male relative can substitute. Before lighting the pyre, a spiritual leader recites hymns and prayers for the departed soul. When a married woman is buried, her family provides her shroud, and she is dressed as a bride.

In India, three days after the cremation, the ashes are collected and deposited in the Ganges. Families gather at the home for 13 days of reading from the Adi Granth. At the end of the 13 days, a feast occurs for relatives and friends. If the dead person was the leader of the family, a ceremony in which a new turban is placed on the head on the man who assumes leadership of the family takes place. A widow, at the death of her husband, discards her colorful clothes and wears a long white scarf to signify her mourning. After 13 days of mourning, she is given a ritual bath by the women of the household, where she discards her old clothes as well as the white scarf and receives a new set of clothes as a way of saying she is reincorporated into the family.

Life Cycle Rituals of Indigenous Religions

If you've ever been exposed to the cultures of indigenous peoples, you'll marvel at their respect for the land, their acknowledgment of the wisdom of their elders, their concept that family responsibilities embrace the whole village and not just their own family, and their deep spiritual quest to revere the environment. These approaches to life are as natural to indigenous nations as eating and sleeping and drinking. They remind us that God is found in Nature and in the family.

Birth

Indigenous religions recognize that duality exists in the birth of a child. Joy and sorrow, holiness and shamefulness are connected to birth. Women are blessed to be pregnant, but at the same time, they are considered ritually unclean. In many indigenous religions, mothers and fathers withdraw from society for a number of days before the birth. They concentrate on eating good food and trying to protect their child from any evil spirits. In the Kikuyu tribe of East Africa, a mother and child are isolated from the community. The mother goes into seclusion, which represents death, only to give birth, which represents new life.

In the Aboriginal world, you can also find a close connection between birth and death. A child is dreamed into existence by a mythical person who may or may not be reincarnated in the child. The Aborigines acknowledge the physical bond between husband and wife in the creation of a child but consider the ultimate source of the birth to be the spiritual dream. When the child grows up and prepares for death, there will be another dream, which will call the child to the next world. For them, death and life are one.

Puberty rituals

In indigenous religions, you find both an instinctive and a matured notion that real success comes by entering into the world of the spirit. Children are taught to treasure the land, to belong to the tribe, and to face the hardness and ordeals of everyday life. When youngsters reach adolescence, members of the tribe expect them to endure a physical and spiritual time of testing. Young people are often isolated from the community, asked to fast for days, and endure hardships such as circumcision to prove that they are strong enough and mature enough to embrace the demands of being a young adult. In the Masai tribe of East Africa, young boys between 12 and 16 go into seclusion for four days. They wear female attire, shave their heads, and then are circumcised in order to be considered an adult, or warrior, among the Masai. Girls cut or pierce themselves, sometimes in their thighs and other times in their ears or other parts of their face. In many African tribes, females are circumcised at the very young age of 3 or 4 and what is left of their genitals is sewn together.

In the Native American Hopi tribe, young children grow up exposed to *katsina,* or masks, that are faces worn by Hopi dancers to make the spirit present. Adolescent boys study the character of the different masks, the values of the different masks, and go off to meditate and pray so that they may enter into the character of the mask. The real rite of passage is not so much the wearing of the mask as much as the becoming one with the mask. This level of spirituality is necessary for a Hopi Indian to be considered an adult.

Another experience that Native American children undergo is called the *vision quest.* Young people at puberty are encouraged to enter into a period of fasting, meditation, and physical challenge. They go out into the wilderness and bear the loneliness of the environment so that they can receive visions from the spirits that will guide the rest of their lives. They ask that the spirit always be close and supportive for their lifetime. Later on, these young people enter the sweat lodge to purify their souls, to renew their spirits, to ask for healing, and to become one again with the spirits of their ancestors. (See the related sidebar titled "Sweating it all out.")

In the Aboriginal context, adolescence is a period of preparation for adulthood. Young girls learn how to take care of a home. They will leave that home as early as 12 years old to take on the responsibilities of running the household for a future husband. At the same time, boys expect to be circumcised, to ritually scar their bodies, to play with fire, or to have certain hair removed. These actions prove their willingness to be an adult.

Marriage

Many societies speak of the value of marriage. While marriage is recognized throughout the world, in many African cultures, marriage as a rite of passage is incomplete until procreation has occurred. In many tribes, the female has to prove fertility before she marries. Children are brought up in not only family context but also a tribal context. When one marries a spouse, the person also marries that person's family and that person's tribe. Arranged marriages are common and usually include a betrothal period that involves gift giving and family interactions. The marriage is recognized when the couple goes to live together publicly or have a child.

Sweating it all out

In the United States, sweat lodges are designed in a variety of ways, depending upon where the tribe lives. In the North, a tent is constructed, and hot water is poured over steaming rocks and coal. In the Southwest, a hut is fashioned out of mud and heated by the sun. In both instances, the initiates enter the structure for a number of hours and are prevented from eating or drinking. As the sweat pours out of their bodies, they may begin to hallucinate, perhaps from the heat or lack of water. This experience becomes a cornerstone for change. Originally, these structures were used for bathing and only later became associated with an experience of the Divine.

In indigenous religions, other forms of marriage include elopement, capture during war, and the *Levirate Law,* which says that if a husband were to die, then his wife would be expected to marry a brother of the deceased man. Polygamy still exists but is less common. Some women even encourage their husbands to take on other wives who would help with the household chores.

Death

A dichotomy exists in the way the indigenous religions deal with death. On the one hand, death is considered as much a part of nature as flowers take seed and grow, blossom, and then pass out of existence. The Inuit community believes that when a person gets older and is no longer able to function well, they should leave the community, walk away, and die by themselves. This approach seems stoic and contrary to the value of the community. In many ways, the Inuit see it as a wise way of acknowledging the passage of time.

Indigenous people often celebrate death with music, conversation, celebrations, and flowers. In most African communities, the whole community turns out to acknowledge the sacred life of the person who has died and to place him safely into the ground. Often, each person touches the corpse of the dead one as a way of saying farewell.

Part IV
Religious Ethics

In this part . . .

Religious ethics are the moral principles that guide religions and that set the standard for what is and isn't acceptable behavior. Surprisingly similar from one religion to the next, these fundamental principles flow from the core beliefs and ancient wisdom of religion, as well as its teachers and traditions.

This part helps you understand some of the fundamental principles of the world's different religions. We also examine how religions — ancient traditions that they are — are responding to dilemmas, possibilities, and issues of the modern world.

Chapter 10

Personal Virtues

● ●

In This Chapter

▶ Looking at the commonality of the golden rule

▶ Understanding religions' views on compassion and humility

▶ Knowing how respect shapes family and society

▶ Recognizing why hope gets us through despair

▶ Figuring out why honesty isn't always the best policy

▶ Discovering how patience pays off

● ●

*V*irtues are standards for ethical, moral conduct — they enable you to look at yourself in the mirror without cringing. In this chapter, you find out about the commonality of personal virtues among the world's religions. Personal virtues, such as humility, gratitude, and patience honor God or, in Eastern religions, reflect a higher state of being. To discover which *public* virtues are common, head to Chapter 11.

The Golden Rule: A Universal Principle

As a small child, you may have grabbed a toy from your playmate, who, of course, immediately started to wail. You'd then hear your mom/dad/teacher say something like, "Well, how would you like it if someone did that to you?!"

Sound familiar? The lesson these adults were trying to teach is what is popularly known in the West as the "golden rule." This rule commands people to get beyond their own selfishness and self-absorbed isolation. The golden rule serves as a reminder that what hurts us hurts others, and that what heals us, heals others. (See the related sidebar titled "Luke 6:27-36" later in this chapter.)

Luke 6:27-36

In the New Testament, Luke extends the golden rule far beyond loving your neighbor by introducing the Christian ethic of also loving your enemy:

But I say unto you which hear, Love your enemies, do good to them which hate you. Bless them that curse you, and pray for them which despitefully use you. And unto him that smiteth thee on the one cheek offer also the other; and him that taketh away thy cloak forbid not to take thy coat also. Give to every man that asketh of thee; and of him that taketh away thy goods ask them not again. And as ye would that men should do to you, do ye also to them like-wise. For if ye love them which love you, what thank have ye? for sinners also love those that love them. And if ye do good to them which do good to you, what thank have ye? for sinners also do even the same. And if ye lend to them of whom ye hope to receive, what thank have ye? for sinners also lend to sinners, to receive as much again. But love ye your enemies, and do good, and lend, hoping for nothing again; and your reward shall be great, and ye shall be the children of the Highest: for he is kind unto the unthankful and to the evil. Be ye therefore merciful, as your Father also is merciful.

In nearly all the world's religions, personal morality begins with this simple concept: Treat others as you would like to be treated. As such, the golden rule is perhaps the most basic of the personal virtues.

The different faiths all have their own version of this universal message:

- ✔ "Not one of you is a believer until he desires for his brother what he desires for himself" (40 Hadith of an-Nawawi 13, Islam).

- ✔ "Wound not others, do no one injury by thought or deed, utter no word to pain thy fellow creatures" (The Law Code of Manu, Hinduism).

- ✔ "Do not do to others what you would not like yourself" (The Analects 12:2, Confucianism).

- ✔ "If you do not wish to be mistreated by others, do not mistreat anyone yourself" (Counsels of Adurbad 92, Zoroastrianism).

- ✔ "We obtain salvation by loving our fellow man and God" (Granth Japji 21, Sikhism).

- ✔ "Having made oneself the example, one should neither slay nor cause to slay. . . . As I am, so are other beings; thus let one not strike another, nor get another struck. That is the meaning" (Dhammapada, Buddhism).

- ✔ "One should not behave towards others in a way which is disagreeable to oneself. This is the essence of morality. All other activities are due to selfish desire" (Anusansana Parva 113.8, Hinduism).

- ✔ "Thou shalt love thy neighbor as thyself" (Leviticus 19:18, Judaism).
- ✔ "Therefore, all things whatsoever ye would that men should do to you, do ye even so to them . . ." (Matthew 7:12, Christianity).

Compassion: 1 Feel Your Pain

The word compassion means, "to suffer with." Having compassion means that you can feel others' pain. In Christianity, Judaism, and Islam, showing compassion to others is how believers imitate the infinite kindness and mercy that God showers upon them. (See the related sidebar titled "Musical chairs" later in this chapter. Although humans' capacity for compassion and kindness isn't limitless, as God's is, believers strive to nurture it, even when doing so is hard, because it brings them closer to God.

One of the central virtues of Buddhism is *karuna,* understanding and identifying with the suffering of all living beings. Karuna is the reason that some people who achieve enlightenment return to this world as Bodhisattvas to teach others. Their compassion is so great, they return to a world that needs them. In Hinduism, compassion is called *daya,* and, along with charity and self-control, it is one of the three central virtues in Hinduism.

Humility: Remembering Your Place

In the monotheistic religions, humility is a sign of respect for God and awareness that all blessings flow from God to whom all thanks are due. In Judaism, for example, Moses is considered virtuous primarily because of his humility.

Christianity provides the classic religious statement of humility in the Sermon on the Mount, "Blessed be the meek for they shall inherit the earth" (Matthew 5:5). Jesus' point here, which other religious traditions echo, is that the secular world recognizes and rewards power and wealth, but the religious world lifts up the ones whom the world has passed over and crushed. Humility, therefore, is not just a virtue, but also an opposite virtue from the ones that the nonreligious world prizes.

In Islam (which itself means *surrender*), humility is a primary virtue. Muslims demonstrate their awareness of the greatness of God and humankind's place in the world by observing the Five Pillars of their faith. Each pillar (see Chapter 5 for details) reinforces the proper order of the universe.

Taoism focuses believers' thoughts on the awesome beauty and wonder of Nature. As we ponder the magnificence of Nature, we learn to respect our place relative to the stars and the seasons — a humbling experience.

Musical chairs

In Judaism, God has two thrones: a throne of compassion and a throne of judgment. According to a rabbinic legend *(midrash),* the angels opposed God's decision to create the world. Every rational argument about the inevitable evil and sinfulness of people that the angels offered up to God was true. So what did God do? God got up from the throne of judgment and sat on the throne of mercy. From that throne, God created the world. During the Jewish penitential season, the prayers urge God to rise from his throne of judgment when he judges us and to sit on his throne of mercy.

Through humility, Buddhists can release anger and learn to live a life free from attachments and suffering. (See the related sidebar titled "Honest Abe on being humble" later in this chapter.)

"Why art thou angry? Be not angry Tusa, meekness is best for thee, and to restrain anger, conceit and hypocrisy is best. It is for this that we live the righteous life" (Sutta Nipata).

Respect: Minding Your Ps and Qs

Respect for parents, respect for ancestors, respect for teachers and clergy — all find powerful and universal support as a virtue in the world's religions.

In Judaism and Christianity, respect for parents, literally honor (*kavod,* in Hebrew), is one of the Ten Commandments. Zoroastrianism advises: "Honor your father and mother, listen to them and obey them" (Counsels of Adurbad 90). In Islam, the Qur'an enjoins Muslims to honor and cherish their parents.

"And thy Lord has decreed that you . . . do good to your parents. If either or both of them reach old age with thee, do not speak one word of contempt to them nor repel them, but speak to them in terms on honor . . . and say 'My Lord, have mercy on them as they brought me up when I was little' " (Qur'an 17, 23-24).

You can see the virtue of respect in the ancestor worship common in both China and Africa. In China, ancestors, although dead, still have a presence. They are the wise ones who created and continued the great traditions of the past and they are the ones to whom you look for information and encouragement. In China, the burial customs reflects this respect for ancestors. (For details on Chinese burial customs, see Chapter 9.)

Honest Abe on being humble

Occasionally, a political leader emerges who understands the virtue of humility and have the need for the entire nation, not just individuals, to practice it. In the United States, Abraham Lincoln was such a leader. In his proclamation of a national day of fasting, humility, and prayer, Lincoln wrote these memorable words:

We have been the recipients of the choicest bounties of Heaven. We have been preserved, these many years, in peace and prosperity. We have grown in numbers, wealth and power, as no other nation has ever grown. But we have forgotten God. We have forgotten the gracious hand which preserved us in peace, and multiplied and enriched and strengthened us; and we have vainly imagined, in the deceitfulness of our hearts, that all these blessings were produced by some superior wisdom and virtue of our own. Intoxicated with unbroken success, we have become too self-sufficient to feel the necessity of redeeming and preserving grace, too proud to pray to the God that made us! It behooves us, then to humble ourselves before the offended Power, to confess our national sins, and to pray for clemency and forgiveness.

His point? That the U.S. Civil War was God's punishment for a proud and arrogant nation.

In African, Australian Aboriginal, and Native American tribal religions, people often pray not to God but to dead relatives and holy people of the tribe. They respect and worship the ancestors who are worthy of such veneration — those who lived good and fruitful lives.

The virtue of respect for elders extends to respect for all in a position of authority, particularly teachers, clergy, and shamans. This honor establishes social and familial relations and provides a way to communicate the wisdom of the past to new generations.

Hope: Living in a Scary World

Many of the sacred Jewish, Christian, and Islamic texts and rituals include the idea of hope. In Christianity, it's one of the three cardinal virtues (the other two being faith and love). In Islam, it's the understanding that Allah knows all; what happens, happens for a reason, and the faithful will be rewarded in paradise and the irreligious punished in hell.

In the world's religions, hope is made possible by human limitations. Most people don't know the future and, because they don't know it, they fear it. Hope reduces this fear. In religion, hope is closely linked with what comes after death. (See the related sidebar titled, "Psalm 23," later in this chapter.)

Psalm 23

This great poem, attributed to King David, remains one of the classic texts (found in the Hebrew Bible) that teaches hope:

1. The Lord is my shepherd, I shall not want;

2. He makes me lie down in green pastures. He leads me beside still waters;

3. he restores my soul. He leads me in paths of righteousness for his name's sake.

4. Even though I walk through the valley of the shadow of death, I fear no evil; for thou art with me; thy rod and thy staff, they comfort me.

5. Thou preparest a table before me in the presence of my enemies; thou anointest my head with oil, my cup overflows.

6. Surely goodness and mercy shall follow me all the days of my life; and I shall dwell in the house of the Lord for ever.

For Christians, the hope that sustains them is the hope for the speedy second coming of Jesus as the Christ and eternal life in Heaven. This hope sustains Christians through what they often perceive to be the immorality of the earthly kingdom.

In Zoroastrianism, Islam, and, to a lesser extent, Judaism, the hope is life or some form of existence after death. That belief in the world to come is a sustaining virtue. Knowing that death isn't the end helps people believe that no burden is too great to bear and that they won't be separated forever from the people they love.

Of course, monotheistic faiths aren't the only ones that consider hope a virtue. In Buddhism, hope springs from the idea that *any* person can attain enlightenment.

Religious hopefulness is not the same thing as optimism. Optimism is the attitude that things are great. Religious hopefulness is actually built upon the idea that things aren't so great, but that we don't see the whole picture. The incompleteness of human knowing is met by the hope that the world holds more promise than we can see from our limited perspective.

Bliss: Happy, Happy, Joy, Joy

The virtue of joy (also called bliss or happiness) is central to faith because it reminds believers that, although faith doesn't promise a life of ease, it does promise a life of happiness. Religious joys connect happiness with selflessness rather than with selfishness, and in this way it offers a real alternative to the "buy it and you'll be happy" mentality of a culture based on consumerism. Every religion teaches the lesson of joy in similar, yet different, ways.

Joy in Judaism and Christianity

In Judaism, joy *(simha, rina,* or *sason)* has many senses. The Psalmist tells us to "serve the Lord in joy," and joy is a central theme throughout the Psalms:

- ✔ "But let all those that take refuge in thee rejoice, Let them ever shout for joy, because thou defendest them: Let them also that love thy name be joyful in thee" (Psalm 5:11).

- ✔ "Thou wilt show me the path of life: In thy presence is fullness of joy; In thy right hand there are pleasures for evermore" (Psalm 16:11).

- ✔ "For his anger is but for a moment; His favor is for a lifetime: Weeping may tarry for the night, But joy cometh in the morning" (Psalm 30:5).

- ✔ "And my soul shall be joyful in Jehovah: It shall rejoice in his salvation" (Psalm 35:9).

- ✔ "Restore unto me the joy of thy salvation; And uphold me with a willing spirit" (Psalm 51:12).

- ✔ "My lips shall shout for joy when I sing praises unto thee; And my soul, which thou hast redeemed" (Psalm 71:23).

- ✔ "They that sow in tears shall reap in joy" (Psalm 126:5).

- ✔ "Let my tongue cleave to the roof of my mouth, if I remember thee not; If I prefer not Jerusalem above my chief joy" (Psalm 137:6).

These uses of joy connect it to an appreciation of God's love and caring, a trust in God's salvation, and hope that the promise of tomorrow will wipe away the burdens of the present.

In the New Testament, the personal quality of joyousness comes from knowing that God loves you (charisma) and partaking in the act of loving unification with God through communion (the Eucharist). Like Jews, Christians believe that joy is a gift of God and a response to God's salvation and love. According to Christians, the death and resurrection of Jesus brings the joy of salvation to Christians. They see Jesus' suffering as a model for living: Even in their own struggles and pain, they can still have the joy of knowing that they're following the example of Jesus' life. In this way, joy can co-exist with pain, because joy transforms the pain into an example of God's love as it once was with Jesus.

Bliss in Eastern religions

In the East, both Buddhism and Hinduism are aimed at a letting go of attachments and emotions and illusions of this world. You may think that joy could seem to be one of those attachments. But, in fact, many Eastern religions have a deep sense of joy, or more accurately, bliss.

The Sanskrit word for joy/bliss is *ananda*. Ananda is one of the main attributes of Brahman (the spiritual source of the universe) and is the very highest state a person can reach before he or she disappears into the universal self of Brahman. Ananda is the bliss that comes from finally breaking free of the attachments of this world. It is the joy of release.

The Buddhist word for all the suffering in the world is *dukkha,* and the opposite of it is *sukha,* which means joy. However, sukha isn't really a synonym for the word joy, as it's used in the West. Buddhism is more intent on releasing attachment from the world than Hinduism, and so it has no real positive meaning for joy. Joy, or sukha, is a quality that helps someone meditate better: "It is a natural law that the mind of a happy person is able to become focused" (Anguttara Nikaya, X.2). Nirvana, complete enlightenment, is associated with joy but not exactly: "Nirvana is . . . called The Everlasting Joy which has neither enjoyer nor non-enjoyer" (Sutra of Hui Neng 7).

In China, the symbol for happiness is *fu.* Fu means good luck, wealth, and so on, and a flying bat is its symbol. Fu has five parts: long life, wealth, health, virtue, and the ability to fulfill one's appointed tasks. These are the virtues of happiness, and the god of happiness is Fu Chen. In Confucianism and Taoism, the material side of joy is present but not that important. In Taoism, joy comes by living in harmony with the Tao. You achieve harmony in Confucianism by not making waves, but by assuming and accepting your place in society.

In certain periods of Chinese history, Taoism became a way of protesting the rigidity of the social structures of Confucianism. By looking to Nature, you could see freedom and change. So, the Way for Taoism became revolutionary, teaching the idea of independence from the drudgery of fitting into a rigid Confucian society.

Honesty: Cross My Heart

Words can be more damaging than bullets and more healing than medicine. This is why every religion makes a virtue of speaking in a morally proper way. This virtue of honesty can be divided into three categories:

✔ Telling the truth

✔ Using right speech

✔ Living an honest life

When to tell the truth and when not to

Telling the truth in court, as well as not swearing or gossiping or slandering people's good names, are absolute virtues, akin to not killing or stealing. However, it's not an absolute virtue. Because telling the truth isn't always the right thing to do, religious ethics make exceptions. If telling the truth would hurt a person's feelings or endanger their life, then truth-telling takes a second place.

✔ Hinduism teaches with great wisdom that speaking the truth is always proper, but speaking in a way that is beneficial to the listener's spiritual growth is even better.

✔ Judaism commands that one always say that the bride is beautiful.

✔ Lying to protect a life is also acceptable: Think about it, if you were hiding Jews from the Nazis during World War II, and Nazis came to your house and asked if you were hiding Jews, you obviously should lie to them to protect human life!

Right speech

In the Western religions, right speech is part of avoiding harm to others; in the East, it is a way to purify one's life from defilement. Both ideas convey the spiritual power of speech and the spiritual need to make our words healing and hopeful, kind and truthful. For this reason, most religions discourage slander, gossip, lying, and cursing:

✔ Right speech is the third step in the eightfold path of Buddhism.

✔ Two of the Ten Commandments are about bad speech: "Thou shalt not take the name of the Lord in vain," and "Thou shalt not bear false witness."

✔ According to the Jewish law, if you deceive someone, you're also guilty of violating the commandment against stealing because you are "stealing knowledge" (Geneivat da'at).

Honesty, the best policy

Honesty is similar to right speech, but it goes beyond simply telling the truth. Honesty is *living* the truth; it's not just right speech, it's right action.

- ✔ **The Hebrew Bible demands as a matter of religious law** that one maintains honest weights and measures in one's business. The rabbinic tradition in Judaism continues the strict demand for honesty in business:

   "When a person appears before the throne of judgment, the first question he is asked is not, 'Have you believed in God?' or 'Have you prayed or performed ritual acts,' but 'Have you dealt honorably, faithfully in all your dealings with your fellowmen?'" (Talmud, Shabbat 31a).

- ✔ **In Christianity, Paul expands the concept of honesty.** In his letter to the Romans, he teaches: "Recompense to no man evil for evil. Provide things honest in the sight of all men" (Romans 12:17). Telling the truth is a key component of honesty in a letter to the Ephesians: "Wherefore putting away lying, speak every man truth with his neighbor: for we are members one of another" (Ephesians 4:25).

- ✔ **In Islam, honesty and honoring promises made in Allah's name are important:** "Fulfill the covenant of God once you have pledged it, and do not break any oaths once they have been sworn to. You have set up God as a Guarantee for yourselves; God knows everything you are doing" (Qur'an 16.92).

- ✔ **In Zoroastrianism, the prophet Zarathushtra or Zoroaster prayed:** "Grant to those present, O Ahura Mazda (God) power through truth and good thoughts" (Gathas 29.10).

In the East, honesty is part of the quest for purity that leads to release, enlightenment, and harmony with the way of the universe:

- ✔ **Jainism sees honesty as part of that preparation:** "Straightforwardness and honesty in the activities of one's body, speech, and mind lead to an auspicious path" (Tattvarthasutra 6.23).

- ✔ **Hinduism teaches honesty as a key part of pure conduct:** "Let your conduct be marked by truthfulness in word, deed, and thought" (Taittiriya Upanishad 1.11.1).

- ✔ **Taoism also sees honesty as a way of imitating the way of the universe:** "Be honest like Heaven in conducting your affairs" (Tract of the Quiet Way).

- ✔ **Shinto teaches that dishonesty is a sure way to punishment:** "If you plot and connive to deceive people, you may fool them for a while, and profit thereby, but you will without fail be visited by divine punishment. To be utterly honest may have the appearance of inflexibility and self-righteousness, but in the end, such a person will receive the blessings of sun and moon. Follow honesty without fail" (Oracle of Amaterasu at the Kotai Shrine).

> ↙ **In Confucianism, Tseng Tzu said: "Each day I examine myself in three ways:** In doing things for others, have I been disloyal? In my interactions with friends, have I been untrustworthy? Have I not practiced what I have preached?" (Analects 1:4).

Curiosity: Asking Critical Questions

If religion is about seeking the truth, seeking salvation, or seeking release, then the tools of that quest are spiritual questions.

The virtue of curiosity isn't the same thing as doubt or lack of faith. Questions help a spiritual seeker understand more deeply or enable a teacher to explain more fully an aspect of faith. For this reason, many religions encourage active questioning and curiosity about the world, about God, about the universe, and about the sacred teachings of the faith.

One of the great works of Buddhism is the Questions of Melinda, written in first or second century, C.E. This book contains questions posed by King Melinda (Menander) to the monk, Nagasena, about the nature of truth. It develops the question-and-answer format that's still central to many wisdom traditions, including the Upanishads in Hindu traditions.

Judaism has always based its educational system on the process of asking and answering questions. Jewish law developed through a process of response (called *she'elot u'teshuvot,* or questions and answers) in which people asked rabbis questions and the rabbis wrote back answers. The process of study of the Talmud in a *yeshiva* (a men's school for higher religious study) is a lively, spirited back-and-forth discussion between students who study in pairs. This behavior of the most intellectually and spiritually gifted set an example for all members of the Jewish community. (See the related sidebar titled "How to know whether you're dead or not" later in this chapter.)

Patience: It's a Virtue (So Are Diligence and Perseverance)

Many of us — particularly those in Western cultures — live in a world in which most of what we do or watch or play is over pretty quickly. Moreover, if it doesn't end fast enough for us, we can fast-forward through it or turn it off. Religion isn't like that. Faith requires the virtues patience, diligence, and perseverance because its rewards aren't immediate, and it doesn't promise a life without struggle or pain.

How to know whether you're dead or not

A story from Judaism perfectly illustrates the virtue of questioning: The Hasidic rebbe, Simcha Bunim, once went on a walk with his disciples. Along the way, he and his entourage encountered a group of Jews who were engaged in casual conversation. The rebbe said to his disciples, "Do you see those Jews over there? They're dead."

The disciples were confused. Finally, one of them spoke up, "What do you mean, dead? They look perfectly alive to me."

"They are dead," the Rebbe said, "because they have stopped asking questions and searching for the right answers." The Hasidim walked on, pondering his statement.

Finally, one of the bolder disciples approached the rebbe and asked, "Then how do I know that I am not dead?"

The Rebbe turned to him and answered, "Because you asked."

✔ When Siddhartha Gautama, the Buddha, left his palatial home, he spent many years fasting. At the end of that time, he realized that it didn't lead him to enlightenment. He spent the next 44 years patiently teaching. Buddhist meditation practice and ethical practice are filled with this virtue of patience and slow deliberate advance.

✔ Confucius taught that it doesn't matter how slowly you go "as long as you do not stop." What this means is that without the patience to keep living and growing and questioning, no answers will ever come.

✔ In Jewish tradition, Job serves as the primary example of patience as a virtue. Job was an innocent man who refused to curse God despite his sufferings. The rabbinic teaching of patience is reflected by a famous passage from the Talmud: "You are not required to finish the work, but you are also not free to refrain from doing the work" (Avot 2:16).

✔ Christians nurture patience and diligence through their expectation that Jesus will return and finish the work of the Messiah: "And we desire that each one of you may show the same diligence unto the fullness of hope even to the end: that ye be not sluggish, but imitators of them who through faith and patience inherit the promises" (Hebrews 6:11-12).

✔ Islam teaches patience and trust in Allah in the face of obstacles.

• **From the Qur'an:** "So be patient; surely the promise of Allah is true" (40.55).

• **From hadith:** "Muslims who live in the midst of society and bear with patience the afflictions that come to them are better than those who shun society and cannot bear any wrong done to them." (Abu Da'ud, 817-889 C.E.; one of the six chief compilers of Islamic tradition).

✔ Zoroastrian theology instructs its followers: "Wisdom comes through patience" (Denkard 6.240).

FROM THE HOLY BOOKS

Obtaining all and conquering all with gratitude

According to a beautiful Hindu teaching, Satapatha Brahmana 1.7.2.1-5, gratitude is the repayment of a debt to the past and the future:

When a man is born, whoever he may be, there is born simultaneously a debt to the gods, to the sages, to the ancestors, and to men.

When he performs sacrifice it is the debt to the gods which is concerned. It is on their behalf, therefore, that he is taking action when he sacrifices or makes oblation.

And when he recites the Vedas it is the debt to the sages which is concerned. It is on their behalf, therefore, that he is taking

action, for it is said of one who has recited the Vedas that he is the guardian of the treasure store of the sages.

And when he desires offspring, it is the debt to the ancestors which is concerned. It is on their behalf, therefore, that he is taking action, so that their offspring may continue, without interruption.

And when he entertains guests, it is the debt to man which is concerned. It is on their behalf, therefore, that he is taking action if he entertains guests and gives them food and drink. The man who does all these things has performed a true work; he has obtained all, conquered all.

Gratitude and Thankfulness: Saying Please and Thank You

In the Western monotheistic religions, gratitude comes from the belief that everything we have — our lives and the blessings of our lives — is a gift from God. In Eastern religions, gratitude is a way to achieve purity because, by feeling grateful, we give up the idea that we own anything or exist as an individual entity. (See the related sidebar titled "Obtaining all and conquering all with gratitude" later in this chapter.)

As a virtue, gratitude spills over into rituals like blessings over food, celebrations of holy days, and the commemorations of life cycle events. The virtue of thankfulness is so basic that Jewish teaching regards it as a duty even after the Messiah comes and all other duties are suspended: "The rabbis taught, 'In the world to come, the Messiah will abolish all the sacrifices of the Torah, but not the thanksgiving sacrifice, and in the world to come the Messiah will abolish all the prayers of the *Siddur* (the prayer book), but not the prayer of thanksgiving' " (Vayikra rabba 9:7).

Gratitude is the glue that holds together decent people and creates civil society. According to the Buddha, "The unworthy man is ungrateful, forgetful of benefits done for him. This ingratitude, this forgetfulness is congenial to mean people . . .

But the worthy person is grateful and mindful of benefits done to him. This gratitude, this mindfulness, is congenial to the best people" (Anguttara Nikaya i.6).

The Yoruba tribe of Nigeria teaches the same thing: "One upon whom we bestow kindness but will not express gratitude is worse than a robber who carries away our belongings."

Purity: Everything You Always Wanted to Know but Were Afraid to Ask

The striving for purity within Judaism, Christianity, and Islam is really a way of coping with our basic spiritual dilemma: We are embodied souls. Our bodies produce animal and spiritual urges. We have the animal urge to eat, for example, but we can eat to excess and gain weight. We have the need to procreate and enjoy sex, but that can lead to sexual promiscuity. The virtue of purity is a way of keeping the urges of our souls ahead in the race against the urges of our bodies. Spiritual purity means being free from the desires of our animal nature so that our spiritual nature has a chance to prevail.

Sexual purity: It's not just for prudes

One of the biggest intoxicants in the world is sex, so it's no surprise that the world religions have something to say about avoiding or moderating its use. Spiritual purity can refer to clean thoughts, but it also refers to clean bodies and clean sexual practices.

Modesty in dress

In Islam, female modesty is highly commanded. The Qur'an (for example, 24:31) specifies that a woman dress modestly, and, according to Islamic tradition, that means in a way that conceals her body so as not to arouse the sexual desire of men. Her dress shouldn't be see-through, overly short, or overly tight, for example. (For her husband, however, she should try to look as pleasing as possible.) Beyond this, she can wear anything she wants or that culture in which she lives demands.

Garments traditionally associated with Islamic codes of modesty by women include the following:

✔ *Hijab* (veil): A headscarf (which can usually be of any material or color) that hides the woman's hair from view

> ✔ **Chador:** The long black cloak and veil that covers a woman's entire body, frequently worn nowadays in places such as Iran
>
> ✔ **Burqa:** A long veil that covers a woman's entire body

Although their restrictions are not as stringent, Islamic men are also expected to dress modestly and to avoid ostentation.

Of course, Islam isn't the only religion that expects modesty from its believers. Certain Christian sects, such as the Amish and the Mennonite, also require modest attire, as does Hasidic Judaism. Any people holding certain vocations within a religion (think nuns and priests, for example) are expected to dress modestly.

The role of marriage

All religions acknowledge the power of the sex drive, and most teach that it is acceptable only within religiously sanctioned union — marriage. Therefore, one way to keep sexual urges within the bounds of acceptable religious expression is to promote marriage.

Muslims see human sexuality as a gift from Allah that gives the couple a small glimpse of paradise. Because it's a gift from God, Muslims don't view sex as sinful, but they do believe that it can lead to despair and pain if people don't consider the moral implications of the act. For that reason, sexual relations must take place only within a marriage.

Zoroastrianism, Judaism, and Christianity share this view. The biblical verses that people often cite to emphasize that sexuality is a gift from God and that it's his intention that we use it — responsibly, of course — is this: "Be fruitful and multiply and fill the earth . . . " (Genesis 1:28).

Sexual relations with one's spouse is considered a double commandment on the Sabbath, and lack of sexual relations is a valid reason for a divorce in Judaism, Zoroastrianism, and Islam. All three faiths also require followers to clean themselves after sex.

Sex as an expression of faith

In Hinduism, self-control, which includes sexual self-control *(dama),* is one of the three basic virtues (along with charity and compassion). By practicing sexual self-control, Hindus can avoid the sin of lust *(kama).* Having said that, Hinduism has some very powerful sexual imagery. The goddess Kali and the God Shiva both have sexual images. The *linga,* or *lingam,* is a symbol of the male sexual organ. The *yoni,* a stone with a hole in it symbolizing the female genitals, is also a part of certain Hindu rituals. The yoni and lingam are present in some form in virtually every Hindu temple as a symbol of divine unity.

Tantric Buddhism and Hinduism also include a ritual for sexual intercourse called *maithuna*. In this form of yoga, sex is elevated to a spiritual act. Tantrism teaches that through the manipulation of your body, you can merge with the Divine. Intercourse is a metaphor for the wonderfulness of the experience of being lost in the Oneness of the Universe.

Celibacy: No sex for you

Judaism and Zoroastrianism don't encourage celibacy; rabbis and magi have always been allowed to marry. Muslims view celibacy with suspicion. They see it as an act of ingratitude for one of God's greatest gifts — yet some Muslim mystics or Sufis do practice celibacy as a form of renouncing the world to focus on God. In other religions — Catholicism and Theravada Buddhism, for example, which have celibate clergy it's an expression of faith.

Buddhists monks and nuns

Theravada Buddhism, as it is lived in the community of monks and nuns, is one of the most restrictive (or modest) regarding celibacy. If you consider that the goal of Buddhism is to extinguish the flames of worldly passions and to let go all earthly attachments, you can understand — and maybe even appreciate — these limitations on Buddhist monks and nuns. In addition to giving up all sexual behavior, the monks and nuns in these communities must also give up other physical pleasures, such as

- ✔ Eating after midday
- ✔ Worldly amusements
- ✔ Jewelry, bodily adornments, and perfume
- ✔ High and luxurious beds

Catholic priests

The Catholic Church considered but rejected celibacy for priests; and popes and priests were allowed to be married until 1139, when an ecumenical council made celibacy a requirement for priests. The creation of a celibate clergy in the Catholic Church is based on two verses from the New Testament:

- ✔ A passage in Matthew (19:12), where the unmarried Jesus defends his celibacy: "For there are some eunuchs, which were so born from their mother's womb: and there are some eunuchs, which were made eunuchs of men: and there be eunuchs, which have made themselves eunuchs for the kingdom of heaven's sake. He that is able to receive it, let him receive it."

- ✔ Paul's first letter to the Corinthians, in which he encourages that married couples abstain from sex temporarily and the unmarried people remain unmarried. (He thought that the second coming of Jesus was soon at hand.)

The economic problem the Church faced was clear. Priests who married would give away church property to their children as their inheritance, and of course the cost of paying married clergy is much greater than the cost of paying celibate clergy. (Protestants rejected this decision because of the value they saw in having married clergy and also because they rejected the authority of the Pope who required celibacy for Catholic priests.)

On a more spiritual note, Catholics defend celibacy as a way of offering up a great sacrifice in order to love others more fully and model the sacrifice of Jesus. Christianity, especially during the Middle Ages, had a lot of trouble with sex as sinful because it was thought to distract men and women from God.

Purity from drugs and other intoxicants

All religions include guidelines of conduct regarding the way people deal with alcohol, drugs, and other stimulants. The spiritual high that religion produces is supposed to be enough, and the world of physical pleasure is often seen as a seduction away from the life of faith.

Islam also has a strong position on temperance, based on the idea that Allah owns our bodies. Therefore, anything that we do to harm them is forbidden, and this means drinking alcohol and taking drugs for any reason other than medicinal.

Don't think that all religions are opposed to all intoxicants or sexual behavior, however. In many Christian religions, wine is used for religious purposes and is a symbol of joy; God is even praised for bringing forth "the fruit of the vine." In some traditions, intoxicants are used to heighten religious rituals and direct physical pleasure is seen as a gateway into a spiritual dimension.

Chapter 11

Public Virtues

All public virtues are manifestations of personal virtues. Truly believing in the golden rule — in kindness, in honesty, or in any of the other personal virtues (covered in Chapter 10), means that you're probably going to act accordingly. Possessing the personal virtue of humility, for example, leads to the public virtue of tolerance; possessing the personal virtue of compassion leads to the public virtues of *ahimsa* (nonviolence) and charity; the personal virtue of faith leads to the public virtue of evangelism; and so on.

This chapter covers the public virtues: those qualities that religions seek to instill in society through the faithful. Whereas Chapter 10 covers the qualities individuals should strive for within themselves, this chapter examines the qualities that, according to the world's religions, people should strive for within their communities and the world.

Charity: Sharing the Wealth

The personal virtue of compassion can be just an attitude or a kindly disposition to others; charity, on the other hand, is an act of kindness through which people share their blessings with others. In this way, charity is a public virtue that Jews, Christians, Muslims, Hindus, and members of other faiths believe to have spiritual consequences. Zoroastrians, for example, believe: "Be generous so that your soul will reach paradise" (Counsels of Adurbad 80).

Eight levels of charity

The most famous treatment of the idea of charity in Judaism comes from Spanish rabbi and philosopher Maimonides (1135-1204). He described levels of charity, from lowest to highest:

1. To give grudgingly

2. To not give enough, but in good spirits

3. To give only when asked

4. To give without being asked

5. To give when you don't know the identity of the recipient, but the recipient knows yours

6. To give when you know the identity of the recipient, but the recipient doesn't know yours

7. To give where neither of you knows the other's identity

8. To help a person become self-sufficient so that he or she will not need to accept charity in the future

Christian charity

In Christianity, charity means unselfish or sacrificial love for others. Charity (along with faith and hope) is one of the three central Christian virtues. Thomas Aquinas (1225-74 C.E.), the Italian theologian and philosopher, considered charity the foundation of all other Christian virtues. According to Christian theology, people don't give of themselves because the object of charity is worthy. They give because, by giving, both the giver and recipient are transformed.

Jewish tzedaka

The Hebrew word for charity is *tzedaka*. The Jewish concept of charity is that giving to charity is not beyond the call of duty. Charity is a duty. Because everything we have is on loan from God, we are duty-bound to share our gifts from God with those who have not been given enough:

"For the poor shall never cease out of the land: therefore I command thee, saying, Thou shalt open thine hand wide unto thy brother, to thy poor, and to thy needy, in thy land" (Deuteronomy 9:11).

In addition, many biblical laws in the Hebrew Bible had the sole purpose of providing charity to the poor. Fields and vineyards couldn't be completely harvested, enabling the poor to come into the fields and glean after the reapers. In the seventh year and the fiftieth year, nothing could be harvested, debts were forgiven, and bondservants were set free, all to make the Jewish idea of charity not just an ideal but also a practical virtue. (See the related sidebar titled "Eight levels of charity" later in this chapter.)

Islamic zakat

Charity, particularly giving alms to the poor, is central in Islam, as represented by its inclusion in the Five Pillars of Islam. An economically self-sufficient Muslim is expected to give alms in an act called *zakat* in Arabic. Giving to charity shows that one's faith in Allah is true, that he or she isn't controlled by material possessions.

The prophet Muhammad often cited charity as a central virtue of Islam: "A man once asked the Prophet what the best thing was in Islam, and he replied, "It is to feed the hungry and to give the greeting of peace both to those one knows and to those one does not know" (Hadith of Bukhari).

In Islam, this "charity" isn't so much giving because of sympathy for a cause or because of a catastrophe. Rather, it's a regular, sacrificial giving that, in addition to helping the needy, reaffirms these Islamic ideas (much like charitable offerings at church):

- ✔ Everything belongs to God, even those material possessions people think they own. By sacrificing these things for the sake of God, people are really just giving things back to their rightful owner.

- ✔ Nothing should be hoarded. Society works best when things — including money and resources — flow naturally. By giving things away that you don't need or use, you give people who *can* use them or may need them the opportunity to do so. In this way, you save yourself from greed and you save others from envy and jealousy.

Islam also developed another element of charity called the *waqf*. The waqf is a way of endowing money or land to be devoted to the maintenance of mosques, shrines, schools, hospitals, and other public works in Muslim lands. The waqf is exempt from all taxation or seizure by the state.

Charity in Eastern religions

In Hinduism, *bhakti* comes close to the idea of charity in the west. Bhakti is the devotion of yourself to a god that may motivate you to act compassionately toward others.

In Buddhism, the word for a Buddhist monk, *bhiksu,* or nun, *bhiksuni,* means "beggar," and the tradition of giving alms to the *sangha,* the community of monks, is as old as Buddhism itself. The only possessions a monk can own are a robe, a piece of thread and a needle, a razor, and a begging bowl into which people place food (called *pinda* or *pincama*) for the monks every morning.

Repentance, Forgiveness, Reconciliation: Repaying Evil with Good

Repentance. Forgiveness. Reconciliation. All these words convey the virtue of repaying evil with good. People do this when they forgive people who've hurt them and when they repent for their own sins against others. (For detail on sin, check out the discussion of sin and suffering in Chapter 5.)

The natural impulse of many people who've been hurt is to get even — to return hurt for hurt. For that reason, repentance and forgiveness are perhaps two of the central virtues of all religions. When people practice these virtues, they actively seek reconciliation with those whom they've harmed or who have harmed them.

To err is human . . .

Although the specifics differ from religion to religion, reconciliation — with people or with God — generally follows three parts: acknowledging the sin, atoning for the sin, and being forgiven.

Oops, sorry about that: Confession of sins

In Judaism and Islam, you confess your sins in public prayer. In Catholicism, you can confess in public prayer or in a private confession with a priest. In Zoroastrianism, the recitation of confessional formulas can be either in public or in private.

In Judaism, the fast day of Yom Kippur and the ten days preceding it are dedicated to prayers of confession *(vidui).* Confessing sins in public helps people who may be hesitant to confess their sins privately. On these days of repentance, the format of the public confession is in the plural "For the sin that *we* have committed by . . . ."

Forgive me? Seeking forgiveness

In most religions, you must seek forgiveness face to face with the person you've hurt. In Judaism, the phrase, "I ask your *mehila* (forgiveness) for what

I have done to you," is used. Moreover, Jews are required to return three times to a person who refuses to forgive them.

The Catholic practice of forgiveness is different from the way Judaism and Islam teach it. A Catholic priest can offer forgiveness of sins without the sinner ever having to appear before the person he or she hurt. Called *absolution of sins,* it is part of the Christian sacrament of penance. The priest may urge such face-to-face forgiveness as part of the sinner's penance, but such a meeting isn't essential. The priest can also establish ways for the sinner to repent that don't involve righting the wrong with the other person. For example, a priest can order a person who stole money from another person to give the stolen money to charity instead of giving it back to the person. (See the related sidebar titled "An enduring ability to forgive" later in this chapter.)

Ahh, . . . clean at last: Getting right with God

The thing about moral failings is that once they occur, they're impossible to take them back. The act of repentance and reconciliation helps restore relationships, but it doesn't free us from shame and a sense of defilement. That happens after we do what we can to make things better. Then God enters and cleans up the effects of our sin on our own sense of ourselves. God makes us clean.

And they shall come thither, and they shall take away all the detestable things thereof and all the abominations thereof from thence. And I will give them one heart, and I will put a new spirit within you; and I will take the stony heart out of their flesh, and will give them a heart of flesh; that they may walk in my statutes, and keep mine ordinances, and do them: and they shall be my people, and I will be their God (Ezekiel 11:18-20).

To forgive, divine

In monotheistic religions, the command to forgive comes from the belief that because God has forgiven us for our sins, we should forgive others for theirs. In Christianity, Jesus exemplifies this forgiveness by forgiving those who murdered him. In Judaism, the holy day of Yom Kippur is devoted to offering forgiveness and seeking it from God and from others. Ramadan, the sacred month of Islam, is devoted to acts of charity and forgiveness. Ramadan is rooted in God's merciful nature, and its success depends upon the sinner's sincere desire to repent before others and engage in acts of kindness and charity.

In the Eastern religions, forgiveness is another way of releasing attachments to things that block the path to enlightenment. By holding onto anger, we keep ourselves from moving forward in our spiritual journey.

An enduring ability to forgive

Jesus taught the absolute duty to forgive in Matthew 18:21-22:

> Then came Peter and said to him, Lord, how oft shall my brother sin against me, and I forgive him? until seven times? Jesus saith unto him, I say not unto thee, Until seven times; but, Until seventy times seven.

If you go by the math, you may think that Jesus meant that 490 is the limit. Most Christians, however, agree he was speaking figuratively, not literally.

Obedience: Doing Your Duty

One of the most ancient religious virtues and perhaps one of the hardest for modern minds to grasp is the idea of obedience. If you don't like the word *obedience,* you can substitute *duty, discipline,* or *obligation,* but they mean the same thing: People shouldn't just do what they want, but what they are commanded to do. Dharma, the religious law that governs conduct and the written truths of the religions' founders, is one the foundations of Hinduism, Buddhism, and Jainism, for example. Dharma demands that people follow the path of their inherited status (in the Hindu caste system, for example) and accept traditional attitudes to find enlightenment.

Other religious virtues, like kindness and charity, are hard to argue against. Most people, however, may cast a suspicious eye at the virtue of obedience. Here's why:

- ✔ Obedience goes against the grain of modern thought. Modern culture (particularly in the West) prizes individualism, freedom, and self-determination — things that seem to be contrary to what obedience requires.

- ✔ Obedience to authority is a cornerstone of many religious ideologies. Confucianism, for example, puts a strong emphasis on obedience to the political order. The purpose of such obedience is to restore harmony and peace to society. What do you do, however, when that political authority is corrupt? You cannot, for example, be an obedient and moral Nazi.

This section looks at what the religions of the world mean when they speak of the virtue of obedience.

Obedience to God: The biggie

The word *religion* stems from the Latin *religare,* which means, "to bind back again." Religion binds people to God through duty. In Arabic, religion is *al-din,* which comes from the root meaning "debt." Religion is humankind's way of repaying its debt to God for all the blessings he bestows.

The virtue of obedience in the monotheistic faiths begins with the covenant *(brit)* between God and the Jewish people. This covenant calls for the people to obey God; in return, God will love and protect the people.

The model of obedience to God as a sign of the covenant shows itself in rituals (such as circumcision) and moral values. The very word *Islam,* for example, means surrender. Islam is surrender in loving obedience to the will of Allah. Through that obedience, the Muslim finds reward and meaning, order and strength.

Disobedience of God by the first couple — Adam and Eve in Judaism, Christianity, and Islam, Mashya and Mashyana in Zoroastrianism — is said to have caused the fall of humanity from paradise, leading to life and death.

Every form of human obedience to other human beings (discussed in the following sections) is modeled on the duty of obedience to God.

Obedience to the state

The religious virtue of obedience states that you should obey the law of your land and be a good citizen. (See the related sidebar titled "The powers that be" later in this chapter.) Even Jesus was happy to pay the half-shekel tax levied by the government to show the importance of Christians' obeying the law. Jesus also taught his disciples to obey the traditional law of Judaism, even though the teachers of that law didn't always follow it.

Render therefore unto Caesar the things that are Caesar's; and unto God the things that are God's (Matthew 22:21).

The Talmud states, *"dina d'malchuta dina,"* that is, "the law of the state is the law," and Jews must obey it unless it conflicts with Jewish law, in which case they must disobey the law or move to another state.

Confucianism is much more firm on the obligation of a person to obey the state. The state is the supreme authority in all matters.

The religious concept of obedience to state authority comes from these concerns:

- ✔ Without some authority, society would collapse into chaos; thus, even if the state is not right all the time, as long as the state is basically just, people are religiously obligated to obey its rulings.

- ✔ Some religions don't consider what happens on earth in politics as important as salvation or enlightenment; therefore, obeying the state and then spending one's time in religious pursuits is much more spiritually wise.

Obedience to parents

Nearly all religions expect children to obey their parents. In Christianity and Judaism, honoring your father and your mother is one of the Ten Commandments; the Hebrew Bible (Old Testament) tells believers to "Honor your father and your mother, that your days may be long in the land which the Lord your God gives you" (Exodus 20:12). The Qur'an enjoins Muslims to treat their parents kindly and with respect: "Your Lord orders that you . . . be kind to your parents. . ." (17: 23). The Confucian Analects give directions to children: "A young man's duty is to behave well to his parents at a home and to his elders abroad . . ." (1:6).

Of course, these laws don't mean that you must do something bad if your parents order you to. Instead, the laws affirm that the status of being a parent is worthy of respect from children. The respect comes from the sacrifices made by parents, the act of giving you life, and the wisdom that all religions accord to those who are older than us.

FROM THE HOLY BOOKS

The powers that be

Paul's letter to the Romans (13:1-7) urges people to obey the laws of the land:

Let every soul be in subjection to the higher powers: for there is no power but of God; and the powers that be are ordained of God. Therefore he that resisteth the power, withstandeth the ordinance of God: and they that withstand shall receive to themselves judgment. For rulers are not a terror to the good work, but to the evil. And wouldest thou have no fear of the power? do that which is good, and thou shalt have praise from the same: for he is a minister of God to thee for good. But if thou do that which is

evil, be afraid; for he beareth not the sword in vain: for he is a minister of God, an avenger for wrath to him that doeth evil.

Wherefore ye must needs be in subjection, not only because of the wrath, but also for conscience's sake. For this cause ye pay tribute also; for they are ministers of God's service, attending continually upon this very thing.

Render to all their dues: tribute to whom tribute is due; custom to whom custom; fear to whom fear; honor to whom honor.

Obedience and the role of women

The controversy of the place of women within religious traditions has been an especially hot topic during the twentieth century. All major world religions are patriarchal or male-dominated, and women all over the world have made a concerted effort to be recognized as full members and to gain equal status within their respective religious traditions.

Within the churches, mosques, synagogues, and temples

Most of the sacred literature of the world religions has been interpreted for hundreds, if not thousands, of years by clerics who had little interest in expanding the rights and roles of women. Today, women are more educated and thus have been researching and reinterpreting key scriptures that have been used to relegate them to subordinate positions. Slowly, ever so slowly, some of the most prominent religious traditions have recognized women and appointed them to important positions.

Traditions such as Methodist, Presbyterian, Episcopal, some Lutheran, Reform and Conservative Judaism, and more ordain women. Within the traditions of India, some women have claimed the status of a *sannyasin* (renouncer who becomes a Guru or Swami), and the numbers of women within Theravada Buddhism are growing. You can find an occasional woman priestess officiating at *puja* (rituals) in Hindu temples. In Mahayana Buddhism, women Bodhisattvas are venerated, and women have been recognized as religious leaders in China, Korea, and Japan.

While Amaterasu is still worshipped as the founding Goddess of Shinto, few if any women priestesses officiate at her altar. At the beginning of the twenty-first century, the following religious traditions do not ordain women to the highest offices: Islam, Orthodox Judaism, Latter-day Saints, Lutheran Missouri Synod, Southern Baptists, Roman Catholicism, and many Pentecostal groups.

Within the home

In many religious traditions, women are subordinate to their husbands, who are considered the head of the family. Traditionally, the Christian churches expected the husband to rule the wife, and many still do, using the following passage from the Bible as justification:

"Wives, be in subjection unto your own husbands, as unto the Lord. For the husband is the head of the wife, and Christ also is the head of the church, being himself the savior of the body. But as the church is subject to Christ, so let the wives also be to their husbands in everything" (Ephesians 5:22-24).

The Bible also acknowledges the importance of the wife's role:

"Let the husband render unto the wife her due: and likewise also the wife unto the husband. The wife hath not power over her own body, but the husband: and likewise also the husband hath not power over his own body, but the wife" (I Corinthians 7:3-4).

According to Islam, Allah created an ordered universe in which every living thing, including humans (who have an unfortunate tendency to forget this), has a unique place and purpose. This perfection of design requires that everything, including people, fulfill their designated roles. In the Muslim family, the husband's rightful place is as ruler of his family; the wife's is as ruler of the house. By accepting their roles and performing them well, they please Allah equally.

When human law and divine law are at odds

Religion doesn't require blind obedience to secular laws. When the law of the land is immoral, obedience to that law is also immoral. In that situation, people should obey the dictates of their faith. In this way, religion can be a force for positive change. For example,

- During the nineteenth century in the United States, the law of the land made it illegal to harbor or aid runaway slaves. Many people, believing with certainty people are equal in the eyes of God and that slavery was a perversion of religion (despite what Southern clergy said), helped thousands of fleeing slaves to freedom.

- Mohandas Gandhi led a nonviolent revolt that resulted in the independence of India from British rule.

- Martin Luther King, Jr. urged a religiously motivated nonviolent resistance to immoral laws that denied human and civil rights to black Americans in the 1960s.

The main point of obedience is that no earthly power can order you to violate the law of truth and the universe and God. Siddhartha Gautama (the Buddha) gave up a kingship to serve the truth of freedom. Moses gave up a principality under Pharaoh to wander as a shepherd in the desert. Jesus gave his life to show the way beyond this world of lies and corruption and power. Look at the abolitionists who fought against slavery; they were religious people. Look at Gandhi, who fought the power of the British Empire without a single bullet. Look at Martin Luther King, Jr., who fought injustice by using his pulpit and his faith. Look at Joan of Arc who went to the flames rather than betray God's words. Although revolutionaries, they obeyed the dictates of their conscience and their faith. That's what religious obedience is.

GOING DEEPER

Keeping the peace with Gandhi

Mohandas Gandhi (1869-1948) used the virtue of ahimsa as the foundation of his idea of nonviolent opposition to evil. He used it in leading the Indian nationalist movement against British domination of India. He learned many of his ideas from a close Jain friend, Raychand, as well as from his mother.

The virtue of ahimsa is connected to other virtues such as

✔ *Aparigraha,* which is giving up all material possessions that bind us to the world of wealth and power

✔ *Samabhava,* which is the virtue of being unmoved and unaffected by either pain or pleasure, triumph or defeat

✔ *Satyagraha,* out of which Gandhi developed political strategies based upon nonviolence and self-sacrifice.

The fact that he was assassinated in January 1948 by a fanatical Hindu is a perfect example of the difficulty that true pacifists have in overcoming the use of violence to achieve political objectives.

Ahimsa: Respecting Life and Practicing Nonviolence

For Eastern religions, the roots of nonviolence are the concepts that all living things are on a journey to enlightenment (and therefore should be left to make their way) and that people struggle to abandon the self and its emotions (including anger, jealousy, and desire) that stop them from reaching enlightenment.

For Western religions, the root of nonviolence is the concept that, because God made everyone, every person bears the imprint of his holiness equally.

In Eastern religions: A way of life

In Hinduism, Buddhism, Jainism, and all the religions originating in South Asia, the word for this virtue of nonviolence or tolerance and kindness is *ahimsa,* and it means far more than just refusing to kill a human being, even in self-defense. Ahimsa also means never killing an animal for food, and in the case of some very pious Jains, it means wearing a cloth over one's mouth, called a *mukhavastrik,* and sweeping the path ahead of them as they walk to avoid inadvertently killing even a lowly insect.

Fighting evil with words of peace

Paul, in his letter to the Ephesians (6:10-17), makes clear that the way for religious people to combat evil is not with armor and weapons but with God's saving words:

"Finally, my brethren, be strong in the Lord, and in the power of his might. Put on the whole armor of God, that ye may be able to stand against the wiles of the devil. For we wrestle not against flesh and blood, but against principalities, against powers, against the rulers of the darkness of this world, against spiritual wicked-ness in high places. Wherefore take unto you the whole armor of God, that ye may be able to withstand in the evil day, and having done all, to stand. Stand therefore, having your loins gird about with truth, and having on the breastplate of righteousness; And your feet shod with the preparation of the gospel of peace; Above all, taking the shield of faith, wherewith ye shall be able to quench all the fiery darts of the wicked. And take the helmet of salvation, and the sword of the Spirit, which is the word of God."

The virtue of ahimsa doesn't require just non-malevolence, the refusal to cause harm; it also requires benevolence, doing good and respecting the sanctity of all living creatures by treating them well. The idea behind ahimsa is that all living things, called *jiva,* have a path through rebirth to higher levels, and by killing or injuring another jiva's journey, you add a load of karma to your own journey and delay and impede your own liberation.

Ahimsa is just one of the Hindu virtues *(guna-gunas)* that apply to people of all castes, but it is the greatest virtue. (See the related sidebar titled "Keeping the peace with Gandhi" later in this chapter.)

In Western religions: A struggle

According to religious tradition (Islam, Christianity, and Judaism), Moses, the one prophet who spoke to God directly, brought the Ten Commandments down from Mount Sinai. One of those commandments was this: Thou shalt not kill. Right?

Not quite.

In Hebrew, this commandment is *lo tirtzach.* The common English translation ("Thou shalt not kill") is simply wrong. The Hebrew word used in this command-ment is not the word for kill, *harag,* but the word for murder. The commandment should be translated "Thou shalt not murder." Murder is killing for no morally sound reason, and that is what is prohibited in the Ten Commandments.

In Christianity, Islam, and Judaism, understanding and implementing the virtue of nonviolence has been a struggle and the topic of theological debate. These religions have traditions that support armed resistance as well as commandments that demand respect for life. The question, then, is when (if ever) is taking life morally acceptable.

Christianity: Back and forth on the issue

The Christian teachings about nonviolence went through two very different stages: before Christianity was the state religion of Rome and after it was the state religion of Rome.

Before Christianity became the official religion of the Roman Empire (324 C.E.), pacifism and nonviolence were hallmarks of the faith. The teachings of Jesus almost sound like the Buddha in their absolute renunciation of all violence:

- ✔ "Ye have heard that it hath been said, An eye for an eye, and a tooth for a tooth: But I say unto you, That ye resist not evil: but whosoever shall smite thee on thy right cheek, turn to him the other also" (Matthew 5:38-39).

- ✔ "And unto him that smiteth thee on the one cheek offer also the other; and him that taketh away thy cloak forbid not to take thy coat also" (Luke 6:29).

- ✔ "Then said Jesus unto him, Put up again thy sword into his place: for all they that take the sword shall perish with the sword" (Matthew 26:52).

After Christianity became the state religion of Rome, Christian theologians began to figure out ways to approve Christian participation in wars. Saint Augustine (354-430 C.E.), an early church father, made it official church teaching that Christians could go to war, provided that

- ✔ The action was for the defense of the common security of the nation.

- ✔ The public authorities were not corrupt.

According to the thinking at the time, if you kill to defend your life and the freedom of your country, you're protecting yourself and those you love from an unjust assault by an outsider attacker. The killing, therefore, is in self-defense. Even though your attacker's life is just as sacred as yours, their actions in attacking you are neither sacred nor just. The self-defense argument defends your right not just to respect the lives of others, but also to protect your own life and the lives of your family and friends and fellow citizens who have been unjustly attacked.

Even though the church, following St. Augustine, endorsed killing in wartime, the pacifist tradition in Christianity remained alive in some Protestant traditions, including the Mennonite, Amish, and Bruderhof communities, as well as the Anabaptists and the Quakers, or the Society of Friends. (See the related sidebar titled "Fighting evil with words of peace" later in this chapter.)

In Judaism

Killing is morally and spiritually acceptable in Judaism in these situations:

- For capital punishment
- In self defense
- In commanded wars of national defense (*milhemet mitzvah*)

The Talmud teaches the following tough lesson in the morality of self-defense, *bah l'hargecha, hashkem l'hargo,* "If someone comes to kill you, you must rise early and kill them first."

In the Bible, Deuteronomy 21 includes several laws about warfare that make clear that even permitted wars have moral limits. Consider these examples of proper conduct during war:

- You can't cut down one's enemy's fruit trees, because it takes so long for a tree to grow back up again and bear fruit.
- When you lay siege to a city, you first have to give people a chance to run away.
- You must never put salt in the fields, because salt makes everything die for many years.

These laws serve to prohibit ancient war crimes; their lesson for people today is that, even when you have to kill to protect yourself, you can't do it any way you want, and you can't do it with a smile.

Judaism also contains a nonviolent tradition. The pacifist words of the prophet Zechariah — "Not by might, nor by power, but by my spirit, saith the Lord of hosts" (Zechariah 4:6) — were chosen by the rabbis to be read on Chanukah, which celebrates the military victory of the Maccabees in 165 B.C.E.

In Islam

Islam (a term which derives from the word *salam,* or peace) has a long history of tolerance. Two of the main tenets of the faith are forgiveness and returning good for evil. Unlike many of their Christian contemporaries, Islamic countries in the Middle Ages were models of religious tolerance, based on Qur'anic ideas, such as

✔ "Let there be no compulsion in religion" (2:257).

✔ "For every one of you, We appointed a law and a way. And if Allah had pleased He would have made you a single people . . ." (5: 48).

Islam teaches tolerance and respect for individual decisions, but it doesn't teach pacifism or absolute nonviolence. Turning the other cheek so that an oppressor has free rein over you or watching a tyrant subjugate a people and not acting to help is not considered a virtue in Islam. In Islam, the point is to do what is right; sometimes, doing what is right requires the use of force:

✔ "Why should you not fight in the cause of Allah and of those who, being weak, are ill-treated and oppressed?" (4:75).

✔ "And if Allah did not repel some people by others, cloisters, and churches, and synagogues, and mosques in which Allah's name is much remembered, would have been pulled down. And surely Allah will help those who help Him" (22:40).

According to Islam, the only acceptable wars are defensive or to right a wrong — to restore peace and freedom of worship, for example, or to eliminate tyranny. And wars should last only until the aggressor lays down his weapons. Force must never be used to convert people to Islam, to settle border or political disputes, to wage wars of aggression or ambition, or to conquer and subjugate people.

Isaiah 40:17, 21-24

Western religions teach that nations are good or bad, but never the way to salvation and never the central object of devotion, which must be, in the West, God alone. The prophet Isaiah said it with great power and simple eloquence:

17. All the nations are as nothing before him, they are accounted by him as less than nothing and emptiness.

21. Have you not known? Have you not heard? Has it not been told you from the beginning? Have you not understood from the foundations of the earth?

22. It is he who sits above the circle of the earth, and its inhabitants are like grasshoppers; who stretches out the heavens like a curtain, and spreads them like a tent to dwell in;

23. who brings princes to nought, and makes the rulers of the earth as nothing.

24. Scarcely are they planted, scarcely sown, scarcely has their stem taken root in the earth, when he blows upon them, and they wither, and the tempest carries them off like stubble.

Evangelism: Spreading the Faith

For some religions, it's not enough that people know and accept the truth of their faith. These believers must personally and collectively go out into the world and share their "good news" with others with the intent of converting them. Christianity, in particular, is a religion that actively pursues members of other faiths to accept the Christian truth of Christ. The biblical verse that invokes the missionary zeal is this:

"Go ye therefore, and teach all nations, baptizing them in the name of the Father, and of the Son, and of the Holy Ghost" (Matthew 28:19).

Some famous evangelical movements include

- ✔ **The Jesuit order of the Roman Catholic Church:** Jesuits are ordained priests who live in community, are responsible only to the Pope, and are responsible for conquering the world for Christ. Provocative films such as *The Mission* and *The Black Robe* chronicle their exploits and successes.

- ✔ **Missionary activity of the Latter-day Saints:** Young men, aged 19-21, and young women, aged 21-23, are strongly urged to give two years of their lives as missionaries for the Church. If they choose to do missionary work, which can (but doesn't necessarily) take these young people to far away countries, their parents must financially sponsor them.

- ✔ **Doorstep preaching of Jehovah's Witnesses:** Most members of local congregations are expected to devote as much time as they can in doorstep preaching in which members go door to door in assigned neighborhoods, preaching and handing out literature.

Where East and West meet

The virtue of perfection embraces the idea of non-resistance to evil. It is in this concept that Eastern religions (such as Buddhism, Jainism, and Hinduism) and the Western religion of Christianity meet. Perfect living that leads to nirvana and perfect living that leads to Christian salvation both require a life that renounces *all* force and violence in achieving aims.

This idea is clear in Matthew 5:44-48:

> But I say unto you, Love your enemies, bless them that curse you, do good to them that hate you, and pray for them which despitefully use you, and persecute you; That ye may be the children of your Father which is in heaven: for he maketh his sun to rise on the evil and on the good, and sendeth rain on the just and on the unjust. For if ye love them which love you, what reward have ye? do not even the publicans the same? And if ye salute your brethren only, what do ye more than others? do not even the publicans so? Be ye therefore perfect, even as your Father which is in heaven is perfect.

Of course, many people with evangelical spirits aren't preaching missionaries or actively trying to convert others. These people share the "good news" of their faith by leading good lives in accordance with their faith, helping people in need, and caring for the sick. In this way, they serve as examples of the principles of their faith.

For other religions, such as Judaism and Zoroastrianism, converting people isn't particularly important.

Justice: Doing Right

Almost every religious tradition is interested in the welfare of people. In the Bible, the command to pursue justice is absolute and is the only way to live on the land: "Justice, justice you shall pursue that thou mayest live, and inherit the land which the Lord thy God giveth thee" (Deuteronomy 16:20).

Interestingly, this biblical commandment is to *pursue* justice, not *do* justice. We can't always do justice or even know what the just thing is to do. What we can do is to try always to fight for justice, pursue justice, work for justice. Those endeavors are in our control, and that's what God requires. By pursuing justice on earth, people attempt to imitate, honor, and reflect the God who made them. In essence, human acts of justice merely mirror God's.

The virtue of justice is not only rooted in the nature of God, but also in the experience of the Jewish people as slaves in Egypt and Babylonia, and for Muslims through the Qur'an. It was that notion of justice based on God's will that is said to have led the Iranian (Zoroastrian) monarch Cyrus (549-530 B.C.E.) to free the Jews from captivity in Babylonia.

"O ye who believe! Stand out firmly for justice, as witness to God, even as against yourselves, or your parents, or your kin, and whether it concerns rich or poor: for God can best protect both. Follow not the lusts of your hearts lest you swerve, and if you distort justice or decline to do justice, verily God/Allah is well acquainted with all that you do" (Qur'an 4.135).

In Western religion, God commands justice for orphans and widows, the oppressed, the meek, the poor, and the vulnerable. God/Allah is always on the side of the victims. A powerful God who cares for those with no power is one of the primary reasons that the monotheistic faiths have endured for so long and have created such a powerful moral ethic for people to live by.

Quietism in Christianity

The West does have a rich sense of spiritual tranquility, or quietism. The prophet Isaiah in the Hebrew Bible, who is a passionate defender of justice, is also aware of the value of tranquility: "In sitting still and rest shall ye be saved. In quietness and in trust shall be your strength" (Isaiah 30:15).

In Christianity, quietism has had its defenders. "Desire nothing, refuse nothing" was the motto of Frances de Sales (1567-1622). He influenced a generation of Catholic mystics who called themselves quietists. They were following the sentiments of Jesus that to be born into a Christian life one must die to oneself and be born again in God's love: "And he called unto him the multitude with his disciples, and said unto them, If any man would come after me, let him deny himself, and take up his cross, and follow me. For whosoever would save his life shall lose it; and whosoever shall lose his life for my sake and the gospel's shall save it. For what doth it profit a man, to gain the whole world, and forfeit his life?" (Mark 8:34-36, ASV).

Tranquility: Finding Peace

Thinking of tranquility as a public virtue may be hard, because it seems focused on the individual rather than the community. Yet achieving personal tranquility affects the way we live with others.

Tranquility enables you to

- ✔ Live with other people without anger or jealousy or envy.
- ✔ Respond to the absurdities of life without indignation.
- ✔ Accept your lot in life without complaint.
- ✔ Treat everyone with dignity.
- ✔ Abandon your ego and your self-centeredness.

In essence, tranquility helps us to live with others by reminding us that what is in us is more important than what is owned by us; or, as Lao-Tzu said perfectly, "The important part of the cup is the empty part inside."

In Theravada and some Mahayana Buddhist sects, tranquility is not a way to control yourself, but a way to realize that you have no self. (See the related sidebar titled "Quietism in Christianity" later in this chapter.) This self-renunciation is a key to becoming a Theravada monk, a *bhiksu:*

"He who has no thought of I or mine whatsoever toward either his mind or body, he who does not grieve for that which he does not have, he is indeed called a bhiksu" (Dhammapada 367).

Knowing that there is no self helps to overcome pain: "All states are without self. When one sees this in wisdom, then he becomes dispassionate toward the painful. This is the path to purity" (Dhammapada 279).

Tolerance: Accepting Other Ways up the Mountain

Tolerance is the virtue of accepting the legitimacy of other belief systems even though you may hold your own belief system to be true. The religious traditions have deep and various teachings about tolerance.

Following are some samples of how the world's religions view this public virtue:

- ✔ "At any time, in any form and accepted name, if one is shorn of all attachment, that one is you alone. My Lord! You are one although variously appearing" (Jainism, Hemachandra Anyayogavyavacchedika 29).

- ✔ "The One Being sages call by many names" (Hinduism, Rig-Veda 1.164.46).

- ✔ "In the world there are many different roads but the destination is the same. There are a hundred deliberations but the result is one" (Confucianism, I Ching, appended remarks 2.5).

- ✔ "There are different gifts but the same Spirit. There are different ministries but the same Lord. There are different works but the same God who accomplishes all of them in everyone . . . it is one and the same Spirit who produces all these gifts, distributing them to each as He wills" (Christianity, I Corinthians 12:4-11).

- ✔ "Say, We believe in God, and in what has been revealed to us, and what was revealed to Abraham, Ishmael, Isaac, Jacob, and the Tribes, and in what was given to Moses, Jesus, and the Prophets from their Lord. We make no distinction between any of them, and to God do we submit" (Islam, Qur'an, 3.84).

- ✔ "Just as the sin offering atones for Israel, so righteousness atones for the peoples of the world" (Judaism, Talmud, Baba Batra 10b).

✔ "The Hindus and the Muslims have but one and the same God, what can a mullah or a sheikh do?" (Sikhism, Adi Granth, Bhairo, p.1158).

✔ "The Buddha declared to the bodhisattva Aksayamati, 'Good man, if there are beings in the land who can be conveyed to deliverance by the body of a Buddha, the bodhisattva Avalokitesvara preaches the truth by displaying the body of a Buddha. To those who can be conveyed to deliverance by the body of Brahma he preaches the Truth by displaying the body of Brahma. To those who can be conveyed to deliverance by the body of Shakra he preaches the Truth by displaying the body of the god Shakra. To those who can be conveyed to deliverance by the body of the god Ishvara . . . an elder . . . a householder . . . an official . . . a woman . . . a boy or girl . . . a god, dragon, spirit, angel, demon, garuda bird, centaur, serpent, human or nonhuman, he preaches Dharma by displaying the appropriate body . . . . The bodhisattva Avalokitesvara, by resorting to a variety of forms, travels the world, conveying the beings to salvation" (Buddhism, Lotus Sutra 25).

Tolerance requires acknowledging that, although you may think your religion is the one true faith, you can learn from and respect other faiths as well. The trick to doing that is personal, spiritual humility.

If you were God, or if God spoke to you regularly or if you were a Buddha or a Bodhisattva, you could probably speak the truth without error. The rest of us, however, should remain humble about everything we learn and everything we teach because we might be wrong, and we won't know for sure until after we die. Then it'll be too late to call home and straighten everything out!

Humility doesn't mean that you have to deny your faith; it just means that you should affirm your faith gently and lovingly and without judgment of others and with deep respect for the ways that other seekers make their spiritual journeys.

Community: Gathering Together

A tenet of every religion is that people are meant to be a part of a community of faith and good deeds. The Talmud shares a saying with the Masai tribe of Africa: "Sticks in a bundle are unbreakable. Sticks alone can be broken by a child." The sentiment behind this statement is that, alone, human beings are vulnerable; yet, when they are together, they have strength and purpose. Two main forms of spiritual community exist: the family and the faith community.

In the religious context, families hold a special place. They're not just procreating units; they're the foundation of religious expression. The virtue of familial love brings the ethics and rituals of religion into our lives in the most effective and powerful way. The family's mission is to do good in the world and act as a link in the chain of tradition, providing the bridge between what came before and what will come later.

All the people in the religion compose the community of faith. Its centers are houses of worship and study, but its mission is, along with families and individuals, to do the work of God or Enlightenment in the world.

- ✔ In Islam, the name for the community of all Muslims is *umma*. The umma is in itself a holy thing, transcending all divisions within Islam.

- ✔ For Catholics, the community is the Church, which transcends all cultural barriers.

- ✔ For Jews, the community is called *Am Yisrael*, or just Yisrael. Its unity is fundamental and almost organic: "All Israel are bound together one to another." Judaism takes community even into its laws about prayer, requiring a community of ten Jewish adults (men only, in Orthodox Judaism), called a *minyan*, for all formal prayer services. The overwhelming commandment is to stay a part of the Jewish community no matter what the costs: "Do not separate yourself from the community" (Mishna Avot 2.4).

- ✔ The Zoroastrian community is called the *behdinan*, or members of the good faith, bound together in the expectation that they will strive to have good thoughts, speak good words, and do good deeds to each other and to every other human.

- ✔ The Buddhist community is the *Sangha* (the community of believers), one of the Three Jewels of Buddhism (the other two being the Buddha and the Dharma, the teachings of the faith).

Some religious communities separate themselves from the general society. Groups such as Hasidic Jews, Amish Christians, some Buddhist monks, Trappist and Benedictine Catholic monks, and others choose to construct isolated religious communities that protect them from the seductions and distractions of modern society. The challenge of isolated spiritual communities is to be open to what the outside world is learning.

Most religious communities, however, try to integrate into the general culture. The challenge these communities face is to not lose their religious identity — and to keep the faith even though members spend so much time outside it.

No matter how the community structures itself, what every effective religious community offers is a life of morally acceptable spiritual purpose.

Chapter 12

Religion and Some Really Hot Ethical Issues

*R*eligion isn't just about blessings, fasting, and rituals; it's also about the big moral issues of our life and times. This chapter examines the religious responses to some of the defining moral dilemmas of our time such as abortion, euthanasia, and genetic engineering.

One concern some people have regarding religious responses to these issues is that the response is relevant only to the believers. Religious arguments against acts like abortion and euthanasia, for example, are generally based on the religious belief that God owns our bodies. This argument doesn't make much sense to people who either don't believe in God or don't believe that humans' bodies are not their own. Similarly, the idea that killing gives you bad karma for your next life doesn't make sense to folks who don't believe in reincarnation.

While the concern is a valid one to a degree, the responses of religion to the issues that humankind faces today are relevant for believers and nonbelievers alike. These views are valid, not necessarily because they're the true or the right responses, but because they're the true and right responses for millions of people, and they shape and affect the cultures in which we live. Whether you consider that a good thing or a bad thing, it's a fact.

Abortion: Who Can End a Pregnancy?

The medical arena divides abortions into three types:

- **Miscarriage:** Sometimes called spontaneous abortion, miscarriages occur when the fetus dies by natural causes. Miscarriage poses no moral issue because it's spontaneous and not the result of any human action.

- **Therapeutic abortion:** This type of abortion occurs to save the life or, in some definitions, also the health, of the mother who is at medical risk because of the pregnancy. Some religions (such as Judaism, Islam, and Zoroastrianism) approve this type of abortion, while others (such as Catholicism and many branches of Protestant Christianity, particularly evangelical Christians) oppose it. Even Catholic theology, however, which opposes therapeutic abortions to save the life of the mother, actually approves many therapeutic abortions under the Catholic doctrine of *double effect,* whereby an abortion is morally acceptable if, in trying to save the life of the mother, an abortion is produced as a side effect.

- **Elective abortion:** In this procedure, the fetus is aborted to end an unwanted pregnancy that poses no particular medical risk for the woman. This type of abortion is the focus of the huge cultural and religious debate. Elective abortion accounts for the majority of the abortions performed in the United States each year since 1973, when abortion became legal.

The focus of the debate about abortion falls on two questions:

- When is a fetus considered a person — that is, a being that possesses a soul?

- Who owns a person's body?

When is a fetus a person?

Many religions, including several Christian denominations and Islam, take the viewpoint that a fetus is a person beginning at conception and, as such, possesses basic human rights, including the right to life.

Many biblical passages not only mention fetuses, but refer to them as entities created by God:

- "Did not he who made me in the womb make them? Did not the same one form us both within our mothers?" (Job 31:15).

- "From birth I was cast upon you; from my mother's womb you have been my God" (Psalms 22:10).

✔ "For you created my inmost being; you knit me together in my mother's womb" (Psalms 139:13).

✔ "As you do not know the path of the wind, or how the body is formed in a mother's womb, so you cannot understand the work of God, the Maker of all things" (Ecclesiastes 11:5).

✔ "This is what the Lord says — he who made you, who formed you in the womb, and who will help you: Do not be afraid, O Jacob, my servant, Jeshurun, whom I have chosen" (Isaiah 44:2).

The Qur'an states that children are gifts from God, with passages such as

✔ "Kill not your children for fear of want; . . . for verily killing them is a great sin" (Qur'an 17:31).

✔ "Slay not your children for fear of poverty — We will provide for you and for them . . . and kill not the soul which Allah has made sacred . . ." (Qur'an 6:151).

Yet, medieval Muslim theologians reached a consensus that elective abortion was permissible (although not desirable) as long as the fetus wasn't fully formed, which they believed happened at 120 days after conception. After 120 days, the mother's health had to be a risk to justify abortion. In that case, the actual life of the mother takes priority over the potential life of the infant.

Even though Judaism doesn't consider the fetus to be a person *(lav nefesh hu)*, Judaism nevertheless forbids abortion unless the life of the mother is at stake. Judaism also forbids abortion, even if the mother's life is at stake if the fetus is partially delivered.

How does Judaism use pro-choice beliefs to justify pro-life conclusions? The answer is complex, but the main point is that Judaism frames the abortion question another way. The question for Judaism is not whether the fetus is or isn't a person but whether the fetus is or isn't innocent. How could the fetus be anything but innocent? According to Jewish law, anything or anyone who attacks you unjustly and threatens your life is called a pursuer *(rodef* in Hebrew). If you can't get away to safety, you are morally and religiously entitled to kill a pursuer. If the fetus is a pursuer, you can have the abortion. A fetus can be a pursuer, for example, if a pregnant woman had uterine cancer and needed chemotherapy or radiation treatment. The treatment would abort the fetus, but if the mother waits for the baby to be born before she seeks the necessary treatment, she may die. In this case, the fetus is a pursuer because it threatens the life of the mother, even though it doesn't intend to. A fetus that poses no threat to the mother's life is innocent (that is, not a pursuer), and Jewish law prohibits killing any living innocent thing *(ba'al tashchit)*.

A little misreading that led to a big question

The original Christian opposition to abortion came from a mistranslation of a verse in a passage from Exodus. In the Greek translation of the Hebrew Bible, the Hebrew word for harm *(ason)* was translated as "form," so the verse mistakenly read, "If there is no form [to the fetus], then . . . " instead of "if there is no harm to the mother . . . "

So then, a big Christian issue became determining the moment of *ensoulment,* the moment when the soul enters the body of the fetus and gives it the "form" of a human being.

Following Aristotle, many believed that the fetus had no form until 40 days for boys and 90 days for girls. This started Christianity down the road to deciding when the fetus was a person. Judaism, which had the original translation, never cared much for the debate over fetal form. Judaism tended to follow Aristotle in agreeing that the fetus was "mere water" until 40 days.

Hinduism opposes abortion because if you abort a pregnancy, you're interfering with the cycle of rebirth.

Pro-choice religious people cite a variety of texts to show that the fetus isn't a person. One of the most contentious verses is the only verse in the Bible that specifically refers to miscarriage:

"If men who are fighting hit a pregnant woman and she gives birth prematurely but there is no harm [to her], the offender must be fined whatever the woman's husband demands and the court allows. But if there is harm [to her], then you are to take life for life, eye for eye, tooth for tooth, hand for hand, foot for foot, burn for burn, wound for wound, bruise for bruise" (Exodus 21:22-25).

The point here is that, if the fetus were considered a person, then the death of the fetus described in this passage would be a capital crime. Instead, the death requires a monetary payment.

Who owns a person's body?

The view of many monotheistic faiths is that God owns our bodies; therefore, we don't have rights over something we don't own. The biblical passages that support the idea that God owns our bodies are the creation story in Genesis and this verse in Ezekiel: "All souls are mine" (18:4).

This issue doesn't affect only women (men don't own their own bodies, either), and it has ramifications beyond the abortion issue. Because of the concept that our bodies are not our own, many religions outline what is and isn't acceptable use or treatment of the body. A few religions, for example, forbid the use of contraceptives and prohibit masturbation. Abortion is simply another issue that falls within the idea that our bodies aren't our own. As a result, according to most religions, women are not the only ones who should decide whether to continue a pregnancy.

The notion of absolute personal rights over one's body is a relatively modern idea — one that pro-choice supporters, even religious pro-choice supporters, use to explain why a woman should be the one to make decisions about her body, especially in this age of equality and deeper understanding of human autonomy.

Euthanasia and Suicide: Who Can End Life?

Euthanasia comes from the Greek words meaning "good death." Nowadays, the term refers to painless death or death to end interminable and fruitless suffering. The ethical issues surrounding euthanasia involve choices between ordinary versus extraordinary treatment, voluntary versus involuntary death, and assisted suicide.

The main reason euthanasia is a big ethical concern is because of medical advances that can extend the time of a person's life without extending the quality of a person's life. Medical treatments that cannot cure but can delay and obstruct the inevitable arrival of death seem to many people a cruel form of torture.

Types of euthanasia

Euthanasia occurs in two forms: active and passive, although the line between them can get quite fuzzy:

- ✔ **Active euthanasia:** Taking a deliberate action to intentionally end a person's life at that person's request.
- ✔ **Passive euthanasia:** Withdrawing medical procedures that are not therapeutic, with the aim of letting death happen more quickly, if death is going to occur without the procedures.

Active euthanasia may involve increasing pain-killing drugs until the overdose kills the person (this is called "snowing a patient," in some hospital parlance). Passive euthanasia may involve taking a patient off a respirator.

Religious positions on euthanasia

Deliberately taking a life, even a painful one, is quite a bit different from withdrawing treatment and letting nature take its course, which, in most cases, inevitably will end in death. For these reasons, every religious tradition considers active euthanasia wrong and opposes it as murder. Passive euthanasia is another matter, one that is much harder to call.

When death is imminent

If the action involves stopping medical treatment which only purpose is to delay death and not heal, there is good religious justification for accepting that act as a moral act. Judaism, for example, specifically prohibits doing anything to hasten the death of a dying person, but it allows the removal of "obstacles to death." In one picturesque example, a woodchopper is making noise outside the room of a dying person and this noise is keeping the dying person from dying. The law is that the woodchopper must stop. From this, many rabbis have ruled that removing medical obstacles to death is also permitted.

When the quality of life is the issue

Other situations aren't so clear. What happens, for example, when a person in a persistent vegetative state will never awaken from a coma and is being fed through stomach-feeding tubes or intravenous lines. His or her condition isn't life threatening. Can you remove feeding tubes as an act of passive euthanasia, or must you continue to feed and hydrate the patient no matter what the physical condition? Some say depriving such a patient of food and water is the same as starving the person death; as such, it's active euthanasia and murder. Others say that such a person is dying and that feeding in such an unnatural way causes more pain and serves only to delay death.

Some religious traditions don't view suffering as evil, but as a test and a challenge and part of the spiritual journey of life into death. Zoroastrianism, for example, sees life as a struggle against evil. Evil is regarded as the source of pain, suffering, and death. So to take life in order to remove suffering from another or oneself is to commit a major evil action that supposedly bars the soul from heaven. Islam also is against any form of euthanasia. The reason is that all things, including disability and suffering, come from Allah. To surrender to Allah's will means to trust that he knows best and accept that which he gives you. In dealing with end-of-life issues, Muslims believe in accepting tragedy with fortitude and making the suffering person as comfortable as possible:

Calling all doctors/scientists/legal minds/ethicists

Euthanasia is an example of how ancient religions must now begin to update their moral codes to accommodate previously unimaginable circumstances. In the old days, death came early and quickly. Our modern capability of postponing death without really healing a person has complicated the old rules. The old rules are not obsolete, however. What the world needs now are new and creative religious leaders who are as well versed in modern medicine and law as they are in ancient theology.

"And no soul can die but with Allah's permission — the term is fixed" (Qur'an 3:144).

Quality-of-life arguments for euthanasia are generally outside the religious frame of moral reference. Quality of life doesn't matter to religious morality. If our lives have high quality, that's good. Nevertheless, even lives that are full of suffering and pain are still gifts from God.

Suffering, euthanasia, and Eastern religions

Buddhist literature rarely discusses euthanasia. Strong Zen traditions exist in Japan that tolerate suicide, and stories are told of how Siddhartha Gautama allowed monks to kill themselves. Theravada Buddhism in Thailand, on the other hand, appears to be decidedly against any form of euthanasia.

Hindus consider all life sacred and so would be generally against the taking of life. They argue the issue of euthanasia from the point of view of motive. Taking a life for personal gain is always wrong, but taking life out of compassion for the individual might be acceptable.

Nevertheless, many of these religious traditions see life as a journey toward enlightenment that can take several lifetimes to achieve. The primary task of these journeys is to be purified of attachments, including our attachment to such issues as quality of life.

What about suicide?

Most Western religious traditions condemn suicide for many of the same reasons they condemn active euthanasia. Taking your own life — for whatever the reason — shows lack of faith and trust in God.

In Islam, suicide is as illegal as murder. God, who alone knows the reasons for why things are the way they are, creates and owns all souls. Life is a test, and suffering has purpose, even though you may not understand what that purpose is. Besides, suicide doesn't really stop suffering; it simply compounds the problems. The reason is that, on earth, souls have less awareness of the truth; after death, however, things become more apparent. Only after death can people can fully realize how their actions hurt others. This knowledge plagues them because they are unable to make amends.

Many Christian traditions see suicide as unforgivable. The reason? Suicide is a mortal sin, that is, a sin committed deliberately and in full knowledge of the act. The only way to get back into God's good graces after you commit a mortal sin is to repent. See the problem with suicide? You can't repent because you're dead.

Nowadays, some Christian traditions, including Roman Catholicism, have softened their stance on suicide being an unforgivable sin. They use the mindset of the person to determine how responsible they are for their actions. The argument is that most people are not themselves and not in control of their actions when they become desperate enough or depressed enough to see death as the only solution. Therefore, the desperate act of suicide doesn't automatically cut people off from God's grace (but it's still a bad idea).

Genetic Engineering: Who Creates Life?

The religious command to heal is absolute and unwavering. A few Christian groups believe that transfusions of blood are a violation of the biblical commandment not to eat blood. So Christian denominations, such as Christian Science and Jehovah's Witness, refuse medical treatment. Most religious traditions, however, authorize any clinically proven application of medical science that has the chance of healing.

Seen in this light, healing by giving us a new gene to replace a defective one is no different than healing by giving us a new kidney to replace a defective kidney. The biblical commandment, *rapo yirapeh* from Exodus, "In healing you shall surely heal," refers to the ends, not the means. Religious ethics thus approve any new miracle cure, no matter how unique and different it is from the past, so long as it heals disease.

The promise and the threat

Genetic engineering holds the promise of not only coping with the symptoms of disease, but also of eliminating their causes. Gene-replacement surgery or gene therapy may some day wipe out inherited genetic diseases. The outlook for these and other such positive achievements in genetics is astounding.

On the other hand, the prospect of genetic engineering run amok confronts us with horrors that more than match the miracles of healing:

- ✔ Genetically altered bacteria could wipe out all life in the seas or on land, because nature had never evolved a defense against it.
- ✔ Genetically altered food could alter the humans who eat it.
- ✔ Genetically engineered people may, in some way, lack the mysterious element that makes people human.

In a world of unrestrained and unaccountable genetic engineering, the same science that can produce miracles of healing can also produce abominations of vanity. Cloning could produce a genetically identical version of you in every generation. Genetic counselors would meet with parents to go over all the choices about what traits they want implanted in their child (if it would be their child. After all, how many people of average size, average intelligence, and average talent could produce a child with the brain of an Einstein, the athletic ability of a Michael Jordan, and the artistic talent of a Picasso?).

Genetic engineering to protect against disease and disability (a good thing, according to most people) easily morphs into an acceptance of genetic engineering for other reasons. That easy transition is what scares people. How far down the slope can you go before you end up sliding uncontrollably to the bottom?

Ask yourself this question: "If some genetic engineer could offer my new baby an additional 20 points of intelligence, would I refuse that for my child?" Then while you're at it, why not choose the nose shape and hair color and height you prefer. Designer clothing is merely a casual arrogance, but the concept of designer babies is human arrogance gone bad.

The religious response

If you look at all the sacred texts of all the world's religions, you probably won't be surprised to discover that not one of them contains a single reference to genetic engineering! The holy books do, however, contain some suggestive passages.

In Genesis, when God makes all the living things on the earth, this is the description:

> ✔ "Then God said, 'Let the land produce vegetation: seed-bearing plants and trees on the land that bear fruit with seed in it, according to their various kinds.' And it was so" (Genesis 1:11).
>
> ✔ "So God created the great creatures of the sea and every living and moving thing with which the water teems, according to their kinds, and every winged bird according to its kind. And God saw that it was good" (Genesis 1:21).

So, what's the idea of the Creation account? Perhaps it's the ancient religious wisdom that says what God has created, we have no permission to alter, and particularly no permission to alter in ways that have nothing to do with healing and everything to do with human vanity.

Capital Punishment

Capital punishment is a tough issue for religions — and not because it pits a religious ethic against secular culture, as do the issues of abortion and homosexuality. The topic of capital punishment also isn't a recent issue, like euthanasia and genetic engineering. Capital punishment is difficult, because the religions of the world are divided about what is right.

Some religions oppose capital punishment vigorously; others endorse it vigorously. Some endorse it in theory, but in practice teach that it should never or hardly ever be done. In the case of capital punishment, you can probably find religious support for any position.

Buddhism and Hinduism employ similar reasoning for both euthanasia and capital punishment. When is it allowable to kill? In general, Hindus practice nonviolence to any living thing. Yet, if you're Hindu and a member of the warrior caste, you can — and must — kill in defense of your country and to ensure that you have a good birth in the next life. Buddhists may or may not follow the same principles; it depends on the country in which the religion is practiced and on the type of Buddhism.

In the monotheistic faiths of Judaism, Christianity, and Islam, the views on capital punishment are affected by the fact that the Hebrew Bible is clearly in favor of it. Many crimes described in the Bible are capital offenses, including working on the Sabbath and insulting one's parents. It's not clear if Sabbath violators and parent insulters were actually executed, but the message is clear:

"If there is serious injury, you are to take life for life, eye for eye, tooth for tooth, hand for hand, foot for foot, burn for burn, wound for wound, bruise for bruise" (Exodus 21:23).

The form of execution was stoning, in which the convicts were placed in a pit and the witnesses and judges threw stones at them until they died. After the biblical period, the rabbis preserved the general support of capital punishment in Judaism, but they severely limited its application. The rabbis put in rules of evidence for capital cases that made executing someone virtually impossible. For example, two witnesses had to see the crime, and they had to warn the person before he or she did it.

Note the following:

> "The judge says to the witness: Perhaps you saw a man pursuing his fellow into a ruin. You followed him and found him, sword in hand, with blood dripping from it, while the murdered man lay writhing in pain. If this is what you saw, you saw nothing" (Talmud, Sanhedrin 37b).

The writer of the Gospel of Matthew was ambivalent about the biblical laws of capital punishment. In the Sermon on the Mount, Jesus criticizes the idea of retribution:

"You have heard that it was said, 'Eye for eye, and tooth for tooth.' But I tell you, Do not resist an evil person. If someone strikes you on the right cheek, turn to him the other also. And if someone wants to sue you and take your tunic, let him have your cloak as well. If someone forces you to go one mile, go with him two miles" (Matthew 5:38-41).

Later Christian teachers such as Augustine (Letters, 133) were not as pacifist as Matthew's gospel. They allowed that the state could execute criminals in accordance with Christian law. Despite leaders such as Pope John Paul II, who has been extremely critical of capital punishment, the Catechism of the Catholic Church still states that the state has the right to punish criminals by appropriate penalties, "not excluding, in cases of extreme gravity, the death penalty." Following centuries of Church-sponsored executions of heretics, the stance of Pope John Paul II is a radical departure from past teachings and past practice.

In Islam, capital punishment is allowable for the gravest of crimes:

- Murder

- Committing adultery in public

- Attacking Islam in such a way as to harm it or the people who practice it, if the attacker is a former Muslim

In the case of murder, the victim's family gets to choose between retribution and forgiveness, and forgiveness is the preferred option. In the case of adultery, execution is rarely necessary because the act must occur in public and

GOING DEEPER

An eye for an eye: Believe it or not, it was a good thing

This passage from Exodus 21:23: ". . . if there is serious injury, you are to take life for life, eye for eye, tooth for tooth, hand for hand, foot for foot, burn for burn, wound for wound, bruise for bruise" — is widely misunderstood. It seems cruel and unjust to the modern mind, but consider the world in which it was written. This passage was a way to eliminate the escalation of blood feuds. It specifies what is adequate retribution: One life for one life, not ten for one, which then led to ten others and ten more after that. In addition, post-biblical Jewish teachers interpret the text as a guide for monetary damages, not a command to put out a man's eye if he put out yours.

be witnessed by four people. In the case of attacking the religious community, perhaps the gravest crime, the person can be forgiven if he or she repents.

In Zoroastrianism, too, capital punishment is permissible in the case of major crimes, such as murder.

Despite the general support for capital punishment in many of the world's religions, you can find many groups who reject it: Check out Soka Gakkai, a Buddhist sect, or the Quaker, Mennonite, Amish, and Bruderhof traditions.

Homosexuality and Lesbianism

No moral issue other than abortion is the source of more public debate and discussion than the issues concerning gay rights. One issue is the question of whether homosexuality and lesbianism are morally disordered states. Not every religious leader or group can agree on that. Some groups officially condemn homosexuality, while groups with other denominations support gay people.

Sacred texts and homosexuality

For the most part, the response of the world's religions is to condemn homosexuality. Some religions condemn it outright; others condemn the actions, not the orientation (in other words, you can be homosexual as long as you don't engage in homosexual activities). Because most religions see the purpose of sex as procreation rather than pleasure, homosexuality is either discouraged or condemned. Zoroastrianism, for instance, claims that the devil created homosexuality.

You can find pretty strong language and imagery in the holy books of the Western religions that makes clear — from the Christian, Jewish, and Islamic perspective at least — that homosexuality is an unnatural act.

Consider the story in Genesis 19, for example, in which Lot tries to protect the two angels from homosexual rape:

The two angels arrived at Sodom in the evening, and Lot was sitting in the gateway of the city. When he saw them, he got up to meet them and bowed down with his face to the ground. "My lords," he said, "please turn aside to your servant's house. You can wash your feet and spend the night and then go on your way early in the morning." "No," they answered, "we will spend the night in the square." However, he insisted so strongly that they did go with him and entered his house. He prepared a meal for them, baking bread without yeast, and they ate. Before they had gone to bed, all the men from every part of the city of Sodom — both young and old — surrounded the house. They called to Lot, "Where are the men who came to you tonight? Bring them out to us so that we can have sex with them." Lot went outside to meet them and shut the door behind him and said, "No, my friends. Don't do this wicked thing. Look, I have two daughters who have never slept with a man. Let me bring them out to you, and you can do what you like with them. But don't do anything to these men, for they have come under the protection of my roof" (19:1-8).

Obviously, Lot, a fairly upright man who was spared from the destruction of Sodom, finds homosexuality disturbing enough that he's willing to hand over his two daughters to the rapists, instead.

Other passages from the Old and New Testaments and the Qur'an also deal with homosexuality:

- ✔ "Do not lie with a man as one lies with a woman; that is detestable" (Leviticus 18:22).

- ✔ "Because of this, God gave them over to shameful lusts. Even their women exchanged natural relations for unnatural ones. In the same way the men also abandoned natural relations with women and were inflamed with lust for one another. Men committed indecent acts with other men, and received in themselves the due penalty for their perversion" (Romans 1:26-27).

✔ "Do you not know that the wicked will not inherit the kingdom of God? Do not be deceived: Neither the sexually immoral nor idolaters nor adulterers nor male prostitutes nor homosexual offenders nor thieves nor the greedy nor drunkards nor slanderers nor swindlers will inherit the kingdom of God" (I Corinthians 6:9-10).

✔ "But we know that the law is good, if a man use it lawfully, as knowing this, that law is not made for a righteous man, but for the lawless and unruly, for the ungodly and sinners, for the unholy and profane, for murderers of fathers and murderers of mothers, for manslayers, for fornicators, for abusers of themselves with men, for men stealers, for liars, for false swearers, and if there be any other thing contrary to the sound doctrine" (I Timothy 1:8-10).

✔ "Do you come to the males from among the creatures, and leave your wives whom your Lord has created for you? Nay, you are a people exceeding limits" (Qur'an 26:165-166).

The debate

The arguments offered in response to this univocal tradition condemning homosexuality are the following:

✔ These texts reflect primitive and incorrect understandings of human sexuality. Because homosexuality and lesbianism are natural forms of human sexuality, these old prohibitions should go the way of other foolish and damaging prohibitions against behavior that hurts no one. Bad ideas are not made better, they argue, just because they are old ideas.

✔ Gayness is not chosen but is innate. It's like being left-handed. This sexual orientation isn't the majority orientation, but it *is* normal and natural for some. How could God make something that was innate and also sinful?

✔ Gayness is a non-coercive form of real love. A truly loving God would never condemn honest consensual love between two people.

In response, those who feel that homosexuality is morally disordered make these arguments:

✔ The fact that homosexual inclinations are innate in some people doesn't prove that this inclination is morally or spiritually proper. One can have an inclination toward many morally disordered behaviors, from substance abuse to sexual attraction to children, but the innate nature of these desires doesn't give moral value to their manifestations.

✔ The fact that gay love is consensual doesn't make it holy or morally proper. Adultery can be consensual, and it's wrong. Incest between adult

> parents and adult children can be consensual, and it's wrong. Agreeing to have sex does not mean that the agreement is worthy of sanctification or moral approval.

> ✔ The heterosexual family is not an arbitrary cultural phenomenon. Men marry women, and women marry men to create families. Such unions can produce children, reduce promiscuous behavior, and provide both with male and female models of parenting.

The situation today: Not black and white

Hardly a week goes by that newspapers don't have some story or feature related to same-sex relationships and religion. When Disney decided to offer benefits to same-sex couples, for example, the social statement implied by Disney's actions upset many people. Other groups applauded what they considered a progressive and courageous act.

Episcopalians were the first denomination to ordain a practicing gay woman, and Reform Judaism ordains openly gay rabbis. Methodists and Presbyterians are considering whether or not to ordain gays. For years, Dignity/USA, a Catholic lay movement, has supported gay Catholics with the same types of rituals that are found in Roman Catholic churches. Obviously, this roiling debate has strong advocates — religious and secular — on both sides.

Separation of Church and State

The separation of church and state is primarily an American construction, grounded in the first amendment to the U.S. constitution:

> Congress shall make no law respecting an establishment of religion, or prohibiting the free exercise thereof; or abridging the freedom of speech, or of the press; or the right of the people peaceably to assemble, and to petition the government for a redress of grievances.

Despite its majority Christian population and its traditional fondness for prayers, the United States has a long (albeit imperfect) history of religious tolerance. Within the United States, the issues of religion-and-state separation revolve around issues such as prayer in school, funding for parochial schools, and, most recently, the state support of faith-based charities.

In general, members of religions that have experienced the most persecution at the hands of unfriendly governments (such as Jews, the Baha'i Faith,

Latter-day Saints, and Quakers) are most in favor of strict separation. Those religions that are in the majority — or that most feel the need for state support of their educational institutions — are usually in favor of a more loose definition of the separation doctrine of the First Amendment.

Although many countries have state-sponsored religions, perhaps the religion least inclined to buy into the American insistence on separation of church and state is Islam. With the exception of Turkey, and, to a lesser extent, Iraq and Syria, there are really no examples of completely secular Muslim countries. Yet, only a few Muslim countries such as Saudi Arabia and Iran actually use religious law as the national legal system. The generally widespread closeness between religion and politics is based on injunctions in the Qur'an and the *hadith* (or traditions) that Muslims should create societies whose moral structure are modeled after the community that developed during the prophet Muhammad's lifetime In this way, Islam is almost inseparably linked with politics and government.

Part V
All (Other) Things Holy

The 5th Wave   By Rich Tennant

"You don't have to tell me the kitchen's a spiritual center of the house. God knows I pray for a good matzo kugel every Passover."

In this part . . .

Religions accept two realities: that which we can see and that which we can access only through spiritual discipline and insight. How separate these realities are depends on the religion. In Native American faiths, for example, that which we see — the physical earth — is itself holy. In other religions, like many Eastern religions, all that we see is illusion; the "real" reality is an entity or prime force beyond the illusion, the understanding of which we can achieve only through enlightenment.

No matter how far away the ultimate reality is, all religions offer ways in which the devout can encounter it or get a glimpse of its splendor. In this regard, all religions consider certain things holy — that is, divine, or so close to the Divine that they deserve special reverence. What's holy? Locations, people, books, certain animals, you name it. Moreover, some religions probably consider these things sacred.

Chapter 13

Holy Books

• •

In This Chapter

▶ Keying into the karma of Hindu holy text

▶ Telling Tao tales

▶ Looking into Buddhist sacred text

▶ Understanding what Confucius really said

▶ Getting to know the Hebrew and Christian Bibles

▶ Finding out about the Qur'an

▶ Making the sign of the Z: Zoroastrianism

▶ Exploring Sikhism's Adi Granth

▶ Delving into the Book of Mormon

▶ Investigating indigenous writings

• •

The assortment of sacred texts or holy books available for study reflects the diversity of the world religions. All these texts and myriad other texts provide the core teachings of their respective religious traditions. These writings convey the beliefs, the rituals, and the ethics that make the religion what it is.

Consider just a few of the many sacred texts that exist:

✔ The Adi Granth in Sikhism

✔ The Book of Certitude in Baha'i

✔ The Digambara Canons in Jainism

✔ The Five Classics in Confucianism

✔ The New Testament and (for Mormons only) the Book of Mormon in Christianity

✔ The Qur'an in Islam

✔ The Torah and Talmud in Judaism

✔ The Vedas in Hinduism

Hindu Holy Books

Hinduism's sacred texts include the Vedas, Upanishads, Bhagavad-Gita, Mahabharata, and Ramayana. These scriptures are divided into two categories:

- *Shruti* **(that which is heard):** Shruti literature came from sages (called *rishis*) who were said to have written down the texts without any changes whatsoever from their eternal form; in other words, these texts were *revealed* as opposed to being created. The Vedas, including the Upanishads texts, are the most important examples of shruti.

- *Smriti* **(that which is remembered)** The smriti are those stories, legends, and laws that were written down but not specifically revealed. The smriti have come to represent an oral tradition of law and social customs of Hinduism. The three most important works of smriti literature are the Mahabharata, the Bhagavad-Gita (which is actually contained within the Mahabharata), and the Ramayana.

The Vedas

Hinduism includes four official Vedas. The oldest and most prominent is the Rig-Veda, or songs of knowledge. The Rig-Veda contains more than 1,000 hymns. In general, each hymn is addressed to gods such as Indra, the warrior who overcame the power of evil, or Agni, the god of fire who linked earth and heaven.

The Rig-Veda teaches that life is illusory, fleeting, and has no meaning without sacrifice. It also introduces the most important social element of Hindu tradition, the caste system. When the Aryans, a conquering people from the north who brought the Vedic literature with them, came to India, they introduced the caste system that had just four divisions at first.

The Law Code of Manu explains the duties of the castes:

- **Brahmin:** The priests and scholars
- **Kshatriya:** The warriors and rulers
- **Vaisya:** The tradespeople, merchants, and farmers
- **Sudra:** The laborers and serfs, artisans, and slaves.

Later, another group, the Unscheduled Castes (formerly called the untouchables) was introduced.

In addition to the Rig-Veda, the other Vedas are

✔ The Sama Veda, which concentrates on the divine chants.

✔ The Yajur Veda, which speaks of the sacrificial rituals.

✔ The Atharva Veda, which focuses on the incarnations.

The Upanishads, known as the mystery writings, are also classified as Vedic literature.

The Upanishads

The Upanishads, written around 600 B.C.E., recount the oral teachings of Hindu sages. These teachings reach back to about 1000 B.C.E. The teaching based on the Upanishads is called Vedanta (end of the Vedas) and is the central theological teaching of Hinduism.

The Upanishads deal with the nature of ultimate reality and speculate on the relationship between the individual soul (*atman*) and the soul of the ultimate reality and god of the universe, Brahman. The nature of reincarnation and the nature of creation are also primary themes of the Upanishads.

The Mahabharata

The Mahabharata, often called the fifth Veda, is a huge epic of 110,000 couplets that recounts the war between the Pandavas, a family that symbolizes the spirits of goodness, and the Kauravas, who symbolize evil. Unlike the other Vedas that primarily focused on the importance of sacrificial ritual, the Mahabharata promoted *bhakti* (devotion to the lord.) In addition, unlike the Vedas, the Mahabharata was meant to be heard by all people, the rich and the poor, men and women alike. Book six of the Mahabharata is the Bhagavad-Gita.

The Bhagavad-Gita

Considered the highlight of smriti literature, the Bhagavad-Gita includes a famous dialog between Krishna, an avatar who is an incarnation of Vishnu (the Hindu god who protects and preserves) and Arjuna, a warrior prince.

Krishna appears on earth at intervals to fight evil (kind of like Superman without the cape). In this story, he is Arjuna's good friend and charioteer. Krishna tries to convince Arjuna that going to battle against the evil opposition is wise. Arjuna's refusal to fight is based on compassion and grief. As a warrior, his place in society is to wage war, which will help him to have a better birth in the next life. However, as the warriors line up on the battle-field, he sees members of his own family on the enemy side. Hence, his dilemma: to choose for himself, his family, or the gods. Arjuna argues that going to battle would destroy the family and hurt his cousins. Krishna argues that the more noble action is to dispassionately perform his duty with faith and without desire for personal gain. Arjuna finally comes to see the wisdom of Krishna's argument and agrees to fight.

The Ramayana

The Ramayana is one of the most popular Hindu poems. Composed originally in Sanskrit, probably around 300 B.C.E., it tells the life story of Prince Rama:

> In the country of Ayodhya, Prince Rama is exiled to the forest because of the jealousy of the evil Queen Kaikeyi (Rama's stepmother) who was one of King Dasharatha's (Rama's father) three wives. Prince Rama's beautiful wife, Princess Sita, and his half-brother, Lakshmana, insist on joining him in his exile. The evil Kaikeyi asks King Dasharatha to make *her* son, Bharata, king and to continue Rama's exile for 14 years. The king, heart-broken, gives in to Kaikeyi's wish: He makes Bharata the king and then dies.

> Meanwhile, back in the forest, the demon king Ravana abducts Sita and carries her off to Lanka (Sri Lanka, formerly Ceylon). Rama, with the help of a friendly army of monkeys, attacks Lanka, rescues Sita, and kills the demon king, Ravana. Rama becomes king, but rumors persist that Sita did not remain faithful while in the demon king's domain. Even though Rama believes that Sita was chaste, he exiles her from the kingdom and back into the forest, where she meets Valmiki (the guy reputed to be the author of the poem) and gives birth to Rama's twin sons. The family is eventually reunited when the sons come of age, but, still plagued by rumors of infidelity, Sita asks the earth to swallow her. It does, and the story ends.

The point of the story is that doing the right thing in accordance with the law (dharma) is often painful and self-sacrificial, but it's still the right thing to do.

Tao Holy Books

Founded more than 2,000 years ago, Taoism advocates simplicity and self-lessness in conformity with the Tao, the organizing principle of the universe. According to the law of Tao (literally, the Way), everything reverts to its start-ing point, and the whole is contained in its parts. The way to tranquility is to allow the Tao to flow unchallenged, moving everything from a state of nonbe-ing to being to nonbeing. The sacred texts of Taoism include the Tao Te Ching, Chuang Tzu, and the Tsai Chih Chung.

The Tao Te Ching

The Tao Te Ching is more a philosophical text than a religious text. Although the great Taoist teacher Lao-Tzu, who was a contemporary of Confucius in the sixth century B.C.E., is the one who gets the credit for writing Tao Te Ching, no one really knows whether he was the actual author. The entire book has fewer than 6,000 words, but that doesn't make it easy reading: The text is cryptic and metaphorical. (For more information about Lao-Tzu, see Chapter 14.)

The Tao Te Ching was essentially a guidebook for Chinese rulers. According to the work, the way to rule effectively is to follow the idea of nonassertive action — basically, action in inaction. According to the Tao Te Ching, actively not acting can be even more effective than running around like a chicken with its head cut off. It teaches this lesson through paradoxes: the way to advance, for example, is to yield.

Themes central to the work include:

✔ **The idea of the Tao:** The Tao (pronounced *dow*) is the unchanging principle of the universe. Our role as human beings is to find a way to live in harmony with the Tao. Doing so means that we will also live in harmony with other people and nature.

✔ **The idea of the Te:** The Te is not the Tao; it's the power of the Tao, the unconscious functioning of the physical self. By being in tune to the Te, you can live in harmony with the forces of nature.

✔ **The concept of yin-yang:** Yin and yang are the two complementary (that is, opposing) forces of existence. Yin is female, passive, dark, absorbing, and sustaining. It is conceived of as the earth. Yang is dominant, male, light, heat, and penetrating. It is conceived of as heaven. These two elements, together, form all life and all phenomena.

The Tao Te Ching urges people to follow Nature, not the structures of society, arguing against the strict code of order that is found in the Confucian Analects.

Chuang Tzu

Chuang Tzu was both a person and the name of the book he wrote. Chuang Tzu lived from 369-286 B.C.E. in China. His work is more personal and less political than the Tao Te Ching. The book continues the idea of the Tao as a creative force and unifying Way of the universe.

The Tao, according to Chuang Tzu, is a force we must feel and know by intuition, not think or seek to describe. The *Chuang Tzu* urges yielding and encourages personal mysticism and reflection and creative inaction. Instead of filling the mind with ideas, the *Chuang Tzu* asserts, the Tao can best be found by emptying the mind.

Sacred Writings of Buddhism

Buddhism has two primary schools of thought. The Theravadan form, known as the doctrine of the elders, is practiced in Burma, Sri Lanka, Thailand, Cambodia, Vietnam, and Laos. This form emphasizes the role of the individual in transforming the universe. In order to do this, the person must arrive at wisdom; gain insight into the nature of reality, the causes of anxiety and suffering; and achieve the awareness that everything is an illusion.

The Mahayana form of Buddhism is practiced in Nepal, China, Tibet, Korea, and Japan. This Buddhist sect believes that we are not alone in this world but that we are helped in our spiritual journey by bodhisattvas. (A bodhisattva is a semi-divine being who voluntarily renounces nirvana to return to the earth to help others attain salvation.) The goal of every Buddhist is to be a person of compassion. This quality is not automatic but must be cultivated by connecting with a bodhisattva.

The sacred texts of Buddhism include

- **The Tripitaka:** The Tripitaka, literally "three baskets," is the collection of Buddhist scriptures most important in the Theravadan branch of Buddhism. Compiled between 500 B.C.E. (the time of the Buddha) and the beginning of the Common Era, the Tripitaka contains three divisions, or baskets:

  - *Vinaya Pitaka:* This division contains the rules, regulations, and disciplinary codes for life in a Buddhist monastery.

  - *Sutta Pitaka:* The second division includes the stories of the life and teachings (dharma) of Siddhartha Gautama (the first Buddha).

  - *Abhidhamma Pitaka:* The third basket is an ancient dictionary that defines religious terms and discusses elements of existence and causal relationships.

- **The Dhammapada:** The Dhammapada is an anthology of Buddhist proverbs and maxims that present the teachings of another Buddhist sect, Theravadan Buddhism. Its message is spiritual in nature and defines the right path to wisdom as the enlightened path for existence in this transitory world.

- **The Siksha Samukhya:** The Siksha Samukhya present sutras (the scriptural words of Buddha) written by Santideva, who, like Buddha, renounced the world. Santideva embraced the Mahayana form of Buddhism.

- **Mahayana texts:** Some of the most popular include the Tibetan Book of the Dead, the Translation of the Word of the Buddha, the Translation of the Treatises, the Great Scripture Store (Chinese), the Lotus Sutra, and the Heart Sutras.

Buddhist scriptures reflect the personality of the Buddha: Blessed in life to live in a protected environment, he chose to leave the security of his family life to search for the inner meaning of life. He believed that life had deeper questions, which only could be answered over time and with the person's willingness to search within. When Buddha saw the unhappiness in life, he came to see that suffering could be relieved only by understanding that so much of life is an illusion and that we are all on a journey toward completion. When Buddha attained enlightenment, he sought to pass it on to his disciples. His scriptures reflect the story of the man, but more importantly, the path to nirvana and freedom from suffering. (For more information about Buddha, see Chapter 14.)

Confucian Texts

Confucius (551-479 B.C.E.) considered himself the transmitter of the wisdom of the ancients. He established a religion and a reputation that is recognized throughout the world. Today, the name Confucius is synonymous with the terms *master teacher, philosopher,* and *sage.* (Head to Chapter 14 for details about his life.)

His idea? That humankind could be perfected through the cultivation of the mind. His teachings emphasized devotion to parents and rituals, learning, self-control, and just social activity.

The authoritative texts of Confucianism are the Five Classics (Wu-Ching) and the Four Books (Ssu-Shu).

The Five Classics (Wu-Ching)

The Five Classics are five ancient books that, for 2,000 years, were considered the definitive authorities on Chinese law, education, social structure, literature, and religion.

The Five Classics consist of the following:

- **The Book of History (Shu-Ching):** Written during the Han dynasty (23-220 C.E.), this book describes events dating back to the third millennium B.C.E. Contained within the Shu-Ching are the rules and stories of both wise and wicked rulers of past dynasties. It also includes theories of why heaven supported the sagely rulers and opposed the wicked rulers.

- **The Book of Songs/Poetry (Shih-Ching):** The Book of Songs contains more than 300 songs and poems, some dating back to 1000-500 B.C.E.

✔ **The Book of Rites (Li-Chi):** This describes Chinese religious practices from the eighth to the fifth century B.C.E.

✔ **Book of Changes (I-Ching):** Dating back to approximately 3000 B.C.E., making it one of the oldest sacred texts, the I-Ching contains 64 symbolic hexagrams (see the example in Figure 13-1), that, if properly interpreted and understood, offer insight into human behavior. The I-Ching is recognized as one of the most popular of the holy books of the Eastern religions.

✔ **The Book of Spring and Autumn (Ch'un Ch'iu):** A chronology, compiled between 722-481 B.C.E., of Confucius' home state of Lu. Confucius may have actually dictated this book.

The Four Books (Ssu-Shu)

Each of the books that compose the Four Books existed independently years before being published as a unit in 1190. Knowing this material served as the basis for civil service examines in China for hundreds of years, until the early twentieth century.

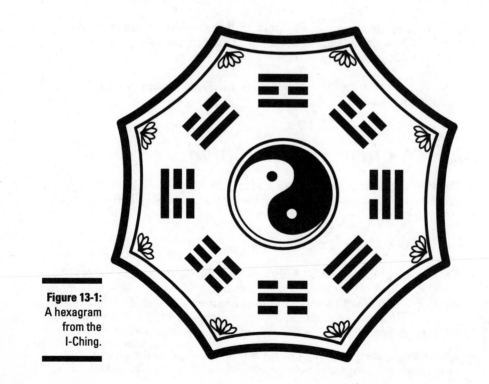

Figure 13-1:
A hexagram
from the
I-Ching.

Great Learning (Ta-Hseuh)

Written between 500-200 B.C.E., the Ta-Hseuh is a book of instruction about how to conduct the rituals properly. Its main message is that the ruler's integrity has a direct effect on government.

Doctrine of the Mean (Chung-Yung)

The most mystical of the Confucian works, Chung-Yung emphasizes the Way toward the realization of *chun tzu* (the perfectly cultivated self).

Analects (Lun Yu)

The Analects are a collection of Confucius' sayings, compiled by his disciples more than 70 years after his death. This collection is a significant part of the Four Books. In addition to including main ideas of Confucian thought — perpetuation of culture, respectful conduct of affairs, loyalty to superiors, and keeping of promises — the Analects also include glimpses of Confucius' life, as related by his disciples.

The Book of Mencius (Meng-Tzu)

Mencius is considered one of the most renowned Confucian scholars. In the Meng-Tzu, Mencius asserts that righteousness is more important than life itself. One of the strongest interpretations of Confucius' teachings, Mencius believed that people could achieve the Way only through constant self-refinement or self-cultivation.

Shinto Texts

Shinto (known as following the way of kami, or the gods) is the religious tradition indigenous to Japan. It intertwines with Confucianism and Buddhism to mold Japan's culture, ethics, and philosophy about life and death. Shinto emphasizes *makoto,* meaning the completeness that an individual achieves through inner harmony and sincerity. (For more details about kami, see Chapter 9.)

Although Shinto doesn't have a comprehensive scripture or canon, specific rituals do appear in a Shinto mythological works, including the following:

- ✔ **The Kojiki (Records of Ancient Matters):** This work was completed in 712 C.E., and it includes a wide range of stories about the various Shinto deities, ranging from their births to their battles and deaths. The first part of the Kojiki includes the story, "The Beginning of Heaven and Earth." In this mythological tale of the kami, Shinto followers learn of the births of the five heavenly deities.

With its myriad of deities, virtually one for every natural object and phenomena, such as the sun, the wind, fire, the mountains, rivers, and trees, the kami are often referred to as a collective whole in Shinto rituals and writings.

✔ **The Nihon Shoki (Chronicles of Japan):** This work continues the documentation of Shinto mythology and rituals begun in the Kojiki. Completed in 720 C.E., this book records the role of the kami in creating Japan and the Japanese imperial lineage. As written in the Nihon Shoki, the divine pair Izanagi and Izanami brought forth Amaterasu, the sun goddess and ancestress of the Japanese emperor. Her symbol is the sun, which was consequently placed on the Japanese flag.

In addition to the Shinto classics outlined in the preceding list, later sources (from the Kamakura period to the present) of Shinto rituals and practices are found in the poetry and stories by Shinto priests and scholars. A well-known example of Shinto poetry is the Man'yoshu, a collection of poems written during the Nara period (700-1150 C.E.).

Jain Holy Books

Jainism is an Indian religion that dates back at least to the sixth century B.C.E., and perhaps as far back as 1500 B.C.E. According to Jain tradition, Jain teachings began during the prehistory of this cosmic age. Contained within the sacred text of Jainism is the story of the evolution of the Jain tradition through a series of 24 Tirthankaras ("makers of the river crossing" or "the highest level of liberated souls"). Mahavira was the last in this series of Tirthankaras, and he is viewed as the official founder of the formalized Jain religion. (For more information about Mahavira, see Chapter 14.)

The sacred writings are found in the Jain Canon, and they are called the Agamas (traditions). The sacred Canon was handed down orally in the monastic communities; it wasn't until about 500 C.E. that someone actually wrote down the sacred text.

In the fifth century C.E., the Jains split into the two branches: the Svetambara branch and the Digambara branch. These groups share many of the same sacred texts, but each branch preserved a different version of the Canon:

✔ **The Svetambara Canon,** collected in the sixth century, C.E., consists of 45 books, the oldest of which are the 11 Angas (limbs), believed to be the teachings of Mahavira. The Angas include dialogs between Mahavira and one of his disciples. Another disciple recorded these conversations, thus preserving them for future generations.

> ✔ **The Digambara Canon,** according to Jain tradition, is based on a group of writings that sages composed centuries after Mahavira's death. Two of the most important of these writings are the Prakrit Karmaprabhrita (the chapters on karma — an individual's karmic substance is formed on the consequences of an individual's actions and is then mixed with his soul substance, or *jiva*) and the Kasayaprabhrita (chapters on the passions). These writings date back to the second or third centuries C.E.

Reinforced throughout all Jain sacred literature is the understanding that the Jain community is based on the monastic life. Jains practice nonviolence, honesty, and celibacy, and moving beyond the attachments and hatreds of this world. To be a Jain is to accept and practice the Three Jewels *(ratna-traya)* of right belief, right knowledge, and right conduct.

The Hebrew Bible

The Hebrew Bible contains the story of how God created the world and how a group of people came to know and love their God. Written in Hebrew, the Hebrew Bible is called the tanakh, an acronym made up of the first letter of the three sections of the Hebrew Bible: The Torah (t); the prophets, nevi'im (n); and the writings, Ketuvim, (k).

Some people call the Hebrew Bible the Old Testament — a name that makes sense only for those who accept the New Testament (the Christian holy book) as divinely revealed, which Jews do not. In addition, in Christian printings of the Hebrew Bible (called the Old Testament), Prophets appears as the third section and not the second. The reason is that Christians believe that the Hebrew prophets include a foretelling of the coming of Jesus. Jews don't believe any such references exist.

Part 1: The Pentateuch, or the Torah

The Hebrew Bible begins with the Pentateuch, or the Torah. (It's also called the *humash,* or the Five Books of Moses.) The Pentateuch covers history from the time of Abraham, whom Jews consider to be the first Jew, to the end of Jewish Exodus from Egypt and entry into the promised land of Canaan, which occurred in roughly around 1200 B.C.E.

Probably edited and put in written form around the time of King David (1000 B.C.E.), the Pentateuch consists of five books (hence the name Pentateuch):

> ✔ **Genesis:** Genesis includes the creation story and, in addition to other stories, the tale of the life and times of Adam and Eve. The longest story in Genesis is the story of Joseph and his brothers.

- ✔ **Exodus:** Exodus tells the story of the liberation of the Israelites from Egypt by God through Moses, and the years they spent wandering in the desert.

- ✔ **Leviticus and Numbers:** Leviticus and Numbers have fewer stories and more laws that describe the sacrificial offerings and the Jewish priesthood that administered the rituals of Judaism in biblical times.

- ✔ **Deuteronomy:** Deuteronomy picks up the narrative again, repeats the Ten Commandments and several laws, and describes the final entry into the land of Canaan and the death of Moses, the only prophet who, according to the tradition, spoke to God directly and not through visions or dreams. (For more information about Moses, see Chapter 14.)

Part 2: Prophets, or Nevi'im

The second part of the Hebrew Bible is called Nevi'im, Prophets. This section includes the historical books of Joshua, Judges, 1 and 2 Samuel, and 1 and 2 Kings. The text then turns to the major prophets:

- ✔ **Jeremiah:** Prophet who preached that divine justice is inescapable and warned Jews against rejecting God.

- ✔ **Isaiah:** Prophet who believed that the covenant between Israel and God was contingent on the people's conduct. He warned the Israelites that their misbehavior had broken the covenant and that God would punish them through a human agent, specifically a conqueror.

- ✔ **Ezekiel:** Prophet whose early statements warned of the destruction of Judah but whose later statements foretold of a new covenant that God would make with the restored house of Israel.

Prophets wraps up with the minor prophets including:

- ✔ Hosea (last king of Israel)
- ✔ Amos (the prophet of doom)
- ✔ Jonah (of whale fame)
- ✔ Zephaniah (who proclaimed the approaching divine judgment)
- ✔ Zechariah (who urged the Jews to rebuild the Temple of Jerusalem).
- ✔ Joel (who urges people to repent)
- ✔ Obadiah (who foretold of the destruction of the Edomites)
- ✔ Micah (who predicted the fall of Samaria and the destruction of Judah)
- ✔ Nahum (who predicted the fall of Nineveh, the capital of the Assyrian empire)
- ✔ Habakkuk (who predicted the coming Babylonian invasion)

✔ Haggai (who encouraged exiles to return to rebuild the Temple of Jerusalem)

✔ Malachi (who rebuked the returning exiles for doubting God's love)

Part 3: Writings, or Ketuvim

The third part of the Hebrew Bible is called Ketuvim (writings), and it includes a variety of miscellaneous books:

✔ **Psalms:** Includes 150 psalms (sacred songs or poems), making this the biggest section of the Ketuvim.

✔ **Proverbs:** Contains sayings attributed to Solomon and others.

✔ **Job:** Contains the story of Job, a man who didn't lose faith in God, despite his great suffering.

✔ **Song of Songs** (also called the Song of Solomon): Contains a love poem, traditionally attributed to Solomon, the king of Israel who built the first Temple of Jerusalem.

✔ **Ruth:** Tells the story of Ruth, a widow devoted to her mother-in-law, Naomi.

✔ **Lamentations:** Includes lamentations regarding the destruction of Jerusalem.

✔ **Ecclesiastes:** A book of teachings.

✔ **Esther:** Tells the story of Esther, who saved her people from slaughter.

✔ **Daniel:** Contains stories and prophecies of Daniel, the Hebrew prophet whose faith saved him in the lions' den.

✔ **Ezra:** Contains the life story and teaching of Ezra, a Hebrew prophet and religious reformer.

✔ **Nehemiah:** Recounts the work of Nehemiah, a Hebrew leader during the fifth century.

✔ **Chronicles I and II:** Books of history.

The Christian Bible

Christians believe that Jesus is an incarnation of God as man. He was born into a Jewish family and lived as a Jew his whole life. The Christian Bible includes the Old Testament, the New Testament, and additional works. The New Testament is the main sacred text of Christianity; it records the stories about Jesus' ministry, what he said, what he did, and how he became Messiah, Lord, and Savior.

The four Gospels

The New Testament begins with the four Gospels (gospel means "good news"): Matthew, Mark, Luke, and John.

The Gospel of Matthew

Matthew was one of the Twelve Apostles and, according to Christian tradition, he was the one who wrote the Gospel of Matthew. The gospel is written to Jewish-Christian communities in an environment that was predominantly Jewish.

In this gospel, Matthew portrays Jesus as the new Moses — the teacher and lawgiver. It also includes the Beatitudes, which resemble the Ten Commandments in that they contain guidelines as to how to live. They call Christians to work on humility, peacefulness, and prayerfulness, and the willingness to fast, to mourn, and to undergo persecution.

The Gospel of Mark

No one really knows the identity of the writer of the Gospel of Mark. He isn't mentioned in the list of the disciples. In addition, other references to Mark (such as a John-Mark in Acts of the Apostles and another Mark in Paul's letters) don't shed much light on the matter. According to an early church writer, however, Mark followed Peter, one of Jesus' disciples, and copied down Peter's words. Those are the words contained in the Gospel of Mark.

The Gospel of Mark has a different audience than the Gospel of Matthew. Some suggest that Mark wrote to a Latin community, gearing the text to the gentile, that is, the non-Jewish, community, whose members struggled with the idea of following Jesus because he was a Jew.

The Gospel of Luke

A person who never met Jesus wrote the Gospel of Luke. Luke portrays Jesus as prayerful, as a natural teacher, and as someone devoted to the salvation of all people. His gospel is particularly partial to women, and of all the gospel writers, Luke most completely portrays Jesus as one who uses parables, that is, stories with a meaning, to reach his audience.

The Gospel of John

According to Christian tradition, John was one of the first of Jesus' disciples. His gospel, the Gospel of John, is written differently than the other Gospels. It is more poetic and symbolic than the other gospels, and it portrays Jesus as pre-existent and divine. Jesus is the *logos,* that is, the word. Jesus was present with God at the creation of the world and chose to come on earth in human form so that he could redeem humankind. Jesus is the bread of life (John 6), the light of the world (John 8), the good shepherd (John 10), the way, the truth, and the life (John 14).

For John, disciples are called to believe in Jesus with their entire mind, heart, and soul. Through this belief, they will obtain eternal life.

Other stuff in the New Testament

In addition to the four Gospels, the New Testament also contains the following:

- ✔ **The Acts of the Apostles:** Stories about the beginnings of Christianity.

- ✔ **Epistles:** Twenty-one letters attributed to Peter, Paul, James, John, Jude, and others. These writings address specific spiritual and social problems in the early Christian community.

- ✔ **The Book of Revelation:** Stories about the end of time. It was written during a period of time in which the early Christian community was undergoing persecution for faith. The book is filled with symbolism, dream sequences, and visions, which remind those being persecuted that their suffering will end soon and that a new life with God will bring peace for all eternity.

But wait! There's more!

The Christian Bible also includes elements for which authorship is fuzzy enough to put it into a different category, called *apocrypha*. The word apocrypha means hidden. Many biblical scholars suggest that the apocryphal books have been hidden or withdrawn from mainstream use because the text is viewed as containing mysterious or esoteric lore. Biblical scholars continue to explore the question of whether or not apocryphal books contain heretical writing.

Hebrew Apocrypha

The Hebrew Apocrypha adds 15 books to the Bible that the original Hebrew canon didn't contain. The Hebrew Apocryphal books are as follows:

- ✔ **Tobit:** Tells the story of Tobit, a Hebrew captive in Nineveh.

- ✔ **Judith:** Tells the story of Judith, a Jewish woman who saved her people by killing Holofernes, a general in Nebuchadnezzar's army.

- ✔ **The Additions to the Book of Esther:** Provides more info on the biblical Esther.

- ✔ **The Wisdom of Solomon:** Additional works attributed to Solomon.

- ✔ **Ecclesiastes:** A book of proverbs.

- ✔ **Baruch:** Book attributed to Baruch, Jeremiah's scribe.

- ✔ **The Letter of Jeremiah:** Warns the exile Jews against worshipping idols.

- ✔ **The Prayer of Azariah and the Song of the Three Jews:** Tells of three young men who are thrown into a fiery furnace. Their actions (prayer by one of the three men, Azariah, and praise from all three, glorifying God) lead an angel to save them.

- ✔ **Susanna:** Tells the story of Susanna, a woman falsely accused of adultery.

- ✔ **Bel and the Dragon:** The prophet Daniel has a hand in destroying two Babylonian idols, Bel and a great dragon.

- ✔ **1 and 2 Maccabees:** Tells of the successful revolt against the Syrians by the Maccabees, a family of Jewish patriots, who later ruled Palestine.

- ✔ **1 and 2 Esdras:** Tells more about Ezra, the Hebrew scribe and prophet.

- ✔ **The Prayer of Manasseh:** Book attributed to Manasseh, a seventh-century king of Judah

In addition to the preceding books, the Eastern Orthodox religions accept 3 Maccabees, 4 Maccabees, and Psalm 151.

At the end of the fourth century, Pope Damasus commissioned Jerome, the most learned biblical scholar available, to prepare a Latin version of the scriptures. Jerome followed the Hebrew canon and then added a second category for the apocryphal books. Subsequent copyists weren't always careful in indicating that these books were additional works. This uncertainty was clarified at the Council of Trent in 1546 C.E. when the Western church included the apocryphal books in the Old Testament. The reformers, known as Protestants, stuck by the Hebrew canon.

Christian Apocrypha

In addition to the Hebrew Apocryphal books, Christian Apocryphal books have also been discovered. These books present information about the beliefs and practices found in the various movements of early Christianity.

Some of the Christian Apocryphal books are the following:

- ✔ **Infancy Gospels:** These include the Gospel of James, the Infancy Gospel of Thomas, Arabic Gospel of the Infancy, and the History of Joseph the Carpenter.

- ✔ **The Passion Gospels:** These include the Gospel of Peter, the Gospel of Nicodemus, the Gospel of Bartholomew, the Book of John the Evangelist, and the Assumption of the Virgin.

- ✔ **The Acts:** These include the Acts of John, Acts of Paul, Acts of Peter, Acts of Andrew, Acts of Thomas, and Acts of Philip.

- ✔ **The Epistles:** These include the Epistle of Abgar, Epistle to the Laodiceans, Paul and Seneca, and the Epistle of the Apostles.

- ✔ **The Sayings Gospels:** These include the Gospel of Thomas and the Nag Hammadi manuscripts.

The Christian church never accepted any of these Apocryphal books as canonical. However, it is interesting to note that 3 Maccabees contains teachings such as the Doctrine of Purgatory and the Efficacy of Prayers and Masses for the Dead. The important thing about the Apocrypha is that these books fill in the religious climate of the roughly 300 years between the end of the Hebrew Bible at about 250 B.C.E. and the beginning of the New Testament at about 50 C.E. They show us a time of deep turmoil and religious conflict. There was a strong tradition at the time that the world was coming to an end and that a great battle between good and evil would occur.

Islam: The Qur'an

The Qur'an, which is an Arabic word meaning "the recitation," contains words that the prophet Muhammad received from Allah through the angel Gabriel. Not inspired, written, or created, the Qur'an is, according to Muslims, the actual transcribed word of God in God's own language — Arabic. In that way, the Qur'an is perfect in form and content. As such, it is different from the holy books of other religions that were created by human authors. Muhammad's own writings and teachings are in the hadith. (For more information about Muhammad, see Chapter 14.)

Basic structure

The prophet Muhammad received the Qur'an in bits and pieces over a period of 23 years. By the time it was complete, the Qur'an contained 114 surahs or chapters of varying length. The surahs are not arranged in the order in which Muhammad received them. With the exception of the first surah, "The Opening," the other surahs are arranged from longest to shortest. This arrangement, however, is believed to be deliberate and divinely directed.

Each surah contains verses, or *ayat* (meaning signs), and all but one surah (the ninth) begins with the words "In the name of Allah, the Most Beneficent, the Most Merciful . . . " called the Bismallah. In addition, each surah deals with a particular topic, revealed through the surah's title.

The first surah, called the al Fatihah (The Opening) is beautiful; its simple eloquence contains the essence of Islam. It is used in daily prayers and at many religious moments: "In the name of Allah, the Most Beneficent, the Most Merciful. Praise be to Allah, the Lord of the Worlds, the Beneficent, the Merciful, Master of the Day of Requital. Thee do we serve, and Thee do we beseech for help. Guide us on the right path, The path of those upon whom Thou hast bestowed favors, Not those upon whom wrath is brought down, nor those who go astray."

Main theological points

The Qur'an, written in Arabic and approximately the same length as the New Testament, provides the guidelines for living a life that is pleasing to Allah. By following the straight path — submitting your life and will to Allah — believers grow closer to God.

To understand the Qur'an you need to understand the Islamic interpretations of God, creation, the human self, the Day of Judgment, and more. These ideas combine with the guidelines for living (the Five Pillars of Islam) and are explored within the Qur'an's many surahs:

- ✔ **The nature of God:** Allah, as the creator, is unique and singular. The Qur'an notes 99 attributes, or names, of God. For the Muslim, God is invisible, is all knowing, and has awe-inspiring power, a power that instills a certain amount of fear among the followers of Islam. This emotion inspires adherence to the Islamic code of existence. Muslims following the straight path will reap the benefits and love of Allah; Muslims who don't follow this path will face Allah's wrath.

- ✔ **The concept of creation:** The story of creation is based on the belief that Allah deliberately created the world and everything in it with the simple command "Be!" He is its craftsman. As Allah's creation, the universe shows perfect design and order, and all things are possessed by and come from Allah.

- ✔ **The human self:** Human beings are the most important of Allah's creations. According to Qur'anic law, all individuals are born inherently good. Islam doesn't have a doctrine of original sin. The closest thing that comes to this is humankind's tendency toward arrogance that leads people to forget their place in Allah's world and to commit acts that are contrary to the spirit and law of Islam. To remind people of their proper place, Muslims must surrender to the code (the Five Pillars) of Islam. The concept of struggling to become everything that Allah would want in a human being is termed *jihad.*

- ✔ **The Day of Judgment:** The Qur'an portrays life as a "fleeting gift." For this reason, people must adhere to the Islamic code of existence or face the wrath of Allah at the time of "reckoning." When they die, souls are judged as to whether they should be sent to the heavens or the hells — places graphically described in the Qur'an. The bottom line: Each soul, accountable for the use of time on earth, must stand alone, without the benefit of intercession or excuses, and be judged. Allah is the final judge.

- ✔ **Other religions:** The Qur'an accepts the revelations of the Torah and New Testament. These revelations are incomplete and flawed, however. The revelation to Muhammad — the Qur'an — is the culmination of God's revelations, completing and correcting the revelations that came before. Muhammad, therefore, is the final prophet.

Zoroastrian Holy Books

The Zoroastrian scripture is the Avesta "Pure Instruction," which includes the following:

- ✔ **The Gathas or "Songs, Hymns":** Zarathustra himself is believed to have composed these works. The *magi,* or priests, transmitted the Gathas orally for centuries, with some variations and additions. Around the fifth to seventh centuries C.E., the Gathas were finally written down.

- ✔ **The Yashts "Hymns (to Divine Beings)" and the Videvdad (Code to Ward off Evil Spirits):** These texts compose the rest of the Avesta. Prayers, such as the *Asham Vohu* "Righteousness is Good" (recited by priests and laity in daily religious observances), are gathered together in a text known as the Khorde Avesta or "Shorter Avesta."

Next in importance are religious narrations written in Pahlavi, a Middle Iranian language. Among the vast amount of Pahlavi literature is the Zand, or commentary, on the Avesta. In addition, the Arda Wiraz Namag, or "Book of the Righteous Wiraz," preserves a description of a voyage through heaven, limbo, and hell.

Sikh Holy Books

The Sikh religion, founded by Guru Nanak (1469-1539), is the youngest of the world's monotheistic religions. (For a closer look at Guru Nanak, head to Chapter 14.)

The basic tenets of the Sikh religion are as follows:

- ✔ A deep belief in a single God, who has many names, is essentially One and unknowable, and who should be both loved and feared

- ✔ A rejection of the caste system and a commitment to the community

- ✔ A belief in the guru as a mediator of divine grace and the closest person to God

- ✔ A belief that the struggle to achieve liberation from the cycle of rebirth and death is hampered by innate human self-centeredness

- ✔ The moral obligation to help in the liberation of all others after personal liberation has been achieved

The role of the guru

The Sikh scriptures present God as the Creator, the Supreme One. God for the Sikh is truth and reality as opposed to falsehood and illusion. God is beyond description. God is the fullness of life. Because of this, God chooses different gurus to keep society on the right path toward moksha. The guru doesn't replace God, but leads one to God. The guru is the servant of God who shows others the path of truth. Important in the Sikh religion, according to Nanak (the first guru of Sikhs), is the need for people to associate with other holy people so that they can live in a right way. Nanak, through Divine guidance, hoped to bring people together. For him, divisions such as Muslim or Hindu didn't exist; he saw only people.

The Adi Granth

The compilation of the Sikh holy writings is known as the Adi Granth. As the Adi Granth evolved through the contributions of the various gurus — starting with the fifth guru, Arjun Dev in 1604 and lasting through Gobind Singh, the tenth and last guru in 1708 — it gained the special designation of "divine guru." (A guru is similar to a teacher, one who points a person in the best direction in life.) See the related sidebar titled "The role of the guru" later in this chapter.

Since that declaration, Sikhs consider the Adi Granth to be "the Book" — similar to the place that the Bibles hold for Christians and Jews and the Qur'an holds for Muslims. The Adi Granth is revered, and its writings, which help people to find the path to the eternal, are considered holy.

A compilation of poems and hymns that guide and direct the Sikh community in its dealings with God and man, the Adi Granth has three sections:

- ✔ The first, core part of the Adi Granth, is a long poem by Nanak, the first guru and founder of Sikhism, which articulates the fundamentals of Sikhism.

- ✔ The second is a collection of songs called *ragas,* composed by the first five gurus.

- ✔ The final section is a collection of commentaries of songs and hymns related to Hindu saints and Sufi mystics.

Contained within the Adi Granth is the Sikh theology begun by Guru Nanak.

The Dasam Granth and the Janam Sakhis

The second most important scriptural book of the Sikhs, the Dasam Granth, furthers Sikh theology. Written by Gobind Singh, during the seventeenth century, the Dasam Granth, which means "book of the tenth guru," includes poetry gathered from the bards of his time and focuses on mythological stories.

The Janam Sakhis (Life Stories) celebrates the life of Guru Nanak, who is considered the greatest teacher and spiritual leader of his time.

Holy Texts of the Baha'i Faith

The Baha'i Faith believes that God is essentially unknowable, but that he communicates the need for unity among all people through special messengers. The Bab, who received promptings from God and founded Babism, which was the forerunner of the Baha'i Faith, initiated this spiritual message. Baha'i is a breakaway sect of Islam and embraces many of the same goals of other monotheistic faiths.

The Bab predicted that God would send a divine teacher. That divine teacher turned out to be the Baha'u'llah, who was revered in the Baha'i teachings as the latest of God's messengers. The Baha'i Faith believes that God has spoken the divine message first through Adam, then through the Jewish prophets, then Jesus, Muhammad, and, for this age, most directly, through Baha'u'llah. (For more information about the Bab and Baha'u'llah, see Chapter 14.)

The sacred texts of the Baha'i Faith, written by Baha'u'llah, are the Most Holy Book, The Book of Certitude, The Seven Valleys, and The Hidden Words. These texts are spiritual in nature and ethical in content. They recognize the immortality of the soul and view heaven and hell as indicators of how far a person has progressed spiritually. In addition, the message is not only inspirational and prophetic; it is also considered divine because it comes directly from God. The Baha'i Faith believes that the writings of Baha'u'llah are more like the writings of the Qur'an, which came directly from Allah to Muhammad (through the angel Gabriel).

Baha'u'llah wrote:

- ✔ **The Most Holy Book,** which gives a full count of the laws and ordinances of the Baha'i Faith.

- ✔ **The Book of Certitude, The Seven Valleys, and The Hidden Words.** These writings envision a glorious new creation where all of humanity will be united under the holy teachings of Baha'u'llah. To achieve this, humankind must reject all forms of prejudice, treat all people equally, show concern for the poor, eliminate both great poverty and great wealth, create an international language, and ultimately create a society based on justice and equality.

Baha'i scriptures teach that people should love each other, respect each other, and live in a collaborative, rather than confrontational way. Adherents to the Baha'i Faith sign a Covenant to Baha'u'llah, a way of acknowledging their desire to respond to God through the message of Baha'u'llah.

The Church of Jesus Christ of Latter-day Saints: The Book of Mormon

The Book of Mormon is the most holy book in the Church of Jesus Christ of Latter-day Saints. According to Mormon theology, ancient prophets wrote of the history of Hebrews who came to America from Jerusalem about 600 B.C.E. The prophet/historian named Mormon abridged these texts and wrote them on gold plates. When the book was completed (circa 421 C.E.), Mormon's son Moroni sealed it and hid the sacred record until God indicated the time when it should come forth. About 1,400 hundred years later, in 1823, the resurrected ancient prophet Moroni, in the form of an angel, visited Joseph Smith (1805-1844) and delivered the engraved sheets of metal containing the Book of Mormon. Joseph Smith translated the text. (See the related sidebar titled "The mystery of the disappearing metal plates" later in this chapter.)

Smith founded the church, based on this restored gospel, in preparation for the second coming of Christ. His followers called Smith "the prophet" because, in the tradition of Old and New Testament prophets, he depended on revelation from God for his teachings. (For more information about Joseph Smith, see Chapter 14.)

The Book of Mormon, made up of 15 main parts, each designated by its principal author, offers an account of two civilizations that existed in ancient North America:

- One civilization came from Jerusalem around 600 B.C.E. and separated into two nations, the Nephites and the Lamanites.
- The other civilization reportedly came much earlier and was known as the Jaredites.

After many thousands of years, all except the Lamanites were reported destroyed. The Lamanites are viewed as the principal ancestors of the Native Americans.

Mormons consider the Book of Mormon a sacred record of peoples in ancient America as well as a guide that outlines the plan of salvation, the way to peace and eternal salvation, and the teachings of the gospel. They also believe that it contains sacred revelations about the gospel of Christ. In this way, the Book of Mormon is a supplement to the Bible. It bridges the gap between the apostolic church initiated by Jesus and the restored church that God called on Smith to reinstate in America.

In addition to being engraved upon sheets of metal, four kinds of metal record plates are spoken of in The Book of Mormon:

- **The Plates of Nephi:** These are both the Small and Large Plates of Nephi. The Small Plates are devoted to spiritual matters and the teachings of the prophets. The Large Plates provide a secular history of the ancient civilizations.

- **The Plates of Mormon:** These plates contain an abridgement written by Mormon of the Large Plates of Nephi. Mormon also provided a continuation of the ancient history, along with additions by his son Moroni.

- **The Plates of Ether:** These offer a history of the Jaredites. Moroni also abridged this record and inserted his own comments along with the general history of this ancient civilization. Moroni called this work the Book of Ether.

- **The Plates of Brass:** These plates contain the five books of Moses, an ancient historical record of Jews, and prophecies from earlier prophets. According to tradition, the people of Lehi brought the information that was on these plates when they migrated from Jerusalem to America.

The mystery of the disappearing metal plates

Because no one other than Joseph Smith saw the plates, and because he returned them to Moroni when he was done with them, no one really knows what the metal plates were. It's interesting to think about the possibility of the existence of the Book of Mormon plates since a copper scroll of writing that dates back over 2,000 years has been found at the Dead Sea in Israel.

Chapter 14

Holy People

. . . .

In This Chapter

▶ Understanding the lives of people who around whom religions grew

▶ Taking a look at messengers of the Divine

▶ Getting to know the theologians and scholars who shaped religious thought

▶ Meeting a few of today's religious leaders and (extra)ordinary people who made a difference

. . . .

Some religions are based on the teachings of a single founder. Buddhism, for example, is based on the teaching of Siddhartha Gautama; Christianity is based on the teachings of Jesus; Islam is based on the teachings of Muhammad; and Zoroastrianism is based on the devotional poetry of Zarathushtra (otherwise known as Zoroaster). Other religions that trace the foundations of their beliefs back to a particular person are Sikhism (founded by Guru Nanak) and Mormonism (founded by Joseph Smith). Some religions, like Judaism and Hinduism, however, aren't based on the teachings of one person, but on the accumulated teachings of many. All religions, however, have special people whose lives and teachings represent the essence of the faith and offer examples of faith's promise.

This chapter looks at a few of the key holy figures from the various world religions, as well as some of the most respected contemporary men and women of faith. The common thread among them all is the power of their living faith and luminous goodness.

Founders of Faith

All religions have to begin somewhere. (Even religions that believers claim have always existed have a point in historical time when people became aware of them.) Many religions begin with a divine revelation shared through a particular messenger. In some instances, such as Christianity and Taoism, this messenger (Jesus, in the case of Christianity, and Lao-Tzu, in the case of Taoism) is considered divine. In other religions, such as Islam, Zoroastrianism, and Buddhism, the messengers are human — special humans, that's true, but human nonetheless.

Whether divine or not, these people, who attracted communities of believers, represent the purest form of the revelation (after all, they're the ones to whom the "truth" was revealed). Although God, nature, or a divine essence is the basis of faith, these people are faith's founders.

Jesus: Human and divine

What little is known about Jesus comes from the Gospels of the New Testament. Jesus was born in Bethlehem to Mary, whose husband was a carpenter named Joseph. He was raised in Nazareth (a town in Galilee). He became a carpenter. When he was 30 years old, he sought out John the Baptist for baptism. After his baptism, Jesus began his public ministry by retreating into the desert for 40 days, where, according to Christian tradition, he experienced temptations from the devil that he overcame. Upon his return from the desert, Jesus recruited disciples, including those who became the Twelve Apostles. Jesus then took up preaching, largely through parables — short stories with moral or religious messages. Through his ministry, Jesus gained a reputation as a healer of the sick and afflicted and a performer of miracles. When he was 33 years old, the Roman authorities arrested him. He was tried before the Roman procurator, Pontius Pilate. Found guilty of inciting rebellion against the Roman government, Jesus was crucified.

For Christians, however, that very brief overview doesn't begin to cover the half of it. For them, Jesus is the face of God. He is the Messiah, the Christ, the Anointed One. Jesus is the second person of the Trinity, the three-part Godhead: God the Father, creator of heaven and earth; God the Son, who became human in the form of Jesus Christ; and God the Holy Spirit, who sanctifies humankind. Although divine, he chose to come to earth to redeem the sins of humankind (Philippians 2:5-11), which he did through his death and resurrection.

According to Christian tradition, after he was resurrected from the dead, Jesus ascended to heaven to sit at the right hand of God, where he will meet all who die to offer them a new life in the next world. The second coming of Jesus, called in Greek the *parousia,* will, according to Christian belief, provide the opportunity for Jesus to finish his Messianic work and defeat the forces of evil on earth.

Muhammad: The "Seal of the Prophets" and Father of Islam

The final prophet of God, according to Islam, is Muhammad (570-632 C.E.). Muhammad was born in Mecca around 570 C.E. According to legend, his mother heard a heavenly voice when he was born, and it was said that a light shone from her womb all the way to Syria. Despite the picturesque image surrounding his birth, tragedy touched Muhammad's life early. His father had died shortly before his birth; his mother died when he was six. His grandfather, who cared for him after his mother's death died when he eight. Muhammad's uncle then took responsibility for him. Although not wealthy, Muhammad's uncle welcomed him into his family.

When Muhammad reached adulthood, he took a job with a wealthy merchant, named Khadijah. Although he was more than ten years younger than her, Muhammad impressed Khadijah. She married this hard-working and honest man. The couple had two sons, who died young, and four daughters, one of whom provided him with grandsons. During Khadijah's life, Muhammad did not take another wife.

Through his marriage, Muhammad gained not only wealth and a strong political standing in the community, but a loving wife who was the first to believe in his prophetic abilities — even before he himself did.

As much as Muslims revere Muhammad, they don't consider him divine. (The earthly emanation of God's divinity is the Qur'an.) Nevertheless, Mohammed was the last and the greatest of God's prophets. For this reason, Muslims call him the "Seal of the Prophets."

The revelation of the Qur'an

Muhammad often withdrew into the desert for solace and meditation. Although not the first of his people to believe in a single God, Muhammad was the one who came to believe that Allah's powers were far greater and more magnificent than anyone up to that point could imagine. God was what his name — *al-ilah* — indicated: the Divinity.

It was during one of his spiritual retreats, when he was about 40 years old, that the angel Gabriel appeared to Muhammad. Through Gabriel, God began the *recitation,* the Qur'an, of his laws and will. Muhammad, often in a trance-like state, would repeat God's exact words as they came to him, committing them to memory and later having them transcribed. These revelations continued over the next 23 years.

Life in Mecca

Muhammad, anointed by God and with God's own words to proclaim, began to preach the message of Allah to the people of Mecca. His message was not well received for a couple of reasons:

✔ He preached of one god, not several, to an audience that largely believed in many gods and goddesses. The idea of a single God not only threatened Meccans' faith, but also their revenue. Quite a bit of money came into the city as the result of pilgrimages to the shrines of the many deities.

✔ His message, although more religious than political, condemned the depravity of the Meccans and the unjust social order under which they lived.

Muhammad didn't find a much friendlier reception with the Jews in Mecca. They didn't believe that he was a prophet or that the Qur'an was the word of God.

As the hostilities grew, the attacks on Muhammad and his few followers became more severe. Around this time, a delegation from the city of Medina (actually it was named Yathrib at the time) came to ask Muhammad for help. Their city was in chaos because of tribal rivalries, and the members of the delegation needed someone not associated with any particular faction within the city tribes to restore order and lead the city. Muhammad was their man. After receiving a sign of from God that he should go, Muhammad left Mecca for Medina in 622. This journey, called the *Hijrah,* marks the beginning of the Islamic calendar.

Life in Medina

Medina provided a better setting for Muhammad. He became not only the town's spiritual leader, but also its political and administrative leader as well. Muhammad built a coalition between the town's many factions, which included Arabs who hadn't converted to Islam, the Muslims who had come with him from Mecca, and Jews. Although this coalition didn't last (the tensions with the Jewish inhabitants of the town increased, resulting in their conversion to Islam or expulsion from Mecca), it established Muhammad's reputation as an able administrator and statesman.

Muhammad also gained the reputation as an able soldier and military strategist. He formed alliances with nomadic tribes and won several military victories. One of the most symbolic was his conquest of Mecca, the town that he had once fled.

About two and a half years after his conquest of Mecca, Muhammad died.

Zoroaster (Zarathushtra): Father of Zoroastrianism

The prophet Zoroaster is the founder of Zoroastrianism. (His actual name, Zarathushtra, is a compound word possibly meaning "possessor of old camels." The form Zoroaster, by which he's commonly identified in the West), comes the ancient Greek version of his name: Zoroastres.

Not a lot is really known about Zoroaster, and what people *do know* (or think they know) comes from glimpses available from his Gathas, or songs to God. These songs suggest that Zoroaster was a devotional poet whose words spiritually united a community of followers around him.

TECHNICAL STUFF

A prophet's life

As Zoroastrians experienced centuries of contact with Jews, Christians, and Muslims, they gradually transformed the prophet's life story to fit the established Near Eastern model of a holy man.

His revised sacred biography — with signs of auspicious birth, childhood miracles, revelation after years of wandering and contemplation, an initial ministry that met with limited success in his homeland, his flight to a nearby region when he gained a royal patron, and, finally, his success as a prophet — that survives, fits Zoroaster into the general image also seen in religious leaders like Moses, Jesus, and Muhammad.

Following is the life of Zoroaster, according to legend and his own songs:

✔ He probably lived and preached some time between the seventeenth and fifteenth centuries B.C.E.

✔ His homeland was somewhere in the region stretching from northwestern Afghanistan to the eastern shores of the Caspian Sea. In other words, he lived in what is now present-day Central Asia.

✔ When he was 20, Zoroaster left home. He spent a decade wandering and contemplating. During this time, he received a revelation and returned home to preach the religion of Ahura Mazda, "the Lord Wisdom," who is the supreme deity of Zoroastrianism.

✔ The clergy of the older cults in his native land opposed Zoroaster, and he had to seek refuge at the court of a neighboring ruler named Vishtaspa, who accepted the religion. In Vishtaspa's court, Zoroaster preached and gained many followers.

✔ When he was 77, a priest of another sect assassinated him. Or so it is written.

Siddhartha Gautama: The Buddha

The term Buddha isn't a name but a title. It means "enlightened one," and according to Buddhist theology, there are innumerable Buddhas. The Buddha to which people now refer, the one who existed in the world in which we exist, is the Buddha Siddhartha Gautama. According to Buddhist tradition, the Buddha had many lives before he was born as Gautama. It was in this life that he finally experienced the ultimate enlightenment and the ultimate release — *parinirvana* — an end to the cycle of being reborn.

The Buddha is represented in several statues throughout the Eastern world. One such statue is Amida Buddha in Kamadura, Japan. (See Figure 14-1.)

A little personal history

When Siddhartha Gautama (circa 563–483 B.C.E.) came into the world, an astrologer told his wealthy father that his newborn son would become either a monarch or a monk. His father, fearing the loss of his son to religion, surrounded Gautama with possessions, relationships, and luxurious living conditions. When he was 16, Siddhartha married and had a child.

He lived, unquestioning, in extravagance and luxury until he reached the age of 29, when he decided to leave the confines of the family estate. Beyond the walls of the palace, Gautama encountered an old man, a sick man, a corpse, and a monk. Seeing the first three people made him question the true nature of existence; seeing the monk made him question how one could have inner tranquility amid such misery. Realizing that his own life had been sheltered and that the world was actually filled with pain and sorrow, Gautama went looking for answers. This revelation led him to pursue the path of asceticism and a life of self-denial, which he thought would lead him to peace.

Figure 14-1:
A statue of
Siddartha
Gautama,
the Buddha.

Seeing the light

In his early attempts at living austerely, Gautama just became frustrated. Despite fasting, meditating, and denying all pleasures and comforts, he just became unhappier. While denying himself, he met a young maiden who asked him if he was hungry. He asked her if she could appease his hunger. Not realizing that he was looking for spiritual fulfillment, she offered him food to eat under a large tree (which was the Bohdi tree, the tree of wisdom).

Sitting under the tree, Gautama came to realize what he was looking for: an awakening in his soul and an illumination in his spirit. This spiritual moment led him to understand that life's meaning was not found in deprivation but in balance. He didn't have to be spiritually ascetic to be aware and fulfilled. He began to understand his own calling and started to preach a doctrine of inclusion and the Middle Path for 45 years.

Living and teaching the Middle Path

The Middle Path, more a concept than a doctrine, describes a journey in which human beings attempt to lead a life with no extremes, or the middle way. Gautama practiced yoga and taught the Four Noble Truths:

- **Truth One:** Existence is always tainted by sorrow and dissatisfaction.
- **Truth Two:** The cause of sorrow and dissatisfaction is human desire and attachment to people and things.
- **Truth Three:** Human beings can achieve freedom or release in nirvana.
- **Truth Four:** The Noble Eightfold Path is the way to find release:
    - Right understanding
    - Right thought
    - Right speech
    - Right conduct
    - Right livelihood
    - Right effort
    - Right mindfulness
    - Right concentration

Gautama encouraged his disciples, whether rich or poor, male or female, ignorant or learned, to abstain from killing any living thing and to seek time for meditation. He also performed miracles and eventually died of an illness in the city of Sravasti.

For Gautama, the goal of life was to discover the cause of sorrow and the way to escape it. If we can eradicate the desire for sensual enjoyment, all sorrows and pains will end. The soul will enjoy nirvana, and the cycle of rebirths will be completed.

Gautama encouraged his followers to be aware, to seek meaning and balance, and to recognize that certain human problems will not be changed. The world, according to Gautama, will always be fraught with problems. While many in the West would seek to resolve the problems of the world, Gautama encouraged his followers to meditate on them. The real transformation for Gautama came not in the elimination of the problem but in the transformation of the disciple.

Confucius: Teacher, sage, and man of moral conduct

Confucius (551-479 B.C.E.) was a contemporary of Siddhartha Gautama (the Buddha). Although not a religious leader in the same way that Siddhartha Gautama, Jesus, Mahavira, and others were, Confucius' ideas, his philosophy of education, and his respect for authority and family permeates almost all Asian cultures, including the cultures of Korea, Japan, and China. (See Figure 14-2.)

Confucius (the Latinized version of his real name, K'ung-fu-tzu) was born into a family that encouraged learning and nobility. His father died when he was 3 years old. Despite this loss, Confucius showed remarkable maturity and scholarship. As a young adult, Confucius held minor government positions. By the time he was 22, he opened a school, and by his 30s, he was one of the preeminent teachers in China. He believed that learning, itself a personal journey to self-realization, had social consequences. The life of a learned person was one of unending self-improvement and social interaction.

Coming from a culture in which wealth and power determined social order and people's place within it, Confucius had the radical idea that personal virtue — and not social status — was the key to human dignity and social order. A master teacher, Confucius believed that the key to virtue was the cultivation of the mind — that is, education in the six arts: ritual, archery, calligraphy, math, music, and charioteering — arts that he himself had mastered. To Confucius, education was more than a way to build knowledge; it was also a way to build character.

In his 40s and 50s, as the minister of justice for his home state of Lu and as counselor to the king, Confucius was able to put his ideas about social order and education into practice. He created humanities programs for potential leaders and made education available for all. Under his influence, the state prospered. When jealous rivals plotted his overthrow, he resigned his post and wandered for 13 years, looking for other governments and other people who would listen to his counsel. When he was 69, he returned to Lu, where he spent his last three years encouraging people to study, to practice virtue, and to lead noble lives. He died in 479 B.C.E. and was buried at Kufow.

Figure 14-2:
Confucius,
the great
Chinese
philosopher
and sage.

CONFUCIUS
Le plus celebre Philosophe de la Chine.

While Confucius saw himself as a man and never claimed to be divine, many in China erected temples in his honor, and his place of burial is a pilgrimage site for his followers. He left an intricate code of moral, social, political, and religious teachings, the most noted of which are the Analects.

Lao-Tzu: The "Old Master" of Taoism

Several legends relate to who — and what — Lao-Tzu was. Some even speculate whether he was a real person or a combination of many people. Reasons for the uncertainty include the following:

- Lao-Tzu isn't an actual name. It's an honorary Chinese name meaning "Old Master."

- The work that Lao-Tzu is credited with writing, the Tao Te Ching, probably wasn't the product of one man.

What little is actually known about Lao-Tzu comes from a historian who wrote around 100 B.C.E that Lao-Tzu's family name was Li, that he was born in a village in what is now Hunan Province, and that he was a *shih* (a scholar who specialized in astrology and divination) in the court of the Chou dynasty, which ruled from about 1111 to 255 B.C.E. Therefore, if he did live, it was from roughly from 600 to 200 B.C.E.

Other information about Lao-Tzu is based on legend:

- ✔ Lao-Tzu was conceived by a shooting star; in other legends, his mother carried him for 72 years before his birth. He was then born as a wise old man with white hair.

- ✔ In the annals of both Taoism and Confucianism, Lao-Tzu was believed to be the teacher of Confucius.

- ✔ Lao-Tzu is credited with writing the Tao Te Ching, the most sacred text in Taoism. In fact, one name for the work is the Book of Lao-Tzu. According to legend, he wrote this book at the request of the guardian of the Hsien-ku pass, through which he wanted to travel. After writing the book, Lao-Tzu disappeared and was never seen again.

  The Tao Te Ching teaches about the Tao, or "the Way." People should live according to the Tao. The Tao is the unity and the creative force behind all the things in the seen and unseen world. By following the Tao, people can achieve inner peace, courage, generosity, and leadership.

- ✔ After his disappearance, people believe that he has returned to earth throughout history, each time assuming a different personality (one of which, according to some, was as the Buddha himself). As these different people, Lao-Tzu guided people in the way of the Te.

Regardless of what can and can't be proven about his existence, Lao-Tzu is revered in China as a great philosopher to the Confucians. To the Taoists, Lao-Tzu is the *Lao-chun,* the savior and revealer of ancient texts, himself a god.

Mahavira: The "Great Hero" in Jainism

Mahavira (599-527 B.C.E.), a contemporary of the Buddha, was the main spiritual force behind Jainism. Mahavira so reformed and reformulated Jainism and the Jain monastic order and brought order to the teachings of the faith, that he is considered the single most important force in the religion of Jainism.

Mahavira means "Great Hero" in Sanskrit. Mahavira's personal name was Vardhamana, and he grew up luxury near Patna in Bihar, India. When he was 30, after the death of his parents, he left his family (his wife and child) and, like the Buddha, became a wandering ascetic and monk.

According to tradition, Mahavira wore one garment for more than a year. After that, he gave up clothing altogether and walked around naked. He had no possessions, meditated day and night, and stayed wherever he could find a place to sleep. After 12 years of this, he achieved *kevala-jnana,* the highest stage of enlightenment possible to a human being. Considered to be the last of the 24 Tirthankara (Jain saints), Mahavira revived the waning influence of Jainism.

Mahavira taught absolute nonviolence, vegetarianism, and the virtues of self-denial and poverty, as well as the five vows of personal renunciation (which Jain monks and, in some cases, nuns take).

Following are the five vows of personal renunciation:

- Renunciation of killing
- Renunciation of lying
- Renunciation of stealing
- Renunciation of materialism
- Renunciation of sex

Along with the Buddha, Mahavira was also one of the most forceful opponents of India's caste system and of the Vedic animal sacrifices, called *yajna.*

Mahavira died of a hunger fast at age 72. Because the Jains believe that the soul, or *jina,* leaves the body and goes to the farthest reaches of the universe, no communication with or prayers to Mahavira are possible.

Because of Mahavira's teachings — particularly the doctrine of *ahimsa,* or total nonviolence — Jains are loath to take any life. The most devout Jains place cloths over their mouths and sweep the streets in front of them as they walk to avoid killing even a small insect. During the rainy season, Jain monks retreat to their monasteries to avoid squashing a bug that lives in the mud. Of course, Mahavira's influence spread well beyond the Jains themselves. His doctrine of ahimsa had a profound influenced Indian culture in general.

Guru Nanak: Founding teacher of Sikhism

Guru Nanak (1469-1538) was the founder and the first guru of the Sikhs. Nanak was born and raised as a Hindu in the village of Talvandi in the Punjab district of India. As a young man with a wife and two sons, Nanak took a job as a steward in Sultanpur Lodhi, an opportunity that put him in contact with Muslim travelers and Hindu pilgrims. He was also able to visit the sacred places of both the Hindus and the Muslims.

During this time, Nanak had a profound mystical experience that compelled him to leave his family and job. For nearly 20 years, he traveled and preached a message of faith that took elements from both the Hindu and Muslim religions. In the 1520s, Nanak returned to the Punjab district and created the town of Kartarpur (the City of God). His followers and their families soon joined him, and the first Sikh community was born.

Reflection, meditation, and spiritual study are the elements that Nanak preached as he developed the beginning elements of the Sikh faith. Nanak's ideas, revealed through his more than 400 hymns, include the following:

✔ God, who is unique and one, created the universe. He manages universal and personal destinies by using both justice and grace.

✔ Religion must be practiced within a person and a true religious pilgrimage is based upon an individual's ability to find liberation within his own heart. To achieve liberation, people must meditate on the Divine Name and both love and fear God.

The Divine Name, or True Name, is used as a summary term that comprises the meaning of God — *Akal Purukh*.

✔ The most profound spiritual experience doesn't come from self-denial but from connecting with your family, living for the good of the community, and following a strict code of ethical behavior.

One of the most important contributions of Guru Nanak was his forceful opposition to the caste system *(varnas)* of Hinduism. Nanak considered these divisions a violation of the divine nature of all people and of their basic spiritual equality. As the first guru, Nanak's writings defined the elements of Sikhism and comprise the first part of the Adi Granth, the Sikhs' most sacred book.

Joseph Smith and Brigham Young: Founders of Mormonism

In the beginning of the Church of Jesus Christ of Latter-day Saints (also known as the Mormon Church), the journey west to its current world headquarters in Salt Lake City, Utah, began with founder Joseph Smith and continued under the leadership of Brigham Young. The Bible and the writings of both Smith and Young are intertwined together to form the basic teachings of the Mormon church, founded by Smith in his attempt for what he called a restoration of the original Christian faith. As young men, both Smith and Young expressed a need to find a new Christian spiritual identity. This desire inspired Smith to found the Church of Jesus Christ of Latter-day Saints and for Young to become one of his most ardent followers.

Joseph Smith

Smith began to question Christianity at an early age. Growing up in poverty in western New York, Smith claimed that he began to have visions when he was 14 years old. In these visions, God shared a "great revelation" about Christianity. In 1827, Smith said that an angel directed him to find what Smith described as the golden plates. These plates contained text that Smith translated into the Book of Mormon, the guidelines for the new religion Smith founded in 1830.

The golden plates revealed that

- ✔ God evolved from mankind and that men may evolve into gods.

- ✔ The parts of the Trinity are three separate divinities.

- ✔ Souls pre-exist (that is, they're not created).

- ✔ Justification is by faith and following the rules of the church.

When Smith established his first church in Fayette, New York, it met resistance, so he and his followers began their move west. Smith's next brief stops were in Ohio and Missouri, where local people drove them away by killing believers and burning their properties. Smith and his followers finally settled in Nauvoo, Illinois, in 1839. The Church of Jesus Christ Latter-day Saints grew in popularity, and its membership grew to more than 20,000.

The church population made Nauvoo the largest town in Illinois and put Smith in a position of power. He served as mayor, commanded the local militia, and eventually declared himself a candidate for the U.S. presidency in 1844. The local press, not affiliated with the church, condemned this action. Smith retaliated against the newspaper and was jailed along with his brother Hyrum. An angry mob stormed the jail and murdered both Smith and his brother.

Upon Smith's death, the church declared him a martyr, and Brigham Young assumed the leadership of the church.

Brigham Young

Brigham Young, a follower of Mormonism since 1830, was baptized by one of Joseph Smith's brothers in 1832 and became a powerful church missionary. Young was Smith's first lieutenant, a role that groomed him for the leadership that he would assume upon Smith's death.

By 1846, when persecution of the Mormons in Illinois intensified, Young led the journey farther west to Salt Lake City, Utah, a location that he called "the new Jerusalem" for the Church of Jesus Christ of Latter-day Saints. Young became president of the church in 1847 and continued to direct its affairs until his death in 1877.

The Bab and Baha'u'llah: Founders of the Baha'i Faith

Two men — the Bab and Baha'u'llah — are at the spiritual center of the religion's birth. The Baha'i faith is based on Babism (founded by the Iranian Mirza Ali Muhammad of Shiraz — the Bab — in 1844) and holds the following to be true:

- ✔ All the founders of the world's great religions — including the Bab and Baha'u'llah — are human manifestations of God.

- ✔ Each manifestation of God was part of God's plan to educate humankind in stages.

- ✔ The Bab and Baha'u'llah's purpose was to eliminate all barriers — economic, political, racial, and religious — that divide humankind and to establish one, unified faith.

The Bab

Mirza Ali Muhammad was a young Persian (Iranian) merchant who became known as the Bab, a title that means "the gateway," when he announced that he was the bearer of a divine message that would transform the spiritual life of the human race. In his major work, the Bayan, the Bab foretold of the appearance of a second messenger from God, one who was far greater than himself and whose mission was to usher in the "age of peace and justice" promised in Islam, Judaism, Christianity, and all the major world religions.

In many ways, the Bab heralded the coming of Baha'u'llah, the divine teacher who would be recognized as the official founder of the Baha'i Faith.

He was executed for treason in Iran in 1850.

Baha'u'llah

Although Baha'u'llah (original name Mirza Hoseyn Ali Nuri) was born into a noble family in Tehran, Iran, in 1817, he showed little interest in the perpetuation of a life of wealth. Instead, he found great spiritual satisfaction and purpose by ministering to the poor. A Shi'ite Muslim, Baha'u'llah aligned himself with the Bab. Following the Bab's execution, Baha'u'llah was exiled with other of the Bab's followers from Iran. In 1867, Baha'u'llah declared himself al'Mahdi, the twelfth and missing imam, whose appearance, Muslims believe, will herald the end of time.

Baha'u'llah was a prolific writer; he contended that his faith in God enabled him to write more than 100 volumes. His writings, which he claimed came directly from God, dealt with social and ethical teachings, laws and ordinances, and the mystical life.

When Baha'u'llah died in 1892, he was succeeded by his son, Abdu'l-baha'.

Mary Baker Eddy: Founder of the Christian Science Church

Mary Baker Eddy (1821-1910) was the founder of the Christian Science Church. As a child, she suffered from poor health, and health problems continued to plague her as she grew to adulthood. Through years of suffering, Eddy frequently turned to the Bible for consolation.

In the early 1860s, she met Dr. Phineas Quimby, who healed her without the use of medication. She believed that he had somehow reconnected with the healing power attributed to Jesus. When Quimby died in 1866, Eddy's illness returned and was exacerbated by a severe fall. Near death, she called for her Bible and read a passage from Matthew, in which Jesus cures a man with palsy. After reflecting and meditating on this passage, she recovered.

Her experiences with illness and healing led her to question whether organized religions repressed the healing side of God. She taught that healing comes from God and that God's will is to make all of us better. She asked her followers to rely more on faith than medicine, to call on prayer more than doctors, and to grow to expect that God would heal.

In 1879, Eddy organized the first Christian Science Church — the First Church of Christ, Scientist — in Boston, Massachusetts. She wrote the authoritative work of her movement, *Science and Health, with Key to the Scriptures,* and founded the newspaper, *The Christian Science Monitor.* Her religion gained in popularity in the United States and abroad. She remained active in the Christian Science movement until she died on December 3, 1910.

Famous Messengers of God

Within the context of religious traditions, some people stand out as appearing to be divinely inspired and divinely led. The message they share reaffirms the truths held by the community or reveals a new truth that enhances the connection between human beings and the Divine. Abraham's life, for example, is a testament to his unswerving faith in God.

This section takes a look at a few people who, although they didn't start new religions, profoundly affected the religious traditions that existed and that were to come.

Abraham: Father of many faiths

Evidence for Abraham's life exists only in biblical sources. According to the Hebrew Bible, Abraham (circa 1800 B.C.E.), which means "father of the many," is the first person Yahweh (God) called. In Genesis 12, God tells Abraham to leave his homeland, make a covenant with God, and take on the role of the father of faith in Judaism. (Christians and Muslims consider him the father of their faiths, too.) The sign of this covenant is circumcision. (In Judaism, male children are circumcised when they're 8 days old.)

In Christianity, you can find a deep reverence for Abraham because of his willingness to not only to believe in God but also to sacrifice all for God, including his son, Isaac.

Muslims trace their ancestry back to Abraham through his firstborn son Ishmael, born to Hagar, who was Sarah's (Abraham's wife) maidservant. In addition to being the father of the religion, Abraham is one of the most important figures in Islam because his willingness to sacrifice his son (Ishmael, in this version) shows an ultimate surrender to Allah's will. For Muslims, Abraham is also the one who, assisted by Ishmael, built the Ka'bah, the shrine in the center of the great mosque in Mecca and the most sacred place for Muslims.

Striking the deal: The covenant

The story of Abraham may begin in the second millennium B.C.E. when God asked him to leave his native land of Haran to journey to an unknown territory in Canaan. In return for submitting to God's will, God made a promise to Abraham: "I will make of you a great nation." In other words, God would be the God for Israel, and Israel, through Abraham, would be God's special people.

Abraham complied, taking his wife Sarah, their servants (including Sarah's maidservant, Hagar), a few relatives (including Lot and his family), and others into Canaan. Along the way, God continued to talk to Abraham, indicating what land Abraham or his descendents would eventually possess, and Abraham constructed altars to God. As he traveled, Abraham's possessions and wealth grew.

Abraham seemed to have it all. Except for an heir.

Abraham's kids: Ishmael and Isaac

Abraham, the man who was supposed to be the father of a great nation, had no children. His wife Sarah was infertile. Moreover, although God promised Abraham that his descendents would be as numerous as the stars in the sky, Abraham was thinking that one of his servants would end up being his heir. As it turned out, Abraham ended up with two sons: Ishmael and Isaac.

Ishmael

Ishmael was the son of Abraham and Hagar, his wife's maidservant. Sarah, who hadn't conceived, offered her servant Hagar to Abraham, thinking to build her own family with Hagar's children. Sure enough, Hagar conceived a child, a son who would be named Ishmael.

According to Christian tradition: Hagar was a concubine, which made Ishmael illegitimate. According to Islamic tradition: Hagar was Abraham's second wife.

Abraham is said to have been 86 when Ishmael was born.

Isaac

When Abraham was 99 years old, God appeared to him and said, "I am El Shaddai. Walk in my ways and be blameless. I will establish my covenant between me and you, and I will make you exceedingly numerous" (Genesis 17:1). God also promised Abraham and Sarah that they would have a child named Isaac, which they did. (See the related sidebar titled "A house divided" later in this chapter.)

Abraham was 100 and Sarah was 90 when Isaac was born.

The sacrifice

Abraham believed that God wanted him to sacrifice his son as a show of faith. Islam and Christianity have different versions of the events surrounding the intended sacrifice:

In Christian tradition,

- ✔ The request for the sacrifice comes from God, who wants to test Abraham's faith.
- ✔ Isaac is the child to be sacrificed.
- ✔ Isaac doesn't know he's to be sacrificed and questions Abraham as they near the place where the sacrifice is to be made.

In Islamic tradition,

- ✔ Abraham has a dream, which he interprets to mean that God wants him to sacrifice his child.
- ✔ Ishmael is the child to be sacrificed.
- ✔ Ishmael knows of the sacrifice and agrees to it, himself surrendering to God's will

Regardless of how he came to perform the sacrifice (through a direct command from God or a dream), Abraham surrenders to God's will. Abraham went to Mount Moriah (today's Jerusalem) and prepared to sacrifice Isaac/Ishmael for God. At the last minute, however, God stays his hand and provides a ram to be sacrificed instead.

In Palestine, archeological evidence suggests children were actually sacrificed. The remains of some children, for example, are found in the walls surrounding cities and others are buried under the floors of homes. When God prevents Abraham from sacrificing his son, the message is clear: God doesn't want human sacrifice.

A house divided

All was not well with two wives and two sons in the same house. The person who seemed to have the most trouble with the arrangement? Sarah. On the day that Isaac, Sarah's son, was weaned, Abraham had a great feast for him. Sarah, thinking that Ishmael was mocking her son, demanded that Abraham send Ishmael and Hagar away, claiming that Ishmael wouldn't get any of Isaac's inheritance.

Heavy-hearted, Abraham exiled Hagar and his son Ishmael, sending them into the desert with some food and a skin of water. When the water finally gave out, and the two were dying of thirst, an angel of God spoke to the weeping Hagar, telling her that he had heard their cries. She was to go to her son, whom she had left under a bush with the skin of water, and lift him up, for God would make him into a great nation. When Hagar opened her eyes, she saw a well of water, provided by God.

Moses: Israelite and prophet

Moses (who may have lived around 1200 B.C.E.) is an important person to Judaism, Christianity, and Islam. His life is known only from the Bible and Qur'an.

People revere Moses for the following reasons:

- ✔ He is the prophet who led the Israelites from oppression in Egypt to freedom in the Promised Land.

- ✔ He is recognized for receiving the Ten Commandments from God on Mount Sinai.

- ✔ He is the only prophet to whom God spoke directly, rather than through messenger angels or visions. For this reason, Moses' prophecy can never be changed or invalidated.

As described in the Bible, Moses was a Hebrew foundling, raised and educated in the Egyptian court, where he spent the first 40 years of his life. He fled Egypt after killing an Egyptian who was beating a slave. He ended up in Midian (in northwest Arabia), where he became a shepherd and got married. One day, while tending his flock, he saw a bush that burned but wasn't consumed by the fire; here, God spoke to him, telling him to return to Egypt and free the Israelites from bondage. Moses returned to Egypt, eventually secured the release of the Israelites (after sending plagues to convince the pharaoh), and led them into the desert, where they wandered for 40 years, looking for the Promised Land. During the 40 years of wandering, God gave Moses the Ten Commandments and established the covenant between himself and the people of Israel.

Moses never made it into the Promised Land himself, though, because God prevented it as punishment for a lack of faith. The crime? When God commanded Moses in the desert wanderings to speak to a rock to yield water, Moses hit it instead (Numbers 20:7-13).

Before he died, Moses blessed each of the twelve tribes. He encouraged his people to observe all the words of the law. He then climbed Mount Nebo to look at the land that God had promised, but which he would never enter. Moses died on Mount Nebo and was buried in the land of Moab.

According to tradition, Moses wrote the first five books of the Hebrew Bible (the Pentateuch). Although this probably isn't accurate, he was certainly the inspiration behind the Torah.

Wovoka: Native American prophet and "New Messiah"

Wovoka, also called Jack Wilson, was a Paiute, born deep within the Utah Territory in 1858. He was a medicine man, who in the early part of his life lived among the white settlers. In 1889, Wovoka claimed to have a vision in which God told him that within two years the ancestors of his people would rise from dead, buffalo would appear again on the plains, and the white settlers would disappear, enabling all indigenous peoples — both living and dead — to live freely on the land.

To accomplish this "return to the past," Wovoka said that the people must remain peaceful and participate in an ancient dance — the Ghost Dance — that would show their faith and culminate in the resurrection of the dead.

Because of the hope it gave to Native Americans, the Ghost Dance quickly became popular among many tribes. By the time it reached the Sioux Indians in South Dakota, the U.S. Army was convinced that, because of the frenzy surrounding Wovoka and the Ghost Dance religion, the Sioux would lead an uprising. The tragic result was the Army's massacre of about 300 Sioux men, women, and children at Wounded Knee, South Dakota, on December 29, 1890. Soon afterward, Wovoka and his messianic movement faded away. Wovoka died at the Walker River Indian Reservation in October 1932.

The Smart Guys: Theologians and Scholars

Theologians are people who study God and the relationship between God, the universe, and humans. In some instances, the ideas of theologians and scholars, such as Maimonides or Thomas Aquinas, may spur debate within the religion, but they don't divide the religion. In other instances (think Martin Luther and the Protestant Reformation), the ideas are so radically different from the accepted theology that a schism forms.

Augustine of Hippo: Western theologian extraordinaire

Aurelius Augustinus of Hippo (354–430 C.E.), also known as St. Augustine, was one of the fathers of the Western Christian church. One of the most important theologians of late antiquity, his numerous writings still influence religious scholars today.

Augustine lived during the decline of the Roman civilization on the African continent. He was born in an area that was known as Hippo Regius (today, it would be part of Algeria) and was raised as a Manichaen (a religion that taught that an evil god was responsible for the evil in the world). Although his mother was a devout Christian and his father was a pagan, Augustine experimented with an assortment of religions during his youth as he struggled to find his spiritual identity — a journey that Augustine documented in one of his most famous works, *Confessions,* an account of his coming to believe that Christianity is the source of divine truth.

Augustine traveled to Rome and Milan, where he settled for a while and landed a teaching position at the university. Bishop Ambrose (after his death, Saint Ambrose), the bishop of Milan, strongly influenced Augustine during this time. This influence led to Augustine's conversion to monastic Christianity in 386 C.E.

Augustine believed that, by opening his mind and heart to Christian doctrine, he was able to completely open himself up to perfect love, that which delights and freely rejoices in God. During his life, Augustine equated will and love, thus enabling him to understand that acceptance of God is constituted by the love of God and the love of one another in God. Augustine shared his point of view on Christian theology in his writings, which include

- *On Christian Doctrine:* A sort of how-to book on preparing to become a preacher and how to study the scriptures
- *The City of God:* A work that details Christianity's place in history
- *On the Trinity:* An explanation of the Christian concept of God

Maimonides: Revered scholar of Judaism

His influence recorded throughout the annals of medieval Judaism, Moses Maimonides (1135-1204) established his role as the foremost intellectual figure of medieval Judaism because of his ideas about philosophy, religion, and medicine.

Maimonides was born and raised in Cordoba, Spain. In his early 20s, he and his family moved from Spain to Morocco, then to Palestine, and eventually to Egypt, where they settled. In Egypt, Maimonides became a physician with a brilliant reputation, leading to his position as personal physician to the Sultan Saladin and his son.

Some of Maimonides's most well-known writings include

- **Essays about the Mishna** (the first part of the Talmud): This includes the Thirteen Articles of Faith, which summarize the teachings of Judaism.

- **The Mishneh Torah** (The Torah Reviewed): His work in which he systematized the code of Jewish law and doctrine.

- **Guide of the Perplexed** *(Dalalat al-ha'ir-in):* His great philosophical work, which he spent more than 15 years writing. The guide's message asks Jews to discover a rational philosophy of Judaism. Many of the faithful viewed this idea as controversial, thus stimulating the future generations of philosophers and religious scholars to reflect upon Maimonides' recommendation about looking at Judaism in a new, rational light.

Although Maimonides died more than 800 years ago, many of his works, especially his writings on the sciences (medicine, astronomy, and physics) continue to be read and studied today.

St. Thomas Aquinas: Christian theologian and scholar

In the eyes of the Roman Catholic Church, St. Thomas Aquinas (1225-1274), or Thomas of Aquino, born in the castle of Roccasecca, near Naples, Italy, is the Church's greatest medieval theologian and scholar. His formal recognition by the Church began years after his death, when Pope John XXII canonized him in 1323. Then, in 1567, Pope Pius V officially declared Thomas a doctor of the Church, and, in 1880, Pope Leo XIII made him the patron of the Roman Catholic schools — an honor that seemed especially appropriate because of Thomas's role in the revival of learning that had begun in Western Europe toward the latter part of the eleventh century.

During the revival of learning, which spanned more than 200 years, teachers were called *schoolmen,* or scholastics. These teachers accepted Christian doctrine, but their studies expanded to include Greek philosophers. Because of his devotion to lecturing and preaching in the service of his order (Thomas joined the Dominicans, an order of mendicant preaching friars — that is, men who had no personal property of their own and existed primarily by begging), Thomas was acknowledged as the greatest of the schoolmen and as the angelic doctor.

Much of Thomas's study focused on the works of Aristotle. Thomas took upon himself the task of making Aristotle's teachings blend with Christian doctrine. By doing this, Thomas was able to share his philosophy of two sources of knowledge: revelation (theology) and reason (philosophy).

Thomas was a prolific writer and his most significant works are *Summa Contra Gentiles* and *Summa Theologiae.* These works form the classical systematization of Roman Catholic theology. Thomas taught that revelation is a divine source of knowledge and that revealed truths must be accepted, even if a person is not fully capable of understanding them.

Martin Luther: Father of the Protestant Reformation

Martin Luther (1483-1546) was ordained an Augustinian monk in 1507 and became a professor of Biblical literature at Wittenberg University, Germany, in 1512. From his study of the epistles (or letters) of St. Paul, Luther concluded that Jesus was the sole mediator between God and humanity; therefore, according to Luther, forgiveness of sin and the attainment of salvation came from God's grace alone. These teachings put him in direct conflict with the Catholic Church, which taught that faith and good works save people.

In 1517, when the Archbishop of Mainz sponsored a sale of indulgences (partial pardons for sins committed) to pay for his appointment at Mainz and to pay for the construction of St. Peter's in Rome, Luther posted his famous *Ninety-Five Theses* on the church door at Wittenberg. (See the sidebar, "Indulgences: A good idea that got out of hand," in this chapter for more information about indulgences.)

This was the first salvo between the Roman Catholic Church and Martin Luther, at the time an ordained Catholic priest. The battle between Luther's ideas and the Church's ended when the Church excommunicated him (that is, kicked him out) in 1521.

Luther's excommunication didn't cow him, however. He got busy translating the Bible into German and organizing evangelical churches throughout

Germany. He abolished confession and private mass. Priests were allowed to marry. Convents and monasteries were abandoned. His churches were founded on these principles:

- ✔ Salvation came through faith alone and not good works.

- ✔ Christ alone, not priests, could forgive sins.

- ✔ There are only two sacraments: baptism and the Eucharist, or communion. (The Catholic Church has seven sacraments.)

- ✔ Jesus is only symbolically present in the Eucharist. This idea conflicted with the Catholic notion of *transubstantiation,* that the bread and wine are transformed into the body and blood of Christ during the mass.

- ✔ The Bible is the final authority of God.

In trying to reform the Catholic Church, Luther succeeded in starting the Protestant Reformation. Most Protestant denominations adopted Luther's doctrines, especially the final authority of the Bible and justification by faith. For hundreds of years following this schism, Roman Catholics and Protestants went their separate ways. Finally, during the 1960s, a period in Catholic history known as Vatican II, the Catholic Church termed Protestants "separated brothers," that is, they were no longer considered enemies of the Church.

Indulgences: A good idea that got out of hand

Here's how penance is supposed to work: When you sin, you repent. The stain of the sin is wiped clean from your heavenly record, but you still have to atone — or pay — for the sin on earth. Divine justice and charity demand this. If you don't pay for your sin while you're living, then you are stuck in purgatory when you die and have to pay for your sins there. (Purgatory is a sort of holding station for souls who've repented their sins but who aren't quite ready for the bliss of heaven.)

You pay for sins in all sorts of ways. For example, you can do good deeds, fast for a specified period of time, say special prayers or give alms to the poor, or pay money to be used for religious purposes.

Sounds like a good idea: You create pain through sin; you do something good to atone for the pain your sin caused.

By the Middle Ages, however, this good idea had fallen on bad times. Everyone knows that people are going to sin. It's part of human nature. Some unscrupulous clergy (and official collectors, called *quaestors*) used this fact to make money for themselves or raise money for the church. They did this by selling indulgences. People who bought indulgences considered it insurance. They'd give their money (or whatever was required), get their indulgence, and then, if they sinned, consider their debt of atonement paid, without the need for real sorrow or confession.

In 1562, the Council of Trent finally put an end to the abuses surrounding indulgences. Today, indulgences are applied to the souls of the dead (not the future transgressions of the living), and the church officials don't grant the indulgences directly. Instead, *you* pray to God to accept your deeds as atonement for the souls left in purgatory.

Contemporary Religious Leaders and Activists

Certain religions look to a particular leader for guidance in matters of faith. Catholicism is one such religion. The head of the Catholic Church is the Pope. Tibetan Buddhism is another example. The Dalai Lama is the spiritual as well as temporal leader of Tibetan people. In both cases, according to the traditions of the different faiths, the Divine selects these people to lead believers on earth.

Of course, not all profoundly religious people end up as a Dalai Lama or a Pope. Some just end up changing the world — or trying to change the world — for the better.

Tenzin Gyatso: The fourteenth Dalai Lama

Tenzin Gyatso (a name that means "Ocean of Wisdom") is also known as His Holiness, the Fourteenth Dalai Lama. The Dalai Lama is the spiritual and earthly leader-in-exile of the Tibetan people and Tibetan Buddhism. He is revered because he is considered an enlightened being, embodying the compassion of past, present, and future Dalai Lamas.

The Dalai Lama has a worldwide following of people who support his universal appeal for interfaith respect and understanding.

Tenzin Gyatso was born in a small village called Takster in northeastern Tibet in 1935. According to Tibetan Buddhism, the Dalai Lama is the reincarnation of his predecessor and is identified through a combination of oracles, dreams, and visions. The current Dalai Lama was only 2 years old when he was first recognized as the reincarnation of an earlier Dalai Lama.

The Dalai Lama's formal spiritual training began almost immediately, and for more than 20 years, he was trained, tested, and thoroughly educated in the canon of monastic discipline and the study of metaphysics. In 1950, when he was 16 years old, the Dalai Lama was thrust onto the political stage when he became the head of the state and government of Tibet. The Dalai Lama remained in power in Tibet until 1959, when the Chinese occupied the country and forced him into exile.

Although he now lives in India, the Dalai Lama has been steadfast in his devotion to Tibet, its people, and its rich heritage. He travels throughout the world and speaks on behalf of Tibet, spirituality, and the importance of recognizing the commonality of faiths and the need for unity among different religions.

Among his many honors, the Dalai Lama received the Nobel Peace Prize in 1989 in recognition of his efforts to preserve the cultural heritage of Tibet.

Karol Wojtyla (Pope John Paul II)

As the leader of the Roman Catholic Church, Pope John Paul II, born Karol Wojtyla in Wadowice, Poland, to working-class parents in 1920, is one of the most powerful men on earth and has been an active participant on behalf of peace on the global political stage.

John Paul began his studies for the priesthood during the middle of World War II at an illegal seminary. This action, along with his underground activities that included helping Polish Jews escape from Nazi persecution and his participation in an underground theater group that performed anti-Nazi plays, illustrates his deep commitment to helping people. He was ordained in 1946 and quickly rose through the ranks of the Church in Poland. Elected pope in 1978, when he was 58 years old, John Paul was the first non-Italian pope in more than 450 years and is one of the most well-traveled popes in the history of the papacy. Because of John Paul's extensive travels — to date, more than 100 countries — he has been dubbed the "pilgrim pope."

John Paul has survived several assassination attempts — including being shot by a Turkish political dissident in St. Peter's Square on May 13, 1981. The strength of his faith empowers Paul. He is a pope who has accomplished many "firsts" for the papacy.

Among John Paul's accomplishments are the following:

✔ When John Paul returned to his native Poland in 1979, he became the first pope to visit a Communist country.

✔ John Paul is the first pope to visit a United States president in the White House (during a 1979, six-city tour of the U.S.).

✔ In 1983, John Paul approved the first revision of the Church's canon law since it had been modified in 1917.

✔ In 1989, John Paul reopened diplomatic discussion about the spiritual channels between Rome and, at that time, the Soviet Union. (Mikhail Gorbachev went to the Vatican in 1989.)

✔ John Paul is the first pope to visit Communist Cuba. (This historic visit occurred in 1997, following Fidel Castro's 1996 Vatican visit.)

✔ In 2000, John Paul offered the Church's first formal expression of sorrow about the Nazi persecution of the Jews during World War II. He is the first pope ever to pray in a synagogue and a mosque. He also opened official diplomatic relations between the Vatican and the State of Israel.

Mohandas Gandhi: Hindu leader and man of peace

Mohandas K. Gandhi (1869-1948), a world-famous spiritual leader and devout Hindu, was a deeply religious man who believed that God is Truth. Gandhi's teaching was based on the simple principle that when people seek out the Truth, they seek to know God.

History books throughout the world describe Mahatma (the Sanskrit term for "great soul," and his official title) Gandhi, shown in Figure 14-3, as a great man who advocated nonviolence (ahimsa) or the passive resistance, which he called *satyagraha* (defined by Gandhi as "holding onto the truth") through a virtuous form of conflict resolution and political action. Gandhi was a social reformer, the leader of India's nationalist movement, and an advocate of a chaste, modern Hinduism.

Figure 14-3: Mohandas Gandhi was an advocate of non-violent resistance.

Gandhi was raised as a Hindu in humble beginnings in India and was formally educated in England. He was deeply influenced by his mother's Hindu faith and the faith of one his closest friends, Rajchandra Rajivbhai, a Jain.

Through the course of his travels in Europe and then in South Africa, where he lived and practiced law, Gandhi was driven by his passion to help people. Shocked at the racism he witnessed in South Africa, for example, Gandhi became an advocate for other Indians in Africa and participated in non-violent resistance that led to jail. When he returned to India, he entered politics to protest the role of the British in India and set about achieving independence through nonviolent resistance of British rule and law. He led his people in non-violent protests and numerous marches — including the famous march to the sea to protest the British tax on salt — to build a nationalist movement. Gandhi became the center of India's transition from British control to independence.

Having studied the great works from the world's major religions — including Hinduism, Christianity, Judaism, and Islam — he came to the conclusion that all religions are true but flawed because they are interpreted (and misinterpreted) by imperfect humans.

Influenced by the Bhagavad-Gita, a sacred Hindu text, Gandhi began the process of simplifying his life. He freely abandoned the wealth he achieved as a young lawyer, following the ideas of non-possession *(aparigraha)* and equability *(samabhava;* that is, not allowing joy or sorrow, success or failure to affect him). He also tended the sick and dying.

During this tumultuous time, the Hindus and Muslims began a civil war. Through his numerous attempts to "teach by example," Gandhi continued to travel throughout the country and meet with both Hindus and Muslims to try to break down the barriers between the faiths.

Gandhi taught non-cooperation with the government or any civil authority that enacted oppressive legislation. In order to draw attention to oppressive laws or politics, he fasted for many days. Gandhi continued this spiritual journey until his assassination by a Hindu extremist in 1948.

Martin Luther King, Jr.: Social activist

The Reverend Dr. Martin Luther King, Jr., (1929-1968) is one of the most honored social activists and spiritual forces of the twentieth century. His speeches, writings, and actions — such as his civil rights marches throughout the South — are part of United States history. Dr. King's commitment to nonviolent direct action and his philosophy about nondestructive social change, which he learned by studying the teachings of Gandhi, galvanized the conscience of America and forced Americans to confront racial inequalities within their society.

A Baptist minister, King's speeches were filled with references to the Exodus from Egypt as the example of all liberations. Through his religious approach to the problem of racism, he brought a powerful, prophetic voice to America. Racism, he claimed, was not just a social mistake but also a sin against God.

Highlights of his extraordinary life include the following:

- When Rosa Parks refused to give up her seat on a bus in Montgomery, Alabama, King led the first day of the bus boycott in Montgomery (December 1955). The boycott itself lasted for almost two years.

- In 1957, King became one of the founders of the Southern Christian Leadership Conference, an organization established to assist local groups working for the full equality of African Americans.

- On August 28, 1963, King delivered his famous "I Have a Dream" speech on the steps of the Lincoln Memorial in Washington, D.C., at the first large-scale integrated protest march.

- In 1964, King was awarded the Nobel Peace Prize. Thirty-five years old at the time, King was the youngest man, the second American, and the third African-American to be so honored.

- In late March 1965, King led more than 25,000 people on a civil rights march from Selma to Montgomery, Alabama.

Martin Luther King, Jr., was assassinated April 4, 1968, in Memphis, Tennessee. Following the passage of Public Law 98-144, President Reagan signed the proclamation declaring Martin Luther King, Jr.'s birthday as a national holiday.

Mother Teresa: Devoted missionary and "servant of God"

The beauty of Mother Teresa's lifelong mission of love and devotion to the destitute and dying is found in the simplicity of her message — every person is entitled to die with dignity.

Born Agnes Gonxha Bojaxhiu on August 27, 1910, in Skopje, Macedonia, Mother Teresa was 18 years old when she decided to become a nun. After first joining the order of the Sisters of Loreto, a group of Irish nuns with a mission in Calcutta, India, she was sent to teach in India. Living among the poor in the slums of Calcutta, she decided to form a new religious order, the Missionaries of Charity. Based upon what Mother Teresa called "divine inspiration," she began this new chapter in her life of serving God by serving people.

Mother Teresa is known throughout the world for her charitable work for impoverished people. The acknowledgments of her devotion to the victims of this world range from the Nobel Peace Prize she received in 1979 to the many honorary degrees she received from academic institutions throughout the world.

Mother Teresa wasn't in it for the laurels. She received her calling at an early age and often talked about the joy she found in helping the most broken bodies. One look into her eyes as she walked the halls of the Nirmal Hriday (Place for the Pure of Heart) — the home for the terminally ill she founded in Calcutta — showed the spiritual joy or divine inspiration she seemed to derive from the people she cared for. In addition to the Nirmal Hriday, she later founded Shanti Nagar (Town of Peace), a leper colony that was built near Asansol in West Bengal.

The Vatican officially recognized the extraordinary work of the Missionaries of Charity in 1950, and, as a result, the order was able to open up more centers, orphanages, schools, and health-care facilities to treat the impoverished people of India and beyond. The order has established centers throughout the world, including a home in Rome, one in the Harlem section of New York City, and many centers throughout South Africa. The result is that Mother Teresa's mission has expanded to include a multi-cultural diversity of people.

When Mother Teresa passed away in 1997, there were orders of the Missionaries of Charity in more than 90 countries and included more than 4,000 nuns and many thousands of volunteers. Her work continues.

Chapter 15

Holy Places

• •

In This Chapter

▶ Jaunting through Jerusalem

▶ Diving into India's holy rivers

▶ Making your way through Mecca and Medina

▶ Catching up with the Pope in Vatican City

▶ Trekking west to Utah and the Mormons' Promised Land

▶ Exploring sacred sites of a few other religions

• •

Most religions have locations they deem holy, places where, for believers, the Divine breaks through. Sometimes, these are places of natural splendor so remarkable that, according to the faithful, they could only be the product of divine will. Sometimes, the places aren't much to look at but important events in the religion's history happened there. Sometimes, the places simply represent a location that, for whatever reason, holds structures devoted solely for the worship of the Divine.

People flock to holy places as pilgrims. (Where allowed, non-believers flock to these places, too, but they generally come as tourists.) An important point to remember is that, regardless of the history behind what makes a sacred place sacred, these locations are important because, in the minds of believers, they are the places where heaven and earth meet.

This chapter takes you on a tour of some of the world's most famous holy places and explains the sanctity of these places to the respective religions. (For information on houses of worship, go to Chapter 16.)

Jerusalem: Hot Spot and Holy City

Between 2000 and 3000 B.C.E., Jerusalem came to be a city. In some ways, it is (and was) a town like any other town. It exists in physical space (but not much space at that — a little more than a square mile), miles from any significant waterway, trade route, or larger city. It has citizens, but not many — only about half a million, give or take a few thousand. The city has been called various names — Jerusalem, Zion, and Aelia Capitolina, for example — by the different groups who have controlled it. (See the related sidebar titled "Urusalim: City of Peace" later in this chapter.)

Jerusalem is unlike other towns, however, because all the Abrahamic faiths consider it sacred. For Judaism and Christianity, Jerusalem is the holiest place on earth; for Muslims, it's the third-holiest place (after Mecca and Medina).

Judaism, Christianity, and Islam all believe that Jerusalem is the place where Abraham proved his faith in God. According to tradition, the Temple Mount in Jerusalem is the site of Mount Moriah, where Abraham was about to sacrifice his son before God stopped him and provided a ram instead. (For more information about Abraham, his faith, and the stories behind this test, head to Chapter 14.) Beyond this, each of the Abrahamic faiths has its own reasons for thinking of Jerusalem as a particularly holy place.

Urusalim: City of Peace

The name *Jerusalem* comes from two words, *ir shalom,* which means City of Peace. Despite its name, the city — because of its significance to the world's three great monotheistic religions: Judaism, Christianity, and Islam — has been a quite a hot spot. The battles over Jerusalem started thousands of years ago, and they're still raging.

Following is a very brief list of the people who have controlled, fought to control, attacked, counter-attacked, laid siege to, and plundered the city:

- ✔ Jebusites (probably the original inhabitants)

- ✔ Israelites (starting with the biblical King David, perhaps around 1000 B.C.E.)

- ✔ Egyptians, led by King Shisak, which kicked off 300 years of plundering by others (circa 922 B.C.E.)

- ✔ Assyrians, led by Sennacherib (circa 701 B.C.E.)

- ✔ Babylonians, led by Nebuchadnezzar (circa 587/586 B.C.E.)

- ✔ Iranians, led by Cyrus II (circa 538 B.C.E.)

- ✔ Macedonians, Greeks, and Selucids (circa 333–167 B.C.E.)

- ✔ Hasmoneans (circa 167–63 B.C.E.)

- ✔ Romans, led by Pompey (63 B.C.E.), followed by the Byzantines

- ✔ Iranians, led by King Khusro II (614 C.E.)

- ✔ Arabs, led by Umar I (638 C.E.), followed by the Fatimids from Egypt and the Seljuk Turks

- ✔ Christian army of the First Crusade (1099)

- ✔ Islamic army of Saladin (1187)

- ✔ Frederick II, emperor of the Holy Roman Empire (1229)

- ✔ Khwarezmian Tartars (1244)

- ✔ Mamluks, from Egypt (1247)

- ✔ Tartars again (1260)

- ✔ Ottoman Turks (1517)

- ✔ British (1920)

- ✔ Israel, the modern nation (1948)

The fighting, unfortunately, continues.

Temple time: The Jewish connection

Jews consider Jerusalem the holiest place on earth. It was in Jerusalem that King Solomon (circa 950 B.C.E.) built the temple, which became the locus of Jewish devotions after King Josiah centralized worship there around the year 621 B.C.E. (Josiah was a reform-minded king of Judah. Among other acts, he commanded the destruction of altars and shrines devoted to idols and began the restoration of the Temple in Jerusalem, which led to the discovery of the Book of Laws.)

The temple Solomon built was destroyed and rebuilt and destroyed and rebuilt and destroyed. The only thing left of the last Temple is the Western Wall, shown in Figure 15-1. Because of the sacredness of the site, Jews place notes into the cracks in the wall. (See the related sidebar titled "If at first you don't succeed, build, build again — Part I" later in this chapter.)

The temple that Solomon built is said to have had several courtyards and an inner sanctuary called the Holy of Holies where the Ark of the Covenant — the chest containing the tablets on which the Ten Commandments were inscribed — was kept. Only the high priest could enter the Holy of the Holies; and he could enter only once a year, on Yom Kippur. When he entered, the high priest had ropes tied to his ankles so that if he died inside the inner chamber, people could pull him out. Even today, Orthodox Jews never walk on the Temple Mount itself because nobody knows the precise place of the Holy of Holies, and it would be a grave sin for a Jew who isn't descended from the high priest to step there.

Figure 15-1:
The Western Wall, in Jerusalem.

If at first you don't succeed, build, build again — Part I

King Solomon built the first temple in Jerusalem around 950 B.C.E. It lasted until 586 B.C.E., when the Babylonians, led by Nebuchadnezzar, destroyed it. During this attack, thousands of Israelites were killed and thousands of others were taken as slaves to Babylon. Years later, when the Israelites were liberated from captivity in Babylonia and allowed to return home by the Zoroastrian monarch of Iran named Cyrus II, Zerubbabel, their appointed leader, began the second temple, which, after a few close calls, was eventually completed around the year 515 B.C.E. This one was desecrated, too. Around 20 B.C.E., Herod the Great rebuilt the temple again, but three times, it seems, wasn't the charm. The Roman army, led by Titus, destroyed that temple in 70 C.E. The Western Wall, called in Hebrew the *kotel ha'ma'aravil,* is believed to be the western side of the Temple built by King Herod. The temple itself has never been rebuilt.

O little town of Jerusalem . . . : The Christian connection

Jerusalem is the holiest of all holy places for Christians for a variety of reasons, all having to do with Jesus. Christians believe that Jesus spent the last days of his life in Jerusalem:

✔ On the Thursday before his arrest and crucifixion (called Holy Thursday in Christian circles), Jesus shared a Seder meal with his apostles. This meal, called the Last Supper, is the basis for the Catholic Mass and the rite of Holy Communion.

✔ The Garden of Gethsemane, where Jesus went to pray before dying, is in Jerusalem.

✔ On his way to the cross, Jesus walked through what is now a marketplace in Jerusalem. Christians call this area the *Via Dolorosa* (the Sorrowful Way). This sacred path recalls the journey of Jesus to his death, recounting the 14 Stations of the Cross.

Christians, especially during the 40-day period of Lent, go to their churches to walk the route of Jesus, to understand the meaning of his death and resurrection. For Christians, to go to the actual site in Jerusalem and walk the 14 stations is a very holy thing to do. (To find out more about the 14 Stations of the Cross, go to Chapter 8.)

✔ It was in Jerusalem that Jesus was crucified (at Calvary), buried (in the cave of Joseph of Arimathea, a secret disciple who supposedly buried

Jesus in his own tomb), and resurrected. Years later, around 326, the Emperor Constantine built a shrine, the Church of the Holy Sepulchre, commemorating the holiness of the place. (See the related sidebar titled "If at first you don't succeed, build, build again — Part II" later in this chapter.)

Up, up, and away: The Muslim connection

Although not the most holy place to Muslims (Mecca and Medina rate first and second place), Jerusalem is important to Islam. Although the Qur'an doesn't actually specify Jerusalem as the starting point of Muhammad's ascent into heaven, which is recorded in Surah 17:1, Muslims interpret the Qur'anic phrase "to the farthest mosque" to mean Jerusalem.

Muslims believe that in 619, on the "Night of Ascent," Muhammad, who was in Medina at the time, was awakened from a sleep and taken to Jerusalem to Temple Mount. From there, Muhammad, accompanied by the angel Gabriel, ascended into Heaven on his horse, Buraq. During this trip, Muhammad received the rules for Muslim prayer; met with important prophets from the past, such as Abraham, Moses, and Jesus; and came into God's presence.

In 691 C.E., the Umayyad Caliph Abd al-Malik built the octagonal Dome of the Rock on the Temple Mount (see Figure 15-2). This dome stands over the rock outcropping that Muslims believe was the end point of Muhammad's night journey from Mecca to Jerusalem and from there to Heaven.

If at first you don't succeed, build, build again — Part II

The Church of the Holy Sepulchre didn't have much better luck than the Temple of Jerusalem; see the sidebar "If at first you don't succeed, build, build again — Part 1" for that tale.

Built in 326 by Constantine the Great, the church lasted almost 300 years before the Iranians and local Jews who disliked the Byzantine Christians destroyed it in 614. The church was partially rebuilt, only to be destroyed by the Fatimid rulers from Egypt in 1010. In 1144, the Crusaders rebuilt the church again, but Saladin, the Islamic conqueror of Jerusalem, booted them out in 1187. (Although Saladin banned pilgrimages, he also forbade anyone to desecrate the church.) Therefore, although not deliberately destroyed, the church fell into disrepair. Through the years, people have attempted major repairs and restoration, but the work has been plagued by a hodgepodge of caretakers, a fire, political and religious unrest in the region, and infighting among the various groups that claim responsibility for the church's various parts.

Figure 15-2:
The Dome
of the Rock,
an Islamic
shrine in
Jerusalem.

The Dome of the Rock is often incorrectly called the Mosque of Umar, but it's not a mosque at all; it's a Muslim shrine. Prayers aren't allowed in the Dome of the Rock; that would be akin to idolatry. The El-Aksah Mosque (where Muslims do pray) is also on the Temple Mount.

The Holy Rivers of Hinduism

Water, which symbolizes purification and sanctification, plays an important role in many religions. In the Hindu faith, the waters of the Ganges River are sacred. The river is associated with Shiva, the Hindu god of destruction and reconstruction.

According to Hindu belief, the Ganges River, personified as a goddess (Ganga), once flowed only to heaven, but she was asked to come to earth to purify the dead. Ganga agreed. To break her fall, which would have shattered the earth, she fell first on Shiva's head.

More sacred than the Ganges alone, however, is the place where the waters of the Ganges converge with the waters from other sacred rivers. For this reason, the holiest place in India is the place where the Ganges River meets the Jamuna and the Sarasvati:

✔ The Jamuna is another (real) river that flows from the Himalayas. Personified as the sister goddess of Ganga, the Jamuna River is associated with Vishnu, Hindu god who protects and preserves the world.

✔ The Sarasvati is a mythical, invisible river. Hindus believe the river is personified as the daughter (or granddaughter or companion, depending on your predilection) of Brahma, the Hindu god who created the universe and all things in it.

These three rivers meet in Allahabad. Every 12 years, millions of Hindus flock to one of four sacred sites to take part in the Kumbh Mela, a huge religious festival. In addition to Allahabad, the festival occurs at Haridwar, which is on the Ganges River; at Ujjain, on the Sipra River; and at Nasik, on the Godavari River.

According to legend, the good and bad gods (the demons) fought over a vessel (or *kumbh*) that contained the elixir of immortality. Things got out of hand, and four drops of the elixir fell to earth, landing on each of the four sacred sites. During each *mela* (or celebration), Hindus believe that the rivers change back to this elixir, giving the pilgrims the opportunity to experience purification. For this reason, during the Kumbh Mela, Hindus bathe in the sacred rivers, believing they will be protected. Dying people who bathe in the rivers believe they will be freed from rebirth (moksha).

The *Guinness Book of Records* records this extraordinary gathering of people as, "the largest number of human beings to ever assemble with a common purpose, in the entire history of mankind." In 2001, nearly 30 million pilgrims took part in the Kumbh Mela.

Calling All Muslims to Mecca

For Muslims, Mecca (in Saudi Arabia) is the most sacred place on earth. It is the place Muslims face when they pray, and it is the destination of the Hajj, the once-in-a-lifetime pilgrimage that Muslims must make if they can. Of course, the city also is historically important to Islam.

Mecca is the place where, according to Muslims,

✔ Adam, finally forgiven by God, reunited with Eve.

✔ God saved Hagar and Ishmael, who were near death after Abraham abandoned them at Sarah's urging.

✔ Muhammad was born and lived a large portion of his life.

✔ God began the revelations of the Qur'an to Muhammad.

Beyond these events, Mecca is sacred because it's the place where the Ka'bah stands. In fact, Muslims pray toward the Ka'bah — not Mecca (otherwise, what direction would Muslims in Mecca face during prayer?). Even then, it's not so much the place, but the purpose of the place, that is the focal point of prayer. (For more information about the Ka'bah, see Chapter 8.)

According to Islamic tradition, the fallen, yet forgiven, Adam built the Ka'bah as a testament to God's mercy and power. Centuries later, Abraham and Ishmael rebuilt the Ka'bah as an act of devotion. In this way, the Ka'bah is an earthly reminder of God's omnipotence and mercy and humankind's appropriate response to that power — supplication and gratitude.

Medina: The Early Political Center of Islam

Medina is the second-most-holy site in Islam. Located in Saudi Arabia, Medina (formerly called Yathrib) was the city that welcomed Muhammad and his followers after he fled Mecca in 622 C.E. Surrounded by acceptance and political opportunity, both Muhammad and the Muslim faith were able to flourish.

In Medina, Muhammad's political and religious influence grew. The main ritual forms of Islam — worship, alms-giving, fasting during Ramadan, and the pilgrimage to Mecca — were formulated in Medina. During Muhammad's time in Medina, he extended his power base by reaching out to neighboring military forces to join him in his quest to establish Mecca as a Muslim place of worship for one God, which he accomplished in 630 C.E.

In Medina, you can also find the following (well, you can find them if you're Muslim; if you're not Muslim, you can only read about them because all these places are off-limits to non-Muslims):

✔ **Famous burial sites:** Muhammad was buried in Medina in the Prophet's Mosque. The first two Sunni Caliphs, Abu Bakir and Umar, are also buried in Medina. These burial sites are significant parts of Muslim pilgrimages to Medina.

✔ **Famous mosques:** The first known mosque, the Mosque of Quba', was built in Medina. Medina also houses the Mosque of the Two Qiblahs at al-Remah. This mosque is a monument to Muhammad's decision to instruct prayerful Muslims to turn to Mecca instead of Jerusalem. A number of other mosques in Medina honor Muhammad's military conquests.

✔ **The Islamic University** is in Medina, which was established in 1961.

The Vatican: A City within a City

Rome is nicknamed the Eternal City. It's the home of grand basilicas and magnificent art. Rome is also the home of the Vatican, an independent state located within the city of Rome that serves as the headquarters of the Roman Catholic Church and the home of the Pope, the church's spiritual leader.

The church established the Vatican in Rome for a couple of reasons:

✔ Rome is the place where Saint Peter and Saint Paul were crucified (circa 64 to 67 C.E.).

✔ Rome is the place (well, one of the places) where the early Christians were persecuted.

The Vatican occupies slightly more than 100 acres of land and has a population of 1,000 people. The Pope is its absolute monarch. The smallest country in the world, the Vatican is the home of some of the world's richest religious art and antiquities.

Spiritual treasures found within the Vatican and connected to Rome are the following:

✔ **The Basilica of St. Peter:** Dominating Vatican Square, this expansive church occupies more than 163,000 square feet. According to church history, the Basilica of St. Peter (shown in Figure 15-3) was constructed over a period of more than 176 years (circa 1450–1626 C.E.) and is built upon the site of the crucifixion of Saint Peter. An altar within the Basilica reportedly stands upon the site of the actual crucifixion of St. Peter. With its statuary — including those of Saints Peter and Paul placed in the front of the Basilica — St. Peter's is one of the largest and most visited basilicas in the world.

✔ **The Sistine Chapel:** Giovanni de 'Dolci, under the commission of Pope Sixtus IV, built the Sistine Chapel between 1473 and 1481 C.E. Although frescos adorn the walls and ceiling, the most famous artwork within the Sistine Chapel is the work of Michelangelo:

  • The Last Judgment, containing more than 390 figures that surround Jesus.

  • Scenes from the Book of Genesis, including The Creation of Light, The Creation of Stars and Planets, and The Creation of Adam.

✔ **The Christian Catacombs:** The city contains more than 60 catacombs. Constructed over a period of more than 300 years (circa 150–450 C.E.), the Catacombs contain the tombs, sculpture, paintings, and inscriptions of the early Christians. Many Christian martyrs and popes — including nine popes from the third century — are buried within the Catacombs.

The Promised Land for Latter-day Saints

In 1822 C.E., the angel Moroni told Joseph Smith where he could find buried gold plates containing God's revelation. Smith published these plates as the Book of Mormon in 1830. This writing set the foundation of the Church of Jesus Christ of Latter-day Saints (also known as the Mormon Church). From its beginning, this faith has been a missionary church. Like the Jews who went through the desert to find the Promised Land, members of the Church of Jesus Christ of Latter-day Saints had to endure great hardship to find their Promised Land — Salt Lake City.

The early church traveled to Missouri and Illinois before making its final successful journey to Salt Lake City. During this pilgrimage, Joseph Smith was killed while imprisoned in Illinois, and Brigham Young assumed his leadership mantle.

Considering Salt Lake City to be the New Zion, a place where believers could practice their faith openly, Brigham Young settled the community there in 1847.

Salt Lake City is home to:

- **The Salt Lake Temple on Temple Square:** Brigham Young laid the cornerstone of the temple in 1853. Because geographic conditions made the construction process extremely difficult, it took almost 40 years to complete the temple. The temple is the main ritual center for Church of Jesus Christ of Latter-day Saints. Only members in good standing may enter the sacred places in the temple.

- **Brigham Young's burial site:** Young is buried at the Mormon Pioneer Memorial Monument in downtown Salt Lake City. This monument also honors the 6,000 pioneers who lost their lives while crossing the Plains between 1847 and the advent of the railroad in 1869.

- **The Family History Library:** This is the world's premiere genealogical archive. This library enables Mormons to not only be aware of their ancestors but to check and see if they were baptized. (Mormons believe people can be baptized after they die.)

- **The Museum of Church History and Art:** This museum recalls Brigham Young's 1847 journey in a covered wagon to Salt Lake City; it also houses an original copy of the 1830 Book of Mormon.

- **The Mormon Tabernacle Choir:** Perhaps the most famous site in Salt Lake City is the home of the Mormon Tabernacle Choir. This dome-shaped auditorium is so acoustically sensitive that a pin dropped at the pulpit can be heard clearly at the back of the hall more than 170 feet away.

During a pilgrimage to Salt Lake City, enthusiastic missionaries greet visitors and offer courses in the Church of Jesus Christ of Latter-day Saints. To this day, the faith has retained its strong missionary status and still asks young people in their 20s to devote two years of their lives to spread the faith given by the angel Moroni to Joseph Smith.

The Holy Pilgrimage Sites of the Baha'i Faith

Haifa and Acra (both in Israel) are revered pilgrimage sites in the Baha'i Faith. Before his death, Baha'u'llah (born Mirza Hoseyn Ali Nuri, 1817–1892 C.E.) selected this area as the site for the administrative world headquarters for the Baha'i Faith. At Haifa, the Baha'i administrative complex includes

- **Lavish gardens,** which Baha'i followers consider one of the great wonders of the modern world because they create an environment that offers a tranquil and meditative setting in the midst of a chaotic urban existence.

- **The Universal House of Justice** (the international governing body of the Baha'i Faith).

✔ **The international archives building,** which possesses relics, writings, and artifacts associated with the lives of the Bab and the Baha'u'llah.

The area also has the burial sites of both the Bab and Baha'u'llah. The Bab (born Sayyid Ali Muhammad Shirazi, 1819/20–1850 C.E.) is buried in a gold-domed shrine on the slopes of Mount Carmel in Haifa. The Baha'u'llah is buried nearby at Bahji, outside of Acra. Because of their special role in the founding and guiding of the Baha'i Faith, the burial places of the Bab and the Baha'u'llah, near Bahji are sacred pilgrimage sites for Baha'i believers.

It's appropriate that these two spiritual leaders be buried near each other. Contemporaries, the Bab envisioned the premise of the Baha'i Faith, and Baha'u'llah developed the faith's teachings, advocating the unity of all people; the need for a universal religion; and the abolition of racial, sexual, class, and religious prejudices.

Two Hills and a Mount: Sacred Jain Sites

Jainism — viewed as the oldest continuous monastic tradition in India — has two sacred sites: the Shatrunjaya Hills (Siddehagiri) of Gujarat (a city of thousands of Jain temples and shrines) and Mount Abu in Rajasthan.

The Shatrunjaya Hills, an area full of Jain temples and shrines, is one of the major pilgrimage sites for Jains. The hills are a holy place for the Svetambara segment of the Jain faith. The Shatrunjaya Hills are associated with the Jain teacher, Pundarika, the grandson of the first *jina* (a spiritually advanced soul; one who is victorious in the journey toward enlightenment). The temples and shrines of Shatrunjaya are spread over nine hilltops and across approximately 20 acres of land. Many of the structures in this area date from approximately 900 to 1649 C.E.

Two primary divisions in Jainism exist: the Digambara, or "sky-clad," monks, who wear no clothes and own nothing; and the Svetambara, or "white-clad," monks and nuns, who wear white robes and have also given up all worldly possessions.

Mount Abu is the location for some of India's greatest architectural wonders. It is the home of one Digambara and five Svetambara temples. Most of the Jain structures there were built between the eleventh and the thirteenth centuries. Within the Abu area is the statue of Bhagwan Bahubali, the first person in this world — according to the Jains — to have attained enlightenment — and considered the holiest Jain shrine. Sculptured vines entwine Bahubali's legs to show that he stood in rapt meditation, unaffected by the world around him. According to Jain religious law, a purification ceremony, anointing the statue from head to toe, is held every twelve years. Many Jains make a pilgrimage to Mount Abu for this event.

Holy Places of Taoism

Also known as Taishan, Mount Tai, located in the Shandong Province of China, is the site of many temples, towers, and other structures that celebrate the Taoist faith. This area is a major pilgrimage point for followers of Taoism.

Some of the major structures at Mount Tai are the following:

- **The Azure Clouds Temple:** Dedicated to the Princess of the Azure Clouds, this complex of buildings dates back to the Song Dynasty (907–1279 C.E.). Women pray here for assistance during pregnancy.

- **The Red Gate Palace:** This site was also dedicated to the Princess of the Azure Clouds, who was the daughter of the god of the Taishan.

- **The White Cloud Temple:** Located in Beijing, this temple is the home of the Chinese Taoist Association. Taoists views this temple as the most important Quanzhen temple in China. The intricate architecture of the White Cloud Temple dates back to the beginning of the Ming dynasty. According to Taoist writings, the White Cloud Temple was built on the site of the Tianchang Temple (circa eighth century C.E.), a Taoist holy place that enshrined a stone statue of Lao-Tzu, the founder of Taoism.

Sacred Sites for Other Religions

For Confucianism, the state of Lu (now in Shandong Province in China), the birthplace of Confucius (551–479 B.C.E.) is the most important pilgrimage site for followers of Confucianism. Confucius was buried in Kufow. Many altars are scattered through Kufow to honor him.

In Buddhism, the holy sites relate to important events in the Buddha's life:

- According to Buddhist writings, Buddhism began under the Bodhi tree at Bodhgaya in India, when the Buddha (Siddhartha Gautama, circa 560–480 B.C.E.) achieved enlightenment. Bodhgaya is one of the many significant places for pilgrimage by followers of Buddhism. Today, the Mahabodhi Temple, built in the form of a slender pyramid, stands east of the Bodhi tree.

- After leaving Bodhgaya, Buddha reportedly traveled to Sarnath, near Varanasi on the Ganges River, the place where he is said to have preached his first sermon. Numerous Buddhist monuments are there, where, according to tradition, Buddha first preached in the deer park (known as *mrigadawa*) of Sarnath. Some of the Buddhist monuments at Sarnath date back to the third century B.C.E.

✔ For Buddhist pilgrims, Lumbini in Kapilavastu (today known as part of Nepal), the birthplace of Buddha, is another major pilgrimage site.

In Iran, Zoroastrian pilgrims go to an ancient holy fire at Sharifabad and to shrines around the city of Yazd. In India, an ancient holy fire burns at Udvada.

Chapter 16

Holy Houses

● ●

In This Chapter

▶ Examining the structure and purpose of synagogues

▶ Taking a tour though the temples of various religions

▶ Understanding the role, purpose, and design of shrines

▶ Delving into the differences among Catholic, Eastern Orthodox, and Protestant churches

▶ Investigating the function and style of mosques

● ●

For some religions, such as Christianity, Judaism, and Islam, communal worship is important. The faithful gather at particular times on particular days and interact in a faith experience. For other religions, like Shinto and Buddhism, for example, individual worship is the focus. In yet other faiths, such as Hinduism and Zoroastrianism, worship can be both individual (daily prayers) and collective (celebrating religious festivals). Although they may get together for prayer, the prayers are generally individual for members of most religions, not collective. Whether communal, individual, or both, most religions have structures that serve as places of worship. Although these structures are often buildings, they don't have to be. Nor do they have to be grand or imposing. A storefront church or mosque can be as central for routine worship as an ancient shrine.

This chapter looks at churches, synagogues, temples, mosques, and shrines to investigate the history, the religious practices, and the reason why so many people flock to them.

Synagogues: Jewish Houses of Worship

A Jewish house of prayer, study, and gathering has many names: beit kenesset, shule, kehilat kodesh, Temple, Congregation, Jewish center, and more. The Greek word *synagogue* is the most generic; it's also the one most people are likely to recognize.

The ark and its environs

The synagogue is a place of study *(beit midrash),* a house of gathering *(beit kenesset),* and a house of prayer *(beit tefilah).* The most important thing in a synagogue is the ark *(aron hakosh),* a container or cabinet that contains the Torah scroll:

✔ The ark represents the Holy of Holies (originally, the inner sanctum of Solomon's Temple that contained the original tablets holding the Ten Commandments). As such, it's the most sacred place in a synagogue and the focal point of prayer. (For more information about the Holy of Holies and the Temple built by the biblical King Solomon, refer to Chapter 15).

✔ The ark has doors as well as an inner curtain, called a *parokhet.* This curtain is named after and modeled from the curtain in the sanctuary in the first temple in Jerusalem.

During certain prayers, the doors and/or curtain of the ark may be opened or closed. Typically, a member of the synagogue opens and closes the doors (or pulls the curtain); being the person to do this is considered an honor.

✔ The ark also has an eternal light *(ner tamid)* that symbolizes the eternal flame that once burned on the Temple Mount.

✔ In most synagogues, the ark has a raised area in front of it called a *bima.* In orthodox synagogues, the bima is often in the middle of the congregation. This is where the Torah is read on Mondays, Thursdays, and on the Sabbath. In other synagogues, the bima is up front.

✔ Synagogues try to put the ark on the wall that faces Jerusalem so that worshippers face Jerusalem during prayer. If the synagogue can't be arranged that way, worshippers face the ark.

In synagogues, you won't find exact representations of any of the holy objects that were once in the Temple (it's forbidden). For example, if a synagogue has a menorah (a candelabrum), it can't be seven-branched like the menorah in the Temple.

Rabbis, cantors, and the role of laypeople

In orthodox synagogues, the seats for men and women are separate: the women are upstairs and the men downstairs, for example, or, if they're on the same floor, the men and women sit in adjacent areas separated by a divider called a *mehitzah.*

In orthodox synagogues, the rabbi and the other men wear skullcaps, called *kipot* in Hebrew and *yarmulkes* in Yiddish. During morning prayers, men also wear phylacteries (called *tefilin*) — small leather boxes with long leather straps. Men wear one box over their foreheads and the other one on their left arms. Inside the leather boxes are slips of parchment inscribed in Hebrew. Each parchment contains a scriptural passage reminding worshippers to keep the Jewish law. Men also wear prayer shawls, called *talis,* during day-time prayers and on the eve of Yom Kippur. In liberal synagogues, the rabbi and male congregants may or may not wear all these items.

A Temple Here, a Temple There

Temples are places where people go to worship or to perform religious ritu-als. Some temples serve basically the same purpose as mosques, synagogues, churches, and the fire temples of Zoroastrians: That is, they're places for believers to gather and worship. Only priests who commune with God (or gods) can go in other temples. Because the purpose of temples varies from religion to religion, so do their designs. Some, like Jain and Buddhist temples, are elaborate and highly decorated; others, like Shinto temples, are simple.

Don't sit under the Bodhi tree with anyone else but me: Buddhist temples

One of Buddhism's most sacred moments was when the Buddha found enlightenment under the Bodhi tree. To commemorate this moment, Buddhists built the Mahabodhi Temple (circa sixth century C.E.) at the site of Buddha's enlightenment. This temple, like most Buddhist temples built later, contains a large statue of the Buddha. At the heart of the Temple is the shrine, which often holds a lock of hair or bone from the Buddha or a from a great Buddhist teacher. Buddhist monks and nuns preside over the Temple.

You won't find regular daily prayers at Buddhist temples. Buddhist temples are places for personal devotion, ancestor worship, meditation, and offerings for the monks and for the Buddha. Individual devotion is so important to Buddhism, in fact, that Buddhists can construct shrines in their own homes. These shrines, like the great temples, help believers remember their ances-tors and Buddhist scriptures.

At home, shrines (or altars) should be located in a separate room or quiet area. The shrine contains the following items:

✔ **An image of Buddha:** This image, whether a statue or picture, repre-sents the Buddha who passed on his teaching and the potential for everyone to attain enlightenment. It is placed on a special shelf high on the wall, in a place of honor.

✔ **A vase or tray with flowers:** The flowers symbolize the impermanence of all living things and are usually arranged to represent some aspect of Buddhist teaching. For example, a single flower represents the unity of all things; four flowers can represent the Four Noble Truths, and so on.

✔ **A candle (or oil lamp, in some traditions):** The lighted candle or lamp symbolizes the light of enlightenment.

✔ **Incense:** Because the fragrance fills the room, incense symbolizes how Buddha's teachings spread throughout the world.

✔ **A miniature stupa:** The relics of the Buddha are buried within a dome-like shrine, or *stupa*. A miniature one on a home altar can represent Buddha's relics, or it can contain family relics.

✔ **Scripture:** Most people have a Buddhist text on or near the altar to both refer to and to remind Buddhists of the Middle Way.

Some Buddhist traditions also include a

✔ **Water-offering cup:** This cup, which is kept full of fresh water, symbolizes the cleansing power of meditation, as well as the desire to both give up worldly possessions and to share with others.

✔ **Food offering:** These can be bowls of fresh fruit or a variety of fresh and delicious foods. This offering feeds the mind and the tongue of the Buddha.

✔ **Music offering:** Symbolized by an instrument such as a bell, cymbal, or flute, music is an offering to the ears of Buddha. Music, or sound, signifies wisdom, and consequently, compassion.

When the Buddha died, his body was cremated and his ashes were divided into ten parts, each part going to a particular Buddhist shrine called a stupa. These shrines are earthly symbols of the Buddha's *parinirvana,* or final death and release from the cycle of death and rebirth. In India, the original stupas were dome-shaped buildings; in places like Japan and China, the stupas are towering structures called pagodas. Regardless of the shape, these structures generally contain some sort of relic or a piece of sacred text and serve as monuments to the Buddha. (For more information about religious shrines, see the section titled "Shrines: Places of Remembrance" later in this chapter.)

Hindu temples: Where people and gods commune

You can find many Hindu temples by the Ganges, signifying the liberating quality of that river's waters. Hindus believe, for example, that bathing in the Ganges can free them from the cycle of death and rebirth. (Chapter 15 has more information on the sacred properties of the Ganges River.) Through the centuries, the simple square design of early Hindu temples evolved to include more complex structures that contain multiple sanctuaries. Of course, temples don't have to be near the Ganges, nor do they have to be elaborate.

All Hindu temples are places where Hindus go to worship the gods through sacred images. The temples contain many clay, brick, wood, or stone images of Hindu gods and deities. Hindus believe that when the temple is inaugurated, these images essentially come "alive" with the presence of the divinities they represent. As a result, worshippers can see the gods, and the gods can also see them; in this way, worshipping in a temple is a concrete way to interact with the divine.

In more elaborate temples, the figures of the gods adorn the walls and the doorways and lead believers through an outer hallway (called a *madapa*) or a series of antechambers deeper into the temple, where the main part of the temple (the *prasada*) is. Within the prasada is a square inner chamber, called the *garba grha*. The garba grha, which literally means "womb house," is the most holy part of the temple and the place where the temple's most sacred object is held.

Jain temples: Bath houses for the gods

Jain temples, modeled after Hindu temples, are square structures containing an inner shrine. Within the shrine are

- **The image of an enlightened one, called a Tirthankara.** According to Jain tradition, a Tirthankara is a savior who has been freed from the cycle of death and rebirth — represented as a river that must be crossed — and who has paved a path that others can follow to enlightenment.

- **The central image of Jainism:** A swastika (don't worry—they had it first) appears beneath a half-moon and three dots that symbolize the Three Jewels—the Buddha, the Dharma (teachings), and the *sangha* (the community of monks).

  According to the Jain sacred texts, the four arms of the swastika represent the four levels of life: those born in one of the seven Jain hells; those born as animals, insects, or plants; those born as ordinary human beings; and those born as divine beings.

When Jains attend a temple service, they leave their shoes outside. They mark their brows with saffron and recite a penitential prayer called the *nissahi*. Then they ask for the right to wash the figure of the Tirthankara. If this request is approved, they remove the jewels and old flowers from the sacred image; wash the Tirthankara with water, milk, and various nectars; and anoint the holy figure with liquid saffron in 14 places from head to toe. This encounter is considered holy and inspiring. With incense burning and songs of praise, the Jains depart, bowing in gratitude and leaving behind a bowl of rice as an offering.

Sikh temples: For high and low

Sikhs, followers of a religion located primarily in the Punjab region of India, have many beautiful temples, but the most holy is the Golden Temple at Amritsar, India. The temple, shown in Figure 16-1, is magnificently adorned with marble, has gilded copper domes, and stands in the middle of a pool of water. You can get to the temple, which features precious stones and frescos, by crossing a single bridge.

Located in a beautiful area where pilgrims hear soothing music, read sacred texts, and meditate on ways of living in a higher way, the Golden Temple unifies the community of Sikhs, who aspire to see the dignity of all people, rich and poor alike. The Golden Temple is a *gurdwara,* a place of worship believed to be the threshold of the guru who has appeared in ten incarnations.

The temple's construction is more than beautiful; it is also symbolic:

✔ Unlike many Hindu temples that are built on platforms, the foundation of the Golden Temple is lower than the surrounding land, to emphasize that the Sikh religion is open to the lowly and the oppressed.

✔ The Golden Temple features four doors, which represent the religion's openness to people of all four castes — Kshatriya, Brahmin, Sudra, and Vaisya — and to any people who want to worship there.

Figure 16-1:
The Golden Temple, in Amritsar, India.

The Temple also includes a central shrine, as well as a raised shrine that holds a copy of the Adi Granth, the most holy book in Sikhism. The faithful come to the Temple and bring garlands of flowers and other offerings such as puffed-rice candy to decorate the platform.

Shrines: Places of Remembrance

A shrine is a sacred place where people commemorate a sacred event or the death of a holy person. A shrine often holds the remnants of a holy person. People who journey to shrines, assuming that holiness of the person inhabits the sacred place, are often looking for divine assistance. Although shrines can be houses of worship, they're usually not. These places are where the sacred moments in the history of a religion occurred, and they're places of pilgrimage and veneration, but they're not generally places for daily worship.

Several religions have shrines that function primarily as places of pilgrimage and worship. People who make pilgrimages generally do so because they want to reinforce or deepen their faith. When Shi'ite Muslims go to the tombs of the Prophets, for example, they're going to reinforce their own faith and to learn from the people who went before them. In Christianity, when people journey to Lourdes (France) or Fatima (Portugal) or any number of other locales, they're going to the places where the Blessed Mother (that's Mary, Jesus' mom) is believed to have miraculously appeared, bringing the message of God to a spiritually "thirsty" humanity. The pilgrims hope to experience God and God's grace in a new way.

Shrines play an important role in the cultural and spiritual life of the Japanese. The most noted Shinto shrine is the Ise Shrine, dedicated to the emperor's family, as well as to the sun goddess Amaterasu.

Shinto is a religion that makes a connection between nature and the divine. The kami are earthly and heavenly divinities that exist in the world we see and the world we don't. For that reason, Gateways to Nature, called Torii, are found all over Japan. The gateways are said to be doors that people can walk through to find Nature. You can find Torii in mountain valleys, on the ocean, and in front of some temples.

Shinto pilgrims visit shrines to seek favors from the kami, divine beings, or gods. In the Shinto shrine, the spirit of the kami resides in the shrine's main hall. Visitors entering the main hall petition the kami by tossing coins in the offering box, ringing a bell on a dangling rope, clapping their hands twice, bowing briefly in prayer, clapping their hands again, and leaving. The purpose of all this is to make sure that the kami (who, it seems, are either very preoccupied or very hard of hearing) will hear the sound of the bell, realize the petitioners' presence, and answer their requests.

Shrines in Japan are often local in that they honor a local kami. Other shrines are built to invoke business or family success. Finally, other shrines are built in honor of great national or political importance. These shrines frequently honor emperors or commemorate the souls of Japan's war dead. The Hachimangu Shrine, for example, is dedicated to the kami of war and martial prowess. The Toshogu Shrine recalls Ievasu, a Japanese general, and the Tenmangu Shrine honors a successful aristocrat.

Generally, the Japanese go to the shrines by themselves. They come to make a request for some pressing need, such as a job, an education, an illness, or peace of mind. On important days, such as the birth of a baby and the beginning of the New Year, families go to the shrines together.

Churches: Alike and Different

In the early Christian community, people gathered to share stories about Jesus, to pray with each other, and to receive the Eucharist, what's called the Lord's Supper today. Strengthened by this experience, they created communities of faith where people shared everything they had (Acts 2:24). The early church needed to function this way because it was small and endured periodic persecutions.

The Emperor Constantine (in 313 C.E.) recognized Christianity as a legitimate religion and declared all people in the Roman Empire to be Christian. The Christian church was suddenly free of persecution, but now it had to find a way to accommodate all the new numbers. Therefore, the religion moved out of underground homes and began to build churches, that is, assembly places, where the entire community could gather and pray. Prayers became more structured, and central to the gathering of people in the church was the celebration of the Mass, the re-enactment of the Last Supper (a Seder meal in which Jesus took bread and wine, saying they would become his body and blood).

For a while, Christianity embodied one group of people that were, at least officially, pretty much on the same page when it came to expressions of faith and worship, the role of the clergy, and the church's hierarchy. Then came 1054 and the schism that divided the early church into essentially two branches — Roman Catholic and Eastern Orthodox. (See the related sidebar titled " A church divided" later in this chapter.) Then, in the sixteenth century, came Martin Luther and the Protestant Reformation, which shook things up even more.

GOING DEEPER

A church divided

The year 1054 was a busy one for the Christian church. What started out as a battle for power between pope (head of the Western Christian church in Rome) and patriarch (head of the Eastern Christian church in Constantinople) ended up dividing the Christian church in two, otherwise known as the Great Schism.

Since its humble beginnings, the Church had been growing and its influence spreading. This growth, combined with the political instability of the time (the latter half of the first millennium, when everyone seemed to want to conquer everyone else), made the Church not only the supreme spiritual leader, but also a major political leader. When Church business branched out from saving souls to ruling kingdoms, however, the Church fell victim to political power struggles.

Think of the pope and the patriarch, before 1054, as vice presidents in charge of Western and Eastern branches of Christianity. Each one did the same job for different regions. They believed the same things, they followed the mandates of the same church councils, and they were, in essence, the VIPs of Christianity, Incorporated. At the time, the patriarch was Michael Cerularius; the pope was Pope Leo IX.

Now Emperor Constantine (who had made Cerularius the patriarch of the Byzantine church) wanted to form an alliance with Pope Leo IX against the Normans (those pesky French invaders who eventually stormed England). Cerularius hated the idea, partly because of his own political ambitions and partly because he believed the Eastern church should be separate and independent from the Roman church. Constantine, however, wanted Rome's (and Leo's) help, so he made concessions to sweeten the pot a bit. To throw a wrench in the works, Cerularius decreed that all Roman churches in Constantinople would have to use the Greek language (not Latin) and follow Greek (not Roman) liturgical practices. When the churches refused, he closed them down.

The alliance between Emperor Constantine and Leo continued, however, and in 1054, Leo sent three delegates to negotiate the deal. Cerularius, still in opposition to the alliance, refused to meet the delegates. With his delegates in Constantinople and the deal still not made, Pope Leo died. One of the delegates, who apparently had had enough of Michael Cerularius' shenanigans, decided to retaliate: He excommunicated Cerularius and all his clergy. Cerularius, not one to take his own excommunication lying down, excommunicated all the delegates in return. With excommunications flying around like handbills and Emperor Constantine unable to get the two groups back together again, the separation was complete.

If you want a happy ending, you'll have to settle for this: In 1965, both the Roman Catholic Church and the Eastern Orthodox Church, in a show of good will, lifted the mutual excommunications of 1,000 years ago.

Catholic churches: Trendsetters (for awhile)

The entire Catholic Mass centers on the Eucharist, or the Lord's Supper. The beginning part of the Mass prepares Catholics to accept the Eucharist. The heart of the Mass is Holy Communion itself, when Catholics actually consume the Eucharist. The Mass ends with an injunction to go forth in unity and in reverence of God.

Many people think of Catholic Masses as "busy" and of Catholic churches—particularly older ones—as ornate (or lavish, depending on your point of view). Probably what they're reacting to is "richness" of the environment: There's a lot to look at, a lot to listen to, and, during the Mass, all sorts of proscribed movements and responses. All these actions have a purpose, however. For believers, the experience of the Mass is supposed to be more than an intellectual exercise. To be the transforming experience it is meant to be, the Mass deliberately involves the mind, the soul, and the body. One way the Catholic Church does this is to tap into all the senses so that worshippers experience the Mass through smell, sight, sound, taste, and touch.

The church and its parts

Several churches, particularly Roman Catholic churches, are built in the shape of a cross (if you're looking at it from above as, presumably, God is). In these churches, the altar is often placed at "the crossing"—the place where the halls (the "horizontal" and "vertical" parts of the cross) meet.

Important features you'll find in Catholic churches include

- **A crucifix:** This is a cross with the figure of Jesus on it.

- **A cloth-covered altar:** Called the altar of sacrifice, this is where the priest prepares the Eucharist. The altar is always at the front of the church and has a niche with a relic in it. This relic is from the saint the church is named after.

  Other items on the altar include:

  - Two candles, always burning.

  - A cup (chalice) to hold the wine, and a dish (paten) to hold the Eucharist wafers. (A small piece of linen is placed over the wafers of bread to protect it from being soiled.)

  - Decanters (cruets) of water and wine to be mixed together.

  - A dish of water for the priest to wash his hands.

  - A missal, the Catholic prayer book for priests.

  - And a partridge in a pear tree (just kidding).

- **A pulpit:** The pulpit, in the sanctuary of the church, is where the priest stands when he reads from the Bible.

- **The tabernacle:** The place where the consecrated Eucharist is kept before it makes its grand appearance on the altar. Near the tabernacle is a red lamp that's lit only when consecrated wafers are inside it.

✔ **A baptismal font:** Often placed either to the side of the altar or at the back of the church, this is where babies are christened.

✔ **Scenes depicting the 14 Stations of the Cross.** These images, which depict the story of Jesus' death, appear on the inside walls of the church.

✔ **A basin of holy water:** Placed at each entrance to the church, this basin of water is used by church members as they enter the church. They touch the water with their fingers and make the sign of the cross on themselves saying, "In the name of the Father, and of the Son, and of the Holy Spirit, Amen." This act recalls one's baptismal commitment and the willingness to live a life for God.

✔ **Confessional booths:** This is where Catholics go for confession. The person confessing (called a penitent) has a choice of confessing to the priest face-to-face or confessing through a screen.

Many Catholic churches also have statues dedicated to Mary (Jesus' mother), Joseph (Mary's husband), and the patron saint of the church, whoever that may be.

Catholic vocabulary lesson

Just about every part of a Catholic church has a name. For example, you don't enter at the front of the church, you enter at the *narthex*. The main hall isn't a main hall, it's a *nave*, and the area that's behind the nave isn't the "area that's behind the nave." it's the *chancel*.

Take a look at the names of other things Catholic:

✔ **Abbess:** Head of a convent

✔ **Abbot:** Head of a monastery

✔ **Ablution cup:** The water-filled dish where the priest washes his hands

✔ **Chapel of the Eucharist:** The tabernacle where the Eucharist is kept

✔ **Chasuble:** Outer garment a priest wears

✔ **Cincture:** The rope belt a priest wears around his waist

✔ **Confession:** The niche in the altar of sacrifice that holds a relic of the saint that the church is named for

✔ **Convent:** Where nuns live

✔ **Friary:** Where brothers live (A brother is a member of a men's religious order who doesn't plan to or isn't ready to become a priest.)

✔ **Hosts:** Communion wafers that have been consecrated

✔ **Missalette:** The book or pamphlet that contains the readings and some of the prayers of the Mass

✔ **Monastery:** Where monks live

✔ **Rectory:** Where priests live

Eastern Orthodox churches: A few alterations here and there

Eastern Orthodox churches include the Greek Orthodox Church and the Russian Orthodox Church. Although similar in many ways to Catholic churches (see the preceding section), you do find a few differences. For example, the altar is behind a screen, called the *iconostasis*. This screen includes the "holy doors" that are opened and closed during various parts of the service. This screen is covered with two-dimensional images (or icons) of Jesus, Mary, or a particular saint.

In addition, Eastern Orthodox Christians use more incense than their Roman Catholic counterparts. The clergy use incense before each important part of the liturgy. Incense wafts among the altar, the sanctuary, the icons, the church building, and the people present. The purpose of the incense is to remind the congregation that, just as smoke filters through the air, God's presence filters through all aspects of their lives. The liturgy is central to the Orthodox faith. There are four different liturgies for the Eucharist.

Other things you may notice about services in Eastern Orthodox churches include:

- ✔ The clergy read the liturgies in the native language of their congregation.

- ✔ The choir sings hymns, without musical accompaniment, alone or with the congregation.

- ✔ The Eucharist in the Orthodox rite is leavened bread. Congregants dip the leavened bread into the wine and then eat the bread and wine together.

- ✔ In the Greek Orthodox rite, the bishop's chair is behind the screen; in the Russian Orthodox Church, the chair is in front of and to the side of the screen.

Protestant churches: No (or few) baubles, bangles, or beads

Early Protestant churches were a reaction against what the reformers considered Catholic excesses. The churches' design and ornamentation (or lack thereof) also reflect Protestant ideas of the relationship between God and humankind: It's direct. *Mano a mano.* It doesn't need interceders. It doesn't need icons. It needs only faith.

Luther and the other Protestant reformers emphasized singing, reading the Word of God, and preaching, so they emphasized simplicity:

The Roots of Protestantism

For many years, the Catholic Church (not-so-affectionately referred to as the Whore of Babylon by the more fanatical Protestants) was a political power as well as a religious power, and it had a substantial amount of wealth. Corrupt clergy also plagued the Catholic Church. One of the big abuses was *simony,* the sale of indulgences. Before the sixteenth century, people protested the Church's abuses, but in the sixteenth century, Martin Luther led an attack on the Church itself.

Martin Luther and others went for the Church's heart:

- Luther claimed that scripture alone (the Bible) is authoritative. People should follow the Bible to find and obey God, not priests, not cardinals or bishops, and not the Pope. With this one simple idea, he proclaimed the entire hierarchical structure of the Catholic Church irrelevant.

- Luther claimed that the Pope and priests had no authority over forgiveness of sins. People could be saved from their sins only through faith, not good works.

- Luther claimed that no amount of money given to the Roman Catholic Church could buy a place in heaven. In other words, the Church really didn't have much say at all in who got into heaven.

Although Luther's original intention was to reform the Catholic Church from within, the Catholic Church decided to boot Luther out (called excommunication). That action led to a major split between Catholics and the protestors, or Protestants. One of the first Protestant churches was the Lutheran Church. Other Protestant churches began to form as, one by one, the political powers within countries such as England, Sweden, and Norway began to confiscate Roman Catholic lands and churches and form state religions.

- Because Protestant churches focus on the sermon, their architectural emphasis is on the pulpit, where the minister preaches; it's not on the altar. Catholic Churches have three focal areas: the altar, the tabernacle, and the pulpit. (The whole point of a Catholic Mass is the Eucharist. Protestant churches occasionally celebrate communion.)

- Because early Protestants rejected the symbols of wealth, which included gold, fine clothes, and jewels worn by church officials, many Protestant churches are sparsely decorated.

- Protestants generally believe in something called the "priesthood of believers," a concept in which believers speak directly to God; they don't need someone, like a priest, to intercede on their behalf. For that reason, Protestant churches don't have confessionals.

- Most Protestant churches prefer the plain symbol of the cross, representative of the risen Christ, rather than the crucifix, with its image of a crucified Christ.

One of the most important developments in Protestantism is the growth of the mega-church. These huge Protestant churches accommodate thousands of worshippers on Sundays, and often broadcast their services over cable television stations. Millions of people tune in to hear dynamic and galvanizing preachers. Mega-churches often have many youth ministers, as well as educational and self-help programs operating in the church. Some people find these churches too commercial, but others appreciate worship services that have the same technical capabilities as movies and television but which preach words of faith and love.

For some, the little white church on the corner may be a thing of the past; for others, small communities where the clergyperson knows them by name are the most spiritually satisfying communities to nurture faith.

Mosques: Places of Ritual Prostration

The word *mosque* comes from the Arabic *masjid,* which means a place of ritual prostration, and that, in a nutshell is what a mosque is. Although mosques, since Muhammad's time, have served various functions — political social, and educational, as well as religious — the main function of a mosque is as a place devoted to the praise and worship of Allah.

The building

A mosque is any place devoted to prayer. It could be a house, a community building, or an open area of ground that was marked off as sacred. In fact, the early mosques were based on the place where Muhammad worshipped: the courtyard of his house. The builders kept the basic design — open space — and added a roof. Many mosques have domed roofs, atop of which is the symbol of Islam: a star cradled by a crescent moon.

- The star has five points, reminding Muslims of the five obligations of Islam.
- The crescent moon reminds Muslims of Allah the Creator and the lunar calendar that marks Islamic holy days.

Attached to many mosques in Muslim countries is a tower, called a minaret, where the *muezzin* (or crier) calls people to prayer. Most mosques also have an ablutions room, a place where the faithful can perform the ritual washing before prayer.

When you enter a mosque, you may notice that

✔ Mosques don't have furniture. Everyone sits on the floor, not in pews or chairs.

✔ In larger mosques, the carpeting often has a design that marks out the prayer lines so that people know where to sit so as to leave enough room for someone else.

✔ The wall that faces Mecca (and the wall Muslims face when they pray) is called the *qiblah*. Set in this wall is a niche or an alcove, called a *mihrab* that points in the direction of Mecca. The mihrab is not an altar (even though it kind of looks like one). Its function is to direct Muslims' minds and thoughts toward God.

✔ To the right of the arch is a raised platform called the *minbar*. Similar to a pulpit, this is where the imam reads the prayers and gives sermons.

✔ Mosques don't have statues or pictures. You won't find images of God, Muhammad, or any of the prophets, for example. Instead, you'll find beautiful calligraphy of verses from the Qur'an.

Famous mosques

The first mosque, called the Prophet's Mosque, was in Muhammad's home in Medina. As the Muslim faith grew, so did the number and types of mosques. Some of the most famous and visited mosques include

✔ **The El-Aksah Mosque in Jerusalem:** Islam's third-holiest place of prayer, this mosque is on the southern side of the Temple Mount by the Dome of the Rock, where Muhammad is believed to have been taken from earth to observe Paradise.

✔ **The Sacred Mosque in Mecca:** This mosque is one of the places visited by Muslims during their pilgrimages to Mecca.

✔ **The Great Mosque of Damascus (Syria):** One of the earliest surviving stone mosques, the Great Mosque was built between 705 and 715 C.E.

✔ **The Qala-un Mosque:** Built in Egypt between 1283 and 1285 C.E., this mosque contained a hospital, a theological college, and a mausoleum.

✔ **The Great Mosque of Cordoba (Spain):** This mosque was later turned into a Christian church.

✔ **The Hassan II Mosque in Casablanca (Morocco):** This mosque is one of the largest mosques in the world.

Chapter 17

Holy Days on the Calendar

• •

In This Chapter

▶ Understanding how lunar, lunisolar, and solar calendars work

▶ Looking at important holy days, religion by religion

• •

Holy days — and their derivative holidays — are important to every religious tradition. Holy days celebrate events and people important to a religion. On holy days, worshippers take special note of their own existence and its meaning within the context of their beliefs. In many nations, these holidays influence government, politics, and, especially, the school calendar.

Each of the world religions uses a calendar to record, remember, and perpetuate significant events as a way to proclaim its identity. By commemorating and acknowledging significant moments in a religion's history, people of faith unite. The holidays and the festivals — remembering both the times of joy and sorrow within a particular faith — help believers understand where they came from and what they're trying to be.

Types of Calendars — Just in Case You're Curious

A calendar is a way of adjusting and keeping track of the natural divisions of time. Folks who come up with calendars look to the heavens and the stars (celestial bodies) as the basis for determining the calendar.

Three basic types of calendars exist:

- ✔ **The lunar calendar:** Dating back to the Sumerians, the lunar calendar is the oldest type of calendar. It is based on synodic months — that is, complete cycles of phases of the moon.

- ✔ **The lunisolar calendar:** In this type of calendar, the months are lunar, and years are solar. According to ancient literature, the formula for the lunisolar calendar most likely originated in Mesopotamia in the third millennium B.C.E.

✔ **The solar calendar:** This type of dating system is based on the time it takes the earth to revolve once around the sun, 365¼ days. Egyptians were among the first people to use a solar calendar, which they created by using the annual reappearance of Sirius, the Dog Star, in the eastern sky, as a fixed point. This event was reported to have coincided with the annual flooding of the Nile River. Early Indo-Europeans also used solar calendars to track seasonal changes and religious days associated with the seasons.

What you need to know about the calendars is that they're all based on the phases of the moon or the movement of Earth around the sun.

Calendars of the World Religions

Because each religion measures time based on significant events that occurred at certain times, practically every religion has its own calendar. In this section, you look at some of the calendars various world religions use today.

The Christian calendar

In the beginning, the Christian calendar was based on the Julian calendar (the one introduced on the instruction of Julius Caesar in 46 B.C.E.). The Julian calendar was good, except it didn't account for the extra quarter of a day that occurred every year — which may not sound like a big deal, but it had the cumulative effect of throwing off the seasons.

In the late 1500s, Pope Gregory XIII corrected the flaw in the Julian calendar. His calendar, called the Gregorian calendar, provides for an ordinary year of 365 days and a leap year of 366 days every fourth year. Pope Gregory made the change so that Easter (the most important Christian holiday) would be celebrated as a spring festival. The timing for Easter Sunday depends on both the vernal equinox and the moon's phases. Where Easter falls determines the calendar positioning of the rest of the Church's movable feasts.

The Roman Catholic Church adopted the Gregorian calendar in 1582. The Protestant countries accepted it in 1752. The Eastern Churches, however, stuck with the Julian calendar. The result? In some years, a month's difference may fall between certain Christian celebrations in the Eastern and Western Christian Churches. Table 17-1 shows many of the significant dates in the Christian calendar.

Table 17-1	Christian Holy Days	
Holy Day	**Time of Year**	**Meaning/Significance**
Easter Sunday	Celebrated between March 21 and April 25 (Between April and May, for the Eastern Orthodox Church, based on its ecclesiastical calendar)	The celebration of the resurrection of Jesus Christ, Easter is the most sacred of the Christian holy days and is celebrated with a special service, feasting, the giving of eggs, and family gatherings.
Christmas	December 25 (January 7 in the Eastern Orthodox Church)	The day that commemorates the birth of Jesus Christ, Christmas is celebrated with an evening service, often on Christmas Eve, feasting, and gift exchange.
Epiphany	A festival that occurs 12 days after Christmas	Celebration of the three magi who brought gifts to celebrate the birth of Jesus.
Ash Wednesday	Marks the first day of Lent and occurs 46 days before Easter Sunday	A time of fasting for Roman Catholics; represents the beginning of the liturgical cycle that concludes with the resurrection of Jesus Christ.
Lent	The 40-day period (not including Sundays) that begins on Ash Wednesday and concludes with Holy Saturday	A period of fasting and prayer that leads up to the celebration of the resurrection of Jesus Christ on Easter Sunday.
Palm Sunday	The Sunday before Easter Sunday	The official beginning of Holy Week (which culminates with Easter Sunday) and celebrates Jesus' triumphal return into Jerusalem.
Holy Thursday (Maundy Thursday)	Celebrated the Thursday of Holy Week	Recognizes the Last Supper and commemorates the last acts of Jesus Christ.
Good Friday (Holy Friday)	Celebrated the Friday of Holy Week	Commemorates the execution of Jesus by the Romans.

(continued)

Table 17-1 (continued)

Holy Day	Time of Year	Meaning/Significance
Ascension Thursday (Ascension Day)	Occurs 40 days after Easter Sunday	Commemorates the ascension of Jesus into heaven.
Pentecost (Whitsunday)	Occurs 50 days after Easter Sunday	Marks the time when the Holy Spirit descended upon the Apostles.

The Jewish calendar

The Jewish calendar used today is lunisolar: The years are solar and the months are lunar.

The year consists of 12 months, based on a 354-day cycle, and it begins at the time of the new moon of Tishrei (the Hebrew name for the time period of September to October).

Following are the months in the Jewish calendar and the corresponding dates in the Western Gregorian calendar:

Jewish Month	Gregorian Equivalent
Nisan	March-April
Iyar	April-May
Sivan	May-June
Tamuz	June-July
Av	July-August
Elul	August-September
Tishrei	September-October
Marheshvan (Chesvan)	October-November
Kislev	November-December
Teves	December-January
Shevat	January-February
Adar 1 and 2*	February-March

To make certain that Jewish harvest festivals don't creep into seasons where no harvest is possible (one problem with lunar calendars), the Jewish lunar calendar periodically adds a second month of Adar to the solar year to even things out.

The counting of the Jewish year begins at the time of creation, calculated on biblical data to coincide with 3761 B.C.E. Thus, the year of 2002 is 5763 in the Jewish calendar. You can find significant Jewish holy days in Table 17-2.

Table 17-2	Jewish Holy Days	
Holy Day	*Time of Year*	*Meaning/Significance*
Rosh Hashanah (New Year)	Between mid-September and early October	During the two days of the New Year, God in heaven symbolically judges Jews. The *shofar* (horn) is blown to awaken people to repentance.
Yom Kippur (Day of Atonement)	The tenth day after the beginning of Rosh Hashanah	Observed as a fast day; allows Jewish people to remain in contemplation and worship.
Passover (Pesach)	Celebrated during the spring (between March and April)	The celebration of the exodus of the Israelites from Egypt; lasts eight days. The first two and last two days of Passover are the most holy, and Jews come together in a special Seder celebration.
Shavuot	Spring (late May into early June)	Celebrates the giving of the Ten Commandments on Mount Sinai; connected with the conclusion of the barley harvest in ancient Israel.
Sukkot (or Tabernacles)	Celebrated during the fall harvest cycle (late September through October)	A nine-day festival that marks the divine protection given to the Israelites during their wandering through the wilderness. Also celebrates the fall harvest season.
Purim	Celebrated during the 14th day of the Hebrew month of Adar	Marks the deliverance of the Jews of Persia from the persecution of Haman (the prime minister of King Ahasuerus).
Hanukkah (Festival of Lights)	Celebrated on the 25th day of the Hebrew month of Kislev	Commemorates the heroic efforts of the Maccabean brothers to lead the war to oust the Syrian/Greek invaders in Israel; celebrates the rebuilding of the Temple.

The Muslim calendar

The Muslim, or Islamic, calendar is based on a lunar cycle and consists of 12 months. A year has 354 or 355 days. The months of the Muslim calendar and their Arabic names are Muharram, Safar, Rabi' al-Awwal, Rabi' al-Thani, Jumada 'al-Awwal, Jumada 'al-Thani, Rajab, Sha'ban, Ramadan, Shawwal, Dhu 'al-Qa'dah, and Dhu 'al-Hijjah.

Because the Muslim calendar doesn't periodically add a month to keep it in line with the solar year, the months move backward through the seasons, occurring 11 days earlier each year.

This calendar begins its dating system in the year 622 C.E., the year that the prophet Muhammad and his followers traveled from Mecca to Medina. (This journey, or migration, is called the *Hijrah*).

Table 17-3 offers some important Muslim holy days.

Table 17-3	Islam Holy Days	
Holy Day	*Time of Year*	*Meaning/Significance*
Ramadan	Celebrated during the ninth month of the Muslim calendar	The holiest of Muslim holidays, Ramadan is a month-long fast that celebrates the time that Muhammad received the Qur'an.
Id al-Fitr (Feast of Breaking the Fast of Ramadan)	Celebrated at the end of the holy month of Ramadan	Id al-Fitr is a joyous celebration that brings together family and friends to exchange blessings and good wishes.
Laylat al-Qadr (Night of Power)	Falls on the eve of the 26th fast day during the holy month of Ramadan	Laylat-al-Qadr is the celebration of the night when the Prophet Muhammad received the revelation of the Qur'an.
Id al-Adha (Feast of Sacrifice)	Celebrated during the 12th month	A three-day festival that culminates the Hajj by recalling the willingness of Abraham to sacrifice his son in obedience to Allah.
Laylat al-Isra' wa al-Mi`raj (Night of Ascension)	Celebrated on the 27th of the month of Rajab	This celebration marks the journey by the prophet Muhammad, escorted by the angel Gabriel, through hell and heaven and into the presence (but not the sight) of God.

Holy Day	Time of Year	Meaning/Significance
al-Hijrah (Muslim New Year)	Celebrated on the first of Muharram of the Muslim calendar	The term *hijrah* means migration. This day is the celebration of the time the prophet Muhammad migrated from Mecca to Medina.
Mawlid al-Nabi	Celebrated on the 12th day of the month of Rabi' al-Awwal.	Commemorates the birthday of Muhammad
Laylat al-Bara'a or Shab-i Barat	Celebrated on the night before the 15th day of the month of Sha'ban.	This is a time when Muslims believe their destinies are set for the coming year. As it occurs shortly before Ramadan, Muslims spend the time preparing for the new year

The Hindu calendar

The Hindu religion follows the Hindu calendar, which dates back to 1000 B.C.E. and is based primarily on the lunar cycle. The year is divided into three periods of four months each. Each period commences with a special religious rite. The names of the months in the Hindu calendar and their corresponding dates in the Western Gregorian calendar follow:

Hindu Month	Gregorian Equivalent
Magha	January-February
Phalguna	February-March
Chaitra	March-April
Vaisakha	April-May
Jyaistha	May-June
Sravana	July-August
Asvina	September-October
Karthika	October-November
Margasirsa	November-December
Pausa	December-January

In the Hindu calendar, the date of a significant religious event follows this form — month, fortnight (either a waxing or waning moon), name of the *tithi* (lunar day) in the fortnight, and the year of the particular era when the event was to have taken place.

See Table 17-4 for a listing of some significant Hindu holy days.

Table 17-4		Hindu Holy Days
Holy Day	*Time of Year*	*Meaning/Significance*
Maha Shivarathri	Mid-February	Maha Shivarathri is a joyous festival dedicated to the god Shiva.
Holi	Celebrated on the full-moon day of the month of Phalguna (February-March)	Holi is the spring festival and the most colorful of the Hindu celebrations. It lasts two days.
Rama Navami	Late March	Rama Navami is the celebration of the birth of Rama, who is viewed as the reincarnation of the god Vishnu.
Janmashtami	Observed on the night of the new moon during the month of Bhadrapada (August-September)	Janmashtami is a joyful celebration of the birth of Lord Krishna.
Dassera	Celebrated over a ten-day period during the month of Asvina (September-October)	Dassera is a festival in which Hindus honor the goddess Durga. One of the main features of this festival is the remembrance of the epic story of Ramayana.
Diwali	Celebrated on Amavasya, the new moon day of the month of Karttika in the Hindu calendar (late October-early November)	A five-day festival that focuses on prayers and meditations to Laksmi (goddess of prosperity), er consort Vishnu, Durga (the goddess of primal energy), and Sarasvati (the goddess of learning).

The Chinese calendar

The ancient Chinese calendar was lunisolar, and the ordinary year contained 12 lunar months. Each month in the Chinese calendar is named after 12 animals that follow one another in rotation. According to Chinese legend, the animals fought as to who was to head the cycle of years. To settle the fighting, the Chinese gods suggested that the animals have a contest — whoever reached the bank of a certain river first would lead the calendar cycle and the rest of the animals would be grouped according to how they placed in the contest.

The animal names of the months (and the Gregorian equivalents), in the order they finished the contest are

Chinese Month	Gregorian Equivalent
Shu (rat)	January-February
Niu (ox)	February-March
Hu (tiger)	March-April
Tu (hare)	April-May
Long (dragon)	May-June
She (snake)	June-July
Ma (horse)	July-August
Yang (goat)	August-September
Hou (monkey)	September-October
Ji (cock)	October-November
Gou (dog)	November-December
Zhu (pig)	December-January

Table 17-5 lists the major events on the Chinese calendar.

Table 17-5	Chinese Festivals	
Festival	*Time of Year*	*Meaning/Significance*
Chinese New Year	Celebrated sometime during January and February, marking the beginning of the first lunar month.	The most important event in the Chinese calendar. Family and friends gather, pay all debts, discard the old year, and prepare for the coming opportunities of the new year. Celebrations usually last for two or three weeks.
Qingming Festival (Grave Sweeping Day)	Beginning of April	People pay respects to the dead. Families visit ancestors' shrines and tombs; remove weeds and leaves; wipe off the gravestones; and make offerings (food, incense, paper "money" and other goods) for use in the afterlife.

(continued)

Table 17-5 *(continued)*

Festival	Time of Year	Meaning/Significance
Dragon Boat Festival (Fifth Moon Festival)	Held on the fifth day of the fifth lunar month (April/May)	Notes the death of Qu Yuan (circa 278 B.C.E.), a loyal nobleman who drowned himself. Citizens threw wrapped rice dumplings into the water to feed his hungry spirit. Regattas and boat races recall the attempts to rescue him. Each boat is decorated with a wood head and tail of a dragon.
Mid-Autumn Festival	Held on the 15th day of the eighth lunar month of the calendar (around September and October)	This major festival recalls an uprising against the Mongols in the 14th C.E. The festivities include lion dancing and children parading with multicolored lanterns.

The Buddhist calendar

The Buddhist calendar combines solar and lunar elements: The year is solar, while all of the religious festivals follow the lunar calendar. Although this calendar tends to vary from country to country and, according to the school of Buddhism (that is, Zen, Tibetan, Theravada, and so on), some of the most important days in the Buddhist calendar are the full-moon days of each month. The names of the Buddhist months (in Pali, the ancient North Indian language) are Citta, Vesaka, Jettha, Asalha, Savana, Potthabada, Assayuja, Kattika, Maggasira, Pussa, Maga, and Phagguna.

See Table 17-6 for a listing of some significant Buddhist holy days.

Table 17-6	Buddhist Holy Days	
Holy Day	Time of Year	Meaning/Significance
Wesak	April 8; celebrated by Mahayana Buddhists	Marks the anniversary of the birth of the Buddha.
Nirvana Day (or Mahaparinirvana)	Mid-February	An observance of the anniversary of the death of the Buddha.
Losar (Tibetan New Year)	Mid-February	The New Year celebration among the Losar Buddhist sect in Tibet.

Holy Day	Time of Year	Meaning/Significance
Bodhi Day (Day of Enlightenment)	December 15	Celebrates the time that Prince Gautama took his place under the Bodhi tree and vowed to remain there until he attained supreme enlightenment.

The Baha'i calendar

The era of the Baha'i Faith dates back to 1844 C.E., when Mirza Ali Muhammad took on the title *Bab* (which means *the Gate*). The Baha'i calendar consists of 19 months. The month names represent various conditions deemed relevant to the faith. The months of the Baha'i calendar, with their Arabic names, and their associated traits follow:

Month Name	Characteristic
Bahá	Splendor
Jalál	Glory
Jamál	Beauty
'Azamat	Grandeur
Núr	Light
Rahmet	Mercy
Kalimát	Words
Kamál	Perfection
Asmá	Names
'Izzat	Might
Mashiyyat	Will
'Illm	Knowledge
Quadrat	Power
Qawl	Speech
Masá'il	Questions
Sharaf	Honor
Sultan	Sovereignty
Mulk	Dominion
'Alá	Loftiness

The cycle of the Baha'i year ends with 19 days of fasting in preparation for Naw-Ruz (the New Year). For the Baha'i, each day starts and ends at sunset. See Table 17-7 for a listing of some important Baha'i holy days.

Table 17-7	Baha'i Holy Days	
Holy Day	*Time of Year*	*Meaning/Significance*
Ayyam-Ha	Adjusts to the solar cycle; begins late February and runs through early March.	Ayyam-Ha are days that adjust the Baha'i calendar each year. This period is a time for special acts of charity, gift giving, and preparing for the Baha'i fast.
Festival of Ridvan	April 21-May 2	The most holy time of the Baha'i year. A 12-day celebration that honors the time when the Baha'u'llah declared he was the prophet that the Bab foretold.
Declaration of the Bab	May 23	The anniversary of the beginnings of the Baha'i Faith. Celebrates the declaration by the Bab that a new and great messenger of God would come and usher in a new age of peace for all humankind.

Part VI
The Part of Tens

The 5th Wave — By Rich Tennant

@RICHTENNANT

"I don't mean to appear unenlightened Mr. Grove, but I don't think an exorcism should be our first line of treatment."

In this part . . .

Want to hear a few religious tales? Ever wonder what sort of jobs religious-minded people are fit for? Then this is the part you're looking for. You'll find ten occupations for the truly devoted and ten famous and not-so-famous religious stories.

Chapter 18

Ten (or so) Jobs for the Devoted

*H*ere's an interesting job description:

WANTED: Dedicated people person with above-average communication skills. Must be able to handle long hours, customer complaints, and noisy children. On-call availability required. Job responsibilities may include any (or all) of the following:

- *Visiting the sick*
- *Comforting the suffering*
- *Presiding at weddings, baptisms, and funerals*
- *Raising capital*
- *Creating, implementing, and overseeing outreach programs*
- *Communicating with God*

Some experience with transubstantiation or interpreting dreams preferred but not required. Vows of poverty and chastity mandatory in some departments. Will train and initiate. Pay variable (begging may be required), benefits package outstanding. For more information, contact God.

Of course, the calling to devote a life to religion doesn't usually come from the classifieds in the Sunday paper. For many people, like those drawn to the religious roles covered in this chapter, the call comes from within.

Roman Catholic Priest

A Catholic priest is drawn to teaching, to offering aid to the downtrodden, and, most importantly, to helping people maintain or find belief in a world that often seems hopeless.

Two basic types of priests exist: *diocesan* (local) priests and *order* priests.

✔ **Diocesan priests** are spiritual leaders of the parish church. They celebrate Mass, hear confessions, visit the sick, preach, and lead people in the sacraments.

Becoming a diocesan priest requires that you make a

• Promise of obedience to the bishop and his successors.

• Promise to live a celibate life.

• Commitment to live and proclaim the gospel.

If you are a married Protestant clergyman who then converts to Catholicism, you may remain married. If you are in an Eastern Rite church and you are studying for the priesthood, you may choose to marry before you are ordained. But if you intend to become a bishop, you must be celibate.

✔ **Order priests** are men who join a community of people dedicated to a particular type of work for the church. Some order priests belong to these communities, for example:

• Jesuit: This order of priests is concerned with education.

• Franciscan: This order focuses on caring for the poor.

• Maryknoll: The priests in this order go to the missions.

Becoming a Catholic priest in a religious order requires one to take a vow of poverty, chastity, and obedience.

From priest to pope: The church hierarchy

As with most other organizations, the priesthood has a hierarchy. Starting from the top, here's a look at the ecclesiastical organization:

✔ **The Pope:** The most well-known priest in the world is the Pope, the "Vicar of Christ." Catholics consider him the holiest man on earth — the spiritual leader of Catholicism and the whole world. He is also the Bishop of Rome.

✔ **Cardinal:** He is known as the "prince of the Church." As a cardinal, one of his jobs is to elect the Pope. In between elections, he advises the Pope on major issues of the world and the Church and helps the Pope maintain the cathedrals in Rome.

✔ **Bishop** (and **Archbishop**): The bishop enjoys the fullness of the priesthood. He is the leader and the teacher of Catholicism in his *diocese.* The term diocese refers to a geographic area. An archbishop is simply the head of an archdiocese, which is a diocese located in a metropolitan area.

✔ **Monsignor:** This is an honorary title given to a priest in recognition of his specific ministry.

✔ **Priest:** This is where a man begins his journey in the clergy. He generally works in a parish, celebrates Mass, hears confessions, visits the sick, counsels people, and represents the church's teachings to the Catholic community.

Deacons rank under priests in the Catholic and Episcopal churches; in nonconformist churches, deacons are elected lay officers. Deacons, who can be married, serve in pastoral and administrative capacities.

Catholic Monk and Nun

Monks are men who find the presence of God in solitude. Their calling is monastic (which means to be solitary), and they live in communities (monasteries) governed by abbots. Monks study theology and the spiritual life and spend a great deal of time in prayer and contemplation, as well as singing the praises of God. Monks start out as brothers, and some become priests, but they don't have to. Like priests, monks take vows of poverty, chastity, and obedience. Monks live in monasteries.

Nuns, or sisters, are religious women who take vows and devote their lives to God through prayer and selfless work for the community. Historically, nuns have educated orphans, been involved in charity work, care for the elderly, care for the sick, and care for those who are mentally or physically challenged. Today, nuns also specialize in professional arenas and have professional jobs.

Women who want to be nuns study for a year in a *novitiate* (a time devoted to prayer and study) to become more proficient in the spiritual life. Then they take a vow of chastity and, like monks, withdraw from the material part of the world. Sometimes, they live in a convent; but today, more often than not, they live in a community or buy a home and live together. Even though nuns don't marry, they wear wedding bands. The reason is that nuns are married to Christ. Nuns voluntarily accept virginity as a way of serving God.

Protestant Minister

A minister is a servant of God. In general, the term minister is reserved for Protestant clergy — men and women who are ordained and serve a local congregation. Some ministers choose to work in a variety of secular fields such as social service agencies, prisons, hospitals, or as chaplains in any institution.

A minister may be someone who goes through a seminary, studies the theology of a particular denomination, and is ordained by that denomination. Other ministers are called by inspiration: They don't study theology formally, but they believe that they've been inspired by the Holy Spirit to preach. (See the related sidebar titled "Minister, preacher, pastor, or priest?" later in this chapter.)

Jewish Rabbi

Rabbis, the intellectual and spiritual leaders of a Jewish community, are "master teachers" of the Torah and sometimes judges and administrators of the Jewish community. In all the traditions of Judaism, with the exception of Orthodox Judaism, women, as well as men, can be rabbis. To become a rabbi, most rabbinical seminaries require a person to have a college degree and to spend four or five years in full-time rabbinical study.

Rabbis can marry and have families, and they don't necessarily have to be leaders of congregations. In Orthodox Judaism, for example, it's common to find men who've been ordained as rabbis but who don't practice as rabbis. These men just took a few extra courses in the *yeshiva* (a school for Talmudic studies) and were ordained.

Overall, however, rabbis preach sermons on the Sabbath and on the High Holy Days of Rosh Hashanah and Yom Kippur. Sometimes, rabbis lead prayers and read from the Torah scroll (sometimes a cantor, or *hazzan,* or an educated layperson helps the rabbi do those ritual tasks). These "pulpit rabbis," who lead congregations, have the traditional duties of clergy: they officiate at rites of passage, teach, preach, make religious rulings for their community, visit the sick, and counsel the bereaved and the suffering. Rabbis can also serve as teachers or chaplains at universities, in hospitals or nursing homes, or at prisons.

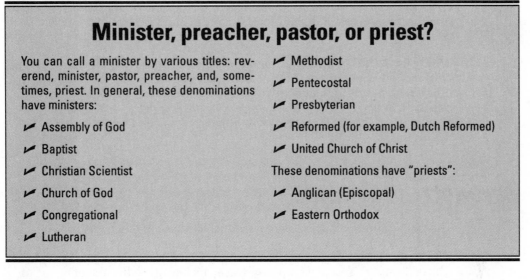

Minister, preacher, pastor, or priest?

You can call a minister by various titles: reverend, minister, pastor, preacher, and, sometimes, priest. In general, these denominations have ministers:

- Assembly of God
- Baptist
- Christian Scientist
- Church of God
- Congregational
- Lutheran

- Methodist
- Pentecostal
- Presbyterian
- Reformed (for example, Dutch Reformed)
- United Church of Christ

These denominations have "priests":

- Anglican (Episcopal)
- Eastern Orthodox

Orthodox rabbis do less preaching and more judging than liberal rabbis. A highly educated Orthodox rabbi whom many call upon to act as a judge of Jewish legal matters is called a *posek*.

Jewish Cantor

The cantor is the person who leads the congregation in chants and hymns. In the prayer service of Judaism, the one who leads the prayers is far more important than the rabbi, who may have a minor role in the prayer service. Leading the prayers is why the cantor's role is so important. In fact, cantors can perform weddings without a rabbi present, but that doesn't happen very often.

To be a cantor, you have to have a good voice. In the old Orthodox *shules* (synagogues), cantors came from the all-male choir that sang with the cantor. Promising voices were nurtured, and the children were encouraged to become cantors. Today, Jewish seminaries offer several years of training for those seeking a career in the cantorate.

Women can't be cantors in Orthodox Judaism; they can in the other movements of Judaism, however.

Muslim Imam

In Islam, the imam is a spiritual leader of a mosque. Because Islam doesn't have professional clergy (except for Sufi Muslims), the imam serves his community in his spare time. He (imams must be men) is the director of Muslim life in the mosque, the planner of holiday feasts, and the administrator of the religious needs of the community.

The imam is chosen from the community because he is learned in the prayers of Islam. Although the role of the imam varies according to the Islamic sect (Shi'ite and Sunni, for example), the primary role of all imams is to lead the members of his mosque — *the communal gathering place* — in daily prayer. (A Muslim prays five times each day, although prayers don't need to be said in the mosque.)

Zoroastrian Magus

The magi (plural of magus) were introduced into Christian belief as the wise men from the east who journeyed to Bethlehem. They were, in fact, Zoroastrian priests from Iran. The contemporary Zoroastrian priesthood, whose members are called *mobeds,* traces its lineage to the ancient magi of Iran. Passed from father to son, priesthood involves long years of studying the liturgies and rituals of Zoroastrianism, starting during childhood. This is followed by formal initiation as a practicing priest via a two-stage ritual process. Once initiated, magi perform prayer services and ceremonies, such as marriage for the laity; tend the holy fires in temples; and guide the community on religious matters.

Buddhist Monk and Nun

The "holy people" of Buddhism are the *bhiksu* (monks) and the *bhiksuni* (nuns). These Sanskrit terms — male and female — for beggar are reserved for people who are ordained. Buddhist monks and nuns begin their training and study of the teachings of the Buddha at an early age. They focus their existence on the meditative life.

Buddhist monks and nuns are members of the Buddhist monastic order and live within a community called a *sangha.* Their traditional responsibilities have been to beg for food and generally to be a source of inspiration and help to other Buddhists. They can perform weddings and funerals, and they teach people the way of the Buddha. Nowadays, the role of Buddhist holy people and spiritual leaders is to inspire the faithful to follow the path of the Middle Way.

Confucian Sage

The sage is the scholar who has devoted his life to the study of Confucius. The sage serves as teacher for men (women aren't allowed to participate in the intensive studies of Confucius with a sage) interested in devoting their lives to embracing the principles of Confucianism. Thus, the primary role of the sage is that of teacher and perpetuator of the principles of Confucius.

Hindu Priest

Hindu priests help people make decisions about life and death. They consult astronomy and help Hindus determine whom to marry, when to marry, and when someone should be cremated. The priest may also serve as the leader of a sect, order, or religious institution that's devoted to the study of Hinduism.

Years of devoted study are required to become a Hindu priest. Hindu Brahmin families introduce their children to the Hindu texts as early as 12 years old. A young man studies about ten years to qualify to become a Hindu priest. The young man's religious teacher assesses the man's qualifications to join the priesthood. Hindu priests perpetuate their existence by passing on their training to subsequent generations. (See the related sidebar titled "A priestly class" later in this chapter.)

Sikh Granthi and Ragi

Since the earliest days of Sikhism, the adherents of the faith have relied on gurus to pass on the wisdom of God. At the death of the tenth and last guru, the power of the guru was passed on to the entire community in the form of the sacred text, the Adi Granth. Sikhs chose not to develop a priestly class; instead, they defined some people as *granthi:* keepers of the most holy, the Adi Granth. The granthi reads the sacred literature while the person who sings the sacred songs is called a *ragi.* The primary responsibilities of these holy men include watching over the Sikh house of worship, protecting the sacred writings, and leading the community in worship.

Jain Monk

The role of the Jain monk (in some sects, the Jains also have nuns, women who have committed their lives to the study and practice of their faith) is to practice the Three Jewels *(ratna-traya)* — right belief, right knowledge, and right conduct. Practicing the Three Jewels is one of the five vows of the Jain monk, which also include vows to not hurt anything, to be truthful, to not take anything that's not given, to renounce possessions, and to remain celibate.

Many monks adopt a wandering way of life so that they can share their faith with other Jains. During the rainy season (Jainism is based in India), a monk may retreat to a temple to avoid the potential of injuring any small creatures that live in the mud.

Shinto Priest and Miko

The Shinto priest is an office primarily associated with the *Koshitsu Shinto* sect (Shinto of the Imperial House). These priests are men *(Shoten)* and women *(Nai-Shoten)* who support the Emperor of Japan in the performance of the rites of the sect. Members in this select group make a life-long commitment to serve and protect the Emperor and his family.

A *miko* is a young woman who functions as a priestess at a Shinto shrine. The role of these women is to dance and assist in Shinto rituals. The miko are often found among the Shinto faithful throughout rural areas of Japan.

Shaman

Generally speaking, shamans — typically men, but women aren't excluded — function as guides for their community in its encounter with the spirit world. Traditionally, shamans experience the divine through ecstasy. The shaman's role is to lead the community in prayers and rituals that are passed down from generation to generation through the perpetuation of storytelling. Shamans embody the interests of their communities and use the power of healing, rituals such as the rain dance, and prayer to guide the community through significant life passages.

Religious folklore includes many stories of how shamans are foretold of their futures and initiated into their roles when spirits visit them. Often elected at an early age by the community, a shaman must undergo several initiations, including one in which the person may be spiritually disassembled and reconstituted as a holy person.

GOING DEEPER

A priestly class

Hindu priests come from the Brahmin class, the highest of the four classes in the Hindu caste system. According to Hindu social theory, the Brahmin was supposedly created from the head or mouth of the creator god (Brahma). This means that members of the Brahmin class should be representative of priestliness, the intellectual life, and the highest of spiritual values. Thus, a Brahmin (men only) may be a:

- Priest
- Religious teacher
- Guardian of the spiritual and intellectual way of life among the Hindu through their perpetuation and preservation of the Vedas.

Chapter 19

Ten Tales for Your Reading Enjoyment

Scripture — words written by religious leaders — form a cornerstone in many faiths. Of course, scripture isn't the only way to teach a faith's lessons. Stories, whether from the scriptures or simply from tradition, also reveal the fundamental religious beliefs. From showing us how the world began to showing how to lead one's life, each religion has a tale to tell.

Creation Stories

Every religion has a creation story, a way of symbolically or literally (depending on the beliefs of the religion) explaining how things came to be. These stories usually describe or explain the nature of existence, the nature of the divine, and the relationship humans have with the gods or God.

God, the Garden, and Adam and Eve: The creation story of Abrahamic faiths

"In the beginning, God created the heavens and the earth." That's how the story traditionally starts, and the next six days were busy ones.

On the first day, God created light. On the second day, he separated the earth from the sky. On the third day, he separated the oceans by sticking a landmass between them and put plants and vegetation on the land. On day four, he created the sun, the moon, and the stars. On day five, God filled the seas and the skies with living creatures. On day six, the day he put animals on the land, and God decided to create Man, which he did by gathering some dust together, molding it into a shape (God's own likeness, actually) and breathing life into it. Then God put this new creature, named Adam, in the garden God had formed (Eden) and gave him the job of working it and caring for it.

Now, Eden had two trees — the Tree of Life and the Tree of the Knowledge of Good and Evil. Before God left Adam in charge and unattended, he told him that he could eat of any tree he liked except for the Tree of Knowledge. If Adam ate from this tree, God said, he would die.

God also realized that Adam didn't have a suitable mate. So he put Adam to sleep, removed a rib, and created Woman, named Eve. Adam loved Eve, and Eve loved Adam. The two lived in Eden in marital and spiritual bliss, until Satan appeared in the Garden one day.

Satan, disguised as a snake, tempted Eve to eat from the Tree of Knowledge, saying that tree's fruit wouldn't kill her or Adam, as God said. Instead, it would give them knowledge akin to God's. Eve, obviously untroubled by a talking snake, ate from the forbidden tree, and Adam, who was with her, took a few bites himself. At once, their eyes were opened and they became aware of things they hadn't been aware of before. They realized, for example, that they were naked. Adam and Eve covered themselves with fig leaves (inspiring untold works of art and off-color jokes) and ducked into the forest to hide.

About this time, God came to the garden and called out to Adam and Eve, who were hesitant to show themselves. When they finally came out of the forest, God noticed the strategically placed fig leaves and asked if they had eaten from the Tree of Knowledge. Adam said, "Eve gave me the fruit."

So God dished out the punishment: In addition to having brought death into the world, Eve would bear children in pain, and Adam would have to toil for food and subsistence. Then he kicked them out of the Garden and placed an angel with a flaming sword at the Garden's gate.

Note: The Islamic version of the creation story is pretty much same. The place where it differs is in Adam and Eve's response to God's question about having eaten from the forbidden tree. In the Qur'anic version, Adam doesn't blame Eve. Instead, they both admit their wrongdoing and ask for forgiveness.

The Zoroastrian creation story parallels the biblical one in many descriptive and thematic ways. The reason the Zoroastrian first couple (named Mashya and Mashyana) fell into sin is believed to be disobedience to God's will — they disobeyed God by attributing creation to the devil and then worshipping not only God but also the devil.

The Okanogan creation story (Native American)

In the beginning, the earth was a human being that the Old One had made out of a woman, saying, "You'll be the mother of all people." Although still alive, the earth's womanly shape changed: Her skin became the soil, her bones became rock and stone, her breath became the wind, and her hair became the grass and trees. When she moved, the earth quaked.

The Old One took some of the woman's flesh and rolled it into balls; then he divided the balls into two groups. From the first group, Old One made the ancients. Some ancients had human form; others had the form of animals that roam through the fields, fly through the sky, and swim in the seas. The ancients, whatever form they had taken, all had the gift of speech and great powers and cunning, more so than the animals or humans whose forms they shared.

From the second group, the Old One molded real animals and people, whom he shaped like the Native Americans. Then he blew on these shapes to bring them to life. Thus, all living things came from the earth. Wherever you look, you see a part of the Earth Mother.

One version of the Hindu creation story

The universe was made entirely of water. Within this water floated a golden egg. Eventually, the egg broke in two. From this egg emerged the *Prajapati,* the lord of all creation. His head became the sky, his feet became the earth, his navel the air, his eye the sun, and his breath the wind.

Through his breath, Prajapati created the *Devas,* gods who flew skyward and produced light. From his flatulence, he created the *Asuras,* who entered the earth as demons, and produced darkness.

Miraculous Conceptions and Virgin Births

A few religions believe that their founders are the offspring of a human woman who was miraculously impregnated by a divine being. In addition to being a shock to these women's unsuspecting husbands or fiancés, such paternity reiterates the specialness or actual divinity of these messengers.

Nonbelievers generally view these accounts as mere stories. Believers view them as retellings of events that actually transpired.

The birth of Buddha

Buddha assumed the form of a glorious white elephant and went to the place where his future mother was lying under the watchful eye of four guardian angels. He plucked a white flower with his trunk and trumpeted loudly. Then he entered the mansion and walked three times around her couch, where she lay dreaming. Buddha, in the shape of an elephant, struck his mother's side with his trunk and entered her womb. Later, when Buddha's mother went into labor, a giant tree bent low so that she could grasp its branches and ease her pains. Four angels received the newborn child in a golden net. The hosts of heaven, delighted at the birth, held a joyful celebration.

The birth of Jesus

The angel Gabriel approached Mary, a young women engaged to a man named Joseph, and told her that she would give birth to a son, called Jesus. Confused, Mary wondered how this was possible: She was a virgin, she said, and had never lain with a man. Gabriel informed her that the Holy Spirit would come to her and overshadow her, at which point, a being, the Son of God, would be conceived in her womb.

When Mary was far along in her pregnancy, she and Joseph had to go to Bethlehem to pay taxes. While there, she went into labor and, with no place to stay, she delivered the baby in a stable, wrapped him in swaddling clothes, and placed him in a manger. At the child's birth, an angel appeared to a group of shepherds and told them the good news — that a savior, called Christ the Lord, was born in Bethlehem — and enjoined them to go to see the child. Then the heavenly host appeared and began to praise God, saying, "Glory to God in the highest, and on earth peace, good will toward men."

When the angels were gone and things had quieted down again, the shepherds traveled to Bethlehem. They found the baby as the angel had told them they would. When they saw the child, they knew that what the angel had said was true, and they told everyone they met of what they had seen and heard. Thus, the word of Jesus' birth spread through the land.

The birth of Zoroaster

Zarathushtra, or Zoroaster, the founder of Zoroastrianism, was conceived when his mother drank milk that miraculously appeared in two white virgin cows after they ate from a sacred plant on which an archangel had carried Zoroaster's spirit to earth. Upon birth, Zarathushtra laughed with joy.

Morality Tales and Lessons for Living

Many religious tales serve as lessons for the faithful. Although they may be based on actual events, they don't have to be, because their importance isn't in how factual they are. These tales are important because they reaffirm a religion's beliefs and expectations and offer guidelines for living.

The parable of the prodigal son (Christianity)

There lived a man who had two sons. The elder worked very hard on his father's farm; the younger, prodigal son, was a happy-go-lucky kid who helped out occasionally. One day, the younger son approached his father and said, "Pop, can I have my share of the inheritance now? I want to go out and see the world." The father, who loved his two sons, complied. He divided his possessions and gave the younger son what was due him.

A few days later, the younger son hit the road with his inheritance. He headed to the big city, took up with a few bad friends and loose women, and spent like crazy until his money — all that his father had given him — was gone. As luck would have it, a famine hit the country just as the son's money ran out, so no one could help him — even if they had been inclined to, which they weren't, being bad and loose. Desperate and hungry, the son took a job as a pig feeder.

One day, as the son was in the fields taking care of the pigs, he realized how far he had fallen. He had started out as a wealthy young man with big dreams; now he was feeding pigs and envying them for the food they had. Then he thought longingly of home and his father, and he decided to return home.

Shamed by his behavior and selfishness, the son approached his father's house. The father saw his younger son in the distance and ran to greet him. Overjoyed, he drew his wayward son in an embrace and kissed him. When the contrite son could catch his breath, he said, "Dad, I've really messed up. I don't deserve to be called your son."

The father pooh-poohed the son's apology and told the servants to bring the best clothes and shoes and to kill a fatted calf because they were going to have a celebration to mark the son's return. Everyone was happy.

While all this was going on, the older son was still working in the field. When he came home and heard the music and dancing, he asked a servant why his father was partying. The servant told him that the celebration was for the younger son, who had finally come home, and that his father had had the fatted calf killed.

About that time, the father came out of the house and told his older son to come in and join the party. Angry and hurt, the older son refused, saying, "All these years I stayed here and did whatever you told me to, and you never even killed a *goat* for me. But let Younger Son waltz back home after wasting all your money on bad friends and loose women, and you kill the prize heifer!"

So the father said to his older son, "Son, you're always with me. Everything I have is yours. But your brother was gone from us, and now he's back. That's worth celebrating." And they all went in and had a good time.

The lesson? If we fail to fulfill what God expects of us in our lives, he will forgive us, his children, if we ask him to. Just as the father always loved his prodigal son, God the Father always loves us — no matter what.

Buddha in the town of Kosambi (Buddhism)

During his preaching tour, after having reached enlightenment, the Buddha came to the town of Kosambi, where he was going to spend some time with his disciples. As it so happened, a wicked man who resented Buddha lived in Kosambi. Moreover, this man, to make things hard for the Buddha, bribed others to tell false stories about him.

With vicious rumors running rampant through the town, people turned away from Buddha and his disciples, denying them food (Buddha and his disciples had no possessions) and abusing them. One day, one of Buddha's disciples, Ananda, suggested that they go to a better town, one where they could do their work and not have to suffer the abuse of misled and wicked people.

When Buddha asked Ananda what they would do if the *next* town were like Kosambi, Ananda replied that they would just go to another town.

Buddha refused, saying that they should stay put and bear the mistreatment with patience. Only after the abuse stopped would they move to another place. Enlightened people, after all, are not swayed by external events — good or bad.

Fan Ki's message of justice (Taoism)

Fan Ki was a man who lived a wicked life. His main love? Stirring up trouble. He instigated fights and incited people to sue each other. He promoted thievery and violence and encouraged men to ruin the reputation of other men's wives and daughters. He was a conniver and a scoundrel, and he spent almost all of his time hatching schemes to bring others to ruin or humiliation.

One day, Fan Ki died; he didn't stay dead, however. He came back to life and had his shocked wife gather all his family and his neighbors together. When everyone was around, Fan Ki told them that he had seen the king of the dark realm who had explained how justice in the afterlife works: In the realm of darkness, the dead are punished for the evil they caused or did. All are thrown onto beds of coals. The heat from the coals is proportional to the wickedness of their crimes. Good people get off lightly; bad people suffer untold torment.

Everyone listened to what Fan Ki had to say, but they figured he was hallucinating. (The stress of dying can do that to a person, you know.) But the king of hell, Yama, had sent Fan Ki back to life as an example to scare everyone else straight and decided the unbelieving people needed a demonstration of how evil acts in life return evil in the afterlife. Fan Ki's torment, because he had had hurt so many people during his life, would be great, indeed.

Under the command of Yama, Fan Ki mutilated himself with a knife, saying that such was the punishment for being angry with his parents and lusting after other men's wives and daughters. Then he cut off his hand, as punishment for having killed so many people. Then he cut out his heart as punishment for causing other people to die from torture. The last thing he cut out was his own tongue, as punishment for his lies and slander of others.

Although dismembered and disemboweled, Fan Ki remained alive, under Yama's orders, writhing on the ground in agony. People came from all over to see him. He remained alive and in agony for six days before Yama finally allowed him to die, his torments serving as a warning to the living.

The bramble bush (Islam)

A man planted a bramble bush in the middle of a road. People were bothered by the bush's location, which impeded their journey up the road. They asked the man to move the bush, but he didn't.

As the bush grew, it became more problematic, and people who journeyed along the road were pricked and scratched by the bush's thorns. With bloody feet and shredded clothing, travelers again asked the man to move it, but again, he didn't.

The bush grew and grew until the road was nearly impassable. Finally, the town's governor spoke to the man about the bush. The man finally agreed to cut it down. "Tomorrow," the man said.

But tomorrow came and went, and the bush remained untouched in the middle of the road. Then another tomorrow passed and another and another, and the bush grew larger.

Finally, the governor called the man to him and said, "You know, the longer you wait, the older and weaker *you* get and the hardier that bush gets. So be quick about it. Cut it down now, while you can."

Appendix

A Few Religions of the World

• •

*W*e organized this book according to themes and topics so that we could easily compare the views that different religions have about the same subjects. Some of you, however, may prefer a religion-by-religion breakdown where you can see how a particular faith views these themes and topics all in one place. You get your wish in this appendix.

Following is a traditional list of the main members of this religion club, arranged alphabetically.

Baha'i Faith

In 1844, a young merchant named Mirza Ali Muhammad (1819-1850) declared that he was destined to transform the spirituality of the human race. He took the name *Bab* — a title that means door or gate in Arabic and which referred to his mission to proclaim one greater than himself. The boldness of the Bab's revelations stirred the Islamic world, because his teachings (Babism) foretold of the coming of a promised Divine Teacher. Because of his teachings, the Bab was deemed a heretic and a dangerous rebel, and he was executed on July 9, 1850.

One of the Bab's disciples was Mirza Hoseyn Ali Nuri, who took the name Baha'u'llah and claimed to be a manifestation of the unknowable God. Baha'u'llah was imprisoned in Persia as the result of his adherence to Babism. During his stay in prison, he received a series of revelations that led to the foundation of the Baha'i Faith.

Baha'u'llah taught his people that there is one God and that all of the citizens of the earth have a common humanity that binds them to each other and to God. Today, this faith flourishes throughout the world.

Sacred texts

The sacred books of the Baha'i Faith include the Bayan, written by the Bab, which promotes a universal law intended to replace the separate laws of

Christianity, Judaism, Islam, and all other religious legal codes. The Bayan foretells of the coming of a second messenger of God, who would be far greater than the Bab and whose mission would be to usher in the age of peace and justice promised in Islam, Judaism, Christianity, and other religions. Other Baha'i sacred texts include the Most Holy Book, the Book of Certitude, and the Seven Valleys.

Core beliefs

The core beliefs of the Baha'i Faith are

- **God is one and is utterly transcendent in his essence.**
- **God created all people equal** — people of all races, all ethnicities, all religions, and both genders.
- **Each person shares a common destiny,** founded by the one God who revealed his message through a variety of prophets such as Buddha, Muhammad, Jesus, and Krishna.
- **The prophets who founded the world's greatest religions have been part of God's plan to progressively educate and illuminate humankind.** The prophet Baha'u'llah's particular task was to overcome religious divisions between people and establish one faith.

Buddhism

Buddhism, founded by Siddhartha Gautama (circa 563-483 B.C.E.), the son of a wealthy and influential nobleman, began as an outgrowth of Hinduism. One day, while wandering outside his sheltered palace, Gautama saw great suffering and decided to begin a search for the meaning of life, giving up everything. He gave up his family and all of the fortune that would have come to him in what is now termed the *Great Renunciation.* He tried various ascetic practices, but they led him only to grow tired and hungry. It wasn't until he sat under a Bodhi tree that he realized that life was about choosing the middle path of action. In this discovery, he found enlightenment and the course of action that he would preach for the next 45 years.

Core beliefs

The core beliefs in Buddhism center on the *Four Noble Truths:* (1) life is about suffering; (2) suffering has a cause; (3) you can suppress suffering; and (4) the way to do that is to follow the Eightfold Path, also called the Middle Path.

Take a closer look at the Four Noble Truths:

✔ **All human life is about suffering.** Nothing lasts — not happiness, not sadness, not good things, or bad. From the moment we are born, our bodies change to eventually die and decay. The world is an illusion. There is no self, no permanence, and the things that we think are necessary are actually fleeting. This state of temporary being is what causes sorrow and suffering.

✔ **The cause of suffering is desire and ignorance.** Being ignorant of the true nature of things, people are always striving to obtain something that they want, and the absence of those things causes them pain.

✔ **Suffering will finally stop when we attain nirvana,** a state of being where we understand the true nature of existence and no longer feel desire.

✔ **The way to attain nirvana is with the Eightfold Path.** The eight parts of this path are to have right views, right thoughts, right speech, right action, right livelihood, right effort, right mindfulness, and right concentration. The Buddhist who would live this middle path accepts the truths as Buddhism outlines them and avoids killing, stealing, lying, abusing sex, and taking intoxicants.

Buddhism has a variety of sects, nearly all of which agree on the preceding Four Noble Truths. Following are some of the areas where they differ:

✔ **Some Buddhist sects accept the caste system of Hinduism as a social reality,** but reject it as a way of indicating that any person is superior to another. Other Buddhist sects reject the caste system entirely. Regardless of the sect, people of any class can achieve nirvana if they live in an enlightened way.

✔ **Some sects don't consider the Buddha to be divine,** but rather the "Enlightened" or "Awakened One." Other sects consider Buddha divine.

Schools of Buddhism

Buddhism is generally divided into two categories: Theravada and Mahayana.

✔ **Theravada Buddhism** is known as the smaller vehicle, because not many people want to walk down the path of celibacy and poverty. Most monks and nuns live in community and give up almost everything, except a robe, a belt, a begging bowl, and a needle and thread. They eat only one meal a day.

✔ **Mahayana Buddhism** is known as the greater vehicle and embraces the majority of Buddhist followers today. Theravada Buddhism looks to the historic Buddha, Siddhartha Gautama, as their leader and spiritual guide. Mahayana Buddhism has so-called Buddhas-in-the-making, or bodhisattvas. A *bodhisattva* is a person who has found the route to liberation or nirvana and, out of compassion for friends and family, does not lose him or herself to the Infinite. Instead, the Bodhisattva comes back to earth to help others to find the way.

Theravada and Mahayana Buddhism are but two of thousands of sects within that religion. Some of the better-known sects include Zen, Shingon, Pure Land, Soka Gakkai, and Lamaism (or Tibetan).

Christianity

Over its 2,000-year history, Christianity has spread to the four corners of the earth. Today, the number of adherents to Christianity is reported to be approximately 2 billion.

Christians believe that Jesus entered human history as the Son of God to redeem humankind through his death and resurrection. After his death, Christians came to believe that Jesus was the Messiah, the anointed one, the Christ. Jesus' followers then became known as Christians. These early Christians shared their food, their money, and their biblical writings, and they became a community of faith. They claimed Jewish roots but saw Christianity as the fulfillment of Judaism. They embraced the Hebrew Bible but wrote the Christian Testament, known as the New Testament.

Sacred texts

The sacred texts in Christianity are the Old Testament (the Hebrew Bible) and the New Testament. The New Testament is composed of the

✔ **Gospels,** the story of the ministry of Jesus

✔ **Acts of the Apostles,** the history of the early Church

✔ **Epistles,** the letters of the early Church

✔ **Book of Revelation,** writings about the end of time

Core beliefs

The core beliefs in Christianity are as follows:

✔ **The world was created by God,** is good, and is influenced by the sin of Adam and Eve.

✔ **Jesus came to earth in human form** to teach humankind about God's love and to sacrifice his life on the cross so that all could enter eternal life with God.

✔ **The purpose of life for the Christian** is to do the will of God in this world and to be judged worthy of heavenly life in the next.

✔ **God is a trinity:** God the Father, who created the world; God the Son, (Jesus) who redeemed the world; and God the Holy Spirit, who sanctifies the world.

Branches of Christianity

The Christian church — essentially the Catholic Church — was unified until 1054, when a split, or *schism,* occurred between the eastern and western churches. This split resulted in the Orthodox communities in Christianity. A later split from Catholicism, which occurred in the sixteenth century, resulted in Protestantism.

Roman Catholicism

The oldest of the branches of Christianity, this church traces its history back to Peter, a disciple of Christ who, according to tradition, became the first pope. Although it began as a relatively small group of people attracted from the lower classes and drawn to the teachings of Jesus, the Church grew and attained power over both spiritual and political realms.

Roman Catholicism asserts that scripture and church tradition are revelatory, that priests are Christ's representatives on earth, and that grace comes through both faith and good works.

Eastern Orthodoxy

Eastern Orthodoxy differs from traditional Roman Catholicism in the following ways:

✔ **It doesn't accept the authority of the Pope.**

✔ **It believes that the Holy Spirit is not equal to the Father and the Son.**

✔ **It allows clergy to marry before being ordained.**

✔ **It allows non-priests to dip the bread (the body of Christ) into the wine (the blood of Christ).**

Protestantism

In the early 1500s, a Protestant Reformation led by Martin Luther challenged the selling of indulgences (see Chapter 14), the distance between the clergy and the people, and some of the teachings of the church. This challenge caused Luther and others, such as John Calvin and Swiss priest Huldrych Zwingli, to create individual churches that sought to reform the Church of Rome.

The most prominent Protestant sects include the following:

- ✔ Anglican
- ✔ Baptist
- ✔ Christian Science
- ✔ Church of God
- ✔ Congregational
- ✔ Lutheran
- ✔ Methodist
- ✔ Pentecostal
- ✔ Presbyterian
- ✔ Quaker
- ✔ Seventh Day Adventist
- ✔ Unitarian

Generally, these sects are community-based, they emphasize the word of God, de-emphasize saints and statues, highlight the importance of preaching, believe that the Eucharist is symbolically present, emphasize singing, and tend to be non-hierarchical.

Confucianism

Confucianism comes from Confucius, a Chinese philosopher who lived in sixth century B.C.E. Confucius spent a good deal of his adult life in government and administrative positions, seeking to convince government leaders of the importance of pursuing peace and equity. In fact, Confucianism is more a way of living than a theology.

Confucius believed in the perfectibility of humankind through the cultivation of the mind. His teachings emphasized devotion to parents and rituals, learning, self-control, and just social activity.

Teachings become spiritual when people act in a correct way with etiquette. Confucianism advocates the importance of the family life. The teachings also promote that the ruler of the country should be known by virtuous conduct.

Sacred texts

The sacred texts of Confucianism are The Five Classics and the Four Books. The most noted part of the Four Books is the Analects, which contain the teachings of Confucius. These books served as a foundation for the Chinese education system for centuries.

Core beliefs

Confucius held that society consisted of five relationships: husband and wife, parent and child, elder and younger brother (or, generally, of elders and youngsters), ruler and minister or subject, and friend and friend. Confucius encouraged followers to have true compassion for one's own role and for the people one would meet. He encouraged each person to live appropriately in his or her chosen relationships.

The essence of Confucianism is called the *jen,* which can be translated as social virtue. Confucius believed people must balance their individual good with ultimate good. In addition, although people are fundamentally good, they need a path, which if adhered to, would lead to deeper virtue. People who put aside virtue for material comfort choose an inferior path.

Expressions of faith

The spirituality of Confucianism can be defined as the call to good conduct. Superior people are the ones who fulfill societal, political, and family obligations. Moral people are active in creating their lives through careful spiritual and intellectual cultivation of the mind and the heart. In order to achieve this, Confucianism places a great deal of emphasis on the role of the family and calls for respect, piety, and deference in one's family interactions. Confucianism teaches righteousness, ritual wisdom, and faithfulness.

Hinduism

Hinduism, the world's oldest religion, dating from around 4000 B.C.E, is deeply connected to the culture of India and its diversity of people, cultures, and belief systems. The religion has no founder, nor does it reflect the teaching of any particular prophet or sage.

Sacred texts

The collection of Hindu sacred texts is called the Vedas. The oldest and most important of these is the Rig-Veda, which explains creation, the deities, the connection between humans and the divine, and so on. Another important sacred text is the Upanishads, which give spiritual advice to believers.

Core concepts

The core concepts in Hinduism are:

- **Moksha:** The main task of this world is to move beyond all desire so that the soul can be released from the cycle of death and rebirth, called *samsara*. Achieving release *(moksha)* can take lifetimes, and Hindus believe that the soul goes through many reincarnations; rebirth is a sign that the person hasn't attained enlightenment or release.

- **Impermanence of life:** According to Hinduism, nothing in life is permanent. By embracing yoga and other forms of prayer, people can choose between the two paths in life — the path of desire and the path of renunciation. Those who seek the path of desire are bound to be unhappy. Their victories are temporary and fleeting. Those who choose the path of renunciation find happiness and, eventually, enlightenment.

- **Karma:** The idea that actions in this life affect future lives and that only by freeing yourself of desire, which keeps you bound to the cycle of death and rebirth, can you attain release.

- **Ahimsa (non-injury):** *Ahimsa* is the foundation of nonviolence toward any living thing. However, the meaning is more complex than simply not actively trying to hurt something. It also means not doing any injury, known or unknown, to any other thing.

- **The sanctity of the cow:** The idea, stemming from the importance of cows in the lives of early Indians, is that the cow represents divine and natural goodness and should be protected.

- **The Caste system:** In Hinduism, human beings are divided into four classes, determined by birth. A person's caste defines the job he or she may do, the person he or she can marry, how he or she is to dress, the religious practices the individual should adhere to, and the level of freedom to move about.

Important divinities

Besides Brahma (or Parusha), the supreme being and the font of all things, Hinduism has many gods. Most notable are Shiva, the destroyer and regenerative god; Vishnu, the affirmer god; and Sakti, the god (sometimes goddess) of creative energy.

Indigenous Religions and Belief Systems

Indigenous peoples have had to deal with the pain of colonization and the plethora of missionaries trying to convert them. The history of such forces has not always been good. Many instances have occurred in which the religious and social practices of the expansionists toward indigenous peoples have resulted in bloody outcomes, such as the Massacre of Wounded Knee in December 1890, when the U.S. Cavalry massacred Chief Big Foot and almost 350 Sioux men, women, and children.

When faced with an unbeatable foe, religions can adapt, flee, or die fighting for their beliefs and way of life. Some indigenous religions have survived, often by maintaining beliefs and rituals of the past while making accommodations to the larger culture.

The belief in a single god or "Creator" varies among indigenous religions and can often be attributed to the influence of Western religions and missionaries bringing a theistic message to the indigenous peoples. Regardless of outside influences, indigenous religions teach sensitivity to the "natural order" and to the people living at one with Nature.

North America

You can also find a rich, cultural diversity among the indigenous religions found in the Americas. Examples of some of the many Native American tribes and their spiritual belief systems are:

- **Cherokee:** The Cherokee make no specific reference to God; they believe that an "unknown source" is responsible for first creating animal and plants, and then for creating man.
- **Hopi:** Their mythology focuses on the origin of the inhabitants of earth.
- **Iroquois:** This tribe's belief system is based on a strong sense of self-determination and a strict moral code of conduct.
- **Navajo:** At the core of the Navajo mythology or belief system is the exploration of creation or the age of beginning.

✔ **Sioux:** The Sioux are committed to protecting the earth and maintaining its peace.

✔ **Zuni:** The spiritual foundation for the Zuni is the elaborate rituals for fertility and rain because of their importance in the continuation of the life cycle.

Following are a few significant Native American prophets and religious figures:

✔ **Handsome Lake (circa 1800):** A member of the Seneca tribe, his visions stressed the message that it was time for Native Americans to hold on to their religious and cultural beliefs and not be overcome by European influences. Handsome Lake delivered his Good Message to the Iroquois people. Shortly after his death, his teachings became the foundation of the renewal of the Longhouse religion (circa 1818 to the present).

✔ **Nicholas Black Elk (1863-1950):** A Sioux religious figure, his life was the story about uniting two religious visions: the symbolic universe of Lakota spirituality and Roman Catholic Christianity.

✔ **The Delaware Prophets (circa 1745-1805):** This group of religious leaders included Neolin, the "old priest," and Wangomen. All claimed to have had encounters with a deity who shared messages that the hardships Native Americans suffered were the result of their being corrupted by the European colonists. The impact of the Delaware Prophets extended beyond the Delaware tribe to the Shawnee, Ottawa, and other Native American tribes in the Ohio area.

Australia

The Aboriginal culture of Australia devotes itself to attaining knowledge of the environment and landscape of Australia. In Aboriginal folklore, you can find stories about the birth of the planet, about struggle, about conflict, and the human frailties that lead people to treasure the spirituality of the land.

For the Aboriginal people, knowledge is attained through a lifetime of studying the land. An Aboriginal elder is revered for his years of living, as well as his insight into the spirit of the land. This reverence supports the core belief that many indigenous religions hold: respect for elders and their wisdom.

Africa

Africa is rich with indigenous religious diversity. Although missionaries have brought world religions (primarily Islam and Christianity) to Africa — and their influences have been incorporated into many of the tribal or community cultures — the strength of the indigenous religions have endured.

Most indigenous African religions feature a high god (the Creator) and a mythology of rupture. (Long ago, the Creator lived close to earth and to human ancestors. One day, a "rupture" occurred, and the Creator moved itself to the sky, and the ancestors were transformed into their present forms as humans.)

In addition to this mythology, most indigenous African religions adhere to a full range of life cycle and annual rituals. The rites of passage for young men and women into adulthood include sacrifices, offerings, meals, and dance — the predominant ritual forms.

Islam

Islam is the third and youngest of the Abrahamic faiths. Founded by the prophet Muhammad, who lived around 570-632 C.E., Islam claims to complete and perfect God's revelations, which began earlier with Judaism and continued through Christianity. Today, there are more than a billion Muslims around the world.

Sacred texts

The sacred text of Islam is the Qur'an, which, according to Islamic tradition, God revealed to Muhammad through the angel Gabriel. According to Muslims, the Qur'an is the actual transcribed word of God. As Jesus is for Christians, for Muslims, the Qur'an is a physical manifestation of the Divine on earth.

Other important texts in Islam include the *hadith,* sayings and guidelines attributed to the prophet Muhammad.

Core beliefs

Central to the core belief system of the Muslim faithful is the doctrine of God: God is One, God is unique, God has created all things, and God sustains all things.

Life for the Muslim is surrender to God. There is no god for Muslims except for God, and they avoid all forms of idolatry and polytheism, including pictures or physical representations of the divine.

Muslims believe that God sent prophets and messengers to communicate his message. These prophets include Abraham, Moses, and Jesus. Muhammad, however, is the last and the greatest of the prophets. While Muhammad is not divine, he is given the unique title, "Seal of the Prophets" to indicate that his prophecy completes and perfects the revelations shared through the earlier prophets.

Muslims believe that there will be a last day, a day of resurrection, and a day of judgment during which each person stands before God, accountable for the way he or she responded to God's mercy and goodness. Those who have lived apart from God in sinful ways will go to hell, or the fire. Those who do good with their lives will enjoy the delights of heaven, or paradise.

Expressions of faith

The religious obligations of Islam are the Five Pillars of Faith. They are the following:

- **Saying the shahadah: "There is no god but God, and Muhammad is his prophet."** The simplicity of this statement captures the centrality of God in the Muslim faith as well as the importance of Muhammad. Observant Muslims utter the shahadah regularly.

- **Muslims perform five ritual prayers a day.** The call to prayer, or *adhan,* happens at rising, at noon, at midafternoon, at sunset, and before retiring. Muslims turn to Mecca, the holy city where Muhammad received his calling.

- **During the ninth month of the lunar Islamic calendar, Muslims observe *Ramadan,*** a holy time where they don't eat, drink, smoke, or have intercourse between sunrise and sunset to remind themselves of the importance of being aware of what they eat, what they say, and what they do in everyday life. This month-long sacrifice leads them to a greater intimacy with God and helps them purify earthly desires.

- **The Muslim faith commands almsgiving.** Each Muslim donates 2½ percent of their money to help others.

- **Muslims who are capable must make the Hajj,** the pilgrimage to Mecca, at least once in a lifetime.

The Muslim place of worship is the mosque, from the Arabic term *masjid,* which means place of prostration. Muslims go to the mosque on Friday at noon. At these holy services, Muslims give praise to God, recite the Qur'an, and listen to learned people giving instruction in the faith. Most prayer services are lead by an imam, one chosen by the community because of his knowledge of the Qur'an. Mosques often serve as places of study, as well as places of prayer.

Islamic sects

The two principal divisions in the Muslim faith are the Sunni and Shi'ite:

The Sunnis form the majority (85 percent) of Muslims. According to Sunni Muslims, when Muhammad died, he didn't designate a successor. The community chose a successor, called a *caliph,* who became the political leader of the community. Sunni Muslims also believe that the community must follow the example of the Sunnah, the ethical and religious code from the sayings and deeds of Muhammad. In this sect, the religious and political authority in Islam rests with the community, guided by Islamic law and a consensus of the Qur'an, the scholars, and the leaders.

The Shi'ite sect believes that Muhammad designated his cousin and son-in-law Ali to be the religious leader of Islam. In this sect, all authority is vested with the imams or mullahs and, ultimately, the ayatollah. The charisma and authority of these leaders guides the teachings of Islam.

Jainism

Jainism, a religion of India that teaches deep respect for all life, began in the sixth century B.C.E. According to the Jain tradition, the world has known 24 *Tirthankaras* (conquerors or saviors), guides who remind Jains that to attain enlightenment they must move beyond material dependence.

The most noted — and last —Tirthankara was Mahavira (fifth century B.C.E.). Mahavira was a *pathmaker,* a teacher who guided his people across the river of transmigration.

Jainism broke into two groups by the first century C.E. The Digambara of southern India felt that true asceticism would lead one to become nude. The Svetambara of western India thought that people could wear a single garment and still be not attached to the things of the world. This debate underscores the severity of the Jain desire to remove people from material possession.

Sacred texts

The Jain sacred writings are the *Agamas* (traditions). The sacred Canon was handed down orally in the monastic communities; it wasn't until about 500 C.E. that someone actually wrote down the sacred text. The two branches of Jainism — Svetambara and Digambara — share many of the same sacred texts, but each branch preserved a different version of the Canon.

Core beliefs

In Jainism, followers seek to become liberated souls *(siddhas)*, free from the cycle of death and rebirth, and believe that liberation *(moksha)* comes through knowledge and self-denial.

Jains seek to remove themselves from desire, believing that through effort, discipline, and knowledge they can control karma, which can weigh down a soul.

Because Jains believe that every living thing has a soul *(jiva)*, they practice *ahimsa,* non-injury to any living being. In the Jain tradition, however, ahimsa doesn't refer solely to actions. In addition to not killing any living thing, Jains also avoid any psychological or intellectual violence.

Expressions of faith

Jains are the most nonviolent of Eastern believers and adopt almost a monastic life. Jain monks take vows to abstain from violence, deceit, theft, attachment to material things, and sex. They also practice the Three Jewels, which are right belief, right knowledge, and right conduct. Monks are so conscious of not offending anyone, that during the rainy season they retire to monastic homes to avoid injuring bugs and other animals that may surface.

The laypeople in the Jain religion adopt a modified monastic approach to life. They commit themselves to almsgiving, meditation, fasting twice a month, and publicly confessing their sins.

Judaism

Judaism is a religion that began about 4,000 years ago. It's the oldest and the first of the Abrahamic faiths, which trace their origins back to Abraham.

Sacred texts

Sacred texts of Judaism are the Hebrew Bible (referred to by Christians as the Old Testament) and the Talmud, which contains the teachings of the rabbis.

Core concepts

Judaism teaches the following:

- ✔ **God is the creator of the world but is not the world.** This single, unique God is also the revealer of a law for humankind that, if followed, produces lives of compassion, love, and justice.
- ✔ **God will redeem the world from evil some day** by sending a Messiah or by performing some other redemptive act. (Judaism doesn't believe or accept the claims that Jesus was the Messiah sent by God.)
- ✔ **The Jews are God's chosen people.** That is, God established a covenant with the Jewish people, who were to act as the transmitters of God's law.

Expressions of faith

To be a Jew, you don't have to believe anything that Judaism teaches; you just have to be born of a Jewish mother. (Some liberal Jews now hold that the child of Jewish father and a non-Jewish mother can be a Jew, but this ruling is highly controversial within Judaism.) Jews who do believe in Judaism observe daily rituals, such as prayer, and observe the Sabbath and the holidays. The specific rituals vary, depending on the form of Judaism.

Judaism has many rituals that are to be performed in the home and very few that must be performed in a synagogue. Jewish prayer requires ten adult Jewish men for Orthodox Judaism. Liberal movements in Judaism allow women to be counted for prayer.

Divisions of Judaism

Modern Judaism is divided into four movements: Orthodox, Conservative, Reform, and Reconstructionist.

Orthodox Jews

Orthodox Jews are the most traditionally observant Jews. Men always wear a head covering when going out, and women dress modestly. Men and women are separated during prayer services. All Orthodox Jews keep kosher all the time, both at home and out of the home. No women can be rabbis or cantors in Orthodox Judaism. No Orthodox Jews will allow their children to marry unconverted non-Jews and will demand an Orthodox conversion for the non-Jew before permitting the marriage.

Orthodox Judaism has two main divisions.

- **Hasidic Judaism:** Hasidic Jews don't generally send their children to any secular schools or universities. At parties, men and women sit and dance separately. Hasidic Jews follow the teachings of a *rebbe,* a mystical wonder-working rabbi who is descended from a line of other Hasidic rebbes.

- **Modern Orthodox Judaism:** Modern Orthodox Jews do send their children to secular universities after usually sending their children to Jewish parochial schools. A modern Orthodox rabbi need not be the heir to a rabbinic dynasty. Men and women are separated in prayer but not always at parties.

Conservative Jews

Conservative Jews follow a less strict interpretation of Jewish law. All Conservative Jewish men wear head coverings in prayer, and many wear them all the time. Men and women are not separated in prayer in Conservative Judaism. Most Conservative Jews keep kosher at home, but some will eat in non-kosher restaurants. Conservative Judaism opposes intermarriage (marriage to a non-Jew). Conservative Jews sometimes send their children to parochial Jewish schools. Women can become Conservative rabbis and cantors.

Reform Jews

The Reform movement in Judaism represents a more liberal interpretation of Jewish law. Some Reform Jews and rabbis wear head coverings in prayer, but very few wear them all the time. Very few Reform Jews keep kosher at home or outside the home. Women can be rabbis and cantors in the Reform Movement. Reform Jews will rarely send their children to Jewish parochial schools.

Reconstructionist Jews

Reconstructionist Jews are similar to Reform Judaism, but they practice Jewish traditional historical customs like keeping kosher. Rabbi Mordecai Kaplan was the founder of Reconstructionist Judaism, and he focused more on the Jewish traditions than on God as the commander and revealer of Jewish law.

Shinto

Shinto means "the way of the kami" or "divine way." Shinto is Japan's indigenous religion, and its origin is as old as the history of the Japanese culture. This religion didn't have a name until Buddhism from China began appearing in Japan (circa 500 C.E.). To distinguish between the worship of the kami and the Buddha, the name of Shinto (the way of the kami) was born. However, it was not until the late twelfth century that the term Shinto was used to refer to a specific body of religious ideas.

The Shinto religion places a stronger emphasis and value on ancestry, social cooperation, and fertility.

Sacred texts

Although Shinto doesn't have scriptural texts, as such, it does have two works that are compilations of the religions oral traditions: *Kohiki* (Records of Ancient Matters) and *Nihon-gi* (Chronicles of Japan). In addition to including the religious traditions of Shinto, these works also offer historical information about Japan, as well some early Japanese literature.

Core beliefs

The religion requires a devotion to family and ancestral traditions and a respect for both living and inanimate things (such as pebbles, sand, and waterfalls). These values were incorporated into the daily religious rituals of believers. Shinto adherents, for example, use ritual prayers as part of their harvest cycle of events. Because of such rituals, Shinto is a form of religious practicethat is inextricably intertwined with everyday life.

The Shinto belief system is expressed in the Four Affirmations:

- ✔ **Tradition and the family:** The family is the foundation for preserving traditions. Their main celebrations center on birth and marriage.
- ✔ **Love of nature:** Nature is sacred, and natural objects are worshipped as sacred spirits.
- ✔ **Ritual purity:** Followers of Shinto take baths, wash their hands, and rinse out their mouths before entering a shrine where they will worship the kami. Many of the sacred shrines are built near flowing water to help the people maintain their state of purity. Twice a year, festivals are held to drive out pollutants or impurities.
- ✔ **Matsuri:** This is the practice of worshipping and honoring gods and ancestral spirits.

Expressions of faith

Shinto followers embrace the way of the *kami* (the deity or deities) in all aspects of their daily lives. These actions are outlined in a constitution that specifies the "General Characteristics of a Life lived in Reverence of Kami":

✔ To be grateful for the blessings of kami and to be diligent in the observance of the Shinto rites, applying oneself to them with sincerity, brightness, and purity of heart.

✔ To be helpful to others through deeds of service without thought of rewards.

✔ To bind oneself in harmonious acknowledgment of the will of the emperor, praying that the country may flourish, while all people live in peace and prosperity.

Sikhism

The founder of Sikhism, Guru Nanak (1469-1539 C.E.), lived in a culture in northwestern India that was influenced by Hinduism and Islam. He found that each of these religions had their limitations. He rejected the caste system and the concept of multiple gods in Hinduism, and he found the Muslim faith too ceremonial. He wanted to create a religion that was simpler and devoted to one goal — preaching love and devotion to one god. He saw God as the same god for people of all religions. For Nanak, the goal of earthly existence was to live a decent and devoted life to God and, eventually, to merge with God. He encouraged followers to blend their spiritual and temporal obligations.

Sacred texts

Central to Sikh preaching is their most famous holy work, the Adi Granth. In Sikhism, gurus are ones who share God's revelations with the world. Nanak was the first guru, and nine others followed him. In the early eighteenth century, the last guru, Gobind Singh, retired the office of guru and vested the guru's authority in the Adi Granth, thus elevating this work to the status of a guru (called Guru Granth Sahib). The Adi Granth, therefore, is a living guru that continues to teach God's revelations.

Core beliefs

The core beliefs in Sikhism include

✔ **The ideas of karma and reincarnation.**

✔ **That the world is veiled in *maya*, or illusion.** Despite this, the believer can soul-advance by observing *dharma*, which is righteous behavior.

✔ **That God cannot be known in any human form,** but that the name of God is *Nam*.

> ✔ **That gurus are the closest embodiment of divinity.** Nanak and the nine gurus that succeeded him were all representatives of the true guru, God. Because the Sikh community believes that there will be only these ten designated gurus, it is now time for the community as a whole to act as a guru to the world.

Expressions of faith

The believing Sikh practices meditation, engages in communal worship, and concentrates on the divine name. The religious person accepts other religions, races, and sects. Critical to the Sikh is an awareness of defending the motherland, having a social consciousness, and making a deep religious commitment.

The word *Sikh* means learner, disciple, or follower. The Sikh religion emphasizes a communal identity, symbolized by men wearing turbans and beards. They greet each other with a unique salutation, *"Sat-sri-akal,"* which celebrates the true, timeless lord.

Taoism

In the sixth century B.C.E., a philosophy of life called Taoism emerged in China. *Tao* means path or way, and it refers to the underlying, imperceptible presence that moves through the universe and is the source of all things. The permanent Tao is unchanging and holds within itself everything and everything's opposite; therefore, the natural way of things is to move from being to not being. Serenity and harmony come from allowing the Tao to move unchallenged.

Core concepts

Taoism recognizes the yin and the yang of life. *Yin* and *yang* are the two opposing but complementary principles. Yin is earth, dark, female, passive, and absorbing. Yang is heaven, male, light, and penetrating. Together yin and yang represent the harmonious interplay of all the opposites in the world. The emphasis is on harmony.

Another Taoist concept is that of inaction. Deliberately intervening in the way of things ruins the natural harmony of the Tao's unimpeded progress. Therefore, the most effective course of action is inaction, or letting things be.

Expressions of faith

The Taoist seeks to empty himself of worldly concerns. The less preoccupied a person is, the freer, the more liberated, the more spontaneous a person becomes. Lao-Tzu, the founder of Taoism, for example, encouraged his followers to abandon restlessness and to take up meditation and simplicity and to move beyond striving for wealth.

Taoist sages and saints strive to reunite with the Tao by internally cleansing themselves of every desire and distraction. In this way, they create a void through which the Tao can move.

Zoroastrianism

Arising from the devotional poetry of Zarathushtra (or Zoroaster), Zoroastrianism is one of the world's oldest religions that still exists. The prophet Zarathushtra lived in Persia (modern-day Iran) around 1600-1400 B.C.E. The supreme deity in this monotheistic faith is Ahura Mazda, "the Lord Wisdom."

Core beliefs

Zoroastrians embrace a threefold path, which promotes "Good thoughts, good words, and good deeds." Followers fight evil and all forms of inequality, pain, and suffering. By so doing, they believe that God's will is fulfilled and eternal life will be achieved.

Expressions of faith

Followers recite liturgy from their sacred scripture, the Avesta, and make pilgrimages to holy fire-temples. Zoroastrians do not worship fire; rather, fire symbolizes justice, the Divine, purification, and inner illumination (enlightenment).

Index

• C •

• 1 •

Notes

Notes

Notes

Notes